Schools and Classrooms

A cultural studies analysis of education

SECOND EDITION

COLIN SYMES AND NOEL PRESTON

 **LONGMAN**

An imprint of
Addison Wesley Longman

Addison Wesley Longman Australia Pty Limited
95 Coventry Street
South Melbourne 3205 Australia

Offices in Sydney, Brisbane and Perth, and associated companies throughout the world.

Copyright © 1997 Addison Wesley Longman Australia Pty Limited
First published 1992
Second edition 1997

All rights reserved. Except under the conditions described in the Copyright Act 1968 of Australia and subsequent amendments, no part of this publication may be reproduced, stored in a retrieval system or transmitted in any form or by any means, electronic, mechanical, photocopying, recording or otherwise, without the prior permission of the copyright owner.

Every effort has been made to trace and acknowledge copyright. However, should any infringement have occurred, the publishers tender their apologies and invite copyright owners to contact them.

Designed By Sarn Potter
Set in 10.5/13.5pt Sabon
Printed by Pearson Australia Demand Print Centre

National Library of Australia
Cataloguing-in-Publication data

The publisher's policy is to use **paper manufactured from sustainable forests**

Schools and classrooms: a cultural studies analysis of education.

2nd ed.
Bibliography
Includes indexes.
ISBN 0 582 81013 2.

1. Educational sociology - Australia. 2. Education - Australia - Aims and objectives.
I. Preston, Noel, 1941– . II. Synes, Colin. III. Title

306.430994

Contents

Acknowledgements   vii
Authors' acknowledgements   viii
Introduction to the second edition   ix
Introduction to the first edition   xi

PART 1
Education: from the pre-modern to the postmodern   1

Chapter 1   The discipline of education   3
    A map of the educationworld   3
    A theory of educational theory   6
    Seeing as seeing as   8
    Research in the educationworld   10
    Education in theory and practice   13
    Notes   16
    Keywords and phrases   16
    Tutorial and field activities   17

Chapter 2   Education and the postmodern turn   19
    A paradigm shift?   19
    Jürgen Habermas and Critical Theory   20
    Jean François Lyotard and the postmodern condition   24
    Michel Foucault and the disciplinary society   28
    The discipline of education   32
    By way of conclusion   34
    Notes   34
    Keywords and phrases   35
    Tutorial and field activities   35

Chapter 3   Education in context   37
    Making education meaningful   37
    Lower-case education   41
    What's in a name?   44
    Childhood and the invention of schooling   45
    Some measure of resistance   50
    Education: intrinsically valuable or instrumental?   52
    Education as transformative   55
    Summary   58
    Notes   58
    Keywords and phrases   59
    Tutorial and field activities   59

Chapter 4   Competing perspectives on education   61
   Putting things into perspective   61
   The liberal perspective: a rationalising education   63
   The instrumental perspective: education for human capital   67
   The progressive perspective: education for individuality   70
   The emancipatory perspective: education for an equitable society   72
   Postscript: in defence of the utopian   78
   Notes   79
   Keywords and phrases   80
   Tutorial and field activities   80

Chapter 5   The curriculum and the course of education   81
   Education and knowledge   81
   A cultural etymology of the curriculum   84
   'The knowledge most worth having'   87
   The curriculum and the knowledge industry   90
   The curriculum and the organisation of knowledge   95
   The structural organisation of school life   100
   The ghost of Plato   102
   The differential distribution of knowledge   106
   In summary   109
   Notes   109
   Keywords and phrases   110
   Tutorial and field activities   110

Chapter 6   Educational as a positional good: equality and schooling   112
   Not making a difference   112
   Meritocracy, or to each according to their abilities   114
   The discourse of equality   119
   Justifying justice   121
   Distributive justice   123
   Justice and equality in schools and classrooms   126
   Being equal to the task   132
   Notes   133
   Keywords and phrases   134
   Tutorial and field activities   134

PART 2
The disciplinary foundations of schooling   137

Chapter 7   School to work, or learning to labour   139
   Beginning work   139

The capitalist divisions of labour 142
Taking a holiday 144
Returning to work 147
Post-Fordist or Taylor-made? 150
Nil sine labore: the work ethic 152
Education and work 155
Mental work and handiwork 162
Conclusion 165
Notes 165
Keywords and phrases 166
Tutorial and field activities 166

Chapter 8 The chronology of the school, or making subjects run on time 168
Starting time 168
Time and the human condition 170
Time is money 175
School time 179
The school and the clockwork sensibility 181
Time and the moral economy 188
Finishing time 191
Notes 192
Keywords and phrases 192
Tutorial and field activities 192

Chapter 9 The character-building building: the architecture of the school 194
Entrance 194
Meaningful architecture 197
Fronting up to the school 202
The panopticon or society's gaze machine 205
The power of school buildings 211
Exit 217
Notes 218
Keywords and phrases 218
Tutorial and field activities 219

Chapter 10 Assessment and examination: getting a measure of the subject 221
On your marks! 221
The terms of assessment 224
An examination of examinations 229
Quantifying natural lottery effects 232

More crosses than ticks: marking as a sign system   235
The aesthetics of assessment   241
A final comment   242
Notes   244
Keywords and phrases   244
Tutorial and field activities   244

Chapter 11   Education and 'The Risk Society':
teaching with an ecological time bomb   246
Booting up   246
'The Risk Society'   247
Out of work   255
Further effects   258
Biting into information technology   260
Educational perspectives on technology   266
Quitting   268
Notes   269
Keywords and phrases   269
Tutorial and field activities   270

PART 3
From discipline to emancipation   271

Chapter 12   Education for a change:
some reflections for practice   273
A recapitulation   273
Setting guidelines for practice   275
Critical pedagogy   277
The transformative teacher   282
Some lessons for teacher education   286
A coda   287
Notes   288

Glossary   290
References   293
Names index   320
Subject index   327

Acknowledgements

We would like to thank the following for permission to reproduce copyright material:

Faber & Faber Ltd for quotation from Tom Stoppard 1993, *Arcadia*, (p. 3)

Cassell Academic for quotation from E. R. Robson 1972, *School Architecture*, Leicester University Press, (p. 194)

The Peters Fraser and Dunlop Group Limited on behalf of Michael Frayn © 1986, *Clockwise*, Methuen, (p. 168)

A. M. Heath & Co for quotation from George Orwell 1954, *Nineteen Eighty Four*, Copyright © Mark Hamilton as literary executor of the estate of the late Sonia Brownell and Martin Secker and Warburg Ltd (p. 19)

Oxford University Press for quotation from Henry Green 1984, *Pack my Bag*, (p. 139)

Pluto Press for quotation from R. W. Connell 1993, *Schools and Social Justice*, (p. 112)

Laurence Pollinger Ltd for quotation from D. H. Lawrence 1975, 'The Novel and Feelings', in J. Williams et al. *Lawrence on Education*, (p. 81)

Sage Publications for quotation from Ulrich Beck 1992, *Risk Society: Towards a New Modernity*, (p. 246)

Victor Gollancz for quotation from A. S. Neill 1974, Summerhill, (p. 221).

Authors' acknowledgements

We would like to thank a number of organisations and individuals who have contributed, both directly and indirectly, to this book in its new edition. First, there are the many students and teachers who have used the book in its first edition and gave us 'chalkface' advice about its merits and demerits; second, are our colleagues at QUT, particularly those within its School of Cultural and Policy Studies, with whom we have worked over the past decade and whose enthusiasm and energy have provided a stimulating context of collegiality and debate.

We would like to dedicate this book to this School, which has provided a number of scholars in education a propitious home in which to develop their careers and establish their reputations. That many of them now occupy senior positions in other institutions, is testimony to the foresight of the School in employing them. Without their assistance, this book would not exist. We would also like to thank the QUT, for permitting us to devote a Professional Development Program around the revision of this book. Indeed, as Noel has moved into the field of applied ethics, it is Colin who has had the time and insights which have most significantly shaped this second edition.

We also have to thank Jean Hilton who prepared the final manuscript of this book, and perfected its headings and layout. We would also like to thank Peter van Vliet at Addison Wesley Longman who encouraged us to prepare this present edition and gave us invaluable support during its preparation. On the personal front, we would like to thank those nearest and dearest to us, who tolerated the caprices and whims that writing a book tends to generate. Among the most important of those people were Coralie Kingston and Sandra Taylor.

Colin Symes & Noel Preston
Brisbane, July 1997.

Introduction to the second edition

Once they are bequeathed to the world, books tend to have a life of their own. This one is no exception. When we first wrote the book in the second half of 1990, we had no idea of its likely fate and reception. At the time of its writing, it was exploring the new theoretical territories, which the various varieties of postmodernism and post-structuralism had conquered and colonised, and which educa-tionalists, with one or two notable exceptions, had yet to appreciate or bring to the attention of their students. With varying degrees of success, the first edition of this book attempted to translate this theory to an audience that was unfamiliar with its terms and underlying assumptions, to make a theory which is not renowned for such, more palatable and approachable.

In preparing this second edition of *Schools and Classrooms*, we were quite surprised that the book had stood the test of fast-moving times (theory like everything else in this postmodern age moves along at a staggering pace) and much of what we thought relevant theory at the time continues to remain relevant. We were also surprised at the degree to which the book anticipates much of what has occurred during the four or so years which have intervened between its first and second editions.

The symptoms of educational conservatism and reactionism, what is sometimes called 'backlash' politics which were being articulated in the late 1980s, have become more intense in the last three or four years or so. Education, at all levels of its operations, has become much more market-driven, more like any other commodity in the postmodern world. Its human capital components have also become more emphasised, and education is increasingly driven by the needs of the economy. In this context, some of the ideas that were broached in the first edition such as post-Fordism and globalisation are now common currency, and part of the framing principles of Australian education in the late twentieth century and beyond, into the next millennium.

Ambivalent though we are towards some of these trends, they are part and parcel of an increasingly rugged landscape that teachers will have to negotiate throughout their careers. The major danger, as we see it, is that within this landscape the more utopian outposts, such as those that centre around social justice and construction of a fairer and more meaningful education, are likely to be places little visited in the new 'educationworld'. The second edition of this book, whose shelf life should mean that it is being used at the turn of the century, is a reminder that these utopian outposts are still worthy of a visit and that every teacher needs them on their itinerary.

When we first wrote *Schools and Classrooms* it was not done so in the most propitious of circumstances. It was written very quickly, in a little over four months. In spite of these rather difficult circumstances, it was a book which almost 'wrote itself' and it has been difficult to revise, given the continuity and narrative integrity of its original arguments. There was never much redundancy in the book. The spirit of the book and its contents, nevertheless, have been preserved but with, we hope, some notable improvements in style and presentation.

The book has been heavily edited and some of its obfuscatory language and convoluted sentences have been modified. We have also 'Harvardised' the references and eliminated many of the endnotes. A number of errors have been amended, though important contradictions and logical consistencies, what are called, in postmodern jargon 'aporia' remain impossible to eliminate in a textbook which takes a panoramic look at a contemporary social theory which is far from unified or marked with much consensus.

These changes have produced a book—we hope—that is far more user-friendly and inviting in its presentation—more in tune with the intellectual sensibilities of a generation of students more used to visual than verbal forms of presentation, and who are not used to consulting dictionaries and reading long sentences. We have also added at the end of each chapter tutorial and field activities, which we hope will extend the book's usefulness, particularly in the tutorial room situation, and add another dimension to its understanding and elucidation.

Introduction to the first edition

In the genus of scholarship and research, textbooks are an important species. They constitute a kind of go-between, conveying to a new generation of scholars and students the latest developments in a discipline. Fulfilling a function somewhat akin to a news bulletin, though one with a somewhat broader time frame and more depth of analysis, they place students in touch with what has been going on in their discipline. They translate some of its more esoteric and less accessible features, effectively permitting them to become familiar to a wider and less specialised audience.

This book is both an introductory and polemical text, designed for students at all levels including the undergraduate. It is not meant to be a definitive account of educational theory in all its diverse forms. Only a text with encyclopedic dimensions could hope to do that! Its aims are somewhat more modest. It is prompted by the belief that since 1968, which is a watershed year for contemporary social theory, a revolution has been occurring in the social sciences, including the field of education. This revolution began with revamped versions of Marxism, especially those of Louis Althusser and Antonio Gramsci, which had considerable impact on our understanding of the way schools function in the context of society, specifically one dominated by a capitalist economic order. Occurring more or less at the same time as neo-Marxism was the emergence of feminism, probably the major theoretical 'ism' of the late twentieth century, which has prompted not just an interest in the oppression of women and the causes of this within the framework of patriarchal society, but also an interest in the domain of sexual politics.

Feminism has also led to a reinvigoration of psychoanalysis, to an interest in the way gendered subjectivity is produced. As a force for social change in the post-1968 climate, feminism's only real rival is the green movement, which constitutes an ideological challenge to the materialism and growth economics of corporate and international capitalism. Within the interstices of both the feminist and environmental movements, there are a number of intellectual movements of considerable interest which have extended and challenged the territory of Marxism. These include critical theory, post-structuralism, deconstructionism and, most recently of all, postmodernism. All of these have had, or are beginning to have, an impact on educational theory and research.

In this book we shall try to trace that impact. But this text constitutes more than just a guide, providing students with some rudimentary understanding of the concepts and language of post-1968 social theory as it applies to education. One of the overriding features of this theory is its commitment to political change, its recognition that all social practices, including those of education, are by their very nature political in character, serving to reproduce dominant interests of various kinds, part of the invisible hand controlling the movement of society through time. Teachers can no more escape from this role of political functionary than any other citizen involved in social practices within the basic institutions of the modern state. But at least they can come to understand this role, its profile and constituent elements, and perhaps change it, so that its politics are differently formed and structured.

One of the unfortunate developments in recent teacher education, more so overseas than in Australia, has been a tendency to marginalise and derogate such understanding, to emphasise the technical rather than the political dimensions of teaching. In our view, teacher education needs to be more theoretical and less technical. This is because teachers need to regard themselves as intellectual workers, as bearers of mental capital, at home in the processes of rational and critical argument, as traders in the 'marketplace of ideas'.

In line with our general assumption that all education is political, we make no apologies for stating our commitment to education as an instrument of social amelioration. For, in addition to its various theoretical exegeses, this book also contains an argument, a thesis, relating to the general discourse of schooling. This is, that schooling in relation to society can be used to generate either a disciplinary or emancipatory form of society. The meaning of these terms, which are now commonly used in social theory, will become clearer as the book unfolds.

For the present, it is enough to indicate that this broadly means that school processes are always transformative in their impact on the lives of individuals, but mostly these processes are directed towards disciplining and controlling individuals or subjects in a way which reproduces rather than reconstructs society. Thus, when we examine the discourse of educational theory and practice, whether at the level of a school prospectus or a philosophy text, it is possible to discern within it disciplinary and emancipatory features.

Although within this book we refer to work in the areas of philosophy, sociology, history and psychology, this book is not intended to be representative of one discipline of education and no other. We believe that educational problems are best understood in an interdisciplinary way, particularly at the introductory level, and that a cultural studies approach, which is broadly the approach adopted in this book, offers the kind of analysis which yields most enlightenment about the provenance and reason for being of most of our practices in the classroom. There are several reasons for this.

Firstly, we believe that cultural studies can provide the kind of aegis needed to bring a variety of perspectives to bear on education and schooling which single-disciplinary approaches, monopolised by particular paradigms, cannot. If the new social theory, which itself is difficult to compartmentalise in terms of a particular discipline, is to be at all edifying, then its epistemology needs to be freely applied, untrammelled by territorial prescription. Moreover, education, perhaps more than any other endeavour, is a social activity which takes place within a historical framework, which is both past and future oriented and traverses the territory of everyday practice as well as that of theory and philosophy. A snapshot or synchronic approach which looks at schooling only in a contemporaneous way, as if its practices were constructed on a day-to-day basis, inheriting nothing from the past, thus eschews an important dimension of pedagogic determination, namely, that classroom practices, especially of the micro-kind, are saturated with references to the past.

In addition, though, education is also an intellectual enterprise. Its practices are grounded in rational belief systems, 'regimes of truth', which have common reference points relating to the basic values of Western culture. These are the values of humanism and the pursuit of knowledge and understanding, as well as broader socio-political issues relating to the nature of fair and just social arrangements and the role that education plays within their generation, broadly the agenda of Enlightenment thought. These are largely philosophical matters—not of the technical and foundationalist sort, but of the more ideological kind, relating to belief systems developed by philosophers and social theorists.

In this book we are trying to argue that educational theory needs to proceed diachronically, with constant reference to the fact that what happens in the classroom is a matter of history. One of the phrases we shall use regularly is that of 'cultural etymology', to signify the fact that the everyday practices of the classroom preserve elements of the past, so that it becomes possible to trace their evolution, much as one can trace the evolution of a word's meaning through sentences preserved in the texts and discourses of the past. In this connection, the practices that we have in mind are those like timetabling, the organisation of school space, the procedures of assessment and examination, the writing of reports on pupils, classroom work and school rules. These practices are not often the focus of inquiry in educational theory; if they are, they tend to be treated in a decontextualised and technicist way. Yet they are absolutely central to the basic architecture of school life, to the maintenance of its disciplinary order and the processes of educational structuration, and their management provides important clues on the kind of impact that schools have on the subjectivity of individuals.

This might seem like a description for yet another ethnography of school life. But the trouble with ethnography is that it rarely goes beyond the present, the here and now, leaving many of the routines of day-to-day practice unexplained! We feel that much can be gained from looking at the classroom in a historical way, in turning the contemporary back to its origins in the latter parts of the eighteenth century when many of the practices that are employed in modern classrooms were invented and established. This might seem like an unnecessarily retrograde step in the last decade of the twentieth century, when surely this pedagogical heritage from the Victorian era has disappeared. Yet this is not the case. The history of pedagogy in that era continues to haunt the present, albeit in rather degraded and diluted forms; moreover, in some parts of the world, notably Britain and the United States, there have been arguments advanced in favour of returning to the values and practices of Victorian education and society generally.

Another reason for examining the education of the early modern period of education is that this period, like our own, was a period of considerable transition, when society was moving into a new social order, one grounded in the imperatives of industrialism. In order to facilitate this transition, new technologies of the self were born—and the school was one of them. These provided mechanisms to produce the kind of sensibility which was needed if the industrial order was to function efficiently. We shall argue that this socio-cultural analysis, much of which is derived from the revisionist forms of history which have been written since 1968, suggests that there is transformative potential in schooling, which hitherto was used to rebuild the sensibility of the whole population through reconstructing childhood, to create a disciplinary society, one which accorded with the demands of the new industrial order. That this was done successfully, though not without some resistance, provides some support for the other major argument in this book, that schooling should be used to produce not a disciplinary society but an emancipatory one based around the values of equity and fairness. Much of the theory in this section of the book's thesis is derived from critical pedagogy which, unlike other theories discussed within this book, has been produced within education itself, admittedly with some assistance from critical theory and Gramscian-style Marxism.

The book is divided into three parts. The first deals with the more generalised issues of schooling and education; the second with specific facets of day-to-day classroom practice; and the third, very briefly, with some suggestions on how these practices could be modified and restructured in line with the demands of an emancipatory social formation.

The initial chapter examines the concepts of theory and practice in education, and argues that theory is only another variety of practice, and one with which we are all familiar. The second half of the chapter provides a more detailed survey of post-1968 theory, with special attention being given to the theoretical perspective of this book and its rationale. This survey is not meant to be exhaustive; it is intended to give an impression of this theory and its usefulness in a rather broad and generalised sense. The following two chapters concern themselves with the nature of education and attempts to trace its 'cultural etymology'. We argue that education is an area in which there are competing perspectives within its dominant discourses; Chapter 3 aims to typify these perspectives. We then proceed to a chapter on the curriculum and raise issues to do with the organisation of knowledge, of how the curriculum leads to valorisation of certain epistemological experiences and the devaluing of others. One theme of the chapter—that of the differential distribution and allocation of knowledge—leads into the next chapter which deals with school population questions, with the matter of classifying pupils, with issues to do with equality and with the maldistribution of opportunity in the schooling system.

From there we venture into the second part of the book, which examines micro-institutional practices within the school, particularly within the framework of theory provided by Michel Foucault. We begin with an examination of school work, specifying its forms and types, and its place within the overall structure of school life. We also suggest that there is a strong isomorphism between school work and work in general. In the following two chapters we examine issues to do with the timetable and the architecture of schools, and we assert that it is within these domains that the kind of surveillance which is at the heart of a disciplinary society occurs.

However, the main exercise of this surveillance, which is characterised by examination and confession, occurs in the area of assessment, the theme of the next chapter. We then go on to examine the question of technology in relation to schooling, arguing that technology has augmented the school's technological processes, providing new mechanisms for disciplining, through the adoption of technical rationality. In the final part of the book we examine some possibilities for change within the prescribed arena of schooling. We argue that these must happen at a localised level and must focus upon the micro-institutional practices of schooling. We suggest that the work of critical pedagogy can be of assistance here. The last chapter mainly deals with its practical ramifications and the way of bringing about more emancipatory social arrangements through the agency of schooling.

In textbooks there is a tendency to overlook endnotes and references— the domain of the bibliography—perhaps because they are situated outside the main body of the text. We want to discourage this practice in relation to this book, for its endnotes are intended to be a supplementary text, one which adds extra commentary and suggests further reading which hopefully will lead the reader to a better appreciation of the literature in the area. We have also tried to use antipodean literature wherever possible, believing that Australian (and also New Zealand) research into education and in the social sciences generally has come of age in the last decade or so, and represents a distinctive tradition. We also think it is important to recognise that the literature on education extends well beyond the academic texts, and encompasses films, novels, newspapers and documentaries; hence we often make reference to them as subsidiary material.

Finally, we have included a glossary. Learning a new discipline is rather like learning a new language. The glossary is intended to provide a kind of phrasebook to assist the learning of this language. It might assist students if they were to photocopy these pages and keep them close by as a handy reference while they read the text.

This book is not intended to be comprehensive in its treatment of school life. We would like to have included chapters on reading and writing, administration and management, to have engaged in a more rigorous analysis of the school subjects and disciplines. In a text of this length only so many themes can be treated. The tone of the book might annoy some readers, especially those with a purist appreciation of post-structuralist and postmodernist theory, who will possibly complain that we have over-simplified Foucault, missed much of the subtlety in Habermas and so on. Teachers, on the other hand, might be disturbed by the picture of schooling that we have presented.

On the other hand, we have set out to produce a gadfly text, one which sets out to annoy and pester the common assumptions about education and its practice, in the hope that in exposing their inadequacies our readers will work for something better in their classrooms and educational situations.

Education: from the pre-modern to the postmodern

The discipline of education

It's wanting to know that makes us matter.
Otherwise we're going out the way we came in.
(Tom Stoppard 1993)

A map of the educationworld

Schools are an inescapable part of the landscape of modern life, figuring prominently within our lives and the organisation of contemporary society. Their day-to-day happenings, as experienced by students and teachers, are distinctive, comprising a series of practices inspired by the curriculum and the imperatives of classroom life. Each population of students is different, as is the school in which it is located, and each teacher brings a particular biography to their teaching which is dissimilar from that of their colleagues. Yet they are also similar in the degree to which they follow certain customs and conventions, practices and moralities, and which make recognisable the distinctive organisational culture that is the modern school. This culture has a long and complex history involving various educational theories and practices, which are periodically subject to change and reform. Taken together these various background elements form part of the social and cultural substratum of the 'educationworld', a term we have adopted from Howard Becker's (1982) institutional aesthetics.

Schools provide a set of foundational experiences which shape our lives, helping to produce our identity and, most importantly, providing one of the mechanisms through which some individuals are able to obtain a degree of positional advantage (Hirsch 1976). They are also one of the mechanisms through which contact with our cultural and moral heritage is established, albeit a contact which is selective and distorted. For as well as having a stake in the future and playing a role in the constant modernisation of society, schools are embedded in the past, acting as a powerful vehicle for the transmission of those values at the heart of the Western tradition. Nor do schools act alone in this enterprise. To them must be added universities and colleges, which are part of the official network of learning (for the most part funded by the state), and which are able to award recognised credentials and which employ qualified teachers. Alongside them there are a variety of other privately funded institutions, which teach a whole range of skills from acupuncture to foreign languages. Then there are many quasi-educational institutions such as museums and libraries, which often employ educational officers, and which, though not organised as teaching institutions awarding credentials, play an important role in transmitting and inculcating dominant cultural values.

Schools are not independent enterprises and laws unto themselves; they are accountable to the state, and they are expected to play a part in satisfying its needs, producing outcomes which further the national interest and are in accordance with government policy. The state's power to determine by statute and legislation the length and duration of schooling, and to influence its overall character, is indicative of the degree to which the day-to-day routines of classroom life are underpinned with general and systematic views of the schooling process.

The advent of mass compulsory schooling has meant that education has become one of the core cultural experiences of modern life, a form of civil conscription through which all children and young people pass in anticipation that they will obtain positional advantage from its benefits. For schools are a comparatively recent addition to the fabric of social life, contributing a new dimension to childhood. Like other core experiences, though, that of schooling has generated its own mythology and folklore, based around meanings and symbols, icons and experiences, apocryphal stories and the like. It is not merely that schooling is consumed as one of the perceived mechanisms of social advancement, but that its meanings and experiences, like many aspects of modern life, are reproduced and re-produced through new additional associations and meanings.

Education, for instance, is a popular subject on talkback radio and in the letters' columns of newspapers. The popularity of films like *Heartbreak High*, now a television series on the ABC, and *Dead Poets' Society*, particularly those in which a charismatic teacher or a subversive student reshapes the daily life of the classroom in radical and unorthodox ways,[1] is indicative of the degree to which schooling is part of a collective imagination, of the measure to which certain educational fantasies strike a sympathetic chord with our own educational ideals.

The community of interest in schooling, in fact, is large and diverse, comprising not just teachers and parents, but also (for instance) employers, parliamentarians, unionists and moral crusaders of various convictions. Moreover, each interest group tends to have its own vision of education, everything from a return to the basics—a form of educational fundamentalism—to one aligned to the nation's economic goals, to national efficiency and the development of an increasingly productive citizenry. In fact, there is no unified and agreed vision as to what constitutes education; on the contrary, most visions of education are characterised by competing and contradictory sentiments.

The whole area of education tends to be one in which rival discourses compete for sovereignty and control. Some of these discourses are more convincing and acceptable than others, but all, no matter how outrageous or far-fetched, contribute to the schooling debate and to the context in which theories about its functions and purposes are formed and generated. A prominent player in the production of new educational discourses is the professional educationalist who specialises in researching the educationworld, describing its ecology and habitat, identifying its inadequacies and endeavouring to invent new and more efficient processes of teaching and learning.

Another prominent player who has come to the fore in recent years, is the policy-maker who works in the educational bureaucracy and is responsible for the articulation of new pedagogic guidelines, designed to reshape the direction of education in the state, to give it new emphases and accents in the light of changing demands and attitudes, research and understanding about the role of schooling in contemporary society. Teachers and students need to be particularly alert to policy and its analysis (Taylor, Rivzi, Lingard & Henry 1997), for, as will be suggested in subsequent chapters, policy has become the principal fuel that drives the engine of the modern school.

Unlike much lay commentary on the school, that of the professional theorist and policy maker is based on the outcomes of research, derived from the application of various educational theories. In this first chapter, we are concerned with examining this theory, and the institutional context from which it gains its legitimacy and authority.

SCHOOLS AND CLASSROOMS

A theory of educational theory

The theory of education is something teachers tend to renounce, particularly when it is not perceived to have a direct bearing on classroom practice. The somewhat 'pragmatic cast of thought' characteristic of many teachers (Gibson 1984; McWilliam 1994), makes them extremely resistant to inquiry of a speculative and analytic kind, which is the essence of educational theory. This is somewhat ironic, given that teachers are part of the knowledge industry, part of a 'marketplace of ideas' in which 'knowledge goods', such as argument and theory, are the principal commodities of trade (Marginson 1995). Moreover, as we shall argue in the concluding chapter of this book, teachers ought to regard themselves as intellectuals, with a commitment to critical inquiry and cultural action.

We have already suggested that the character of educational theorising is co-extensive with everyday thinking, for most teachers, like parents, administrators and even students, have ideas about schooling, broad visions of what education ought to be like, and what constitutes ethical practice in the school. What is called educational theory is only a more sophisticated version of such thinking.

Particularly in a practical endeavour like education, theory is often contrasted unfavourably with practice, as if the two were at loggerheads with one another. Yet there is a relationship (and it is a very interesting one) which can only be understood if the nature of theory and its practice is itself understood. The word 'theory' in connection with education is used somewhat loosely to cover a multitude of epistemological activities, including research, inquiry, thought, understanding, critique and ideas. There are 'theories' in education which are somewhat analogous to those found in science and which provide a basis for research and inquiry; however, unlike the popular view of science, education is not characterised by an overarching methodology which determines the character of all theorising done in its name.

Much educational theory is empirical or positivist in character, and the word 'research' sits quite comfortably alongside it. But there is a great deal of educational theory which does not fit the empirical mould, which is more critical and speculative in character, and which owes more to the methodology of philosophy than that of science. It is with this kind of research—'critique' would be a better word for it—that this book is concerned.

Theories are associated with particular disciplines, which in turn tend to be associated with certain domains of inquiry and programs of research, and these serve to demarcate the disciplines from one another within the overall spectrum of knowledge. Thus science is concerned with the physical and natural world, with decoding its underlying behaviour and material fabric, whereas history is concerned with documenting the past and with making sense of human societies as they have evolved over periods of time. Education as a field of understanding, on the other hand, is concerned with making sense of teaching and learning, and with describing, among other matters, the contexts and conditions in which they typically occur, as well as specifying the role education ought to play in a given social formation or arrangement. It is with this 'ought' dimension that a 'critical' theory of education is, in the main, concerned.

These, as well as the many other forms of knowledge which now exist, reflect not just an expansion in the intellectual repertoire of humankind, but also an extension of the domains of understanding, to encompass institutions and society. The distinctiveness of each form of knowledge or discipline derives in part from these domains, and in part from its particular epistemological approaches (e.g. the extreme empiricism and positivism of science and the high rationality of philosophy). Thus each discipline—or what is sometimes called 'a regime of truth'—consists of an assemblage of features, ranging from its distinctive objects of inquiry through to particular procedures for determining, generating and storing truth (Foucault 1970; Gordon 1980).[2]

Alongside this methodological repertoire is the substantive content of the discipline: its laws, its theories and the specialised knowledge gained from their application. Each discipline also has a distinctive language associated with it, a discourse of stipulated terms and nomenclatures. To this has to be added—in some disciplines at least—complex symbol and notational systems, such as those which are to be found in mathematics and music.

An important aspect of the knowledge process are complex data structures and rules called theories. They constitute systems of computation which attempt to account for the causes and effects of everyday observations, be they in society or the universe (Thagard 1988). Theories are disciplinary specific; they are produced from the methodologies or styles of reasoning that have developed within the various disciplines. Their function is mostly explanatory and predictive, serving to produce accounts of why certain events occur and what outcomes can be expected should certain conditions prevail (Hempel 1966).

Theories are, in fact, like fishing nets designed to catch the world in all its diverse elements; as they gain in sophistication, so their mesh becomes finer and they catch more of the diversity of the world (Popper 1972). Theories are central to the operations of research programs, and through their complex nets knowledge is gathered and harvested. But there is nothing fixed or absolute about theories. The tenure of their application tends to be limited. The accounts of the world they provide are provisional rather than long-standing. And part of their explanatory power derives from the fact that they are falsifiable. Thus within each regime of truth, theories are subject to regular appraisal and refutation once there is enough evidence to falsify them.

Quite wrongly, there is a widespread impression that knowledge, particularly science, has a Whiggish history—that is, its theories are progressive—constantly evolving to higher levels of sophistication and truth. According to some philosophers of science, most notably Kuhn (1973) this view is fallacious. Theories, or what Kuhn terms 'paradigms', are always subject to periodic renewal and internal redesign as the limits of their explanatory potential become apparent through the identification of 'anomalies' that do not match the paradigm's predictions.

The history of science is not a linear one, development following upon development in a never-ending expansion of scientific certainty. On the contrary, its history alternates between periods of normality and revolution and is punctuated with periods of crises and doubt. At such moments, paradigms are challenged before being replaced, causing a complete restructuring of what Kuhn (1974) has called a 'disciplinary matrix'—everything from its research programs to its textbooks, its methodologies and the 'arsenal of exemplars' used in teaching programs. Thus even what is taught in schools is eventually affected by such paradigm changes.

Seeing as seeing as

Theories also influence the way the world is perceived. They act like lenses, bringing focus to certain quarters of inquiry, while diminishing the significance of others. They thereby turn the processes of 'seeing' into 'seeing as'. Like all lenses, theories refract and distort, never accurately reflecting the world that is mediated through them. This spectatorship theory of theory—which is shared by a number of philosophers of science, the most notable being Norwood Russell

Hanson—in fact reflects the etymology of the word which contains allusions to sight, viewing and spectacle. According to Hanson (1969), the processes of initiation into a discipline, which are broadly those associated with the processes of education, result in an individual's observations of the world becoming 'theory laden'. What is seen is seen as something. Thus a trained physicist, although receiving the same sensory information at the retina as the rest of us, processes that information in rather different ways, and apprehends at a different level of amplification features of the physical world that escape the apprehension of lay persons.

Knowledge is thus a key factor in the differentiation of perceptual experience, helping to determine the way the world is perceived and to what, within it, one's attention is likely to be drawn. Epistemological and vocational background, then, are crucial factors in the perception process (Abercrombie 1974; Dretske 1969), enabling radiographers, after a period of training, to see significance in X-rays and physicists to read cyclotron photographs as the 'fingerprints' of subatomic particles. In the case of education, certain theories have led childhood to be reperceived. In this century, for instance, the theories of Piaget have caused childhood to be seen through the lens of cognitive development, as a phase of life characterised by intellectual dispositions different from those of adults. Incidentally, the Piagetian paradigm is one increasingly subject to contestation.

Although paradigms come and go, altering the agenda of research programs and causing the world to be rather differently apprehended, there are certain metaphysical assumptions within a regime of truth which are relatively inviolable and stable, and these remain unaltered, even during periods of paradigm shift. For instance, there are certain assumptions governing science, such as the existence of a world available to empirical interrogation, upon which the whole edifice of science depends. Where education is concerned, this core of ideas consists of the central principles of what is often called the Enlightenment project or the discourse of Liberalism.

The mainstays of this thought and discourse are beliefs in the sovereignty of the individual, in the unfailing merits of progress, in the importance of emancipation and freedom, and above all in the ameliorative power and epistemological importance of rationality (Bowers 1987; Usher & Edwards 1994). A body of theory which challenges these core notions (e.g. post-structuralist and postmodernist theory), which attempts to ground itself in assumptions very different from this discourse, and which looks at traditional problems in a new way, through different sets of lenses, is often marginalised and is forced outside the mainstream of the discipline, to establish itself as a separate body of theory.

To a degree (although it is by no means at the margins of social theory) this is the case with feminist theory which, in some of its versions at least, has held out against the assumptions of Enlightenment philosophy, regarding them as the products of so-called 'male-stream thought', which has always suppressed and distorted the intellectual and caring inclinations of women (Davies 1989; Lloyd 1984; O'Brien 1981; Theile 1986; Weiler 1988). Part of the appeal of postmodernism for feminists is that its assumptions declare war on male-stream thought because of its failure to acknowledge pluralism and diversity, and its allegiance to indefensible binaries such as that between nature and culture.

Research in the educationworld

Theory and knowledge construction takes place in a research culture, which has well-defined characteristics and associated material practices. There is an institutional framework associated with this culture, sometimes called a 'resource' or 'social space' in which ideas and theories are generated and constructed, reported and evaluated (Gooding 1992). The framework acts as a powerful mechanism through which status is conferred upon ideas and theories, and through which certain of them become candidates for circulation. The culture comes to act as a kind of educational go-between, helping to generate a larger audience, be it students or the general public, for the seminal ideas and theories contained within a discipline.

Typically, a research culture is located within institutions called universities where research is combined with teaching responsibilities. However, universities are but one part of the research network which also includes, in Australia, institutes like the CSIRO and the Institute of Family Studies, as well as the research and development (R&D) sections of industrial corporations. Inevitably, certain institutions gain reputations as centres of disciplinary excellence, attracting researchers and students to them and commanding considerable prestige as places in the foreground of research within a particular discipline.

These are places where the 'founders of discourse' are located—the disciplinary equivalent of rock stars, men and women with whom particular paradigms and seminal ideas are associated. But this research culture also crosses institutions and national boundaries via the mechanism of the so-called 'invisible colleges' (Crane 1972; Ben-David 1971),[3] which bring communities of scholars together across the globe, on a regular basis, via conferences, professional associations, journals, books and the Internet, leading to the promotion of certain lines of inquiry and the consolidation of certain disciplinary formations and paradigms. In Chapter 2 we shall discuss globalisation, a subject of much interest among social theorists of the late 1990s, of which scholarly activity, ever since its emergence in the Western tradition, was an important forerunner.

As well as advancing the state of knowledge, much of a research culture is concerned with intellectual quality control, with maintaining standards of scholarship and ensuring that the so-called disinterested pursuit of truth remains uncorrupted by unscrupulous researchers more concerned with enhancing their careers than the condition of knowledge. The culture is in the hands of the communities of scholars, who transmit it to the next generation of scholars through a kind of intellectual apprenticeship, thus reproducing the 'form of life' called research.

This apprenticeship ensures that the community only admits scholars into its midst who are prepared to support the values and morality of the discipline and who possess sufficient epistemological command over its 'disciplinary matrix' to extend its knowledge base. In other words, one of the functions of this apprenticeship is to guarantee that the would-be scholar becomes conversant with the discipline, becomes theory and language laden in ways consistent with its current epistemological condition. In effect, what happens is that the apprentice scholar is gradually initiated into the research community, acquiring its values and etiquette, and passing through its various rituals, while at the same time sacrificing certain modes of awareness and knowing which are considered inappropriate within the disciplinary community. In a small way, readers of this book, which is itself an outcome of the same processes of initiation, are being initiated into this community, specifically that associated with education.

There is thus a textual dimension to a research culture which plays an important role in the production and propagation of knowledge. It is becoming clearer that certain forms of literary exposition like the essay—of which the academic paper is the most specialised example—have become the primary vehicles for promulgating new knowledge, exerting a degree of influence over the way knowledge is organised and structured (Olson 1977). The academic paper, with its particular registers and referencing etiquettes which students learn to write as part of their disciplinary apprenticeship, helps reify a discipline's social network and uphold its values, particularly those to do with intellectual property. The system of internal acknowledgement and networks of citation which identify the sources of ideas, is symbolic of the degree to which research is a textual phenomenon, a specialised genre, with its own literary conventions and narrative style. Forms of research presentation which do not conform to these conventions and style tend not to be considered as candidates of legitimation (Wilson & Cowell 1989).

Indeed, until a theory or piece of research appears in print, it tends to lack 'epistemic authority' and legitimacy. The process of refereeing papers, which precedes publication, is another element of intellectual quality control, another important process in the maintenance of epistemological standards. Journals and books tend to have varying degrees of prestige and status, and constitute a powerful conduit through which a community of scholars is able to assert its authority and to ensure that allegiance to particular paradigms and theoretical viewpoints is maintained. They are also important symbols of the way a discipline is evolving, particularly in terms of its paradigmatic preferences and epistemic directions.

New journals and new series of publications tend to be established when new paradigms and new disciplinary directions emerge. One reason for this is that existing outlets for the circulation of new ideas are often less than receptive to publishing research which transgresses existing paradigms and which challenges the channels of epistemic authority. At the lower levels of disciplinary expertise, textbooks, of which this work is an example, are also an important factor in the dissemination of theory, serving to legitimise certain paradigms and discrediting others, signposting new directions in the trajectory of theory.

But it would be a mistake to think that a research culture is characterised by perfect moral conditions, and that the integrity of scholarship is never compromised or violated. With careers and professional reputations at stake, the evaluation of new contributions to scholarship is not always dispassionate and objective; indeed, in order to protect the tenure of an existing paradigm, scholars will often do anything to bring these contributions into disrepute, from personal abuse to a concerted attempt to demonstrate their spuriousness (Feyerabend 1975). In education, Sir Cyril Burt falsified his findings into intelligence as a way of legitimising an education system stratified along intellectual and social lines; similarly, Lysenko, in another political context, used research in molecular biology to support a type of Lamarckianism in line with Stalinist ideology.

This demonstrates the degree to which a research culture is located in a broader cultural framework which has the power to bring its own values to bear on research, shaping it in accord with such factors as political ideology, the national interest, defence and economic prosperity (Aronowitz 1988). Indeed, one of the major characteristics of the post-industrial society (Bell 1976), which it is said we have entered, is that it is centred around knowledge and information rather than the production of material goods. In line with this, the knowledge and information industry is fast becoming big business in advanced capitalist societies, with the production of knowledge, its storage and retrieval a significant factor in the modern economy, employing a larger and larger percentage of the workforce.

Knowledge has gained a commercial significance, moving 'from being primarily a use-value to being primarily an exchange value' (Frow 1990). Indicative of this is the degree to which the work of universities is now shaped by commercial and entrepreneurial goals. Universities are expected to turn their knowledge goods into commodities, which will earn them dollars to supplement their funding. As a consequence, the construction of educational theory is bedevilled by the need to obtain recognition and acceptance within increasingly corporatised and commercialised institutions.

Education in theory and practice

Like a number of other domains, with which it is often compared, namely medicine, engineering and librarianship, the practice of education was historically prior to its theorisation. This is not to suggest that its practices were necessarily atheoretical; rather it is to suggest that the need to transmit culture and certain social practices, which is the governing principle of education, is a necessary precondition of the existence of something called education.

For countless millennia—before it was associated with schools and notions of what constituted an adequate education—this was the primary sense of education: a process concerned with initiation into adult society, with the total upbringing of children and the passage of those skills considered essential for the preservation of the culture (Mead 1980; Passmore 1980). The invention of schooling only added a new element to this process; it did not modify its overriding function and purpose.

In the not too distant future, it could be that new developments in information technology will turn the school into an institutional dinosaur and that its present functions will be supplanted by a home-based computer linked through the Internet, through mechanisms of virtual learning—though, once again, this would only be a different means to the same end. The same applies to the theory of education: its development, which began with Plato and his recognition that education played a central role in the conservation of society, in maintaining what Feinberg (1983) has called 'intergenerational continuity', has helped to illuminate the processes involved but it has not substantially altered its reason for existence.

There are, nonetheless, a number of reasons why a body of educational theory exists regardless of its possible utility or not. It has already been noted that there is a strong will to know, to understand and to explain, in which individuals, as part of the general creativity of daily life, reprocess their experiences of institutions, particularly when they are disempowered by them, making jokes of them, subjects of graffiti and other forms of counter-hegemonic commentary (de Certeau 1984). This is one form of the sub-stratum of theory.

Another, is the tendency to make commentary about education, be it in conversations or letters to newspapers, wherein a certain preferred view of education is expressed, usually one at loggerheads with that of the mainstream. It is likely that this commentary is informed with a whole hotchpotch of educational impressions, derived from a variety of sources and perspectives including uninformed parental reactions or maybe the publication of a report on literacy standards, given notoriety and mischievous distortion on tabloid television. Whatever its ultimate value or worth as educational truth, the point is that such commentary, for all its pre-theoretical character, seeks to give an explanation about what is happening in schools and classrooms and to state a different view as to what ought to be happening in them.

Another reason for the existence of educational theory is the hope that it will result in the improvement of classroom practice in some small or large way. One reason for inquiring into the practices of schooling is to unmask their inadequacies, to demonstrate their lack of efficiency in achieving certain goals. Another is to provide a better grounding for existing practices and to improve the general preparation of teachers in skills like questioning and conducting discussions. Among those who have been committed to such theory, advancing the cause of pedagogic practice, medicine and engineering are often cited as areas which have obviously benefited from theory and which educationalists could well use as a model for the epistemological development of their own theories (O'Connor 1973).

The general assumption here is that the problems of learning and schooling lend themselves to empirical approaches, and that the variables of the classroom and the students are controllable and predictable. In other words, the achievement of learning is akin to treating an illness or building a bridge. On the other hand, it has been argued that there are aspects of the teaching process which transcend determination, which defy analysis and explication because, as with many practical endeavours, they contain a tacit component (Polanyi 1972) which transcends theoretical explication and which can only be learnt in the classroom, through teaching and contact with students.

The trouble with focusing upon pedagogy and pedagogy alone, is that it obscures contextual questions affecting classroom processes. Schooling (and it is like medicine in this regard) does not happen in a social vacuum. As has already been suggested, it is a social practice, centred, in the main, on the reproduction of the existing social order. It takes place in a society in which conflict and division, inequalities in the distribution of power and opportunity, exist not on a trivial scale but in a way which affects the outcomes of schooling and the issue of pedagogic efficiency.

To eschew this dimension of the schooling process is to neglect what is a major factor in the classroom equation. Reproduction theory (Bowles & Gintis 1976), which stems from a Marxist paradigm, is an important strand of contemporary educational theory and one which has provided convincing explanations as to why it is that schools have not been particularly successful at remedying what are often called 'natural lottery effects', not just the contingencies of socio-economic circumstances, but also more incorrigible lottery effects such as being born black or having a certain ethnic background.

However, there is another level of theory which goes beyond merely describing the processes of schooling or perfecting their foundations, one which focuses upon questioning the existence and functions of schooling per se. The tenor of this theory is often utopian, looking towards optimal social arrangements in which schooling has a function other than to reproduce the caste system of capitalism, in which it educates rather than miseducates. This might mean radical changes along the lines suggested by Illich (1971; 1979)—namely, of eliminating schools altogether and replacing them with less imperfect learning communities such as educational networks or learning webs.

Or it might mean developing a model of schooling which is transformative and emancipatory rather than reproductive and disciplinary, which brings about real cultural and social change, which introduces a mode of teaching and learning which is just and fair, which is genuinely egalitarian and advantages the disadvantaged in some beneficial and useful ways. Instead of education as social reproduction, we should think of education as a process of 'cultural mobilisation', one leading to broad social understandings and the production of a rather different kind of culture (Wexler 1982). Many of these ideas are drawn from the new social theory which has emerged in the last two decades and which we shall examine in the next chapter.

NOTES

1. These films inherit the tradition of the school novel which began with Thomas Hughes' *Tom Brown's Schooldays* and which is a well-developed genre with gender-specific dimensions (Cadogan & Craig 1976; Hooton 1990; Inglis 1981; Musgrave 1985). One only has to think of the degree to which the novel (*bildüngsroman*) about education and the experiences of becoming an adult provides compelling insights into the processes of schooling, to realise that the font of all useful knowledge about schools and classrooms is more comprehensive than that included in educational theory (Buckley 1974; Craig 1995; Moretti 1987). To these fictional recreations of the schooling process, one could also add the 'language and lore of children', the doggerel and verse of the playground which also a provides a rich and insightful commentary on the schooling process (Opie & Opie 1959).
2. In education, the work of Paul Hirst (1974) provides a useful, if much criticised, account of the elements of what he calls the 'public forms of knowledge'.
3. For more on the nature of academic life and its connection with a research culture, see Pierre Bourdieu (1988). For more entertaining accounts of *homo academicus*, it is useful to turn to novels and television series which explore the drama of university life. There have been many of these in recent years, forming a new literary genre, the so-called campus novel. Among the best of these novels (and they date back to the early 1960s) are by David Lodge (1978; 1985) and Anne Oakley (1988).

Keywords and phrases

- educationworld
- epistemology
- natural lottery effects
- paradigm
- policy
- positional good
- resource space

Tutorial and field activities

1. Consult a local edition of Yellow Pages and list from the entry for 'Coaching and Business Colleges' the range of quasi-educational institutions that exist in your local community. Suggest some reasons as to why such institutions exist, and note the major differences between them and formal educational institutions such as schools and universities. What particular constituency of students do they serve?

2. Compile a list of recent films and television series (more ambitious tutorial groups might like to extend this list to include novels, autobiographies and short stories, perhaps even poetry and rock lyrics) in which school and university life are represented. View one such film in class and attempt to ascertain its underlying values with regard to education.

3. Draw a map of the 'educationworld' and attempt to provide a schematic representation of all the various institutions associated with it, including those, such as publishers, uniform retailers and computer manufacturers which have a commercial interest in education.

4. Examine the range of journals dealing with educational issues and theories in your university library and classify them according to their epistemological framework and theoretical orientation. What does this classification tell us about the major disciplines that contribute to education? You might also try and ascertain from whence these journals come and where the authors of their various papers are, in the main, located.

5. Much of the exploration of education dealt with in this book focuses upon the everyday happenings in schools and classrooms, particularly the various micro-practices associated with them—practices which are often central to the cultural organisation of the school and which often contain telling insights about the nature and values that underpin much education. These practices, and there are many of them, are the subject of the various texts associated with schooling such as handbooks, prospectuses, school diaries, timetables, school maps, badges, mottoes, school magazines and so forth. These are examples of educational ephemera, and they also include advertisements and web-sites on the Internet (http://webtt.coled.umn.edu/schools/AU/Queensland.html), and

increasingly school merchandise. As part and parcel of developing an appreciation and understanding of the culture of the school, you should develop a folio containing examples of this educational ephemera. You will probably already have in possession some examples of such, a legacy of your own school days.

When you have such a folio, you might like to compare some of the items of within it with one of your colleagues, who attended a state or private school. Note any differences between the presentation and sophistication of the materials used.

Education and the postmodern turn

He took a twenty-five cent piece out of his pocket. There, too, in tiny clear lettering, the same slogans were inscribed, and on the other face of the coin the head of Big Brother.

Even from the coin the eyes pursued you. On coins, on stamps on the covers of books, on banners, on posters, and on the wrappings of cigarette packets—everywhere. Always the eyes watching you and the voice enveloping you. Asleep or awake, working or eating, indoors or out of doors, in the bath or in bed—no escape. Nothing was your own except the few cubic centimetres inside your skull.

(George Orwell 1954)

A paradigm shift?

In Chapter 1, a theory of epistemological change was outlined. It indicated that a discipline's conceptual frameworks, in response to their perceived inadequacies, undergo not just overhaul and maintenance, but wholesale renewal and replacement. Among other things, the emergence of new theoretical frameworks or paradigms causes old problems to be seen in a new light, and makes it necessary for new research agenda to be enumerated. In the last thirty years or so—or to be more accurate, since 1968, which is often seen as a point when an 'epochal break' occurred (Peters 1995)[1]—contemporary social theory has undergone a paradigmatic shift of almost revolutionary proportions. Thirty years on, and this epochal break is still perceived as a remarkable period of cultural development in many fields including literature, popular music and personal politics. At the level of social theory, where the developments were equally dramatic, not only were the more traditional styles of Marxism reworked to accommodate the developments in late twentieth-century capitalism, but also there was an interest in psychoanalysis and gender politics generally which highlighted the power differentials between men and women.

Overall, the epochal break which occurred in the late 1960s saw a shift away from the modernism which has dominated Western thought since the seventeenth century which was an extremely turbulent period of European history. Given that turbulence, the idea of order, epitomised by Newtonian physics, was embraced as a valuable moral template and extended to society throughout the period of modernism (Toulmin 1990). The late 1960s, then, were an era in which the second half of the twentieth century was reinvented, and whose legacies continue to define the ethos of the present, particularly in the area of cultural and social theory. This is the idea of a postmodern condition, an idea that signifies, among other things, a closure of the modernist project. Postmodernism also encapsulates a feeling of millennial crisis and despair as old values and moral certainties are overturned. A society that is increasingly fragmented, morally confused and marked with transience has emerged (Harvey 1990; MacIntyre 1987), whose character has helped to maintain the cogency of the postmodernist idea.

Jürgen Habermas and Critical Theory

The theories of the Frankfurt School (so named because it was originally based in the German city of Frankfurt) represent one of the outcomes of this attempt to update Marxism and to ensure its continuing relevance in the face of global capitalism and the increased bureaucratisation of the modem state. The work of the Frankfurt school, embracing many scholars (Theodor Adorno, Max Horkheimer, Herbert Marcuse and others, including Eric Fromm at one stage) (Bottomore 1984; Geuss 1982; Held 1980; Kemmis & Carr 1986), covers a wide spectrum of interdisciplinary study which is nevertheless united by its pre-occupation with a theme common to the analyses of seminal thinkers in the social sciences—namely, the ability of capitalism to offset the alienation of the proletariat through the provision of a more comfortable lifestyle and flexible social system, meaning one in which a degree of social mobility is attainable.

The Frankfurt School, and the so-called Critical Theory which stemmed from it, explores the human condition from a similar starting point. With a renewed focus upon the problem of the individual, the

Frankfurt School was also oriented towards Freudian psychoanalysis, interpreting the problems of neuroses, and psychopathologies in general, in terms of the failure of a capitalist society to allow the individual free rein and autonomous sexual expression. In effect, the Frankfurt school updated Marxism, preserving its belief that all problems to do with society stemmed from the economic sphere, but adding to it the plight of a society shackled to the debilitating effects of technical rationality and an efficient division of labour. In effect, it is these factors which have provided capitalism with tools of economic and material success, but at the expense of a genuinely democratic society in which all individuals can participate and find themselves fulfilled. The Frankfurt school is particularly committed to a view of the social sciences which emphasises a comprehensive critique of existing social arrangements. Hence its relevance for education, a field which is related to the full range of these arrangements, particularly those to do with the division of labour and social advancement. Several features of Critical Theory are noteworthy:

1. Unlike classical Marxism with its stress on economic determinism, Critical Theory stresses the importance and possibility of individual action.
2. A major focus for Critical Theory is the critique of technical rationality and its pre-occupation with efficiency, instrumentality and means over ends. The anti-positivist stance which is characteristic of the theory derives not so much from being anti-science, but from a recognition that modern-day science has lost its connection with politics and ethics, which would check the excesses of positivism. In this critique, technical rationality is regarded as the dominant force in the modern world and as one which must be challenged in the name of emancipation.
3. The study of culture is central to Critical Theory, for culture provides a focus for understanding and shaping the possibilities of autonomy and independence from technical and practical interests. In particular, Critical Theory is drawn to the domain of aesthetics because of its capacity to transcend the economic sphere and to produce oppositional forms of cultural production (Lunn 1982; Gibson 1984).

Jürgen Habermas, the major exponent of Critical Theory, developed an exposition of the 'interests' which not only make culture and society possible but also direct our research for knowledge: 'technical' interest, 'practical' interest and 'emancipatory' interest. The scope of Habermas' work (1972; 1974; 1984; 1987) is immense, ranging from political polemics to intensely theoretical discourses on hermeneutics, and it is still in progress. Throughout his work, Habermas reflects the characteristic distrust Critical Theory has for positivism or scientism. He regards the growth of science, technology and bureaucratisation as combining state power and capitalist control in a way that provokes crisis: a crisis of legitimation (stemming from the impotence of authorities); a crisis of motivation (stemming from the powerlessness of the individual); and a crisis of identity (stemming from a lack of a sense of collective identity).

Through his critique of late capitalism, Habermas goes beyond Marx's analysis of the crisis tendencies of 'classical' capitalism. Habermas identifies one aspect of contemporary culture as its reliance on the technocrat who thrives on efficiency, which derives from the relentless quest for a controlled environment, all this in close alliance with what is perceived as marketplace imperatives—of technology's peculiar view of rationality and effectiveness, of progress and even of meaning. Habermas calls this form of rationality 'instrumental rationality'. He argues that the all-pervasive inner logic of instrumental rationality has begun to take over other areas of human culture. The criterion of instrumentality is applied to more and more relationships, replacing reflective or communicative modes as the dominant mode of human interaction with the world. Instrumentality derives from 'the technical interest' which is evidence of the basic human need to control and manage the environment. According to the Habermasian critique, this cultural change has transformed human institutions. In particular, it has provoked a crisis in politics, a crisis for the state so that the scope of politics becomes basically reduced to a question of who can run the economy best—a matter of technical decision making.

Education, as an institution of the state, has become enmeshed in this crisis and is now an object of this same pragmatic, technical decision making: a prisoner of technocratic values. These values are also the values of the marketplace and managerialism, of 'fast capitalism': competition, efficiency, utility, performance indicators, practicability, profitability and a client-centredness that verges on the obsequious. There are numerous business management texts (Peters 1992) which provide evidence of this, and whose language and vocabulary have infiltrated education at all levels and which, in their turn, have appropriated progressive educational notions such as empowerment (Gee 1993).

The impact of the work of critical theorists, including Habermas, has been felt both directly and indirectly by educational theorists (Young 1989). Our discussion of the emancipatory perspective is taken up more fully in Chapter 3; as a critique of the disciplinary mode and tradition in education it is unquestionably reliant on theoretical analyses which emphasise the emancipatory interest identified by Habermas. Critical Theory recognises that an emancipated society is one in which human beings actively control their own destinies, through a heightened understanding of the circumstances in which they live. Furthermore, Critical Theory encourages self-criticism and continuing critique through a praxis method, which implies emancipation from ideological dogmatism and the transformation of authoritarian systems through democratic communication processes. Critical Theory is not without its blind-spots and invites criticism by those on both the left and the right. A major oversight of Critical Theory as developed by Habermas is the absence of a feminist perspective, which is surely a prerequisite to any contemporary social theory claiming to be liberatory (Fraser 1989).

As we have said, the most noteworthy feature of post-1968 social theory is its distrust of orthodox politics and centralised forms of bureaucracy and government control. Soviet totalitarianism, especially in its Stalinist form, and its milder Western equivalents were the main reasons for there being widespread antagonism towards the state and its bureaucracies. Indeed, we need to be cautious in confusing the claims and successes (now perceived as failures by the populations that experienced them) of those countries in Eastern Europe which practised socialism and communism, as being true to the philosophies and principles of Marxism, for they frequently were not. The Soviet system, which remained impervious to democratic accountability, was a corruption of Marxism at all levels of society. The events of the late 1980s in Eastern Europe thus continue to pose a challenge for those who continue to advocate socialism as an alternative to capitalism, to keep its agenda alive in the face of capitalism's pyrrhic victory over the evil empires of the East. And while we are on the matter of discrediting the Marxism exemplified by societies like the Soviet Union, we must also bear in mind that the schooling systems associated with such societies are guilty of the same disciplinary excesses—if not to a more pronounced degree—than those found in capitalist societies like our own. This is indicative of the degree to which the contemporary practices of schooling transcend political ideology, the degree to which all modern societies—be they capitalist or communist—require a disciplined society of the kind described and analysed in this book.

One of the products of the late 1960s disenchantment with so-called grand theories like Marxism and capitalism was the birth of more localised political movements, such as environmentalism and the gay rights movement, and which had single-issue objectives that were not class-based and which transcended political ideology. This growth in these 'micro-political formations' was also accompanied by styles of theorising which, in an analogous way, were antagonistic towards totalising tendencies. Master narratives and grand-theorising which focused on abstractions like class and ideology, were seen as anachronistic and inappropriate, obscuring the subtleties of difference (Hebdige 1988).

This new social theory, most of which initially emerged in France rather than Germany, is associated with postmodernist or post-structuralist theory. While the two are by no means synonymous, for they tend to be associated with different sets of theorists and have rather different origins, there are many similarities. One is the word 'post', which in this context signifies a coming after and also a going beyond a particular theory or paradigm—in this case structuralism and modernism—which were seen to have exhausted themselves and have limited explanatory powers. Certainly there is an extreme pessimism permeating much of the 'post theory' which is not shared by critical theorists. Not only is there a wariness towards expressing any faith in the future or the possibility of constructive social action, but there is also a somewhat nihilistic attitude towards the past, particularly towards the Enlightenment project and humanism generally. In line with this, among some of these theorists, Marx has been totally discredited, replaced by more iconoclastic thinkers such as Friedrich Nietzsche, a deeply pessimistic thinker who had little faith in history or the achievements of the Western tradition.

Jean François Lyotard and the postmodern condition

Of the two, postmodernism is somewhat better known than post-structuralism, particularly as it has been applied in a whole number of contexts outside social theory. The phrase was first adopted in architecture and literature (Peters 1996; Rose 1991) and was then transferred to the other arts. In a context in which modernism had exhausted all artistic possibilities, the only way forward appeared to be to appropriate the aesthetic styles of the past. Thus postmodernism has come to signify an aesthetic style characterised by pastiche and quotation, and also a degree of self-referentiality, evident in the degree to which artworks probe themselves, acknowledge their own materiality as forms. The novels of Paul Auster are a good example. Moreover, there is the recognition that art, contrary to the position held by critical theorists, is part and parcel of the same economic sphere governing commodities in general. In effect, the aesthetic object is not a privileged artefact with special status and transcendent properties but is a product of a commodified aesthetics.

Mainly as the result of the work of Jean François Lyotard (1984a; 1984b), the word 'postmodern' has also come to refer to the cultural condition of the late twentieth century as it makes its inexorable movement to the new millennium. In essence, Lyotard along with a number of recent social theorists, (Beck 1992; Lash & Urry 1994; Featherstone 1991), have suggested that the postmodern condition is, above all, associated with the emergence of globalisation as a dominant cultural practice throughout the Western world. This is evident in the organisation of the late twentieth-century economy, which is increasingly knowledge and information-based, and in the networks of communication technologies such as the Internet and cable television. Such developments have rendered national boundaries increasingly irrelevant, and led to a culture in which the traditional parameters of space and time have undergone 'distanciation' (Giddens 1990) and 'compression' (Harvey 1989). At the same time, as Baudrillard (1988) has emphasised, the quality of culture has also changed, and it has become one in which spectacularity and surfaceness, along with 'simulacra' and the 'hyperreal' are marked features. Indeed, Baudrillard has argued that we are living in a totally new age, unlike any other, in which there is a proliferation of signs and information codes which negate all humanist criteria of value, in which, using the nomenclature of semiotics, signifiers have an independent existence, detached from the signified. We see these signs and codes in advertising, in the media, in education which is increasingly subject to marketisation and to the same forms of promotion as other commodities. Indeed the commodity of cultures and its popular iconography, such as the Coca Cola trade mark, have become as universal as reason was during the Enlightenment era (Bauman 1992). They are the crucifixes of the postmodern age.

It is also a culture in which everything, including the intellectual and aesthetic economy, has been commodified and made subject to the 'invisible hand' of the market. It is an era, then, in which 'homo economicus' appears to have superseded homo sapiens (Peters 1996; Peters & Marshall 1996). Wealth creation and profit have become the dominant moral impulses, governing everything from education to state policy. The marketisation of the public sector which has become economic orthodoxy of most treasuries in the Western world, replacing Keynsian approaches that were dominant in the immediate postwar period, has been orchestrated by neo-liberalists such as Hayek, who argued that the market is able to spontaneously order social formations in more effective ways than governments and bureaucracies. The impact of such marketisation strategies, along with the climate of increased fiscal restraint, are legion and have led to increased competition and to a general run down of public systems of education and health. There is not much evidence to suggest that such strategies ameliorate the quality of public services: in fact, the very opposite and it is the poor and disadvantaged who bear the brunt of their degradation. This is particularly the case with the run down of education services, and which successive governments across the world are accelerating (Ball 1993; Kenway with Bigum & Fitzclarence 1993; Marginson 1995).

Central to the cultural crisis confronting education is what may be termed 'the crisis of knowledge' in a so-called postmodern world. Lyotard rejects as inadequate the understandings or narratives which have shaped Western thinking, certainly since the Enlightenment, but in effect since Plato. These understandings or meta-narratives, as he calls them, portray the emancipation of humanity as the major project for the accumulation, dissemination and application of knowledge. Furthermore, in the Enlightenment view, that emancipation, in its various expressions of freedom, universal peace, the creation of wealth or whatever, is instituted by appealing to 'the great stories' which exemplify the progress of history. This teleological approach has played an important role in the development of our understandings of education and its institutions. To challenge that approach at its epistemological foundations is to demand a radical review of the role and meaning of education: by implication, that review is regarded as essential by Lyotard.

In his Report on Knowledge, Lyotard (1984b) demonstrates that the status of knowledge is altered in societies of advanced technology, or 'computerised societies' as he calls them. In this condition, concern for 'the pure, the just or the beautiful' (values traditionally associated with education and the Enlightenment) are subservient to 'efficiency' and the 'performativity principle'. Indeed, 'an equation between wealth, efficiency and truth is thus established'. It follows that education is confronted by a need to emphasise skills and techniques (rather than content or relational processes). Along with that, Lyotard anticipates the potential replacement of the traditional teacher by memory banks, meaning computer technology (Lyotard 1984b).

Lyotard is explicit about the dangers of this situation: under the performativity principle the computerisation of society could become the 'dream' instrument for controlling and regulating the market system, as well as knowledge itself. Yet Lyotard remains optimistic that this technology will be emancipatory in society and serve the cause of justice to which it is directly committed, provided that the public is given free access to the computer technology, thus giving groups in society the information they usually lack for making knowledgeable decisions.

What then are we (especially as educators) to make of this postmodernist critique? The postmodernists as a group have been charged with nihilism, anarchism, incoherence and a hopeless subjectivity which, according to Habermas, amounts to a neo-conservative reaction against the emancipatory ideals of the Enlightenment. That would appear to be an unjustified characterisation of Lyotard's analysis of the logic of capitalist-technological domination. On the other hand, the political project of postmodernism seems diffuse, imprecise and practically unhelpful, not only because it is deficient in a strategic sense, but also because of its lack of a utopian vision and its abandonment of the ethical foundations of contemporary Western culture (McLaren 1986; Nicholson 1989; Norris 1993). Nevertheless, our view is that it is worth attempting to appropriate postmodernist insights for the purposes of a revised understanding of education. For the moment, it is sufficient to acknowledge that an understanding of the crisis confronting education is enhanced by an appreciation of the critique offered by analyses such as that of Lyotard.

Lyotard's analysis of knowledge in technically advanced societies is merely one representation of postmodernist thought, which demonstrates the crisis of knowledge in the contemporary age. His analysis differs significantly from that of the 'critical theorist'—Habermas for instance; then again, we might have referred to the expositions of chaos theory or holistic views of science (Capra 1984; Gleick 1987; Toulmin 1982) and for which Lyotard has some enthusiasm. These provide radical critiques of post-Newtonian knowledge upon which much curriculum development and educational planning has been based. On any estimate of these views, we face a knowledge crisis with profound implications for educators. Each of these views confronts the fundamental question of what it means to be human in economies which have been constructed by transnational control of capital wedded to extremely sophisticated information technology. In this condition, we are not simply noting a fundamental shift in how we value or what we value as knowledge; rather, we are confronting a transformation in human culture.

SCHOOLS AND CLASSROOMS

Michel Foucault and the disciplinary society

Post-structuralist theory has adopted a more historicist stance than postmodernism and represents a much more systematic body of theory. It emerges out of reaction to semiology and anthropology, in particular the structuralism pioneered by Ferdinand de Saussure in relation to language, so-called 'semiotics', and developed, among others, by Claude Lévi-Strauss and Roland Barthes at the levels of anthropology and culture. To use a term from semiotics, much of structuralism was concerned with 'synchronic' analysis, with identifying the underlying structures embedded in our various sign systems, from clothes and food through to language and music (Gottdiener 1995). It tended to eschew historical and 'diachronic' analysis, namely, the kind of contextual analysis that is concerned with how meanings are shifted and transformed over periods of time.

The late Michel Foucault has been pre-eminent among post-structuralist thinkers; one of its 'rock stars'. Much of his work had an historical focus, and was concerned with unravelling the 'history of the present'. Altogether, Foucault was a rather elusive theorist, difficult to place within a single disciplinary perspective or approach, being at once a historian, philosopher, epistemologist and polemicist, with an iconoclastic and nihilistic attitude towards Western thought, owing more to Nietzsche than Marx (Peters 1996; Rux 1988).[2] His writings breached the conventional categories of knowing, moving between and across disciplines with scant regard for their conventions and methodologies.

Foucault's historiography is typical of this unconventionality. For Foucault did not 'read' history in a linear or sequential way, but saw it as discontinuous and marked with contingencies of various kinds, which reshaped its course; moreover, his scholarship tended to focus upon marginal historical phenomena such as the treatment of the mad, sexual practices and criminality. However Foucault was more than just a social historian, interested in documenting the presence of such phenomena in day-to-day life; he wanted to show and describe the ideas and rationality underpinning them, to show the purpose and intent behind the day-to-day practices and techniques associated with institutions such as penitentiaries, asylums and schools. In particular, Foucault was interested in behavioural transgression and in categories of abnormality, of human subjects who were at the edges of society, and who were therefore objects of special attention, particularly medical and psychiatric attention. Foucault used the terms 'archaeology' and 'genealogy' to describe his mode of historical analysis, which does not so much re-create the past as show the past that underpins the present. In particular, Foucault was interested in the early modern period, the years immediately following the *ancien régime*, and spanning the latter parts of the eighteenth century and the beginning of the nineteenth century when, according to Foucault, the techniques associated with the modern state, the state of reason, were established and dispersed throughout society. Central to these techniques is the relationship between knowledge and power as is the concept of the disciplinary society which this relationship was instrumental in establishing.

Unlike most theorists of power such as Hobbes and Marx (Nyberg 1981), who assume that power is applied in a top-down way by a central agency such as the government, Foucault argued that this is an outmoded view of power, reflecting a style which prevailed in pre-modern societies, when monarchs presided over society and when there were spectacular and horrific demonstrations of its application at public executions, when bodies were eviscerated and dismembered (Foucault 1979). Foucault suggests that power in modern societies has gone underground and become more discreet; it is now omnipresent throughout all levels of society, spreading its tentacles throughout the practices of everyday life in a capillary fashion (Fraser 1989) like the nervous system of the body, sending its 'messages' to all parts of society, including its extremities. Power is not an external force, overarching society in a detached sort of way: rather, it is one which permeates its whole fabric, controlling our actions and desires in small and very detailed ways, in the habits and micro-practices of everyday life, in the drills and routines of training institutions like schools and prisons where the power practices of modern life are incorporated and inculcated. According to Foucault, this change in the disposition of power, which occurred in the early modern period, the period of the first industrial revolution, was brought about to ensure that individuals became productive and useful members of society, and that those who could not, either because they were sick, mad or indigent, were segregated from the community and placed within institutions like asylums, prisons or hospitals. Thus began the 'era of governmentality', of population control, in which the human being became an object of study, of knowledge, a target for statisticians and data gatherers. This led to societies becoming more transparent and visible, to giving up their secrets (Foucault 1979; Hacking 1990; Rose 1990).

This is by no means a novel thesis. Max Weber, who like Foucault was also interested in the underlying mechanisms of modern societies, and thought that the rationality of the bureaucracy upon which they depended, also represented a fusion between discipline and knowledge (Lyon 1995; Metcalfe 1992) What is novel in Foucault's thought is that he relocates the control mechanisms involved and suggests that they are centred on the body as much as the mind, and are involved in controlling its anatomy rather than its belief systems. Foucault uses the word 'bio-power', sometimes translated as 'anatomo-politics', to describe these processes, and they exert themselves in areas like sexuality and other corporeal practices, resulting in the production of docile bodies.

Power enters the picture because the human sciences emerged at virtually the same time as the new techniques for managing power, providing a legitimating epistemology to govern these bodies. The use of the word 'bodies' rather than 'individuals' in this connection is intentional, reminding us that it is the anatomy which is the main target of Foucaultian knowledge. Hence, Foucault's abiding concern with the little practices of contemporary life, with understanding the everyday and the mundane, which are the main locations of modern power.

The main relevance of Foucault's work for education, though, is that he describes various forms of institutional technology which facilitate the application of 'bio-power'. The most exemplary form of this technology—and again it was developed during the early modern period—was Jeremy Bentham's 'panopticon'. This was a design for an ideal prison. It was one in which the behaviour of inmates was subject to continuous inspection and surveillance from a central viewing point, what Foucault (1979) calls the 'eye of power', the place of 'hierarchical observation'. Surveillance is critical to the dispersal of modern power, and its forms in the late twentieth century are legion, encompassing everything from video cameras in shopping malls to the electronic tagging of prisoners (Lyon 1994). Although Bentham's panopticon was never actually constructed, its architectural principles, in conjunction with the idea of surveillance, were incorporated into prisons such as Port Arthur in Tasmania and also (as we shall see in Chapter 9) into other forms of institutional technology, including schools where bodies are distributed in a grid of time and space to optimise their visibility and transparency.

But surveillance is only one aspect of the application of bio-power. There is the epistemological aspect which ties in its application with various specialist disciplines associated with human conduct and behaviour—hence the knowledge/power nexus which is at the heart of Foucault's later theory. Criminology, penology, psychiatry and pedagogy—the human sciences associated with the administration of disciplinary power and disciplinary systems like education—are some of these disciplines, and their practitioners are, in the main, concerned with the surveillance of deviancy through various systems of examination and the diagnosis of various pathologies which would interfere with an individual's productivity and usefulness (see Donzelot 1979). An important part of this process is the compiling of dossiers on individuals which, so to speak, constitute a record of observations made of an individual's performance and behaviour, be it in a prison, a school or wherever. Think of the way, in the school, the student is constantly being examined, tested, reported upon and encouraged to confess his or her aspirations and ambitions in interviews and counselling sessions. Examination and confession are, for Foucault, the primary mechanisms for knowing the subject in a disciplinary society, which is always centred on the 'normalising judgement' and which is enacted through the micro-practices of school, such as those associated with time, space, behaviour, speech, deportment, gestures and sexuality. Thus the various theories of subjectivity associated with Foucault's work emphasise the significance of the everyday discourses of the classroom, and draw attention to the minutiae of pedagogic practice as the governing principles of contemporary subjectivity.

In Chapter 1, it was noted that theories cause us to re-examine the world and see facets of it in a new light, through new theoretical lenses. Foucault's work, like much post-structuralist and postmodernist theory, encourages us to examine not the grand sweep of society, but its micro-practices, as these are manifested in the daily life of institutions like schools and prisons. In its examination of the seemingly banal and smallscale, the timely, the chaotic, fragmentary, heterogenous, the local and the concrete, Foucault's work is typical of much postmodernist thought and it contrasts markedly with the Newtonian search for some universal order and abstract principle inherent in much modernist thought and social theory (Adam 1995; Toulmin 1990). It also rejects much of the dualism that is an inherent part of Western thinking, such as mind/body, thinking/feeling, nature/culture and so on.

Another aspect of Foucault's work was his criticism of Western humanism, with its overriding faith in rationality and the autonomy of the individual, which are, in fact, governing principles of the educational endeavour, justifying its moral claims and reasons for being. He provided a fierce critique of the self-centred Cartesianism of the Western tradition and offered a framework for understanding the human being as a decentred subject, who is the product of discourses that are historically framed and determined. In this respect, his ideas share some accord with other theorists working within the postmodernist and post-structuralist framework (e.g. Jacques Derrida and Jacques Lacan). Derrida's work, in particular, goes against the 'whole grain of Western philosophy' and suggests that philosophy is a form of writing and inscription not truth and that the boundaries of language are the boundaries of thought (Usher & Edwards 1994). In fact, according to Derrida's well-known injunction, there is nothing outside of the text!

Hence the appeal of the post theories for feminist thinkers who have felt excluded from the terrain of 'male-stream' thought, with its commitment to rationality and its apparent neglect of the caring and feeling side of the human condition and who argue for a more liberalised notion of the human subject. Along with Lyotard's attempt to abandon the grand narrative of science, to which we have already referred, the implications of this post theory for education are immense. Just about every assumption that education is founded upon, from its faith in rationality to its belief in individuality, is thrown into question by the theory. Education is fundamentally part of the humanist project, 'a dutiful child of the Enlightenment' (Usher & Edwards 1994) and so questioning it and its role in the generation of better and more rational human beings means setting aside one of the primary goals of education. Indeed, as Usher & Edwards suggest, education finds itself in something of a double bind: in order to liberate it must also incarcerate.

The discipline of education

Following Foucault, we will take it as a given that education is a (if not the) disciplinary science, one concerned with the observation and regulation of human subjects, with the incarceration and binding of the subject, with the production of identity, particularly as it relates to the area of their desires, physical dispositions and cognitive power. The organisation and practices of the school, even its architecture, all reflect this disciplinary function. Interestingly, in this connection, the word 'school' has both disciplinary and epistemological connotations as does the word 'pupil', a word that has now been superseded (Hamilton 1989). We teach disciplines and we discipline at the same time, which is an etymological exemplification of the power/knowledge nexus. It may be no coincidence, but even the word 'school' in its verb form (not often used these days) preserves the behavioural notion of disciplining, of chastising, of remedying transgressive behaviour. Much of the discussion of the purpose of schooling, particularly in philosophy, has focused upon its liberal dimensions, of showing how education contributes to a more moral and politic citizenry, one more informed and in touch with its cultural inheritance. This has tended to detract from recognising the control and disciplining functions of schooling, particularly as they operate in the practices associated with the material fabric of school life, in its timetables and work-scheduling, in its textbooks, in its day-to-day routines, in its buildings and furnishings, in its various forms of documentation from its prospectuses through to its rules of conduct. In an endeavour to show that they are imbued with power dimensions, this book will focus, particularly in its second part, upon the micro-practices of schools and classrooms.

One theory of schooling that we wish to explore in this book, which is derived from post-structuralism, in effect, visualises the school as a technological artefact, as a mechanism for producing and manufacturing individuals or, perhaps we should say, following Foucault, bodies. The idea of a school—or any institution for that matter—being a form of technology (to be precise, a moral technology) might require some adjustment in outlook, as we tend to baulk at the idea of humans being engineered and designed according to precise specifications, to being the products of some kind of institutional assembly line over which they have very little control.

Although we have tended to separate them out, as if they were mutually exclusive paradigms, the theories of the Frankfurt school and of post-structuralism do have some points of contact, in spite of some notable arguments between their major proponents.[3] For a start, the theories are committed to the overthrow of our existing society and to the redesign, if not replacement, of some of its major institutions. Habermas, for instance, is committed to a society where dominance and oppression are absent, where individuals are genuinely autonomous and not the tools of technical rationalism, where there is truthful exchange of ideas according to the principles of 'communicative competence'. Foucault, on the other hand, places his faith in the fact that there is nothing essential about human nature or incorrigible about institutions, that just as modern society has crafted a particular type of human being and designed particular institutions to house them, so some future society dominated by different discourses could result in human beings and institutions having a rather different nature and character (Rux 1988). The points of difference centre on strategies for achieving human emancipation. Those following Habermas seem to place considerable faith in the capacity of individuals to overthrow technical rationality by confronting the state and setting an alternative social arrangement based on Enlightenment and humanist principles of liberty and justice, rationality and truth. Foucault's agenda is somewhat less ambitious and centres on intervening in local sites like prisons and schools and on reforming them in the light of a more libertarian agenda, if needs be, with an abandonment of the humanist inheritance.

By way of a conclusion

In the first two chapters we have achieved several objectives. First, we demystified theory, showing that what is called theory is an elaboration of day-to-day thinking and reflection. We also argued that theory is a way of seeing and apprehending the world, a prescription for perception, a pair of epistemological spectacles through which the world is seen in various and different ways. We then examined the context in which theory is generated. We argued that theory is a feature of a regime of truth, these regimes being part and parcel of a research culture which has well-defined characteristics and for which education is a progressive apprenticeship. We then proceeded to examine the theoretical perspectives of this book, its epistemological spectacles, and the regimes of truth from which they are derived. We noted that this book is exploring the tension between what education is like and what it ought to be like, the tension between education's disciplinary functions as opposed to its emancipatory functions. In the first, education is perceived as a controlling mechanism, one concerned to generate particular kinds of human beings, in line with the demands of society. We noted how pedagogic knowledge advances the control mechanisms of society, facilitating the surveillance and governmentality of individuals. In the second, these demands and the society in which they originate are brought into question, becoming the subjects of the kinds of critical reflection and analysis which leads to action and transformation.

NOTES

1 In 1968 the Western world was close to revolution, at least in cities like Paris and Berlin where there was widespread student activism and a concerted attempt to overthrow capitalism. Meanwhile, on the other side of the Iron Curtain, the first experiments in *perestroika*, which occurred in Prague, were curtailed by the tanks of the Soviet Union, thus leading to a widespread loss of faith (which had already begun with the Stalinist purges of the 1930s) in the possibilities of a Soviet-style social arrangement, and

which eventually found their ultimate realisation in the complete collapse of the Soviet system throughout in eastern Europe by the early 1990s.
2. In one of his last interviews, Foucault said of himself that he was a 'crypto-Marxist, an irrationalist, a nihilist' (Rux 1988). Foucault's major works, other than those referred to in this chapter, are *Madness and Civilization: An Archaeology of Medical Perception* (1975); and the three volumes of the 'genealogy' of sexuality, titled respectively *The History of Sexuality: An Introduction* (1980); *The Uses of Pleasure*, (1988) and *The Care of the Self* (1988). Foucault is often at his most accessible in interviews and over the years there have been various collections of these published. Among the best are those by Gordon (1980) and Kritzman (1988).
3. Rorty (1984) has summarised the nature of this conflict, at least as it has raged between Lyotard and to a lesser extent Foucault, and Habermas.

Keywords and phrases

- Critical Theory
- epistemology
- globalisation
- instrumental rationality
- modernism
- panopticon
- post-structuralism
- postmodernism
- subjectivity
- surveillance
- time–space compression
- time–space distanciation

Tutorial and field activities

1. To what extent has the idea of the postmodern pervaded our everyday sensibility? For example, would you be able to recognise a postmodern narrative if you read it or saw it on film? You might like to read a postmodern novel such as Paul Auster's *New York Trilogy* or see one of his films, such as *Smoke*, and identify their postmodern features. Examine the architecture in your local town or city, and note any buildings that display postmodern features, that for example, have turrets or other forms of non-functionalist ornamentation. Apply the same observations in other cultural domains such as music and fashion. Do you also identify with the postmodern condition, with a feel of anxiety and crisis, that old certainties have fragmented?

2. David Harvey's notion of time–space compression is an extremely useful one. He is arguing that we now live in a world where space as a dimension has much less relevance as a framing principle of everyday life. Explore some of the features of time–

space compression in your life, and its ramifications for education.

3   Are Bauman and Baudrillard right, that we live in a world dominated by the symbols of transnational corporations, that the world of the media, of the cultural industries is as primary in our lives as that of that the actual, physical, empirical world? Should we be perturbed by these developments, by the fact that our culture is increasingly globalised, meaning Americanised, and that national and local expressions of culture are becoming relevant and marginal?

4   Explore the ideas of marketisation and the likelihood that most aspects of public sector will become privatised. What are the likely outcomes on education systems that are increasingly dominated by the market dynamics and that need to seek corporate sponsorship to support their programs and activities? What does it signify about education institutions when their identity cards have a Coca Cola logo on their obverse?

Education in context

He supposed, that except musicians, everyone thought Beethoven a bore, as everyone except mathematicians thought mathematics a bore.

Sitting thus at his beer-table, mentally impassive, he was one day surprised to notice that his mind followed the movement of a Sinfonie. He could not have been more astonished had he suddenly read a new language. Among the marvels of education, this was the most marvellous.

A prison wall that barred his senses on one great side, suddenly fell, of its own accord, without so much as his knowing when it had happened.

(Henry Adams 1995)

Making education meaningful

Although the term 'education' has been used on a number of occasions, it has not been defined. Indeed, education is a much-contested concept which means many and varied things to teachers and educationalists, to parents and students, and to the general community. Rather than attempt a succinct or simple statement of what is meant by education, the next two chapters will outline a series of perspectives relating to what education is and has become, and what it should become and ought to be. This chapter will concentrate on specifying the differences between the various dimensions of education, bearing in mind the distinction developed in the previous chapter between the disciplinary and emancipatory perspectives.

In the first instance, it is useful to outline some of the parameters within which the terms 'education' and 'schooling' are discussed, understood and misconceived. What might appear on the surface to be a mere exercise in semantics is, in fact, quite important for teachers. Increasingly they are called upon to write philosophies of education and to participate in the drafting of strategic planning statements and to write annual reports, in which passing references to the underlying values of education are made. Moreover, debates about these values are part and parcel of the official discourse of education, in which recommendations for future policy directions are based upon bedrock assumptions of what constitutes 'proper education'. At a more local level, similar debates take place within parents and citizens' groups, around the framing of a school development plan and within school staff meetings. Even school students are inclined to ask their teachers about the whys and wherefores of education. At a wider community level, debates about educational values are increasingly subjects of media reportage. In effect, these are examples of the ways in which theory, as it was described in Chapter 1, permeates the practical and public discourses of education at all the various levels of their articulation.

Thus it is useful to examine the meaning of education, to determine the parameter and contents of its semantic frame. But a word of caution: meaning is not something which is absolute or incorrigible, not something which can be found in consulting a dictionary, for language is a kind of closed system; meanings, as the Deconstructionists have suggested, are always deferred, being defined in terms of other words, which are in turn defined by other words and so on. If we examine the 'logical geography' of schooling and education, we discover that these words are used in various ways and have a complex cultural etymology, passing through many phases of usage and application. The word 'education', for instance, like many words associated with the intellectual discourses that have developed in Western cultures, has its origins in the classical languages, in this case, Latin. Its root meaning is shared with other words such as produce, seduce, deduce, induce—words which indicate change of some kind, change to a different state of mood or logical outcome— in effect, of transformation or perhaps liberation. Education, which shares an etymology with the word 'educe', originally meant to 'draw out', 'to lead out'. Contemporary notions of education concerning the realisation of innate potential have adopted the 'leading out' etymology because of its softer overtones rather than the more authoritarian and disciplinary 'drawing out'. This highlights the degree to which there are normative and value dimensions underpinning the notions of education. For instance, we all have an approximate idea of what it means to be well-educated, and we tend to associate it with a range of epistemological capacities and conditions of mind such as being well-read and articulate, at home with ideas and intellectual argument. In addition, there is the family resemblance problem. This encompasses the many processes similar in character to educating which bring about changes in human capacity and disposition (e.g. indoctrination, rote-learning, conditioning, social engineering and training). For various reasons, it is often said that processes such as these do not count as education.

Turning now to the word 'school' with which education is often taken to be synonymous: like the word 'education', it has a long and celebrated history, beginning in antiquity. Its initial meaning contained overtones of leisure, though in its classical sense these were associated with contemplation and deep reflection, generally of a philosophical kind. It was not until the Middle Ages that the word began to acquire its educational connotations when it came to refer to a place where lectures were presented (Ong 1958). We noted in Chapter 1 how the verb form of the word 'school' also has disciplinary connotations which are associated with dealing with difficult behaviour.

Both education and schooling thus possess a normative dimension. By normative we mean that the term involves standards or criteria which must be satisfied if it is to be appropriately applied or not. Within every view of education there is a system of underpinning values, a philosophical paradigm or discourse. This is why it is important to be aware of the discourse in which the word is used. For instance, as we shall see later, many politicians and business executives have a rather different concept of education than academics and teachers. The fact is that all of us, whether we have any background understanding of the subject or not, tend to use the word 'education' and its various derivatives, and most of us have some vague understanding of what is meant by the word. For instance, we tend (rightly or wrongly) to associate education with schools, with what happens in classrooms. Indeed, many of us think that education is synonymous with schooling. We would also associate being educated with credentials (i.e. by assuming the well-educated person has letters after their name) and with the accumulation of 'cultural capital' which involves not just qualities of mind but also the ability to dress and to be at ease with the activities and artefacts associated with high culture (Bourdieu 1984).

It is in these senses that education is not just descriptive of teaching and learning processes, but also contains a normative dimension which enshrines values. Yet, in the past, education was not always associated with schools. As we shall see in the next section of this chapter, these institutions are a recent invention, peculiar to Western societies. Nor has the word 'education' always been associated with the teaching and learning of human beings. Peters, for instance, has shown how the 'social history' of the word once included animals, and quite lowly ones at that, such as silk-worms! (Peters 1972). In fact, equestrians still talk about 'educating' their horses.

Normally, proponents of particular educational theories make their claims in terms of an assertion that what they regard as educational is associated with human betterment, with what Rorty has called 'the enlargement of the moral imagination' (Arcilla 1995). Such claims rest on what have been traditionally described as ethical questions, 'What is the good?', 'What is the good for society?' But the answers to these questions relate to the answers to other perplexing but vital questions, 'Good for whom?', 'For persons?', 'But what or who is a person?', 'How do persons relate to life, the universe and ultimate reality, if there is such?' and, anyway, 'How do we know?' These inquiries constitute metaphysical and epistemological considerations at the heart of the age-long quest of a philosophy that postmodernists have claimed is suspect. The simple point is that theories, or perspectives on what education is, are based on an explicit or implicit philosophical world-view, usually understood within the framework of the rational principles of the Enlightenment and humanism (see also Bowen & Hobson 1974; Gutek 1988; Moore 1977). As we said earlier education is a 'dutiful child of the Enlightenment' and attempts to give, quite literally, flesh and bone to its ideals and philosophies. To this extent, postmodernism and post-structuralism, unlike critical theory, are uneasy with the concept of modern education framed in such normative terms, particularly as they are underpinned with notions of the autonomous subject and foundationalist approaches to knowledge.

On the other hand, indirectly influenced by critical theory and the project of the Enlightenment, the Brazilian philosopher of education, Paulo Freire (1974), indicates the normative character of education when he insists that education is never neutral. As Freire points out, where a particular approach to education expresses what may be termed 'a dominant ideology' or a 'a hegemonic worldview' there may be some pretence by the managers of that educational system to declare their approach 'neutral' or 'value free', or at least to keep implicit their motivating values; in this way, they promote a disciplinary, or what Freire would call a 'domesticating', form of education. Another way of expressing this point is to say that preferences about the purpose and content of education are formed in a cultural context. A philosophical world view is related to the values and symbols around which human culture is fashioned. In this sense, particular expressions of the purpose and content of education relate directly to the norms of particular cultures or sub-cultures. Whether as cultural transformation, cultural transmission or both, institutional forms of education are, in essence, 'cultural action'.

This, indeed, is the term used by Freire (1972) who, in naming one of his texts, suggests the reader make the substitute 'cultural action' for 'education'. This interpretation of the relationship between education and culture (which is advocated by Freire and the many others who have followed him) invites a wide and profound understanding of education; in this view, the pedagogical is always political and the quest for literacy involves a 'naming of the world' which is closely allied to the never-completed task of human beings to make their culture. The normative and cultural aspects of discussions about education can be seen in the current debates about education policy, with their intense concern over holding education accountable to economic needs, presupposing, in effect, a normative and cultural framework.

Lower-case education

As we have already indicated, one of the fundamental confusions in the popular understanding of education is that education and schooling are one and the same. Richmond (1975) has provided a detailed distinction between the two; here, it is sufficient to note that while schools may contribute to education they may also be counter-educational in a similar way that churches may be counter-religious, hospitals counter-health, roads counter-speed. It follows that, on this view of schooling and education, it would be more accurate if state bodies charged with administering school systems reverted to the earlier terminology 'Department of Public Instruction' rather than 'Department of Education'. If this view sounds cynical, it is not meant to be; indeed, arguably, when a more idealised view of education is pursued over and against schooling, then there is a greater chance that schools or Departments of Public Instruction can be challenged to be more effective educational agencies, as hidden values are made more explicit. Such an approach will also enable us to identify that approach which tends to regard education as socialisation and as the producer of a disciplinary society. Such a view is, in effect, another normative account of education.

In a study of the relationship between 'education' and 'socialisation', Nyberg & Egan (1981) identify socialisation as 'preparation for employment, family and community life and the political activities of responsible citizenship'. They argue that, in a regrettable dilution of an essentially educational function, schools have been forced to take on more and more socialising functions in recent years. This pre-occupation contrasts with education which to them is a more 'all-embracing' concept referring to 'a less practical set of dispositions and capacities' which includes 'respect for intellectual life and an historical perspective which enables one to appreciate one's culture'. Bemoaning the fact that even teachers are more socialised than educated, they reject the possibility of a technology of education centred on the efficient production of specified ends.

Harris (1982b) has a made a similar distinction between education and socialisation, but goes further than Nyberg & Egan in suggesting that the capitalist mode of production—and one could add consumption as well—will only tolerate an abridged version of education to operate in schools, what he calls small 'e' education, which is tantamount to socialisation. Anything more would pose a threat to the machinery of capitalism, which does not thrive in conditions of education, where critical minds exist to challenge its imperatives and dogmas, and where individuals are less inclined to be feverish consumers, content instead to spend their leisure in intellectual pursuits like reading and attending concerts and visiting museums, enriching their lives rather than their bank balances.

The thrust of these arguments is very persuasive. Nevertheless, we must be cautious in making too sharp a disjunction between 'education' and 'socialisation'. Dualistic ways of discussing the concept of education serve to underline the necessary distinction between socialisation and education in its fuller and normative sense. However, they are only helpful in framing a normative concept of education useful for developing social policy when the two parts are understood as complementary parts of a whole, two sides of the one coin. We can never simplistically equate 'education' and 'socialisation'. Nonetheless, critically understood, education can never be reduced to such an abstraction that the meaning of 'becoming educated' does not include the meaning of 'becoming socialised'. It is a central thesis of this book that, as cultural action and edification, education stands in an uneasy tension with the society in which it is historically located, while not being divorced from that society.

Most disconcertingly, the socialisation function of educational agencies and policies has usually promoted the exercise of social control as a major aim of institutions like schools, and of their teachers; moreover, as we have seen, this happens with their complete consent. In the view of many critics, that social control function has limited personal autonomy, has stifled the development of democratic, open and participatory societies and has thereby been anti-educational. Harris, like many philosophers influenced by the neo-Marxist paradigm, sees the social control function of education practice as inducting 'people into a set of ongoing social relations' but, more than that, as getting 'people to perceive the world in a distorted way whereby the real existing relations are disguised', so keeping people 'ignorant of what is really going on and how it works in their best interests' (Harris 1979).

In these emancipatory analyses, power is understood to be exercised by the system and its agents, teachers over learners, rather than in a shared environment of empowerment. These insights have focused greater attention on what has been described as the 'hidden curriculum'—that complex of practices and values embodied in school life in such a way that they are taught informally or indirectly in a powerful, if unconscious, way (Henry, Knight, Lingard & Taylor 1988). We shall have more to say about this curriculum in Chapter 4. The hierarchical nature of most school organisations, with their all-powerful administration teams and a pecking order from subject coordinator to the most junior student, is a powerful social control mechanism, all too often inculcating subservience and passivity amongst the future citizens of our hierarchical and partial democracies.

We have already noted in Chapter 1 how knowledge is a control mechanism. This theme will be explored more fully in later chapters of this book, but it is important that we note at this stage that too often, alienation of body from mind, reason from feeling and emotion, action from thought, and self from other results when educational practice operates as social control. Certainly this is the experience of large numbers of secondary school students. It results in the sad, but oft-cited observation that 'school taught her to hate education'. The zeal for learning is lost in a sea of alienation. Such schooling experiences can hardly be called education or educative (Martin 1985). There are parallels between this viewpoint and the analysis of 'power' and 'discipline' developed by Foucault. As we observed in Chapter 2, much of what Foucault has written of prisons and mental asylums can be applied to schools, particularly in the earliest phases of their development, to which we now turn.

SCHOOLS AND CLASSROOMS

What's in a name?

It has already been suggested that though schooling might be a necessary condition of education (depending upon one's concept of it) it is not a sufficient condition. There are plenty of instances of cultures in which 'intergenerational continuity' is secured without schooling. One such instance close to home is that of the Aborigines who, for millennia before the European invasion, transmitted a very sophisticated and complex culture without the need for schools. Even in our own culture, many individuals have achieved considerable academic success without the benefit of schooling; either that, or they left school prematurely. Albert Einstein is a case in point. His marks at school were unimpressive and demonstrate the veracity of Mark Twain's observation that his education was interrupted by his schooling. All of this has provided grist for the mill for the so-called 'deschoolers' like Illich, who have argued that the advantages and benefits of a deschooled society are legion and persuasive.[1]

In spite of these rather jaundiced views about its effects and outcomes, we nevertheless have had over 100 years of universal schooling in the West, and it does not look as though such schooling, in spite of the advocacy of the deschoolers, is about to become extinct. With its ever-lengthening duration, its stranglehold on society seems to be tightening, if anything. Schooling, in this context, refers to a rather large network of institutions, not all of them administered by the government (at least directly), or necessarily compulsory. What we know as primary and secondary schools are the commonest types of schooling which also includes a range of post-compulsory forms of education available at TAFE colleges and universities, as well as specialised institutions concerned with the education of the differently abled. Then there are types of schools which have become extinct, like the industrial and domestic schools. Primary schools were once called elementary schools. The nomenclature of educational institutions tends to vary between different states and national systems, reflecting the changes to the structure of schooling as new policies and educational imperatives develop. For instance, in Australia, secondary schools are called 'high' schools, which reflects American nomenclature, which in turn reflects that of France and Germany. The United Kingdom, on the other hand, has 'comprehensive' schools which are a postwar development, reflecting the abandonment of selective forms of secondary education in the postwar period, when schooling was divided between grammar schools and secondary modern schools. Vestiges of this English tradition of naming have been retained by those private schools, which are known as grammar schools, reflecting a tradition which originated in the Middle Ages, when grammar was one of the principal domains of the curriculum, one of the Liberal Arts.

Childhood and the invention of schooling

With schooling, (and here we are referring to the state-controlled primary and secondary schools), we are looking at a tradition which began to emerge in the UK in the latter parts of the eighteenth century. There had been other dress rehearsals for modern schooling in other parts of Europe. Notable were those in Prussia in the sixteenth century, mainly prompted by print technology and the ready availability of books. Not only did this lead to a proliferation of discourses on childhood, in which conduct was prescribed and practices of rearing outlined, but it also led to recognition of the school as a potential disciplinary apparatus, via which the behaviour of students could be scrutinised closely and programmed according to the dispositions demanded by the state (Luke 1989).

It needs to be borne in mind that the construction of modern childhood has a close connection with the introduction of universal schooling, which transformed its condition, placing a temporal buffer zone between the phases of infancy and adulthood. As is clear from some recent histories on the subject,[2] childhood is not a biological condition, but is, in large measure, a social construction, one which has taken different forms across cultures and across history. For instance, before the existence of the aforementioned buffer zone, the boundary between childhood and adulthood within Western societies was a weak and permeable one, with, on the behavioural front, none of the taboos and prohibitions which now surround it. Children in the past matured very quickly, and were admitted to adult society as soon as they were able. Contrast this with the modern conditions of childhood, which have postponed the admission into adult society until around eighteen, at least in terms of civic and legal rights and responsibilities. Indeed, there is often a hiatus between physical and the civic age at which the onset of adulthood occurs.

In line with this, children have been constructed as innocent and pristine beings, to be protected from all facets of life but especially those connected with its major biological events such as birth, sex and death. Children's experience tends to be heavily censored, removing from its scope anything which smacks of the morally questionable, anything which might corrupt the child or lead it astray. Thus a culture of childhood has arisen which emphasises its distinctive features, its pure and unadulterated nature. The world of toys and children's literature, the distinctive apparel that boys and girls wear, even concern for their welfare and pedagogic well-being, are all products of modem times and, as far as the working classes are concerned, are no more than 100 years old. Before that time, the culture of adults and children was not separately defined, and the activities of both dovetailed into one another, with little concern about whether it was right and proper for children to participate in adult activities. In this context, it has been suggested that the category of childhood as we know it today did not really exist. Children, for instance, not only worked but also gambled, danced and played alongside adults; there also appears to have been a relaxed attitude towards sexual expression. In effect, what schooling did was to consolidate the construction of childhood, emphasising the differences between being an adult and a child, and promoting childhood as a phase of life with its own traits and features which parents and teachers were expected to consider and observe in their treatment and care of children. In order to facilitate this, legislation and laws were developed to protect children from exploitation and abuse (Sherwin 1996).

Some have argued that the traditional construction of childhood, particularly with respect to innocence, which is hard to maintain in an era of television and the widespread commodification of childhood, are changing and harking back to the pre-modern era (Kline 1993; Postman 1982; Meyrowitz 1985). Others have argued that the control over childhood is, if anything, subtler and more sophisticated and that we are witnessing a return to a vision of childhood that re-emphasises innocence and the child's original goodness (Jenks 1996). Not only are teachers involved in the supervision of the child's normal development but increasingly parents, especially mothers, are expected to provide circumstances and conditions which are optimal for the child's learning and cognitive development. In effect, the home has become another domain for the governance and the surveillance of childhood, augmenting that of the classroom (Meredyth & Tyler 1993; Reiger 1986; Walkerdine 1989).

Universal schooling, which placed new demands on children, was instrumental in redefining the conditions of childhood, in transforming its character and in introducing new dimensions of governmentality to the processes of upbringing and child-rearing. As far as the English-speaking nations are concerned, mass compulsory schooling, like much of the culture that we associate with the modern world, including sport, was invented in Britain, in the nineteenth century, and then was subsequently exported to its colonies (Véliz 1994).

This is particularly true of many facets of the contemporary school's ritualistic culture and its related 'symbolic architecture' (Corrigan 1987) which, in the main, have been derived from the English public school of the late nineteenth century. In this context 'symbolic architecture' refers to the semiotic and iconographical features of the modern school, such as those associated with school dress and uniform, badges and mottoes, songs and war cries, house structures and the prefecture. Their adoption in the English public school followed a turbulent period of student discontent and extreme individualism during the early nineteenth century, which reformers such as Thomas Arnold, the headmaster of Rugby, were keen to eradicate. They did so, through the cultivation of so-called 'muscular Christianity' which was as much a product of the sporting field, of games like cricket and rugby, as it was the classroom. Games were seen as a way of cultivating moral virtue (Mangan 1981; Wilkinson 1964). It led to the rise of increased identification with the school as a collective, as a community of students and teachers and with the emergence of feelings of belonging and affiliation, with *esprit d'corps*. A crude correspondence was assumed to operate: loyalty to school meant loyalty to country. Of more pertinence, though, is the fact that these practices of identification in turn led to their material exemplification in such cultural practices as the school song and eventually the school blazer, which was initially a garment of honour, which only those who achieved success in the sporting arena, were entitled to wear. And it is this symbolic architecture that was invented in the English public school that was subsequently employed throughout the Empire, including not just the Dominions such as Australia but also in the colonies, in the Carribean and Africa (Davidson 1990; McCarthy 1995; Rich 1989).

At the humbler level of the working classes the experiments in modern schooling were preceded by forms of proto-education such as that of the Sunday school tradition, which was grounded in a religious paternalism with a strong pastoral emphasis (Hunter 1995), designed to rescue the souls of the dissolute working classes from damnation and to render the great body of them governable by reason (Usher & Edwards 1994). This period of early education also coincided with the transformation from a pre-industrial to an industrial society, and the proliferation of the Protestant work ethic.

Schools thus played an important role in the modernisation of society and the reconstruction of childhood. But they also acted as a social contraceptive, helping to prevent what was perceived to be a general deterioration in the moral and ethical standards of the population, particularly among the poorest classes, at the end of the eighteenth century. Crime, prostitution, dishonesty, alcoholism, disregard for authority and vandalism were all on the increase, especially in urban settings; indeed, they were almost out of control. At the same time, there was a decline in religious observance which was frequently held to be the root cause of this widespread decline in public morality (Laqueur 1976; Jones & Williamson 1979).

It was into this setting that the Sunday school ventured, with its message of hope: that it could restore some semblance of order and health to the 'moral economy', an oft-used phrase at this time, of the nation. The Sunday school movement, which was considerable in its impact on English society, was not just inspired by the philanthropic middle classes who were keen to protect the social order and, at the same time, their own economic interests, but also had considerable support from the working classes themselves. There were other educational initiatives around at the time, also fostered by church organisations such as the development of Roman Catholic parish schools, which also had working-class support. These tended to have a less intrusive impact on the lives of the working class than other forms of embryonic schooling and became a movement which offered notable advantages to them (Purvis 1984).

The whole approach of schooling at this time was predicated on the *tabula rasa* theories of learning, literally the idea that the mind was a blank slate at birth, which then had considerable currency and influence as a result of the philosophical writings of John Locke and Jean-Jacques Rousseau. These insisted that the child had no innate dispositions and that, providing the environment was furbished with the right experiences and sensations, the child's outlook could be suitably organised according to the moral economy of the time. This faith in the capacity of the school to regenerate the outlook of the whole population through re-ordering the experience of children helped justify their segregation from the corrupting influence of their parents, who were considered beyond redemption (Laqueur 1976).

Thus the school was conceived as an apparatus, as a technology to produce a certain kind of sensibility; indeed, it was often referred to as such. The Romantic poet, Samuel Coleridge, called it a 'vast-moral steam engine'; Joseph Lancaster, one of the first architects of the modern school, referred to it as 'an engine of instruction'. This sensibility, initially at least, was one marked by the productive habits of mind, by self-denial and temperance, by general thriftiness and attention to the cares of family life, and to the preparedness for hard work and industriousness. Lessons were centred around the Scriptures, and the ethos of learning was Calvinist in character. The ideal school pupil was one imbued with this sensibility, which was, in effect, the Protestant work ethic which is at the heart of the 'ideal capitalist man or woman' (Laqueur 1976). Thus the schools tended to be organised along quasi-militaristic lines, with extensive attention to rule following; and they played an important role in the diffusion of Protestant values to the working classes, consolidating the capitalist and patriarchal social relations that were marked features of the industrial order.

Through such schools, students thus came to know their place in society, within the customary categories of class and gender. This control and government of the sensibility also extended to the leisure habits of the poorer classes, which were regarded as decadent and depraved. Children were offered rational pastimes, which emphasised the culture of self-improvement and encouraged sobriety and temperance as an alternative to the bear baiting and pugilism, football playing and gambling which were rife and uncontrolled during this period. It was from this desire to protect children from the corrupting influences of the local environment that today's school excursion emerged. Thomas Cook, the architect of modern tourism, organised a day's outing for some three thousand Leicester school students, to protect them from the 'monster intemperance' that was horse racing in the mid-nineteenth century (Feifer 1985).

Australia's early education system displayed many of the same hallmarks as those that marked that of the United Kingdom. Like many other aspects of its early society, the education system of early Australia was, in fact, transported in tact from the 'mother' country. In fact, the same concerns were evident in Australia, particularly as its population was regarded, with its convict origins, as particularly recalcitrant and depraved, needing moral guidance from a Christian perspective. Indeed, the early colonial governments were willing to cede control of education to the clergy right up until the middle nineteenth century when state-controlled education was favoured. Schooling was introduced to assist the moral growth of the colony, to offset its convict beginnings and to reform the criminal elements in its population (Barcan 1980). This was even true of colonies like South Australia which did not have a convict population, but where the ruling class felt that an appropriately fashioned schooling could render the 'lower orders ... less dangerous and unpleasant to be with and to employ' (Miller 1986).

The emphasis on control and on transforming the outlook of students, in governing their mentalities and subjectivity, was because, at the inception of modern schooling, these facets of behaviour were recognised as being within the power of the school to control and manipulate. As schools developed and became integral parts of the infrastructure of the modern state, the tendencies which were already inherent in the Sunday school became more pronounced. Even the justifications for state-organised schooling, which were in the main articulated by the Utilitarians, largely centred on the possibilities of population control, in the moral sense. For instance, as the public purse was involved, arguments had to be found that would justify the expense on a massive expansion of the schooling system. One argument was that, in helping to eliminate dishonesty and the criminal habits, the schools would eventually lower prison populations and thereby their funding could be offset by the need for lesser expenditure on prisons. According to Jeremy Bentham, one of the more prominent of the early Utilitarians, thereby 'state investment on education was socially profitable' (cited in West 1963). To an extent, such expectations were vindicated. Juvenile crime did decrease, and there was evidence that by the middle of the nineteenth century the working classes were more content and satisfied with their lot than they had been towards the end of the eighteenth century (Goldstrom 1977).

What is worth stressing is that the moral benefits of schooling were valued more highly than its intellectual benefits, which were almost a secondary consideration. In effect, the early 'architects' of modern schooling recognised the view that we are advocating in this book: that education had the power to transform the sensibility of a whole population, to equip it with the kind of outlook that was needed if an industrial society was to develop and be maintained. What we need now is a schooling system which once again recognises its transformative possibilities, one that is able to transform the society that it is currently so adept at conserving.

Some measure of resistance

It would be a mistake to think that the introduction of universal, compulsory schooling was followed by mass docility, and that the disciplinary regime of the school was never opposed or subverted. If there is inadequacy in the Foucaultian approach, it is that it does not recognise the counter-strategies and conducts that often emerge within institutions, even of the most brutalised kind, to circumvent surveillance and disciplinary techniques. Giddens (1984), who has criticised this aspect of Foucault's work, has noted how Goffman's (1976) studies of institutions, particularly of asylums, offer a more accurate account of how it is that their patients often subvert disciplinary techniques, creating spaces in which to be autonomous and free agents. Indeed, as is clear from some of the revisionist social histories of the nineteenth-century education, the resistance to many aspects of universal schooling was considerable, particularly in England and Australia.

It was not that the working classes were opposed to the notion of education in its most extended and emancipatory sense; on the contrary, they could see its benefits. However, they resented the form of education that the state imposed on them. Not only were its excesses brutalising, but its routines upset the routines of working-class life, particularly those of its children who were required to contribute to the family's income. Compulsory attendance at school often interfered with the patterns of working life, imposing time demands which meant children could not easily work, even on a part-time basis, without censure from the school. Also, the moral rhetoric of schooling, which, as we have seen, was based around the Bible, contradicted working-class experience, which rarely included Christian charity in its orbit. The result of such ill-feeling was that attendance at school, in spite of the legal requirements, was, as a form of protest, often irregular and sporadic. Another form of protest was widespread vandalism.

But the most dramatic form of protest was industrial, the student strikes which, in spite of the repressive measures taken to crush them, were common in many parts of England in the initial decade of the twentieth century (Humphries 1984). These involved students as well as parents, and represented a defiant confrontation with the authoritarian state, and with the school bureaucracy and its disciplinary regime. This opposition, the tactics of which were derived from the labour movement, was not just directed towards the brutalising environments of schools, but also to their hours and holidays, locations and leaving ages. Nor did the opposition come simply from disgruntled students who, as the victims of the insensitive system, had little to gain from schooling; in the main, the opposition was drawn from the more able students—those who, on the surface at least, had the *most* to gain from schooling.

It is important to recognise that resistance is not destructive. On the contrary, resistance can be transformative and hopeful in the way discussed later in this chapter and in Chapter 3. Indeed, resistance often leads to institutional reforms, to the redesign of education programs and to more humane pedagogic practice. Just as strikes in industry can lead to better wages and improved working conditions, so the same is true in other avenues of life, including schooling. Indeed, the history of school strikes which we have just recalled is an example of an intervention in a local site which Foucault, among others, commends and which theorists of so-called resistance and counter-hegemonic action (Giroux 1981a) see as one of the forerunners of emancipatory practice. In this view, no social site is ever free from some form of opposition and resistance. Even though ethnographic studies (Willis 1979) have shown how forms of school resistance only serve to consolidate existing modes of domination experienced by the working classes, resistance may also be the catalyst for viable emancipatory classroom practice. This has been demonstrated by critical pedagogues such as Shor, whose work we shall discuss in the last chapter of this book. To borrow Friere's language of *conscientisation*, acts of rebellious consciousness, such as those with resistance, can foreshadow a critical consciousness which is genuinely emancipatory.

Education: intrinsically valuable or instrumental?

In analysing the invention of schooling, it becomes apparent that schooling was understood instrumentally, as a technology through which the population could be controlled and directed towards economic ends, and thus placed within a framework of capitalist social relations. As a footnote to this, resistance was at variance with these instrumental ends. So too, though for different reasons, were the conclusions of the school of analytic philosophy of education which was prominent in Britain and Australasia during the 1960s and 1970s. Such philosophy paid great attention to clarifying the concept of education. In so doing, the exponents of this philosophy, led by Richard Peters, advocated an understanding of education as 'intrinsically worthwhile'. To Peters, education has no ends beyond itself. Implicit to it are standards and criteria giving education its intrinsic value. Peters rejected terms like 'training' and 'instruction' as descriptive of education, preferring instead to see education as an initiation into what is valuable, into worthwhile and desirable states of mind. This is to be conducted in a voluntary and rational manner so as to create an intrinsic desire for learning.

We do not intend to provide a fuller exposition of Peters' view nor an exhaustive critique of it. Trenchant critiques of his view and its limitations are available elsewhere (Adelstein 1972; Harris 1979; Kleinig 1982; Sarup 1978). Our interest is to note his strong insistence on the intrinsic nature of education and his strong opposition to an instrumentalist understanding of education, although in his later writings Peters (1975) acknowledges that education does have some instrumental consequences such as 'control over and utilisation of the natural world for human purposes'. Perhaps this is an acknowledgment that, in the end, it is implausible to have a purely intrinsic view of education. As a normative force, education serves some end or good for human beings. In that sense at least it is instrumental (Peters 1961; 1975).

However, it can be maintained that there is a limited value in insisting on the intrinsic character of education. Without that insistence there may be an easy confusion between applications of education—'careers education', 'skills education', 'driver education', 'education for leisure' and so on—activities which share some family resemblance with education. This demarcation may be useful in current debates in which crude instrumentalism, brazen utilitarianism or, as Cherryholmes (1988) calls it, 'vulgar pragmatism', are reducing education practice to skills training and mere vocationalism. It is for this reason that we raise the debate associated with Peters. His concerns serve to highlight the outbreak of instrumentalism that is almost feverish in its intensity which is now infecting the official discourse of education in many parts of the Western world, including Australia. The charge is commonplace that education systems are not appropriately serving the society and world in which they exist.

Following an international trend, the recent debate in Australia and the reform initiatives instituted by education ministers led by a former Minister for Employment, Education and Training (and it is very revealing that his ministry encompassed these three areas) in a previous federal Labor government, John Dawkins, was predicated on the assumption that education should make a contribution to the amelioration of the Australian economy (Birch & Smart 1989). Robery J. Hawke's oft-cited catchcry, the need for Australia to become a 'clever country', captured the spirit of this shift in political thinking. But behind the catchcry was much sophisticated debate and argument, unleashed by a variety of developments, economic and political. The Labor governments of the 1980s were reformist governments, particularly in terms of economic and industrial policy. They were instrumental in globalising Australia's economy and providing a context in which Australia's industries were to become more export-oriented, and more reliant on the production of high quality products and services, including education. There was a recognition that if this was to happen the intellectual and skill capacity of its workforce would have to be developed and intensified, and be more like those of Australia's competitors in northern Europe and south-east Asia. As we shall see in subsequent chapters, where we will discuss these developments in relation to the emergence of a post-Fordist economy, the policies that emerged in the 1980s under the aegis of the Dawkins' ministry were broadly instrumental and designed to improve the human capital component of the economy.

But it was not just the Labor side of politics that was suggesting that education needed to be more accountable in terms of national goals. Andrew Hay (1988), a former president of the Australian Chamber of Commerce, also argued for an education system that was accountable to the needs of the labour force. This would involve an emphasis on basic skills and more rigorous, regular and objective testing methods, supposedly leading to a boost in the nation's productivity. Hay does not provide a philosophical account of the term 'education' to justify his arguments. Nevertheless, enshrined in all he says is an ideological assumption about the normative nature of education. His arguments are an implicit recognition that education embraces cultural action, and is a potent normative force. Nor are such concerns new. They occur whenever economic or social crises emerge, and an explanation for their onset is sought. Indeed, as we saw in a previous section, the introduction of universal schooling stemmed largely from a situation of moral panic about deteriorating standards in the community which, in the face of emerging industrialisation, were no longer tolerable. The economic pressures and turbulent cultural shifts of the 1980 and first half of the 1990s, which have been pronounced and intense, centred on globalisation and the emergence of information-based economies. They have brought into special focus the role of education as a catalyst of economic achievement, as a way of value-adding to the talent pool of the nation.

While there may be substantial differences in content and approach, there is a common experience emerging in Western economies with respect to education (Wirt & Harman 1986; Hartnett & Naish 1986; Shor 1986). Especially in the English-speaking economies, as recession constricts the budget, latent criticism of schools emerges to justify cuts; the productivity of education is questioned and, in turn, any emphasis on a more general approach to education is challenged by over-emphasising a technical and vocational approaches. Through all this, the debate is fuelled over the nature of education itself. In the process, the influence of academic educators on public education policy is diminished. Furthermore, what is evident in these trends is the dominance of instrumentalist, as opposed to intrinsic, views of education. Nevertheless, it is impossible to escape the inevitable conclusion that explanations about the character of education will include justificatory statements. Answers to the question, 'What is education?' emerge if we ask, 'What is education for?' and 'What are the aims of education?'; in so doing, we put aside the distinction between 'intrinsic' and 'extrinsic' views of education.

What confronts us is the realisation that, before we can proceed to outline what is meant by 'education', the normative basis for the concept of education must be clarified. That is, we must declare our ultimate justifications, the norms within education, as normative. The fact that we say they are 'within' suggests correctly that we are looking for intrinsic criteria. In this context, Peters has a point, though we might choose criteria or norms other than his, and though his formal approach is arguably flawed because it refuses to countenance the social and economic conditions in which schooling is located. In contrast, an emancipatory approach to education, particularly in a technocratic society, will address these conditions as antecedent to socio-cultural transformation (Kleinig 1982).

Education as transformative

So far we have asserted the following about the normative nature of education. Education, as we stated earlier, is never ideologically neutral; it is about directly contributing to moral and social enlargement rather than contraction (which would be a contradiction in terms) and that can be, as we have seen, conceived in either a conservative or radical fashion. Therefore, rather than being an instrument of social control as in fact it often *is*, education *ought* to contribute to social change and the cultivation of the transformative and ethical citizenry.

To say this, however, is not to imply that education ought only and always to eschew conservatism. There is a proper conservatism within education—namely, the transmission and preservation of certain cultural values and practices. This conservatism is no adaptive or conforming force, however. Indeed, it can have a dimension which makes it a critical force within existing social practice. Paradoxically, the conservative and the transformative converge in critical education. The capacity to transcend and transform, so essential to human change, is predicated upon the ability to understand and appropriate from our heritage. In fact, it is by the exercise of the human capacity to transcend and transform that we have progressed as a species. More specifically, 'being educated' includes the vision and capacity, if necessary, to transcend and transform what the rest of society takes for granted, viz, conformity to economic imperatives, and obedient adaptation to dominant ideologies and stultifying social controls generally. In other words, we are maintaining that cultural transformation is generally a worthwhile goal: societies are well served in the process and it is a goal true to the human quest for excellence.

In the view of critical pedagogues (Gibson 1986; Simon 1985), transformative education engages the society dialectically. This 'social criticism' goes beyond 'reflective or creative scepticism' in other approaches to critical thinking (McPeck 1981). A praxis method, no longer the mere exercise of critical thought and problem-solving (a cognitive exercise), critical pedagogy is a problem-posing method, focusing on 'the nexus of thought and action in the interest of the liberation of the community or society as a whole ... it contains a transcendent project in which individual freedom merges with social freedom' (Giroux 1983a). This view of education envisages a process of critical reflection and action (praxis) on the social world through which those educating and being educated together achieve an ever-deepening awareness of the socio-cultural and historical reality which shapes their lives. With that, they come to realise their capacity to know and transform reality, and so make a commitment to act for its transformation. This process is characterised by Freire as *conscientisation*.

It is useful to turn again to Freire for a brief outline of an educational philosophy which gives priority to 'education as transformation'. Freire's normative view of education arises from the eclecticism of a philosophical outlook derived from Liberal, Marxist, Existentialist and Christian discourses. His approach supports the view that our main vocation is humanisation and that the desire of human liberation survives no matter how oppressed a person is, or how distorted or repressed their consciousness is. This view links directly to Freire's conviction about the fundamental purpose of education: education is for human liberation. The opposing view, education for domestication, exemplified by disciplinary approaches, is built on a false understanding of individuals as objects to be adapted and managed. This domesticating style corresponds to Freire's 'banking' concept, which is grounded in an unacceptable view, viz, that the individual is merely an observer of a world that is already complete. So Freire advocates a liberatory education which is transformative and problem-posing, while identifying the dominant current practice of education as domesticating, conformist and disciplinary.

The act of knowing is crucial to this critically transformative perspective: 'The fundamental question about education is, what is it to know?'(Freire cited in Wren 1981). Knowledge comes through critical reflection on action (praxis). It is experiential. Where banking education relies on 'second-hand knowledge', 'knowing about', education for liberation believes that knowing is an act performed by a human subject. When that subject comes 'to know', a transformative transaction has taken place between the knower and the known. In this way, the individual contributes to the transformation of culture.

In this view, the understanding of education as initiation is inadequate. To speak, in the fashion of Peters, of education as a process of initiation, where the initiated introduce the uninitiated to the knowledge that society wants them to master, know or remember and above all, conserve, diminishes, in Freire's view, the capacity for education to be transformative, and therefore a humanising enterprise. On the other hand, if knowledge is an act of discovery in which the knower develops a critical consciousness which questions social reality, then education cannot be regarded as a simple transfer (like making a deposit in a bank) from one person to another. From this perspective, education is always a reciprocal, dialogical process.

It has been suggested that Freire's approach (and that of the many critical pedagogues who have been influenced by him) rests on a utopian view of the person in society, and that it lacks effective strategies for implementation because it glosses over the socio-structural impediments which confront liberatory education. However, in the final analysis, we argue that these criticisms cannot be sustained.

There is another criticism which would be serious for this project inasmuch as we are advocating a view of education as cultural action which is not only transforming, but also conserving, what is worthwhile from the past. Bowers (1987) argues that Freire and other liberatory educators practise 'cultural nihilism', that is, they endorse the rejection of cultural heritage and tradition, though this rejection is as nothing compared with the postmoderns. Arguably, Bowers has misread Freire—or at least, he has linked Freire's assertion that human liberation requires that people move beyond 'magical' or 'naive' consciousness with his emphasis on cultural transformation generally and social change in particular situations, to construct a straw person who has no appreciation of traditional values. This misreading belies the fact that Freire's methodology with oppressed indigenous peoples is to empower them to rediscover their traditional cultures by naming what is worthwhile in tradition, as a step towards the making of a culture adequate for present social realities and the rejecting of imperialistic imposition on that culture.[3] However, Bowers' critique does alert us to the danger of cultural nihilism in liberatory philosophies of education such as Freire's, a tendency (dangerous in our view) which can also be attributed to views inspired by postmodernist and post-structuralist theories.

Summary

In this chapter we commenced with an analysis of the concept of education. We argued that both education and schooling are grounded in normative assumptions, assumptions we examined. In examining the invention of schooling, we suggested that disciplinary and instrumentalist imperatives governed the practices of schooling. These have continued through to the present, though not without opposition and resistance. At the same time, we noted that within that account there is a counter-view of education, located in both radical and liberal discourses, which stresses the need for education to transcend vulgar instrumentalism, for education to adopt either a critical or conservative posture towards its surrounding culture. It remains now to describe, analyse and choose among competing orientations, theories, perspectives or paradigms of what education might be. In this quest we must not wander into idealistic or unrealistic notions, but keep a clearer eye on current educational policy and practice and the cultural context in which it is set; nevertheless, we have already expressed a commitment to a transformative and critical—even utopian—approach to this task.

NOTES

1 The deschoolers were particularly vocal *c.* 1968, when there was widespread disenchantment with many facets of contemporary life,

including schools. The most forceful and articulate deschoolers were Everett Reimer (1971) and Ivan Illich (1971). For an account of this movement and the kinds of education (note, not schooling) it spawned, at least in Britain, see Wright (1989).
2   Of these histories the most oft-cited is Philippe Ariès (1962). Its thesis that childhood is a modern invention, which did not exist in the Middle Ages, has been contested by other historians of childhood, most notably by Pollock (1983). Her book challenges some of Ariès' more outlandish assertions about the treatment of children. For accounts of childhood in Australia, see Finch (1996) and Jan Kociumbas (1988; 1997).
3   Certainly this was the stand Freire took in his work with Australian Aborigines in workshops when he visited Australia in 1974 under the auspices of the Australian Council of Churches.

Keywords and phrases

- conscientisation
- counter-conduct
- counter-hegemonic action
- cultural capital
- deschooling
- instrumentalism
- intrinsically worthwhile
- liberal education
- normative
- praxis
- resistance
- socialisation
- training

Tutorial and field activities

1   Collect some definitions of education from members of your family, colleagues, local or university community. Analyse their contents, and attempt to ascertain what extent these definitions contain instrumental or liberal elements.

2   Talk to some older members of the community, your grandparents for instance, about their recollections of schooling in the immediate postwar period. You should attempt to ascertain at what age they left school, and to what type of school they went. Ask them about the differences that have occurred to schools in their lives. Did they have an opportunity to attend university, for instance? Note any significant differences between males and females in their experience of schooling.

3   Discuss Twain's observation that his education was interrupted by his schooling and Henry Adam's notion (contained in the epigraph to this chapter) that most of the most significant

education is accidental rather than formal, a matter of sudden and explicable awakening in the rude and coarse experience of life. What does this tell us about the value of institutionalised education?

4   To what extent can you identify acts of resistance and counter-conduct in your own experience of schooling? Do you remember engaging in resistance and, if so, what forms did it take? Does resistance occur in universities? Where and how is it expressed? Why are university campuses not marked by the disciplinary problems (forms of educational resistance) that are encountered in many primary and secondary schools?

Competing perspectives on education

All the insights, noble thoughts, and works of art that the human race has produced in its creative eras, all that subsequent periods of scholarly study have reduced to concepts and converted into intellectual property— on all this immense body of intellectual values the Glass Bead Game plays like the organist on an organ. And this organ has attained an almost unimaginable perfection; its manuals and pedals range over the entire intellectual cosmos; its stops are almost beyond number. Theoretically this instrument is capable of reproducing in the game the entire intellectual content of the universe.

(Hermann Hesse 1972)

Putting things into perspective

In our initial chapters we have noted that various approaches to educational theory are reflected in dissent and disagreement about the broad purposes of education. This suggests that we can identify, if not alternative paradigms of education, then certainly different perspectives or orientations as to what ought to constitute a valid system of education. We have already identified two such orientations: the disciplinary and the emancipatory. In this chapter we shall extend this analysis and identify more specific orientations within these general categories. Any attempt to classify different perspectives should proceed with some caution: typologies tend to be artificial constructs designed to enable us to analyse and understand underlying presumptions and probable outcomes of different educational emphases.

They are 'artificial' inasmuch as they are rarely present in a pure and actual form in the practice of education; what we generally find is an eclectic mixture of types. Furthermore, typologies can become limiting if they are adhered to in an overly dogmatic and uncritical way. Nevertheless, it remains a worthwhile—even essential—task of the student of education to identify different approaches in order for teachers, policy-makers and the whole educational community to be able to make conscious and informed choices about their preferred approach to education and schooling. In addition, this task can also lead to an appreciation of the various discourse frameworks within which education is located and an appreciation of the types of social arrangement to which they might lead.

There is a long history to the debate which these competing perspectives have generated, a debate which takes place in arenas where education's official discourse is determined and articulated—namely, in the policy arena. In the last decade or so—mainly as a result of the interventions into education at all levels, including the higher education sector that the former Labor government instigated—this debate focused on the issue as to how the education system should contribute to the economy and the needs of the labour market. It was the conclusion of a Senate Standing Committee (1990) on Employment, Education and Training, for instance, that Australia was producing highly-trained technicians but that they were not educated in the broader sense. In the belief that it would lead to the much vaunted 'clever country', the Labor government was determined to redress this situation. It was a clarion call for subsequent policy making on education by the Labour government, and led to an increased emphasis on educational approaches that were both vocational and general, and which were grounded in competency standards (Marginson 1993). The outcomes of such education were intended to meet the needs of the new style labour force that had emerged under the imperatives of a globalised economy.

But such debates are not new. For instance, at the beginning of the twentieth century there was a concerted attempt, led by Frank Tate, to marshal education in the service of the economy (Hyams & Bessant 1972). Such debates will almost inevitably recur, and they occur in most systems of education, because at the root of them is a fundamental and irreconcilable conflict of values and cultural priorities between, on the one side, supporters of education's role as an adaptive and conforming force advancing the economic priorities of the state and, on the other, those who believe that education should be a critical and transforming force, questioning those economic priorities of the state in its role as an instrument of corporate and multinational capital (Beck 1989; Wirth 1972).

The liberal perspective: a rationalising education

Liberal education belongs to a long tradition in Western thought that has its origins in the ideas of Plato. As a philosophical position, it rests primarily on the assertion that the individual person is potentially rational and autonomous (postmodernists like Marshall (1996) would disagree with this) and that fostering that potential is essentially the goal of education. Liberal education is liberating inasmuch as its central role is to 'liberate from the tyranny of the present and the particular and to liberate toward the ideal of the autonomous moral agent' (Bailey 1984). In this sense, liberal education is explicit about its normative potential and purposes. The term 'liberal education' covers a broad range of views and the term is used differently in the United States, where it sometimes has more radical or progressivist associations and where it describes a species of post-compulsory education, namely, that available in the so-called 'liberal arts college'.

By contrast, in the United Kingdom it has somewhat narrower and more conservative connotations. As we are using the term here, liberal education rejects instrumentalism, while focusing on preparation of the whole person for life in the broad sense, rather than work in the narrow sense. Indeed, to do the latter is to corrupt the meaning of education. The best preparation for life is to enlarge the reasoning and moral powers of the individual, particularly through an introduction to the history of Western civilisation and the humanities generally.

It is instructive to examine one recent American liberal education program, and its capacity to effect cultural transformation and to stem instrumentalist incursions into education coinciding with right-wing political trends. The program is contained in Mortimer Adler's *Paidiea Proposal* (1982). Even its name, *paideia*, reeks of classicism, thus reinforcing the belief that this tradition retains its relevance and is worthy of restoration. The proposal advocates a non-vocational, one-track, general education for all students, with no electives permitted (save a second language). This common curriculum has a required core in language, literature, fine arts, mathematics, science, history, geography and the social sciences. Three-fifths of class time comprises didactic lectures by the teacher, which is a form of banking pedagogy. The remainder of the time is divided between Socratic seminars (classicism again!) on required readings and coaching sessions on literacy, numeracy, speech skills and problem-solving. Throughout the proposal, as with liberal education in general, there is a strong commitment to the fundamental units of understanding in the Western tradition, the *disciplines*, as the means for disciplining the mind. Its basic thesis is 'the best education for the best is the best education for all' and its underlying philosophical assumption is the liberal optimism that there is a common human nature and that a common culture can overcome diversity and differences in that nature.

Such thinking has a long tradition. It is grounded in the humanist ideal, which is associated with restraint and at the same time in a virtuosity of the mind, expressed in such activities as philosophy. There is also a concerted attempt to separate culture from nature, to impose a discipline on our ruder and more bestial instincts, so that our second nature comes to displace that of our first through the discipline of civilised pursuits, those associated with morality, taste and truth, and which transcend the exigencies of the here and now. Human perfectibility and self-formation centres on disciplining the mind, while subjecting it to constant and rigorous intellectual exercise, and developing the ability to engage in an ongoing conversation with the cultural inheritance (Bantock 1980; Hirst 1974; Oakeshott 1967).

In their recent recodifications of liberal education, some of the neo-pragmatists (Cavell 1984; Rorty 1977), in spite of their enthusiasms for some facets of postmodernism, have argued that liberal education provides a way of re-making the self, of it enabling to find 'new, better, more interesting, more fruitful ways of speaking' (Rorty 1977). And unlike some of its more conservative exponents, who are unapologetically Eurocentric in their advocacy of a liberal education, Rorty at least, concedes that there is a place for studying non-Western cultures as they can provide an 'edifying' perspective on the nature of mainstream culture.

Nor is the body excluded from such education. It, too, is subject to its own forms of control, for the humanist ideal also encompasses other civilising processes related to eating, deportment, dressing and control of bodily functions—an integral part of the modern mentality—which developed in court society and which have gradually spread via education to all sectors of society (Elias 1978; Hutton 1981). This, then, is the other side of the disciplinary equation.

Its intents are embedded in humanism and its results are intended to be epistemological as much as they are behavioural and corporeal.

If there is a problem with the Adler approach and the powerful tradition of which it is a part, it is that it overlooks the fact that the human situation is not universal but, as the post-structuralists and postmodernists have emphasised, differs with various socio-economic contexts (though there is a concession to this point in the suggestion of special pre-school programs to cover initial impediments). Shor (1986), along with other critics of its goals (Marshall 1996; Martin 1993) has pointed out that the proposal is flawed. It practises authoritarian pedagogy, its foundational reading lists exclude 'unofficial history' (egalitarian, abolitionist, feminist and narrative documents) but, worst of all, it perpetuates simplistic slogans like 'the classless society in America' and 'democracy depends on education'. Altogether, in Shor's view, it combines to legitimise the rhetoric of excellence which has in turn been seized upon by 'vocationatists' and other economic rationalist forces in education, to institute what Shor has called the 'third wave of culture wars' in education in the United States.

Though liberal education should not be condemned because of any one experiment conducted in its name, and though liberal education possesses many virtues that are to be preferred—and indeed from which other perspectives benefit—it remains suspect as a perspective for engaging society and contributing to cultural transformation. Despite its strengths, the question is whether it can provide an adequate view of education in postmodern, post-industrial, technological societies moving into the twenty-first century.

The liberal view of society is focused on the activity of its members as individuals. So, although this view is open to the reconstruction of society, the role of education in that reconstruction is to prepare each individual to participate as a citizen in social development. The socio-structural dimension is omitted or downplayed. Such a view, wittingly or unwittingly, leads to social conservatism and the maintenance of elitism within society, through the possession of a certain type of cultural inheritance that is deeply Eurocentric in outlook and representation. For instance, it is no coincidence that many privileged private schools in societies like Australia are vigorous promoters of the liberal academic curriculum; at the same time, they accentuate individual achievement, competition and excellence. Bowers (1987) correctly identifies that the main weakness of a liberal approach is its failure to see the individual as a socio-cultural being. This failure lies at the heart of its unsuitability as an educational program for mass, technological societies which demand dialectical and praxis approaches to knowledge and social change; such approaches present a more complex discourse than that with which most liberal educationalists are familiar.

The liberal view is hostile to instrumentalism (the subject of the next section), favouring instead a more intrinsic approach to education; it is comfortable with a normative view which stresses education's responsibility to cultivate character and moral autonomy through a 'selective tradition'. In theory, at least, it is uncomfortable with the way education has often promoted undemocratic methods of social control. As a transformative orientation to education it has both limits and possibilities because of its preoccupation with individual emancipation and its ambivalence regarding other areas of social justice (Bishop 1986; Wren 1981). What emancipatory claims a liberal education has are epistemological rather than political; indeed if it has a political agenda then it is conservative rather than transformative, and grounded in a liberal political ideology.

One of the strengths claimed by advocates of the liberal perspective is that, by avoiding pre-occupation with present realities, it cultivates the critical spirit so essential to the educated person, especially in times of postmodern utilitarianism. But is that so? Is critical 'thought' enough or do we need to appropriate critical 'action–reflection', the dialectical or praxis approach to knowledge associated with Freire and other critical theorists which, in the final analysis, rejects individualised or compartmentalised views of knowledge which may be communicated in one way, as banking pedagogies?

Here we locate a crucial issue: is this perspective adequate for educators engaging technocratic culture in transformative ways? Certainly, many believe a liberal or general education is the answer (Marchello 1987). However, it is our view that, though the general education of the liberal tradition will oppose the extremes of technocratic culture and jealously guard the freedom of individuals under threat in a bureaucratic technocracy, it may not of itself provide the social analysis or hard critical edge which specifically engages the technocratic culture. Indeed, the contrast between technocracy and liberal views may be so sharp that it prevents liberal education from appropriating the benefits of technology. It is more likely that the liberal view will be experienced by the student as lacking relevance to her or his cultural experience, so setting up either a type of cognitive dissonance or an outright rejection of liberal and culturally transforming values.

The instrumental perspective: education for human capital

We have already alluded to the vocational approach to education, and we have indicated that education has been caught up in an international trend which has demanded educational reform, in order that schools, tertiary institutions and educational policy overall will be more responsive to economic imperatives. In his 1990 election campaign, the then Australian Prime Minister Robert J. Hawke exhorted his fellow citizens to turn Australia into 'the clever country'. He was suggesting that economic recovery must be education-led. His plan was that education should serve the need for a new resource base, viz, enhanced technological skills, research and development, development of trading languages, particularly those of the Asian region. This plan is in line with what is called 'human capital theory', a theory which holds that human beings are an economic resource whose talents and ability should be harnessed for the benefit of the economy (Schultz 1977). Although this theory has now been discredited and it has been shown that education does not contribute in a substantial way to the performance of an economy, it is an idea whose credibility persists among policy makers and politicians (Marginson 1995). Thus any number of government reports and policies could be cited to indicate the way in which the perspective of human capitalism has heavily infiltrated the discourse of educational planning.

Without doubt, the New South Wales government in its 1989 Scott Report, entitled *Schools renewal: A strategy to revitalise schools within the New South Wales state education system*, provides evidence of this trend. While recognising that there are difficulties in quantifying educational objectives, the report found that 'significant progress is being made in this area'. Furthermore, Scott's report claims that 'progressive introduction of this performance approach to budgeting will improve measurement of the effectiveness and efficiency of school education'. An assessment of these New South Wales developments, has concluded 'that the work of teachers in New South Wales schools is increasingly to be constructed in accordance with a technical orientation toward practice' (Grundy 1990).

Justifications for this approach often come in the guise of an appeal to 'excellence'. That concept becomes the bridge for an alliance between economic rationalists and 'old humanists' or 'classical liberals'. An Australian instance of this is the way Dame

Leonie Kramer (a classical liberal) is identified with calls for reform in education which are effectively and paradoxically promoting a vocational education agenda (Kramer 1987/88). At the same time, proponents of liberal education provide a penetrating criticism of the emphasis on economic utility in education. The liberal distrust for 'the extrinsic' and 'the instrumental' is aroused by the vocational distortion, not that these critics reject vocational training as such. What they object to is that it is located in, and confused with, schools of general education. In particular, they are critical of how economic utility in education perpetuates the questionable assumption that technological change in the context of a competitive free-market economy, set within a globalised trading system, adds up to undoubted 'progress' (Bailey 1984; Gibson, 1986; Holt 1987).

In our view, this instrumentalist perspective is deficient in normative terms because it promotes a narrow utilitarian approach to persons and human society, and also a trivialising distortion of human knowledge. Its efficacy is under question even within its own pragmatic terms: it does not deliver its promise of economic viability, causing some—even from the business world—to suggest that a general, rather than a specifically vocational, education is the best preparation for the workplace. We shall have more to say on this issue in Chapter 10. In any case, it is reasonable to suggest that, at best, schools can only be pre-vocational. Industry itself or other special technical and further education facilities might be providers of job training. Indeed, the sad irony must be noted that much of the impetus to vocational education that was prompted by the Labor government, particularly in important Reports like those of Carmichael, Mayer and Finn, has led to a massive increase in participation rates in post-compulsory education.

Some would say these policy shifts were substantially motivated by the collapse of the youth labour market, caused by the widespread application of automation and computers, and the general rationalisation of the labour markets. In other words, the effort to get schools to prepare increasing numbers of young people for the workplace coincides with the lack of work opportunities confronting those students! A more optimistic construction on these developments is that they were inevitable; for Australia's education system like that of the UK with its separate vocational and academic tracks was perpetuating a 'low ability' nation, with wide disparities between the educationally 'rich' and 'poor' (Young 1993). This was increasingly out-of-step with the fact that much work in the labour market of the late twentieth century is information and knowledge-based. We shall have more to say about this dilemma in Chapter 6, where we shall deal more extensively with the educational needs of a post-Fordist economy.

Before we conclude this section, it is necessary to emphasise how the contemporary manifestations of this economic utility perspective go beyond the vocationalism of the past. The alignment of vocationalism with the technocratic milieu and its all-pervasive instrumental rationality has fostered new practices and policies throughout the education 'industry', which are now deep-seated and increasingly taken for granted. Because of this, simplistic, liberal alternatives or dismissals of the approach as mere vocationalism do not address the profound cultural change impacting on education (Bowers 1982). The technocratic hegemony is such that it can easily co-opt other educational perspectives, even the concern for a general education. There are many indications of this trend: in marked contrast to the liberal approach, the curriculum is being oriented towards subjects with direct utility and economic return, such as business studies, science, mathematics, computing studies, trading languages and Asian studies, and a systems approach of organising curriculum materials into learning packages is increasingly employed. As well, there are calls for standardised and objective testing and competency-based assessment procedures (Bullough, Goldstein & Holt 1984; Apple 1985). Moreover, there tends to be an emphasis on producing a measurable classroom product not dissimilar from that envisaged at the time schools were invented. For, underpinning the skills and knowledge dimension of the new student, is a respect for the values of work, those to do with being industrious and self-disciplined, altogether another expression of the disciplinary mode in action.

Beyond this, the organisation of education systems is now subject to procedures of external evaluation which are based on essentially quantitative criteria in order to judge the 'performance outcomes' of schools, teachers and students, a technocratic version of 'payment by results'. This emphasis on quantitative elements reflects technocratic consciousness. By focusing the attention of students and teachers alike on these measurable outcomes, valuable elements of the education process will be overlooked. All this takes place within the context of corporate planning in the educational system, which makes the system's on-the-ground representative, the school principal, more the manager than the educational leader.

In summary, we conclude that the economic utility perspective, unashamedly instrumentalist and given to social control as it is, enshrines a normative character of technocratic values (efficiency, competitiveness, excellence, managerialism, wealth creation) which is unacceptable to the interpretation of education guiding this book. The social practice we call education cannot, in our view, be reduced to technical processes whose outcomes can be foreknown and subsequently measured. At the same time, we accept that the instrumentalist perspective warrants a serious and engaging response from educators; the dominant code (technicism, managerialism, market participation or whatever) sets an agenda for educators which demands a counter-hegemonic response that is not carelessly dismissive of the concerns raised by the economic utilitarians.

The progressive perspective: education for individuality

This view has been extremely influential in education theory and practice in the twentieth century, but particularly in the postwar period, especially in the pre-school and primary school. As a child-centred and individualistic approach to education, it draws some inspiration from a long-standing tradition which is traceable to the 'romantic naturalism' of the eighteenth century thinker Jean-Jacques Rousseau. This tradition derived much of its cogency from its claim to be in accord with the natural processes of learning, those of the animal world (see Bowen & Hobson 1987). In its initial years at least, the education of the child was supposed to parallel the processes of nature, thus marking a departure from the humanist ideal which attempted to distance learning from any natural factors, to encourage the child embrace culture from an early age. Even activities like reading, which Rousseau regarded as the curse of early learning, were seen as interrupting the child's instinctual rapport with things organic and environmental, which was based around sensation and experience.

Such educational iconoclasm reaches its most fervent expression in educational libertarianism, in the free schools run by A. S. Neill and by Dora Russell (in collaboration with her philosopher husband Bertrand Russell). In these endeavours, the child is in control and the teacher performs a minor role in the educational process. Constraint and regulation are almost entirely absent, with the child being left to their devices, finding themselves through play and self-generated learning. The happenings in school are spontaneous, emerging from the immediate interests of the children, with few planned events or activities other than those that the children invent for themselves (Neill 1974; 1992; Russell, 1980). Free schools (they exist the world over) of the type inspired by Neill are characterised by a healthy anarchism, grounded in the assumption that discipline and regulation are bad for the child's development and result in unhappy adults, overflowing with anxieties and neuroses, repressed sexuality and an unhealthy respect for authority. Their practices are the very obverse of the orthodox school.

In the American context, the educational philosophy of John Dewey (now undergoing a revival) encompassed similar concerns. Integrating European child-centrism with an American pragmatism that stressed social and democratic principles, Dewey contributed much to the reform of traditional schooling with his emphasis on active and interest-based learning. Those who followed Dewey—and there were many—gave themselves the title 'progressivist'.[1] In another manifestation, the progressive approach has a strong therapeutic component: hence 'psychologism' (see Rogers 1983). Teacher-education institutions, particularly their psychology departments, have given considerable emphasis to this perspective. Because of its understanding of the teacher as an empathetic person helping individuals to grow and reach higher levels of self-actualisation, understanding and acceptance, it has sometimes been described as a therapeutic approach to education (Fenstermacher & Soltis 1986). Here, knowledge and knowing is not something remote, conveyed through preselected knowledge packages; on the contrary, learning happens through encounters with self-knowledge related to the quest for personal meaning and identity, with considerable emphasis on personal creativity and self-expression.

Nonetheless, it represents a genuine, if blinkered, alternative to the behaviouristic pedagogy which is more compatible with the technicist and instrumentalist approach. Process rather than content learning is emphasised. The whole emphasis is on the child doing their own thing, in being true to his or herself, or foregoing any imposed or prescribed models. With its allusions to authenticity, there are strong echoes of existentialist philosophy, and most certainly of the humanistic psychology associated with Abraham Maslow and Carl Rogers, as well as Gestalt therapy. The values clarification movement and the confluent education approach were also parts of this trend (Kirschenbaum & Simon 1973).

As we have suggested, this therapeutic ideology has had a profound impact upon the ways schools conceive their practices and form their ideals. This impact can be readily observed from the rhetoric of the typical school prospectus, where there are constant references to the full development of the individual, to developing the area of feelings and emotions. The simplistic analyses and ready-made recipes for teachers (especially evident in Excellence in Teaching and Teaching Effectiveness Training programs) gave great popularity to this approach. For those who recognise that pedagogy is located in a social context, this approach is generally regarded as deficient, a type of 'false consciousness', establishing unreal optimism about the capacity of individuals to determine their own destiny. In practice, it fails to address the question of social justice and social transformation. In fact, it is devoid of social analysis.

Moreover, there is another side to the apparent freedoms of the progressive approach, particularly in its more psychologistic versions. The whole matter of the approach to learning being considered 'natural' contains elements of biological determinism, which need to be treated problematically, especially when they involve girls, for instance, fulfilling their biological roles as nurturers and handmaidens. Also, the approach, despite its frequent references to freedom and liberty, tends to be extremely regulatory, with its own disciplinary and surveillance features, especially when co-opted by mainstream schooling. The gospel according to Jean Piaget (and perhaps Erik Erikson and Lawrence Kohlberg) has been a powerful influence here, with its insistence that there are stages in intellectual and moral development through which children must pass if the processes of growing up are not to be distorted or impeded. Stage theories of development, of which Piaget's is the most notable example, imply that there is a normal process of intellectual evolution, to which all children should conform. These theories are, in fact, extremely regulative in their impact, creating their own modes of Foucaultian surveillance, in that they require teachers to observe and note each child's development, to ensure that it accords, as nearly as possible, to the Piagetian or other developmental paradigms (Walkerdine 1983; 1984). For these reasons, the progressive perspective, contrary to the impression provided of it in teacher education program, tends to be supportive of a disciplinary rather than an emancipatory approach.

The emancipatory perspective: education for an equitable society

Even though we have argued that the three previous perspectives are inadequate, we cannot overlook some of the legitimate questions raised in the previous discussion. To be specific, any alternative orientation should acknowledge and respond to the legitimate concerns of the economic utilitarians and the commitments of liberals and humanists to education for the whole person, while at the same time addressing the necessity and validity of pursuing education in a technocratic and technological environment. Furthermore, we are seeking a perspective that is emancipatory and empowering for teacher and student alike, within a context of social justice.

While there is no concise package that meets these requirements, we can identify a cluster of educational theorists who are addressing this agenda. They are categorised under various labels (e.g. deschoolers, critical pedagogy, the socially-critical, feminist); in this discussion their agenda will be referred to as the emancipatory perspective. Who are these theorists? What are their origins? What are they saying? What are the strengths and weaknesses of their approach? How does their approach fit with other social theory we have located so far? Why is it preferable? These are the issues to be discussed in this section. At this point it might be helpful to some readers to point out the sense in which the term 'critical' is being used. A technical use of the word is being employed here; it is not being used in the sense of negative or carping criticisms; rather, by 'critical' we mean a questioning and insightful analysis of problems with a view to social transformation.

Critical pedagogy is of fairly recent origin, though in the North American context it has connections with the earlier educational movement of social reconstructionism. The more recent expositions of such pedagogy are undoubtedly influenced by the neo-Marxist theory of the Frankfurt school and critical or neo-pragmatism[2] on the one hand, and Freire on the other. In the past decade, probably the most prolific of authors in the quest for a critical pedagogy is Henri Giroux (1983; 1988; and Aronowitz 1985; and Simon 1988), while in the Australian context, educationalists at Deakin University led by Stephen Kemmis have advocated this approach.

Giroux[3] has been a vigorous and controversial exponent of a utopian pedagogy of resistance, a counter-hegemonic approach which not only identifies how school and curriculum practices serve the interests of dominant groups, but also how, through human agency, those same institutions and practices contain possibilities of emancipation. He calls educators to see themselves as 'transformative intellectuals'—updated versions of Gramsci's 'organic intellectuals'. Giroux's approach is thereby different from those other radical theorists who subscribe to all-encompassing neo-Marxist and structural interpretations of social reproduction (see Bowles & Gintis 1976).

Kemmis' advocacy of the socially-critical approach is best summarised in a study for the Victorian Institute of Secondary Education which addressed the problem of the 'school-to-work' transition, in the context of a previous Coalition government's initiative, taken as a response to economic recession (Kemmis, Cole & Suggett 1983). Kemmis' approach advocated a reorganisation of schooling and curriculum, which addressed social and economic questions by overcoming the perceived separateness of school and society, while endorsing the critical role of education in society. This socially critical school is not conceived merely as a training institution for society; rather, social issues are engaged and students gain experience in working on them.

The necessity for an ongoing critique, in which the claims of theory must be confronted with the distinction between the normative vision the critique promotes and the world of education as it actually exists, is central to the critical pedagogy advocated by Giroux and Kemmis. Similarly, a dialectical and praxis approach are pivotal to this orientation. In this sense, critical pedagogy is faithful to critical theory which is more than a 'school of thought'; it is a process of critique.

The emancipatory perspective contrasts with liberal education in several ways. The emphasis on socially and critically reflective processes goes beyond the liberal concern for the transmission of what history reveals as worth knowing, for much of what history bequeaths results from irrational and unjust processes, and as such must be subject to critical reflection. Again, while sharing liberal education's commitment to the discovery of truth and its link with justice, the socially critical perspective emphasises that education is never ideologically neutral and ought to be committed to the attainment of a fairer and more just social arrangement. Similarly, schools should participate in their communities. In the reciprocal relationship between school and society, formal education is shaped by, and responds to, the demands of society and, in turn, helps to shape the society in which it is embedded. In this critically participative model, we see the dialectic at work.

Such an approach does not reject vocational goals in the curriculum entirely; moreover, it treasures much in the traditional humanities. Nor does it necessarily reject proposals to emphasise science and technology related disciplines. However, these curriculum developments are to take place as a result of negotiation undertaken in the interaction between school, local community, teacher, student and the wider society, rather than as a result of decrees from remote bureaucrats or education ministers. In this way, these curriculum developments may open up counter-hegemonic possibilities. The aim is to embrace new initiatives critically and reflectively, while remaining sensitive to the hidden curriculum and to differences within the school population.

It is apparent that this approach is derived from the dialogical and liberatory perspective on education as cultural action found in Freire's aforementioned writings and approaches. Arguably, its strength is that it presents a normative understanding of education which more accurately reflects underlying realities in the 'nature' of persons, society and their culture; it attempts to meet the learner where she or he is, and promotes negotiation and dialogue. Consequently, it focuses the learner on identifying actual problems, analysing them and acting to transform them; the liberation which comes with critical consciousness is thereby realised. A rhythm of action and reflection (praxis) provides the context for this pedagogy of the problem. As praxis, this interaction is action in the social world—political action.

This approach differs from, and improves upon, other educational approaches discussed previously in that it is generated from a critique of the present, not from the generalities of human nature, but from people's social and historical particularities. On the other hand, not constrained by classical Marxist structural interpretations, the contradictions and oppressions of society are confronted in a wider context of social and human relationships.

The emancipatory perspective is open to criticism. For instance, it can be suggested that it shifts the focus away from the individual to the community and society, thereby diminishing education's intrinsic responsibility to develop personal autonomy. However, this is not a deficiency if autonomy is understood within an essentially social and communitarian context. Also, it is claimed that the epistemological model on which critical pedagogy rests plays down the development of rationality and, in its insistence on praxis knowledge, limits the opportunity for many to learn 'about' much worthwhile and necessary information. But surely it is unnecessary to expect people to rediscover for themselves all the knowledge already gained in the past. In any case, this objection is something of a caricature of the socially critical approach which is not opposed to textbooks or lectures, but simply insists that the knowledge which truly educates (i.e. brings about critical consciousness) is appropriated in an experiential, action–reflection context (Freire & Shor 1987).

Another objection is that this approach is impractical. Critics refer to the fate of Freire's programs and the elusive nature of specific curricula and pedagogical initiatives derived from critical theory. This criticism is itself doubtful when matched with the evidence and practice (Ellsworth 1989; Grundy 1987; Halliwell 1989; Lingard 1983). In any case, the validity of a normative perspective is not simply dependent on its implementation; its influence on practice may not always be amenable to quantifiable assessment. This objection may reflect the fact that critical pedagogy appears unwieldy to educational systems and unpopular to politicians.

There is a further, more potent, criticism of the emancipatory perspective. Because the approach is so transparently ideological, some regard it as liable to become a prisoner of political ideologies, losing the capacity to be critical and emancipatory. This criticism, which has been refuted by Snook (1986), also suggests that critical pedagogy promotes a 'new elitism' (the elitism of critical consciousness) and, with that, a tendency to indoctrinate.

The charge that radical pedagogy becomes ideologically bound to predetermined outcomes is made by Bailey (1984), who insists on a truly liberal education as the answer not only to the prejudices and superstitions of primitive ignorance, but to 'the more modern forms of anti-knowledge, embodied in ideology'. Bailey's argument is only finally sustainable if it is possible to be free of ideology, but even the view that all ideology should be regarded with cynicism, distrust and tentativeness can be labelled ideological. Admittedly, the liberal rationalist view does not appear to be ideological in the same ways as the Marxist or the Fascist views, but we would argue that rationality and the uses to which it is put—the qualities, educational practices, perspectives and world-view which flow from it—provide what is, functionally for the liberal rationalist, an ideology (see Cohen 1982). Similarly presenting himself as an advocate of liberal education, David Kemp (1986), now Minister for Education in the current Coalition government, suggests that a commitment to values (again, an implied ideology) is inevitable in education, and that therefore individuals should be free to choose between schools with differing underlying value systems. His current advocacy of more private schools is entirely consistent with this view.

Arguments like this are an important reminder of the ease with which ideologies give sanctity to their proposals and so lose a critical perspective. However, we maintain that the socially critical approach, when faithfully applied, is a superior antidote to the 'anti-knowledge embodied in ideology', in that it has an in-built recognition of the transitoriness of all ideology and the contradictions in social reality. To the dialectic, no 'thesis' (or 'synthesis') is sacrosanct. Still, some Marxists have been guilty of rigidly and absolutely sanctioning their ideology. Liberals have often sanctified their focus on individual freedom to a self-deceptive degree, thereby sanctioning the status quo. Likewise, the latter-day technocrats and economic utilitarians have an unrelenting capacity to dogmatise their position. The emancipatory perspective (informed as it is by critical theory in the Frankfurt school mould) attempts to avoid these tendencies with a bifocal commitment to the individual and society, knowing that the human condition makes it difficult to sustain self-criticism.

Nevertheless, the blind-spots of critical theory are all too apparent, and it is our view that there is a wide body of social theory which must supplement and critique developments within critical pedagogy. There is scope for a measure of rapprochement between some dimensions of postmodernist thought and that of critical education theorists, as McLaren (1986) and Cherryholmes (1988) have pointed out. Indeed, some critical pedagogists are inclined to wander into romanticism in their social analyses and would profit, for instance, from a rigorous dialogue with the critique of power emanating from Foucault.

Looking in another direction, it seems to us that the insights of feminist theory might provide missing dimensions in the construction of a critical pedagogical approach. Fraser is one author who has explicitly identified the weaknesses in Habermas's exposition of critical theories when it comes to questions of gender (Fraser 1989). Feminist theory could form something of a bridge between the critical theory approach and postmodernist discussion. Feminists share with critical theorists a commitment to political transformation and a utopian vision while, together with postmodernists, they are concerned to challenge the Enlightenment-inspired, dualistic and hierarchical ways of interpreting human experience. Indeed, inasmuch as feminists, postmodernists and critical pedagogists (and to this list Giroux would add liberation theologians) are responsive to the historical experience of the oppressed and the underclass, they may surely be drawn into a praxis which will lead to theoretical and interpretative links; in this way, critical theory will evolve. It is hoped that the potential for dialogue in these areas will develop apace in the near future.

Of importance in this dialogue is the challenge to old paradigms and interpretations of human existence being raised by environmentalists. To be credible as a pedagogical perspective, the emancipatory approach must be integrated with an ecocentric rather than an anthropocentric orientation and, with that, a realisation that sustainable economies imply some limits to growth. Again we raise the need to find an educational perspective with an openness to the future, one that is critical of the progress myths of the Enlightenment which have fuelled the technocratic cultural revolution, but which nevertheless engages the possibilities of technological development.

This brief discussion of the relationship of socially critical approaches to other radical social theory and social movements is an indication of the strength of the critical pedagogy perspective: a flexible capacity for ongoing critique. It is an orientation, not a closed paradigm; it is a way of addressing problems, not a set of answers; it is ready to be amended at any time; it is therefore somewhat resistant to precise statements of how it is to be implemented; it is truly 'educational' in the etymological sense of the word, leading out to new and revised forms.

Postscript: in defence of the utopian

In the preceding discussion we have been exploring the interface between what has been described as 'the romantic impulse' and 'the pragmatic impulse' (Fraser 1989). Critical pedagogy is committed to engaging social realities (the pragmatic impulse) but it is not to be bound by them, just as it sees no reason to apologise for a visionary dimension (the romantic impulse). Indeed, in the quest to distil from contemporary social theory an adequate basis for education policy and practice, the emphasis on utopian praxis is critical.

It is critical because, in the final analysis, hope, vision and a sense of a better future sustain human beings in their action to improve the world. It is critical that this utopian perspective be at the core of our understanding of education because, without it, education degenerates into mere training or socialisation. However, this utopian perspective must be more than a cosmetic euphoria, a cheap romanticism. Paradoxically, we would argue (along with feminists, critical pedagogues, liberation theologians, environmentalists and others) that the grounding of the romantic impulse in a realistic hope, which nevertheless is energetic and vital, occurs best when that hope is generated in conjunction with the apparently hopeless, the oppressed, the most disadvantaged in a society. With Giroux we affirm that 'if intellectual practice is to be tied to creating alternative and emancipatory politics of truth, it needs to be grounded in forms of moral and ethical discourse and action that address the suffering and struggles of the oppressed' (Giroux 1988; McLaren 1989; Purpel 1989). Specifically, this means that critical pedagogy will find its sustaining energy and hope to the extent that it is nurtured by involvement with the victims of society, with those who have so little to lose and so much to gain, those who can see through the shallowness and injustice of the culture around them. At all points, the teacher oriented to critical pedagogy will ask of systems, policies, school development plans, classroom practice, etc. 'How does what is happening here impact on the most disadvantaged?'

If this appears to be a hollow claim, then one challenge of this book is to demonstrate its feasibility. If the charge is that the perspective charted in this section is unworkable or idealistic, there is an obligation to examine its implications for specific educational topics and concerns, which is one of the tasks to be accomplished in the rest of the book. The action-implying conceptualisations described so far must be applied without anticipating easy answers. As educationalists in the praxis mould, we take seriously the questions of practical effectiveness. We take them seriously because we accept the proposition that society, the economy and forms of education are constructed in a social context which can never be denied or negated; similarly, practical outcomes are not predetermined or incorrigible. We are responsible for the present and the future, and the exercise of that responsibility requires vision.

NOTES

1. The scope of Dewey's work is immense, and far from restricted to education. He was an old-style grand theorist whose particular form of pragmatism, a philosophy originally developed by Charles Sanders Peirce and William James, was applied to aesthetics, psychology, history, politics and sociology. Some appreciation of the scope of his thinking can be gained from *Democracy and Education* (1937). Also, R. G. Archambault (1966), shows how pragmatic (in the small 'p' sense) a thinker Dewey was. Of the many commentaries on Dewey, that by Wirth (1966) has not been surpassed.
2. Critical pragmatism, a term increasingly used by the American philosopher, Richard Rorty (1983), has its provenance in John Dewey, Charles Sanders Pierce and William James, and other American philosophers, such as the New England Transcendentalists, like Thoreau and Emerson.
3. Besides Giroux in the North American context, we can identify scholars such as Tom Popkewitz, Kathleen Weiler, Peter McLaren, Ira Shor, David Purpel and Mark Ginsburg with this perspective. For an excellent summary of critical pedagogy and its concerns, see McLaren (1989), especially Part 3. Also useful, in that it provides an analysis of critical pedagogy along ethical lines, is Liston (1988).

Keywords and phrases

- critical pedagogy
- dialectic
- free schools
- human capital theory
- liberal education
- libertarianism
- instrumentalism
- praxis
- socially critical schooling
- vocationalism

Tutorial and field activities

1 Liberal educationalists argue that education should declare a moratorium on being work oriented. Discuss this viewpoint. Can it ever be total? Is it realistic that education systems should distance themselves from the economy and the needs of the labour market? Or are schools inevitably the factories of human capital production?

2 Examine Rorty's view that examining cultures dissimilar from our own, can lead to a considerable enlargement of the moral imagination. How does it do so, and why is it necessary that we develop an empathetic communion with culturally diverse groups?

3 Discuss Neill's view of schooling that it should be almost entirely without regulation and disciplinary features. What impact might such schooling have on children? Could we ever imagine a society in which the bulk of schools were of the Summerhill type?

4 Examine some recent examples of university advertisements (see the weekend editions of newspapers like the *Age* and *Sydney Morning Herald*). Analyse the text of their copy and the images that are used to visualise this copy. What does this analysis tell us about the ways in which universities are seeking to appeal to their prospective students? What is the dominant educational perspective utilised in this advertising, and what does it tell us about the current value trajectory of universities in Australia? Apply the same analysis to advertisements produced by high schools.

The curriculum and the course of education

We think we are so civilised, so highly educated and civilised. It is farcical. Because, of course, all our civilisation consists in harping on one string. Or at most on two or three strings. Harp, harp, twingle, twingle-twang! That's our civilisation, always on one note. The note itself is alright. It is the exclusiveness of it that is awful.

(D. H. Lawrence 1973)

Education and knowledge

Schools might exist for a variety of other purposes, but their primary purpose and the one for which teachers are, in the main, prepared, is the transmission of knowledge. In all sectors of education, but particularly in the high school and to an even greater extent in universities, teachers are first and foremost teachers of subjects or disciplines, the basic units of educational knowledge. The other functions of schooling, those connected with socialisation and subjectification; with producing a productive and politic citizenry, occur alongside the transmission of knowledge as one of its important after effects (Harris 1979). Thereby, the organisation of subject disciplines has a disciplinary function. Along with the teacher and the student, knowledge is the other major element of the educationworld, the one which brings the triangle together, providing a measure of justification for the existence of schools in the modern world.

In terms of an earlier definition of education, that of ensuring 'inter-generational continuity', all cultures accumulate over the period of their existence a repertoire of skills and understandings, social practices and knowledge, upon which the survival of a culture is in some measure dependent. The curriculum constitutes the mechanism by which this continuity is maintained. Functioning historically, it represents a bridge between the achievements of the past and the possibilities of the future (Inglis 1985). The curriculum is an important reference point in education, containing a prescription of what knowledge and frames of thinking are deemed valuable and useful at a particular point in time by the powerful in society with a vested interest in the educationworld.

As discussed in Chapter 3, mass compulsory schooling is a comparatively recent invention, being no more than a century old, at least in the English-speaking world. Reiterating some of the arguments already explored in this book, modern society's need for schooling was largely pragmatic and functional, originating in the need to control the moral condition and productive potential of the population in the face of the emergence of industrial capitalism—to produce, in other words, what we have called a 'disciplinary society'. Any more noble ends, to do with the power of education to enlighten the population and enlarge its moral imagination, were matters of lesser concern.

The history of education in the early modern period shows us that home tuition and individualised learning supervised by parents were commonly practised before the advent of universal education, leading to styles of learning that reflected the demands and abilities of pupils in a direct and specific way. Rothblatt's analysis of the patterns of education in Georgian England (cited in Goodson 1988) suggest that the absence of institutionalised schooling did not mean that the society was without the means for learning, or that its population remained illiterate and uneducated. The concerns about these more cottage industry approaches to education were not related to their effectiveness, but to the fact that the tuition involved was never regularised or subject to examination. There were no guarantees that children reared on a diverse range of literature, that might have included potentially seditious materials, might not gravitate towards political subversion and unchristian rebellion (Hurt 1971). With some urging from the philosophers of Utilitarianism and laissez-faire economists who still cast their intellectual shadows over the political and social discourses of the twentieth century, the state came to see the benefits of managing and controlling education through some form of universal schooling.

As it was undergoing modernisation (meaning industrialisation), the state could no longer afford to entrust the processes of education to untrained citizenry,[1] for industrial capitalism required a labour force inculcated with the values of work and respect for property, particularly that in factories and other places of industrial work. Governments also needed sites where they could obtain social statistics and data about the population and make observations about its conduct; schools were ideal places for studying the demographic characteristics of modern societies (Hacking 1990). Contrary to much of the liberal rhetoric on schools, which insists that they have different and more elevated functions connected with ennobling the spirit, schools were primarily the places that inculcated the value parameters of labour power, those connected with being deferent, punctual, industrious, honest, ambitious, recognising the appropriateness of a differential wages structure and so forth (Matthews 1980).

Notwithstanding this interpretation, which might be regarded as a romanticised view of pre-modern approaches to education, we acknowledge that paradoxically universal schooling did confer some benefits and advantages to some sectors of the population. But there were costs. One was that it centralised the control of education in the 'velvet glove' of the state, with the result being that it robbed the working classes of an opportunity to determine their own educational destiny. The history of schooling over the last hundred years has demonstrated that. In effect, that history entrenched the disciplinary purposes of formal schooling at the expense of its emancipatory potential, which has remained latent ever since. The emphasis here on a more critical analysis of the genesis of schooling is necessary in order to restate that potential in the face of a more complex and technocratic social arrangement, in which the disciplinary functions of schooling are becoming more pronounced and subtle.

Many of these issues have particular relevance in relation to the theme of this chapter, namely the curriculum. Within education there is, of course, a considerable body of theory connected with the curriculum. This is concerned with the optimal arrangement of learning processes in the context of the basic specifications of the theory, in terms of competencies and a taxonomy of educational objectives. The names most often associated with this 'minimalist approach' (Wirth 1983) to curriculum theory are Bloom, Tyler, Taba and, to a lesser extent, Bruner. With its quasi-scientific rhetoric and its origins in behaviourism, such curriculum theorising is another instance of the kind of instrumental rationality which is common in educational theory, the most noteworthy feature of which is a tendency to eschew the cultural etymology of schooling, to neglect the socio-cultural factors that influence and control the pedagogic activities of the educationworld (Apple 1985; Cherryholmes 1988;

Eisner 1979, 1985a, 1985b; Grundy 1987; Wirth 1983). It also overlooks the impact of the curriculum on school life and its production of school subjects, be they teachers or students. In this chapter we shall argue that curriculum is a major organising force in the life of the school and the educationworld in general, and that through knowledge, the stock-in-trade of the curriculum—powerful controls are exerted over the minds and bodies, desires and interests of children.

A cultural etymology of the curriculum

Like much of the language of education, including that of 'education' and the names of the school subjects, like 'history' and 'science', the word 'curriculum' is saturated with Graeco-Roman meanings and origins. This tends to reinforce the cultural etymology of the Western tradition, which was not only embedded in the classical cultures of ancient Greece and Rome but, for many centuries, was conducted in the classical languages. What our moral culture owes to the Judaeo-Christian tradition, so our intellectual culture, both secular and sacred, owes to that of ancient Greece and Rome. Many of our plants and animals, for example, have two names: one Anglo-Saxon, with which we are familiar, and another, a Latin name, which trained botanists and zoologists have used since the time of Linnaeus. Another instance of this classical base to our intellectual culture is the fact that, until quite recently at least, graduation ceremonies at many of the more traditional universities were always conducted in that most 'magisterial' of discourses, Latin, the expectation being that their participants would be conversant with this language!

Thus much of the discourse of our intellectual culture, including that of education, is saturated with this cultural inheritance, with both direct and indirect references to its languages, literature, philosophies and ideas. This includes many aspects of the school's 'symbolic architecture' such as its school mottoes, particularly which are, in most cases, Latin quotations (*semper fidelis*; *nil sine labore*), drawn from poets like Horace, Ovid and Virgil. The word 'curriculum', although its current usage is recent in origin, is derived from the Latin word *currere* (Bantock 1980; Hamilton 1989),[2] meaning a race that is run, is also part of this same cultural pedigree. As we shall see later in this chapter, there is a special aptness in this etymology, with its competitive overtones. In effect, the curriculum is the general course that is followed within an educational system and it refers to its general features and to its various epistemological elements.

From another perspective altogether, the curriculum constitutes a selection from the culture of which the educational system is a part. Culture is one of those words familiar in social theory (bequeathed to us by the nineteenth century), like democracy, class, industry and art, which has substantially altered in its meaning during the modern era. It once referred to the processes and practices associated with agriculture; but it has now come to refer to all those understandings and practices that humankind has acquired over the millennia of its existence and deemed worthy of preservation and transmission (Williams 1977; 1981). This means that culture consists not just of art, music and literature (culture with a capital C and which is normatively defined) but also ideas, beliefs, tools, skills, practices, television programs, eating and dress habits, rock music, customs, rites—in fact, everything which is not a product of nature and which is seen critical to the survival of society (Woods & Barrow 1975; Connell 1983).

It is with this more inclusive definition of culture that the determination of curriculum content is concerned. It is useful to conceive of the curriculum as simply an organisation of knowledge for instructional and educational purposes, as a selective representation of what is valuable within our particular culture, diverse and complex though it be. There are other systems of epistemological organisation which serve rather different purposes. There are, for example, the organisations of knowledge provided by encyclopaedias and reference books and the Dewey-Decimal and Library of Congress systems of knowledge classification used by libraries to facilitate the retrieval and storage of information included in books and journals, and more recent forms of information technology such as CD-ROM. None of these systems is totally inclusive and comprehensive, and all of them bring emphases and preferences to the information surveyed or collected, which refracts its selection, and causes omissions to be made and the value preferences of their compilers of these various data bases to be manifested. No library contains every book and journal that has been published, and encyclopedias treat some entries more comprehensively than others. *Larousse*, for example, deals in greater detail with French culture than the *Encyclopaedia Britannica*, thus reflecting its provenance and the interests and concerns of its editors, which are always, to a certain extent, nationalistic rather than global. Atlases, in terms of the amount of space given to certain nations and the distortions evident in certain cartographical representations of the world, are the same (Harley 1988); as are dictionaries; compare for example the Macquarie Dictionary with that of the Oxford Dictionary. Indeed, the term 'reference book' in this connection can be misleading; it is neither comprehensive and it reference tends to be limited and imbued with the cultural biases of its authors.

One can make analogous observations about the curriculum. The trouble is, our culture is now of such gargantuan proportions that clichés like 'knowledge explosion' and 'exponential growth' cannot do it justice. The turning point in our culture, when it was still possible for one person to master the full spectrum of epistemological achievements, appears to have been 1788, the year when the eleventh edition of the *Encyclopaedia Britannica* appeared. Two people were responsible for all its various entries; subsequent editions of the encyclopedia have been compiled by larger and larger number of experts, so that for its 1968 edition, some 10 000 recognised scholars from around the world were consulted! (Bell 1976).

One of the problems for the curriculum planner, particularly in fast-developing areas like computer engineering and medicine, is that knowledge quickly becomes anachronistic and the sheer prodigiousness of the scale of its production is overwhelming, and becoming more so. More books have been published in the last fifty years than all the previous centuries put together. The average person now spends eight hours per day loading themselves with information of some kind! And in 1980 it was calculated that the number of words emanating per day from all information channels including radio, newspapers, television and books was eleven million (Young 1988). The advent of the Internet and newer channels of information would have increased this figure to even more staggering proportions. In such circumstances, the ability of education to provide even a reasonably comprehensive picture of any culture, let alone a complex and multicultural one like that of Australia, has long since passed.

Even education in a small and very specialised area of culture, such as that associated with a particular profession, faces the prospect of almost immediate uselessness. For instance, it has been calculated that some 50 per cent of the knowledge gained in most engineering degrees is obsolete within five years (Waddington 1977). This means that constant re-education and retraining involving periodic updating of qualifications and credentials, is likely to be an inescapable part of everyone's career. At a more speculative level, it could also mean that we might face Tristram Shandy's plight: that it will take more time to keep abreast of the developments in knowledge than to actually apply them!

CURRICULUM AND THE COURSE OF EDUCATION

'The knowledge most worth having'

Admittedly the problems are of a somewhat less pressing magnitude at the school level, although they are not really different in character. Judgements of value, be they intrinsic or extrinsic, are always involved in the curriculum decision-making process. Not everything can be taught, and some things have to be omitted from the curriculum, even though they might be popular among students or deemed valuable by certain vested interests. The matter of determining just what elements within the culture are worthy of inclusion in the curriculum is one of the more perennial and different questions in education which, as we shall see later on in this chapter, can be answered in all manner of ways.

We need to cure ourselves of the illusion that curriculum issues are a matter about which consensus prevails. They are not; indeed, the whole issue of what is included in the curriculum is a 'battleground for an intellectual civil war' (Inglis 1985) in which parents, teachers, students, academics, bureaucrats, representatives of industry and community lobby groups argue for their educational preferences and desires. In essence, this 'civil war' centres on determining whether or not there is a general body of worthwhile knowledge which every generation of children requires in order to become adequate and productive citizens and, if there is, of what that body of knowledge consists. At issue, too, are debates about educational standards, which critics of modern schooling suggest are on the decline as a result of the displacement of traditional teaching methods and the gradual dilution of the academic curriculum. Australia's most vocal apologists for a return to educational fundamentals such as the 3Rs are the members of the Australian Council for Education Standards (ACES), who play a similar role to the Black Paper group in the United Kingdom.

Another related issue—and it is one which has gained a degree of prominence as a result of the efforts of various lobby groups in the community—is the matter of 'dangerous knowledge', knowledge alleged to be inappropriate for young children, either because of its allegedly lascivious and depraved subject-matter or because it transgresses various forms of religious fundamentalism. As was noted in Chapter 2, in the modern age, innocence has been part of the construction of childhood and with it have come strictures designed to prohibit children from encountering the biological facts of life, those to do with death, sex and birth. This has included strict censorship of learning materials and a degree of community unease (less pronounced now than it was in the past) about sex education in schools. Educational innovation has often been hampered by this unease, with right-wing vigilante groups monitoring and sabotaging school materials and worthwhile curriculum schemes such as *Man A Course of Study* (MACOS). A case in point is Queensland's recent history under various National and Labor party governments. Numerous interventions, of which Preston (1990) has given a succinct account, into the curriculum design process have occurred, the most notorious being the decision in 1995 to axe an Aboriginal studies program which included the word 'invasion' in its syllabus.

At various times in the past, certain bodies of knowledge have had greater status in the curriculum. In the Middle Ages, for instance, the 'Seven Liberal Arts' were dominant; in the nineteenth century, it was the classics. In the late twentieth century, it has been argued (Nidditch 1973), that the sciences should become dominant and that the classical humanism which has dominated education since the Renaissance should be regarded as outmoded and anachronistic. Thus the curriculum is always a matter of normative determination, reflecting various preferences and the values of powerful elites within our society, those able to make an input into curriculum implementation. Following on from Marx and Engels, it is often said (and much has been made of it in recent sociology of knowledge) that 'in every epoch the ruling ideas are the ideas of the ruling class'. The school curriculum is thus not constituted in a neutral and apolitical way, but is formed from interests such as technology, business, politics and higher education (Cherryholmes 1988) in a concerted attempt to force into existence useful outcomes from schooling, be they economic or ideological.

Nor is there much agreement about what types of epistemological priorities the curriculum should articulate. Science, poetry, religion and art have all, at one time or another, had their apologists, who would centre the curriculum on these areas because of the supposed benefits they confer on the individual. Thus the traditions represented in the curriculum are inevitably selective, and what is omitted from the curriculum—sometimes called the '*null* curriculum'—is often as telling and significant as that which is included. For instance, until quite recently, the Australian history (similar arguments apply to its literature) that was taught in schools was rarely that: it was British and European, thus tending to reinforce colonial dependence and cultural subservience to the old world. When this was remedied, the Australian history that was taught still tended to be post-invasion history, leaving out the 40 000 years of Aboriginal history that preceded it. Similar silences can be found in other subjects.

Part of the problem (and this reinforces the Marxist view of the situation) is that curriculum determination, by its very character, has tended to marginalise the 'cultural voice' of the disempowered: women, the working class, gays and lesbians, ethnic groups and Aborigines. Until these groups gained some power within the educational community, they were not able to bring their influence to bear on curriculum construction. What this emphasises is the degree to which the curriculum is always in flux, to which it is always an area of contestation and debate, in which rival interests compete for authority and dominance in the hope that a more equitable representation of culture will result. The struggle to find a place for women's studies in universities is a case in point.

As is clear from the research which is now being directed at them, where the high school curriculum is concerned, many of these struggles occur within subject associations, where factions reflecting new disciplinary developments often develop, sometimes causing new subjects to emerge under the auspices of the breakaway groups within their disciplinary community (Cooper 1984).

However, there are other interests which have a stake in the composition of the curriculum. As was indicated earlier, among the most powerful of these is the state. Since the advent of universal and popular schooling, the state has always had a vested interest in monitoring and (if its interests are not being served properly) modifying the content of the curriculum. This began in Prussia in the early part of the nineteenth century and has continued ever since (Lyotard 1984). Every so often, a national statement, usually of concern and containing countless jeremiads about the nation's survival depending upon a restructured education system, is released. In it, new directions for schooling are canvassed, with particular stress on adding elements to the curriculum which better serve immediate national goals. This often occurs at times of 'moral panic', when there is widespread concern about outbreaks of civil unrest and general unruliness among the population. It also occurs at times of economic recession or perceived military threat when there are worries about a decline in economic prosperity and fortune. It is at such times that the state often turns to education as a salvation mechanism, believing that it can solve its moral and economic woes. In the 1980s the United States had its *A nation at risk*, which recommended the restoration of a more conservative ethos in schools (Shor 1986).

Australia has had equivalent documents, though the policy, at least since the publication of the Karmel Report (1974), has been focused more towards extending the population inclusiveness of schooling to encompass minority groups which have not been the main beneficiaries of schooling. In spite of this equity concern, the rhetoric of this policy setting is still undercut with human capital consequences. A more educated population, so the policy intimates, is important if Australia is to prosper in the future, and is to be able to participate effectively in the information and the knowledge-based society. One dimension of this is the tendency towards greater federalism in education; notable is the attempt, under the aegis of the Australian Education Council, to establish a national curriculum as part and parcel of microeconomic reform (DEET 1989).

Via the curriculum, then, the state has developed a mechanism through which to assert values of national interest, those to do with patriotism, perpetuating state ideology or—as in this case of advanced capitalist nations—economic well-being and prosperity, advancing military might and cultural power on the global stage. The curriculum is perceived as a way of promoting national cohesiveness, of extending the skill base and epistemological repertoire of the population, of bringing something distinctive to national character, of consolidating multiculturalism, of generating more respect for citizenship, and so on.

The curriculum and the knowledge industry

We also need to understand the role that the curriculum plays in the propagation of the knowledge industry, which is international rather than national in scale. To a limited extent, we discussed this role when we examined the social dimensions of research in Chapter 1. In this section we wish to explore these dimensions in more depth and detail, specifically bringing out the contribution that education makes to the knowledge industry and economy.

As a number of writers have argued recently, one of the salient features of the post-industrial society is the degree to which it is a knowledge-based society, one in which increasing numbers of the workforce (and teachers are good examples of information workers) are involved in the generation, retrieval, transmission and storage of knowledge (Bell 1976; Jones 1986; Reich 1991) and are involved in occupations that require symbolic and analytic skills involving numbers, words and pictorial representation. The advent of computer technology has increased this trend. Of relevance here—and again this was touched on in Chapter 1—is the degree to which knowledge now has a textual face. Because classrooms tend to be venues of intersubjectivity in which the knowledge exchange process occurs between teachers and pupils largely through the spoken word and exposition, this tends to detract from the fact that knowledge derives most of its epistemic authority from the printed, *not* the spoken, word. Knowledge exists as an ensemble of texts, books and journals, and their electronic equivalents.[3] The library and its various electronic reincarnations are the principal storehouses of knowledge. The printed and electronic word are the primary vehicles for epistemological transactions, and have been instrumental in restyling cognitive processing, adding new dimensions to its possibilities. The hypertextual dimensions of the electronic word will add new sets of possibilities to the processes of knowledge representation and distribution (Lanham 1993).

But it was not always thus. Indeed, in the past—in the classical period before writing gained its sovereignty—there was some considerable contempt for the written word. Plato in his dialogue *Phaedrus* provides an account as to why this was the case. There was some expectation that 'literalising', through inscription processes, thoughts and ideas would have deleterious effects on their representation, and that the perfect vehicle for thought and ideas was discourse and dialogue, the act of speaking, not writing (Ong 1958). Oralcy had pre-eminence over literacy. The advent of electronic forms of communication, particularly in interactive modes of epistemological representation such as the CD-ROM, have brought new dimensions to this divide and posed new challenges to its significance.

One consequence of this technologising of the word is that it has led to the control over the interpretation and dissemination of knowledge. It has reduced epistemological transactions to the domain of experts who act as gatekeepers where knowledge access and distribution is concerned.[4] An outcome of this process is the commodification of knowledge, not just in textbooks, but in the aforementioned computer software packages and in the institution of education itself, in its curricular and socially restrictive practices vis-à-vis access to certain forms of education (e.g. tertiary education), thereby laying the foundations for a disciplinary treatment of knowledge.

The recognition that knowledge can enhance what Lyotard has called the 'performativity' of an economy has meant that knowledge has been integrated into the capitalist economy, giving it an epistemological base. Knowledge has become a commodity which, like all commodities, has the capacity to generate wealth; it has exchange rather than just use value. The Australian government's recent initiatives in higher education have recognised the wealth potential of the knowledge industry in a number of ways. One of them is purely pedagogic, namely that of marketing courses overseas and attracting fee-paying students to Australian tertiary institutions, particularly in the English language courses for overseas students. In fact education has become one of Australia's largest exports, far larger than that of primary industries like wheat and wool.

When we talk of the knowledge industry, we mean one that is market-based, driven by the economy, and is expected to compete for scarce resources, to attract sponsorship and to raise its own funds. State schools are also part of this entrepreneurial adaptation of the knowledge industry, which pervades all sectors of education, including various support services such as research institutions, museums and the computer and publishing industries. Make no mistake about it, knowledge is big business in the late twentieth-century economy.

Questions to do with knowledge traditionally fall within a branch of philosophy known as epistemology. In essence, epistemology has focused on the foundations of knowledge, specifically the questions of its warrantibility, the grounds for truth in various disciplines and so on. This amounts to establishing, among other things, why it is that the knowledge of astronomy has more epistemological validity than that of astrology, or how it is we can make knowledge claims at all. Much epistemology is quite technical and can easily confound its readers, particularly when it comes to elucidating basic questions as to what knowledge actually is. Of late, though, epistemology has tended to move away from purely foundationalist questions[5] and has developed something of a sociological turn. This has caused an increased awareness of the institutional foundations of knowledge and the civic dimensions involved in justifying knowledge claims. In our discussion of paradigms in Chapter 1, we saw how knowledge is a framework for understanding the world, for providing explanations for its regularities and perceived orders. It is simply another version of 'storytelling' (Inglis 1985) albeit one with fairly sophisticated narrative devices and languages for representing the world. And, as with all stories, there are some favourites which command considerable respect and kudos, as do their tellers. For within the storytelling tradition of knowledge, there are heroes and heroines, whose 'stories' are constantly retold and renarrated because they possess considerable explanatory power.

Foucault (1980) has also directed our attention to the institutional factors underlying knowledge and knowledge processes.

When we think of knowledge, as we have already suggested, we tend to think of the domains of inquiry with which they are most often associated: history with time, geography with space, science with the physical universe and so on. But it is not only these domains which give each discipline its distinctiveness, for each discipline—or what Foucault prefers to call a 'regime of truth'—also has a distinctive set of procedures associated with establishing and regulating epistemological conduct within the discipline, for organising its discursive practices. For example, each discipline tends to have particular sets of procedures for determining, generating and storing truth, and these vary at different times and periods of history. Each also has a distinctive language associated with it, a carefully regulated discourse of specialised terms and nomenclatures.

Think of the way the word 'reproduction' takes on specific connotations when used in connection with sociology, as distinct from biology, where it has a different set of connotations altogether; and these connotations are different again from the way the word is used in vernacular contexts. Above and beyond their natural languages, some disciplines have specially developed systems of symbols for representing particular facets of their domains of inquiry. Maps in geography are a case in point, as are the symbol systems in mathematics, chemistry, music, logic, phonology and so on. A major function of schooling is to induct pupils into the decoding of these symbol systems.

Alongside these more formal structures, each 'regime of truth' has a civic dimension. As discussed in Chapter 1, the generation of knowledge does not take place in a social vacuum. Like all social practices, that of knowledge is subject to various moral and ethical controls, such as professional codes of conduct, which help shape the behaviour of those working within a knowledge community, including teachers and students. In its ideal state, the community is supposed to be characterised by the so-called 'disinterested pursuit of truth', which is supposed to be dispassionate and free of those ideological pressures which would hamper or distort the knowledge acquisition process. In all knowledge communities there are systems of intellectual quality control which are supposed to ensure that epistemological standards are not compromised or transgressed (Sklair 1973). Each discipline has a publicly attested set of criteria associated with it, which new knowledge propositions are supposed to satisfy. Failure to do so means that the knowledge involved finds it difficult to enter the channels of distribution (e.g. journals, which exist in a knowledge community to distribute new knowledge).

Of course, in the real rather than the ideal world, these control mechanisms are often circumvented, either quite innocently or with deliberate intent. Major corporations, for instance, have been guilty of falsifying research findings when it is in their interest to hide unflattering evidence which might prejudice the marketing and use of their products. The American chemical company Monsanto had inadvertently discovered the harmful effects of dioxin well before the worldwide inquiries into the effects of 'Agent Orange' on Vietnam veterans. By cleverly disguising research findings, they were able to keep the evidence against dioxin from public knowledge for decades. Scholars and researchers are thus no less susceptible to deception and chicanery than the community at large.

One of the functions of education is to ensure that students develop a commitment to the moral and ethical standards that prevail within the various regimes of truth as they have been passed on from generation to generation of knowledge practitioners; in effect, this is a matter of learning the *discipline* associated with a discipline. For, as well as being a social practice, knowledge is also a historical practice, one whose parameters and conventions are reproduced, admittedly with some modification, in the social and epistemological practices that each generation of researchers inherits from its predecessors. When a teacher discusses the theory of evolution in a high school classroom, the teacher is helping to maintain a theoretical tradition of biology which began in the nineteenth century and which is crucial to the maintenance of a certain scientific tradition of research and scholarship.

In a sense, teachers at all levels of the knowledge community are the representatives, the ambassadors of a certain tradition of scholarship and research which prevails in their discipline. It follows from this that teachers have an ethical obligation to their teaching subjects, and that they respect their subject matter and the values and standards inherent within them. In so doing teachers act as the conduits through which the epistemological inheritance is passed on from generation to generation; if it is passed on correctly, with a minimum of distortion, students are eventually able to engage in 'conversation' (Oakeshott 1967) with this inheritance, to tell and retell its stories, using its languages, its concepts, its theories and methodologies with the facility and confidence of a ranconteur. At least, that is what is supposed to happen in theory. As we shall see later in the chapter, much schooling seems to be concerned with discouraging, rather than encouraging, this conversation, at least for large numbers of students.

The curriculum and the organisation of knowledge

We have argued that the curriculum is a scaled-down version of culture, a young person's guide to the highlights of Western 'civilisation', or at least those which a powerful minority has deemed to be such. Especially where the school curriculum is concerned, there has always been considerable debate about how this model of Western thought should be organised and shaped, and what within it should be given greatest emphasis and force (this is often phrased in terms of the title of this chapter, as the 'knowledge most worth having'). Debates about its content and its rational justification have tended to be the province of philosophy of education and have centred on questions of epistemological worthwhileness, of what knowledge needs to be acquired in order to guarantee an all-round appreciation of culture.

One form of the debate involves identifying the fundamental forms of knowing and ensuring that a representative of each is included in the curriculum. This often involves identifying some irreducible categories of knowing, like the empirical, the aesthetic and the moral, of which the various school disciplines and subjects are representatives.

Another way of approaching this debate is more cultural than epistemological, centring on broader questions as to what individuals will do with the knowledge they acquire at school and what function this knowledge will play in the conservation or regeneration of society. There are countless examples of such curriculum prescriptions. They began in the classical period and were updated in the Middle Ages with the various specifications associated with the seven liberal arts, the Quadrivium (arithmetic, geometry, astronomy and music) and the Trivium (grammar, dialectic and rhetoric), and have continued through to our own day with a number philosophical statements about the matter (Barrow 1976; Barrow and White 1993; Hirst 1972; Phenix 1963; White 1973).

Notwithstanding the fact that foundationalist approaches to knowledge, of which these statements are examples, have been cast into doubt by post-theorists, who, in any case, incline to approaches to knowledge with few boundaries and demarcations, they do have value in terms of understanding what is involved a projecting an ideal organisation for the curriculum. In addition, a number of educationalists in this area have described various typologies which enable ideal curriculum types to be identified, which approximate to our four perspectives: the liberal, the instrumental, the progressive and the emancipatory, as described in the previous chapter (de Castell & Luke 1986; Kemmis, Cole & Suggett 1983; Lawton 1975).

The first, the liberal curriculum, is the most traditional of our orientations. Underlying this approach is the belief that there is a body of essential knowledge, the cultural inheritance, which has stood the test of time and needs to be transmitted to each generation, and which centres on the trilogy of taste, truth and morality. Matthew Arnold, one of the important advocates of this approach, talked about culture being 'the best which has been thought and said in the world' (Arnold 1973). Along with the development of powers of reason and rationality, its advocates argue, this approach leads to moral perfection and cultural amelioration of the population. The curriculum is often associated with mental discipline and rigorous intellectual training, mostly centred on the traditional subjects, those with a strong disciplinary and academic base: science, literature, mathematics, history, which are representatives of truth, taste and morality at their most developed and refined. The interests of culture and its upkeep tend to override those of the individual. In some of its variants, for example, in the *Paideia Proposal* which we discussed in the previous chapter, programs of learning are centred on the 'great' books of Western civilisation, on Plato, Shakespeare, Aristotle and Dante (Adler 1982). The curriculum is a celebration of classical humanism.

One of the more notable features of this orientation is its condemnation of the ordinary and the everyday, the transient and the ephemeral, particularly in relation to mass culture. Some contemporary defences of it, particularly in the US, have argued that liberal education can save our culture from further fragmentation and wrest its decline into epistemological illiteracy (Bloom 1987; Hirsch 1987). However, these concerns, and they tend to be based on simple-minded assumptions about the nature of culture (Peters 1996), are not new. Though writing in the nineteenth century, Arnold was particularly concerned with the crass effects of a capitalism at its worst and which were as nothing in comparison to the crassness of their effects in the late twentieth century. Poetry and literature, in which he wanted to immerse every school child, were supposed to offset the degrading effects of a society concerned more with its material than its moral prosperity (Heyck 1982).

Accompanying these sentiments was a generalised contempt for the purely utilitarian and instrumental. Apart from its power to morally uplift and to give guidance on how to live the good life, knowledge was supposed to be for its own sake, for the development of the mind rather than the economy. Thus, because instrumental knowledge is grounded in the everyday, immediate needs of society, and these are usually economic, liberal educators tend to oppose versions of the curriculum which are have a strong instrumental orientation. Similarly, they oppose strong vocationalism, to the extent that some private schools exclude subjects like accounting from the curriculum, on the grounds that preparation for the workplace is not the responsibility of such schools. To return to the nineteenth century again, when universities looked like being dominated by the professional schools—by medicine, law and engineering—there was considerable defence mounted to keep these schools outside the university and to maintain the university as a preserve of liberal education (Newman 1927; Mill 1971).

To a lesser degree, there has been a re-run of this debate in Australia when Dawkins' reforms for higher education were first mooted in the early 1990s, since when they have developed apace. These proposals stressed the importance of linking most sectors of education, but especially that of higher education, to the needs of the economy via business, information technology, science, mathematics and Asian studies. Those in the faculties of the arts and humanities continue to find it difficult to justify their existence in the face of this demand that universities be more accountable in terms of their utility (Hunter et al. 1991). How can history or the study of Australian literature be justified in terms of their dollar return to the economy? What ethical capacities do they generate which have utility?

A curriculum which places considerable emphasis on vocational instruction, on developing social competencies and on ensuring that schools and universities produce useful outcomes is typical of the instrumental orientation. Human capital theory, about which we have already written, and which treats human beings as just another resource to be exploited by the economy, gives force to this instrumentalism. Indeed, there would be a tendency for liberal educators to oppose using the epithet 'education' in conjunction with this orientation. They would prefer to call it 'training' or 'vocational preparation' (Peters 1966). Any curriculum which leans towards the vocations, whose outcomes are directed towards employment and extending the skill-base of the economy, can be described as being instrumental, either directly through the constituent elements of its curriculum, or indirectly through the hidden curriculum. In the latter sense, for instance, the schooling of the early modern period was instrumental in that it was primarily designed to instil the work ethic

in students. Since then, this has been augmented with an appropriate skill and epistemological base generated from vocational subjects.

The instrumental curriculum, then, is more in tune with the present than the past, more concerned with the contemporary than the preservation of a cultural past. National efficiency is the prevailing goal of education, and all schooling is directed towards this end. Even subjects like physical education have been commandeered into servicing this end. Their emphasis on fitness and health, today as in the past, is often construed as being essential for an efficient workforce.

Certainly, policy on education developed in Australia in the last decade or so, particularly that associated with the Mayer (AEC 1992), Carmichael (NBEET 1992) and Finn (AEC 1991) Reports, has tended to have a strong instrumental focus. As we shall see in a later chapter, this focus is a qualified one and somewhat more sophisticated than previous attempts at establishing a nexus between schooling and work, which tended to emphasise academicism at the expense of vocationalism. The new nexus foreshadowed in these reports is not necessarily the very obverse of a liberal tradition but retains a strong belief in the importance of a general education as the basis for a vocational education. The title of the Mayer Report, 'Putting General Education to Work', provides a neat summation of the new nexus.

Our next orientation is the progressive one. It arises, as we indicated in Chapter 3, from a powerful tradition in Western educational theory which has been especially influential in twentieth-century educational practice, and which has advocated making the interests and needs of the child the pedagogic centre of gravity. This orientation has various versions, the most prominent being derived, in the postwar period at least, from so-called 'Third Force' psychology, that of Rogers and Maslow. In curriculum terms, this orientation tends to be opposed to locating knowledge within strong frames and boundaries, to use Bernstein's (1972) terminology, as tends to happen in the two previous curriculum orientations. It favours more integrated approaches to knowledge organisation, which are said to recreate more faithfully the child's experience of the world, which has a holistic character and which sees the world as 'seamless web' of experience rather than through categories of knowledge.

A more interesting strand of the progressive orientation, though, is the libertarian one, most often associated with the late A. S. Neill and Dora Russell, in which the child is allowed to do his or her own thing, with but a minimum of constraint and regulation. Their ideas originated in a genuine antipathy towards a disciplined and repressive society, which began to impose its damaging effects in child-rearing practices. The only prescription in the educational process is that the child should find him or herself, via the activities to which he or she gravitates. Unlike the previous two orientations, there is no commitment to any extrinsic goal, be it cultural or vocational, and the interests of the child override those of culture or of the economy. There is a strong ethic of individuality which predominates over any collective goals. But, as was said in Chapter 3, the orientation is flawed in that it is, to a large extent, devoid of convincing social analysis. What analysis there is emphasises the importance of individual sovereignty in the face of a repressive and interventionist state. Neill for one, who was profoundly influenced by Wilhelm Reich's theories relating to extreme forms of authoritarianism and the degree to which they lead to sexual repression and puritanism, was extremely anti-government and wanted individuals to assume control of their own lives, to be self- rather than collectively-regulated. He thought that 'Humanity might be cured of its sickness' once it eliminated the 'compulsive family, the disciplined school, the anti-life religion' (Neill, 1974).

Such views fly in the face of our final curriculum orientation. We have called it 'emancipatory' to distinguish it from curriculum arrangements like the others, which tend to have a prior commitment to an existing social arrangement. The word 'emancipatory' is derived from the discourse of critical theory where it is used to refer to styles of reasoning characterised by critique, by a form of reflection which aims at social change and transformation, or what is called 'praxis' by critical theorists. In particular, the orientation is concerned with remedying oppressive social structures, with countering a hegemonic pedagogy that saturates the individual's sensibility with compliance and which denies opportunity and voice to many students, particularly the most disadvantaged and oppressed. Unlike other orientations, which tend to follow top-down models of learning, centred on exposition and the pedagogy of the answer, emancipatory pedagogy is centred on dialogue through the active participation of both students and teachers. Knowledge is not seen as a commodity, but rather as an active process which can inform students' lives and make a difference to them. In other words, there is a concerted attempt to conflate theory with practice, and reflection with action, which is the core of the praxis approach. Committed to developing a genuinely egalitarian approach to education, it rejects the conventional curriculum, centring instead on 'generative themes', on problematising everyday reality (Shor 1980; 1987).

The curriculum is a matter of negotiation involving all relevant parties, especially the community. In this curriculum, no issues are off limits. The orientation also confronts technocratic rationality and all forms of education, like the instrumentalist, which are seen to lead to an eclipse of a critical outlook. In line with this, the curriculum gives a central place to the critical social sciences. Even in fields like computer education, which may become narrowly technicist, this emancipatory perspective would place a priority upon an ethical and social critique of computer technology, with using computers to establish information networks and localised web-sites, with developing and utilising public domain software.

The structural organisation of school life

Whatever its political or moral virtues, a curriculum, like any other human project, takes place within the limitations of a spatio–temporal framework. There is only so much time in a person's life allocated to schooling and this obviously limits the amount of learning which can be transmitted and which in turn is limited by the number of calendar weeks (and hours within them) in the year that are devoted to schooling (Adam 1995). There are also spatial or architectural (broadly defined) constraints which limit the horizons of the curriculum. Science requires laboratories, physical education needs gymnasia, industrial arts must have workshops, home economics kitchens, performing arts theatres and stages, and so on. New subjects can be added to the new curriculum, but not without some cost, in both spatio–temporal and material terms. If a new subject or discipline is added to the curriculum, something has to be subtracted. Think of the material costs, which are considerable, associated with the introduction of information technology into a school. Not only are there on-site costs connected with adding customised rooms to the school and ensuring that there are optimal numbers of computer terminals and ancillary equipment available to ensure that such technology is a viable proposition for large numbers of students, but there are also off-site costs concerned with the preparation of teachers for this new area of learning.

As computer contracts tend to be negotiated between state departments of education and large computer corporations, there is considerable competition for this lucrative area of business. In order to boost their chances of securing such a contract on a California-wide basis, the computer company Macintosh, for example, donated one of their computers to every school in California (Roszak 1986). Nor is this trend restricted to schools within the vicinity of Silicon Valley; it also happening closer to home, in Australia, as we shall see in Chapter 11. Many non-government schools for instance insist that their students now purchase a laptop computer as a condition of enrolment. This is leading to massive disparities between the government and non-government systems of education in terms of their ability to offer comprehensive information technology facilities. At a less sophisticated level of technology, the textbook also benefits from modifications to the school curriculum, particularly as much teaching, even in these days of information technology, is still centred around textbooks.

The ramifications of the curriculum, then, extend well beyond the classroom. In fact, the curriculum is an organising force in the social practices of school life, is part of what we shall call the 'extra-curriculum', providing a basis for its timetable and subject allocations. The curriculum is part of the technology of modern schooling and was invented at much the same time as the classroom, streaming, grading and the timetable; it is a vital prop in 'substantiating the dominant version of schooling', the so-called 'batch production' version of collectivised and simultaneous instruction (Goodson 1988; Hamilton 1989). It caters for a system of schooling serving a mass clientele. In fact, there is a continuum between the curriculum and the fundamental unit of learning, the lesson or period (which becomes the lecture and the tutorial within the university). This extends through to determinations of what array of subjects are likely to be taught within the school to actual syllabus statements.

However, it would be a mistake to think that the translation of the curriculum into individual lesson plans is a one-to-one process, and nothing gets lost (or more significantly added to it). On the contrary, we need to think of the curriculum as a changeable entity, which is not only challenged and redefined in terms of the exigencies of pedagogic situations, but which, with teacherly imagination and appropriate amplification, can be re-interpreted and re-invented to meet local contingencies. The top-down version of curriculum theory is flawed if it eschews the contributions that grassroots practice makes to curriculum redefinition. Teachers operating through subject associations, writing textbooks and developing new pedagogic techniques can modify the curriculum, and can be instrumental in reframing the patterns of the curriculum (see Goodson & Ball 1984). This is where teachers have some scope for counter-hegemonic action. Despite the intensity of the disciplinary forces operating in the traditional school curriculum, there are emancipatory possibilities even within the most conservative of contexts. Take the junior mathematics syllabus, for example: a lesson on the calculation of housing interest rates could be the occasion for a discussion of interest rates and their social impacts. Too often teachers overlook opportunities to make links between school subjects and the social world.

Nevertheless, there are material constraints. Resource allocation, be it time or material resources, is generally tied up with syllabus statements and with the prestige and status that is attendant with certain subjects. As we shall see in the chapter which deals with school and time, there is always competition for subject time, and some subjects, like mathematics and English, and their teachers have more power when it comes to timetable allocation. Much of the power that some teachers are able to command stems from the fact that there is no parity of esteem where the disciplines of the curriculum are concerned. Some subjects have much more esteem, and are more academically privileged, than others—notably the sciences and English. Much of this has to do with the fact that these disciplines are more highly regarded and valued when it comes to university entrance, and so tend to be selected by more academic students, but there is also a cultural etymology factor causing some subjects to have more prestige than others. In the Western tradition (and it is not alone in this regard, for one can find similar tendencies in the Confucian culture of China), theory has always been more venerated than practice, thought more than action and reason more than feeling, particularly among educational elites.

The ghost of Plato

The origins of this tradition, like much else in our intellectual culture, can be traced back to Plato—to be precise, to Plato's version of Utopia, *Republic* (1972). In this idealised picture of society, written in response to a situation in which anarchy threatened the fabric of Athenian society, education plays an important role in preserving 'intergenerational continuity', in ensuring that the structures of the good society (once arrived at) are reproduced systematically from generation to generation. Grounded in the notion that each individual possessed specialised attributes that were fixed at birth and equipped them to be a carpenter or a doctor or a musician, the function of education was largely a sorting and sifting one, a process of ensuring that each individual ended up being located in that occupational niche for which they had some natural predisposition or talent. To do otherwise was seen as a recipe for social chaos, for a situation in which aspiration and ambition overtook predisposition and ability. The idea that education was a mechanism through which an individual might gain some positional advantage was foreign to Plato.

Furthermore, Plato believed that it was possible to discern, within the broad fabric of society, three classes or types of individuals. These corresponded approximately to our ruling, middle and working classes. There are some differences, though, particularly where the ruling class is concerned. Its members were not, as they tend to be in modern societies, the powerful and the wealthy, but philosopher-kings and philosopher-queens whose intellectual qualities and special insights were considered invaluable assets where the efficient functioning and administration of society were concerned. It is important to recognise that women were included among the guardians in *Republic*. In a philosophical tradition, which for the most part is misogynistic in character (Lloyd 1984; Okin 1980), this is very unusual. The main reason for entrusting the management of society to philosophers was epistemological. Plato held that there were certain ideas which were central to social practice, like those of goodness and justice, which were only available to the intellectual insights of philosophers. This was because they were able to transcend the everyday and deliver themselves into a realm where the ideas of goodness and justice resided. This transcendence was necessary because Plato held that the domain of sensory experience, which was forever in a state of flux and transition, was not one in which truths of an absolute kind could possibly be located.

In order to demonstrate these arguments, it is useful to resort to some elementary geometry. One of the universal properties of triangles is that the sum of their internal angles adds up to 180 degrees. Using the theorems of Euclid, it is possible, through using the processes of reasoning and logic, to prove the truth of this property. However, it is another matter to empirically demonstrate this truth. If we were to draw a triangle on a piece of paper and then measure its angles using a protractor, even one with a high degree of resolution, the result would never be *exactly* 180 degrees. The operative word here is *exactly*, for we might be within a few minutes or seconds of achieving this figure, but because of protractor error (no matter how small) and the thickness of the pencil's lead, which would make it difficult to determine where the angles in our triangle actually began and ended, achieving it *exactly* would be an impossibility.[6] Thus we are drawn to the conclusion, as was Plato, that this universal property of triangles, like countless others in geometry and other fields of human inquiry, does not actually exist in the empirical world, the world of experience and sensation. Rather, it exists only as a theoretical and abstract concept located, as far as Plato was concerned, in a transcendent world of immanent forms, which is only available to our powers of intellect and rationality.

Indeed, as is clear from the passages in *Republic* which deal with these matters, Plato had some contempt for the real world, declaring it to be a place of shadows and distortions, opinions and half-intelligent beliefs which only the powers of the philosophers, with their more extended aptitudes, could overcome (see Brent 1978). As is indicated in the diagram that usually accompanies these passages, Plato saw a dividing line between the two worlds which education could serve to bridge via special training in mathematics and philosophy, the disciplines closest to the world of immanent forms. However, given their specialised attributes and the fact that some individuals were predisposed to dwell in the world of shadows (and would be quite content there), not all the members of Plato's Utopia were given the educational opportunities to cross this bridge and to enter the realm above the divided line. The most extended form of education was granted to the philosophers, and it extended over some fifty years, while the working classes, the artisans in *Republic*, only enjoyed a limited form of education, one which was confined to the shadows, to the material and empirical world. Here we see the seeds of a society in which 'unnatural' social mobility was regarded as a threat to the social good—a point which we also address in the next chapter. This view of society foreshadows the development of feudal and pre-modern agrarian societies in which people were expected to be content with their station in life, to repress social ambition and aspiration.

We have entitled this section 'The ghost of Plato', which implies that the sentiments of *Republic* continue to haunt the curriculum and its content even in the latter part of the twentieth century, some two-and-a-half thousand years after they were first expressed. We have already noted that much Western educational theory, particularly that which emerges from the liberal tradition, places considerable emphasis on centering the curriculum not so much on the here and now, the particular and the present, but on the general and on the past, on the abstract and theoretical, on that which has stood the test of time and is an irrevocable part of the Western cultural tradition (Bailey 1984). In effect, a curriculum thus styled endeavours to remove its students from the world of shadows, from the ephemeral world of the here and now to a transcendent world of universal forms and ideas, that transcend refutability and falsification. Indeed, the word 'liberal', which is often used in conjunction with this type of education, is intended to convey its emancipatory effects, for such education as opposed to an illiberal education is supposed to free individuals from their dependence on the real world, and its shadowy and illusory effects.

St Augustine, one of the early Christian advocates of liberal education, was so disenamoured with this real world that he believed that true music only existed in theory, not practice, a view that he also extended to medicine (Howie 1969). According to this kind of logic, in the greater epistemological scheme of things, even though it might be less interesting and exciting, mathematics has more importance than rugby football because its ideas and concepts have persisted over millennia and will continue to persist long after the results of the latest football match have perished. In the previous section, it was also noted that this liberal approach to the curriculum tends to be hostile to instrumentalism, to placing the curriculum in the hands of employers and governments, and to making it relevant and useful. One reason for this (applying much the same logic) is that useful knowledge is part of the world of the shadows, part of the embedded world of flux and transition.

Another facet of this lingering Platonism is the long-standing tendency to value theoretical knowledge over practical knowledge. We can see this in the prestige and status that is attendant with certain subjects in the curriculum. Mathematics, science, history and English, the subjects which are often perceived as theoretical and therefore more demanding of the intellect, have much more status in the school than those subjects which are practical. Demanding more manual than mental dexterity, the latter are more closely allied to the body than the mind and belong to the world below the divided line. The more practical subjects like industrial arts, home economics and physical education typically fall into this second category and have status problems within the school. As often happens with subjects which need to enhance their epistemological reputation, one response to this situation has been to develop a theoretical component in the subject, to give it more importance and, as a consequence, to give the subject more status.

Physical education and home economics have, in the last few years, tended to embrace more and more theory in order to overcome their perceived inferiority. This often involves giving the subject a more scientific or positivistic face, this being especially apparent in physical education, which has adopted a mechanistic approach to the body and sport (Kirk & Tinning 1990). The trouble is that, as far as students are concerned, this has often been at the expense of the subject's primary appeal: that it is practical, that it is largely a hands-on rather than a bookish subject. Whenever a subject changes its name, as with domestic science becoming home economics, or whenever an education institution changes its classification as the Colleges of Advanced of Education did when they became universities, this usually means that they are trying to upgrade their epistemological status.

Most accounts of this dichotomy between the theoretical and the practical tend to suggest that its origins are mainly sociological, having their provenance in a powerful division of labour power within our society, that between mental and manual workers. While it is true that the school plays a large role in reproducing this division, it is true also that, because of the considerable influence of thinkers like Plato, the division is taken for granted, leading to the widespread supposition that academic subjects are more demanding and therefore more worthy of esteem than practical subjects. We shall have more to say about pure and applied knowledge and the spurious assumptions surrounding this division when we come to examine the nature of work in the second part of this book.

The differential distribution of knowledge

In the introduction to this chapter, we noted that the etymology of the word 'curriculum' contained overtones of a race. Races typically have winners and losers, and involve competition. The curriculum is no exception in this regard. It provides the running track along which countless pupils compete for scarce academic rewards. Many never even finish the race, and others are handicapped considerably when they embark on it. The longer the race continues, the less inclusive and more exclusive it becomes. The education race is far from an equitable one. Natural lottery effects advantage some students, such as favourable home circumstances, and disadvantage others. The race takes place against the clock, and within it there are various staging points which take pupils down different tracks and raceways, as happens when pupils elect to specialise in certain subjects, or leave school for university. It is no accident that schooling takes place in an ethos of competition. From its earliest days, when much of the modern technology of schooling was invented, it was claimed that the forces of the market could have an enhancing effect on the outcomes of learning. No less a figure than the architect of modern capitalism, Adam Smith, was instrumental in suggesting that dividing pupils up into classes in which they could compete with one another would foster conscientiousness and emulation (Hamilton 1989).

To date, in this chapter, we have tended to see the curriculum as an initiatory mechanism, enabling students to come to know their culture in all of its diverse forms. Yet this tends to mask the other important function of the curriculum, which is that of creating of an 'intellectual caste system', as Illich (1978) has called it. Far from opening culture to all and sundry, this system creates barriers and obstacles, limiting access to some varieties of knowledge. It is inevitable that knowledge creates some differences between individuals. As we saw in Chapter 1, the acquisition of dissimilar types of knowledge leads to differing modes of perception and specialist understandings and even languages. Thus a scientist walking into a laboratory registers its contents and furnishings in a rather different way than the historian. Such perceptual changes in outlook are just one of the side-effects of the knowledge acquisition process.

Some of the differences created by the curriculum are more social than epistemological leading to the latent recreation and reinforcement of the cultural and economic disparities in our society and its associated social relations. Then there are hidden curriculum effects which act somewhat like subliminal advertising, inserting their messages into sensibilities of students via tacit, rather than explicit, means. Many of the disciplinary consequences of schooling flow on from the content and processes of the hidden curriculum. For instance, much schooling takes place in a competitive context, creating the impression that the world of winners and losers is natural and desirable rather than a problematic social construction. In another way, hidden curriculum factors operate in the subject choices of students, the most obvious instance being the fact that girls have tended to study different arrays of subjects than boys.

However, there are other differences created by the knowledge acquisition process which have a more generalised impact on the school population. Knowledge is one instrument through which the school population is controlled and differentiated, by which its progress is watched and monitored. Educational success, for instance, is usually measured in terms of epistemological capacity, which is examined at various points in the educational race but most significantly at the point of transition from high school to university or college. In these circumstances, credentials and entrance qualifications are used as instruments of educational closure, preventing admission into certain programs of learning (e.g. those available at university). At a point beginning halfway through high school, in the name of specialisation, the curriculum becomes a mechanism for differentiating pupils, for designating them, for tracking and streaming (Goodson 1988). The curriculum thus has come to facilitate hierarchical rather than egalitarian distributions of knowledge. Knowledge acquisition is regularly examined and tested in the schooling process and it has become one of the benchmarks for measuring potential, one of the ways in which knowledge and power are connected (Hextall & Sarup 1978).

One of the more serious side-effects of these processes is the restriction of opportunity. Via the subjects they study, students are soon designated as academic or practical, and this can have a detrimental effect on their career options. In terms of the reproduction of labour power, the curriculum, as noted in the previous section, has become the means for separating mental workers from manual workers, between the conceivers and the executants in the labour process (Braverman 1974). Until we became aware of the problem and its damaging ramifications, the curriculum also tended to be dichotomised along gender lines, girls tending to follow one track of subjects, boys another, thus helping to instantiate patriarchy and capitalist gender relations. With monotonous regularity, girls who were not academic tended to follow the home economics/commercial route, thus tending to reinforce gendered patterns of labour. And those who were academic tended to avoid the hard sciences which were regarded as the boys' terrain, opting either for the humanities or the softer and more feminised sciences like biology and botany.

We also need to be aware that the impact of hidden curriculum operates through both the mind and the body. There is tendency to assume that the corporeal practices associated with the latter are entirely natural and instinctual, and do not contain elements of social construction and discourse formation. Yet as Mauss (1973) noted in the 1930s, the various techniques and habits of the body, be they associated with eating, swimming, walking and even sex, differ between and within cultures, according to the 'habitus' in which individuals are located. Indeed there is a parallel here with Bourdieu's notion of cultural capital and what applies to our various symbolic forms of life also applies to our corporeal practices. In effect, there is also a phenomenon of physical capital, manifested in our corporeal dispositions, and the ways these are managed in the outward expressions of the body in such areas as dress and grooming.

Shilling (1993) has suggested that education plays a significant role in the generation of physical capital through the cultivation of particular corporeal accomplishments, many of which are class and gender specific. For instance, working class males tend to be more physical than their middle class peers, and gravitate towards physical sports such as rugby league and weight training which develop their physiques. This is obviously of use to them outside of school in forms of employment such as labouring which require a strong physique and anatomy. But the construction of the 'unfinished body' extends through other educational activities which also impact on its various accomplishments and in often unexpected ways. Most subjects in the school curriculum result in some adjustment to the individual's psycho-motor proficiency, some subtle regulation of its capacities, be it in the area of keyboard skills and writing or the playing of a musical instrument. Even the voice is no stranger to such manipulation and modulation, to make its register and tone accord with certain class and gender expectations (Poynton 1996). At the more dramatic level, the body's accomplishments are contorted in sometimes dangerous ways in physical education and in dance, which are activities that also require of their participants particular body shapes.

In summary

In this chapter, we have suggested that the curriculum is a central component in the schooling process. We have also suggested that the curriculum is a representation of culture, though not an egalitarian one. We have argued that the cultural etymology of the curriculum can be traced back to Plato and, although other curriculum orientations have emerged to challenge the hegemony of the liberal curriculum, it still remains the dominant orientation within the school. In the latter parts of the chapter, we examined the way in which the curriculum creates divisions and differences among the school population, differences which echo those existing in the divisions of the labour force and which assist the creation of inequalities in the population, the topic of the next chapter.

NOTES

1   We do not wish to be misunderstood here; we are not advocating a permissive approach to education which would return education to lay

persons. On the contrary, we recognise that for the foreseeable future, schools, under the guidance of qualified teachers, will remain the primary sites of education.

2   In this respect it shares something in common with a curriculum vitae (a more educated expression for what is commonly called a 'résumé') which, literally translated, refers to the course of one's life, but actually refers to a document which summarises the highlights of one's biography.

3   Popper suggests that these artefacts have an independent existence, constituting another distinct world, what he calls a 'World Three', alongside World One, that of physical objects and physical states and World Two, that of mental states, of the personal and the subjective (1973).

4   This commenced in the Medieval monasteries, which were the main repositories of knowledge. For a fictional account of this phenomenon, see Umberto Eco (1983), the basis for a recent film of the same title as the book *The Name of the Rose*.

5   This tradition has not been totally abandoned. It continues in the work of Quine, Dummett, Goodman and a number of other eminent philosophers.

6   The calibre of this problem can be best appreciated from the perspective of the Mandesbrot drawings (see Gleick 1987), associated with chaos theory, which indicate that higher-degree magnification of the world reveals that what appears on the surface to be a linear pattern is in fact curvilinear, full of inlets and jagged edges. The same is true of a pencil line.

Keywords and phrases

- cultural capital
- culture
- habitus
- knowledge
- liberal education
- null curriculum
- physical capital

Tutorial and field activities

1   Gather a collection of school mottoes or promotional slogans. The latter are particularly in vogue in universities (e.g. QUTs 'A University for the real world'). Mottoes and slogans present in summary the dominant values pervading education systems. What do the mottoes and slogans you have gathered suggest about the values governing education at the moment.

2   At one stage in this chapter it is suggested that in the current climate subjects like history and literature find it difficult to justify themselves in terms of their dollar return, that is, they

have little, tangible economic utility. Is this true? Does it matter that history and literature do not make a substantial contribution to the development of the nation's economy? What justification can be mounted to defend their existence?

3 Hirsch's book (1987) is subtitled 'What every American needs to know' and in its appendices he supplies a list of '5000 essential names, phrases, dates, and concepts'—items which he considers essential knowledge, which includes, among other matters, knowing who Captain Ahab is, the works of Frédéric Chopin, the contents of the Communist Manifesto, what a *tabula rasa* is, and so on. Are these matters that every Australian needs to know? Is there any point in developing such lists as Hirsch's? What are the dangers of doing so?

4 Think about your subject choices at school and university. What were the factors and grounds governing these choices? Were they the subjects and courses you really wanted to study or were you pushed into them? What justifications, if any, were provided to support these choices?

Educational as a positional good: equality and schooling

If the school system is dealing unjustly with some of its pupils, they are not the only ones to suffer. The quality of education for all the others is degraded ... An education that privileges one child over another is giving the privileged child a corrupted education, even as it gives him or her a social or economic advantage.

(R. W. Connell 1993)

Not making a difference

Preceding chapters have described a view of education which is committed to the promotion of human freedom, democracy and social justice, the underlying philosophy of the emancipatory perspective. Implied in this view is an assumption that equality should be a major goal of schooling. This contrasts with other perspectives we described which enhance the disciplinary consequences of schooling in practice and are more ready to tolerate inequality and, in some instances, are in favour of its existence.

On the face of it, schooling appears to be a vehicle for the promotion of equality. After all, regardless of race, colour, creed, social background, geographical location, disability or other differences, all children are offered a place at school. Modern schooling was established on the principle that it would be universal, free and secular. By and large, in the system that is modern education, all children are able to compete for the same qualifications and credentials.

It may be claimed that if children grasp and make the most of their opportunities, education is a vehicle, though not the only one, for social ascendancy. Yet appearances are not substantiated by the facts.

Many studies show that schooling discriminates against blacks, females, certain ethnic minorities, rural and isolated populations, and children of lower socio-economic status (Anderson & Vervoorn 1983; Branson & Miller 1979; Connell et al. 1982; Hatton 1994; Junor 1991; Henry et al. 1988; Raper 1982; 1984; Western 1983). A study by the Australian Council of Educational Research (1996) has highlighted the degree to which retention rates among students from poorer backgrounds, after a period of dramatic increase in the immediate past, are now on the decline. Indeed, a close examination of social experience leads to the conclusion that schooling is not an instrument of social advancement; on the contrary, it actually compounds and reinforces social inequality. In fact, what is at stake here is not whether students have the equal opportunity of schooling: they do. Rather, it is whether that opportunity proves to be fair and equitable. In fact, the educational outcomes for disadvantaged groups are positively correlated with other social indicators, such as rates of imprisonment and unemployment which are all higher among these groups than other groups within the Australian population and which are, in turn, related to the ownership of wealth and assets (Connell 1991). Indeed, it has been argued (Jones 1982), that much can be inferred about a person's educational achievements along with their social achievements (or lack of them) from knowing their postal code.

There are many indicators[1] of inequity in education systems such as those operating in Australia. For instance, of every 100 students who start secondary school, about 70 complete the secondary years. This figure has increased dramatically during the 1980s and 1990s, partly because the Labor government of the time encouraged students to remain at school beyond the official leaving age and partly because the youth job market contracted dramatically during this same period and continues to do so. An examination of the social distribution of successful high school leavers would reveal a prima facie case for the link between education and factors of gender, class and race. Take the link between parental background and tertiary education entrance: children of professional parents have about a 40 per cent chance, while children of unskilled parents have only a 10 per cent chance, of higher education.

With regard to gender, since 1976, more girls have completed full secondary education than boys. Indeed 54 per cent of university students are now women, many of them in areas like engineering which were formerly the preserve of males. However, the clear gender segmentation in terms of subject choice operates to limit the higher education and work options of young females. Of course, the

position of some minorities, such as Aborigines, is worse still. Again, there has been an improvement in recent years, but in the senior years of secondary schooling there has been a dramatic decline in Aboriginal participation compared with that of the rest of the population.

Meritocracy, or to each according to their abilities

The belief that individuals succeed or fail because of their ability, or lack of it, has widespread currency (even in schools). Ability is understood as a discrete individual characteristic with no regard for the social context of the individual. The ideology of ability bedevils the debate about equality and education and belies the social facts about inequality and education, which are often construed (quite erroneously) as being the problem of the individual and not the social arrangements of which they are a part (Henry et al. 1988; Harris 1982). Consistent with the interpretation adopted throughout this book, we maintain that educational outcomes are socially constructed within the framework of a 'meritocracy'. While there are certainly exceptions where individuals succeed or fail despite their socio-economic context, these instances are no reply to the weight of sociological evidence which indicates that meritocracies, contrary to the claims of their advocates, produce only limited instances of educational redistribution.

This term 'meritocracy', originally coined by Young (1958), refers to a society in which positions of power and status are competed for on the principle of merit and desert rather than birthright or historical endowment, as was the case in pre-modern societies. In the nineteenth century, these societies were increasingly perceived as inefficient and wasteful of the talent reserves of the nation, open to corruption and nepotism, and denying opportunities to persons of real ability and talent. At the same time, it was commonly asserted that many sections of humanity were intellectually inferior because of racial, class and even sexual factors. Women as a group, for example, were seen as the inferiors of men and, because of their reproductive role, as closer to nature, a clear marker of inferiority in the Western tradition. Philosophers (who were invariably male) were particularly guilty of such assertions, inferring that women could not reason, that menstruation interfered with their powers of logical thought and so forth—in effect, that anatomy determined ontology (Lloyd 1984). The idea that human beings share the same intellectual faculties and potential, regardless of sex, race or class, is a comparatively recent one. The struggle for the extension of basic civil and political fights to minority groups has largely occurred only in the twentieth century (Singer 1976).

The influence of Darwinism was a factor in helping to revise notions of equality. When these theories were translated into a sociological form as Social Darwinism, utility and efficiency were seen as especially meritorious, arising from free and natural competition from *all* members of the population, not just a select few. Competition was seen as a way of promoting quality, the consequent gains outweighing the suffering and pain it might cause. Indeed, in its most radical forms, Social Darwinism opposed egalitarian social policies, on the grounds that they interfered with nature's evolutionary 'impulses': it was believed that the weak and poor were nature's genetic mistakes, destined, like any other inferior animal, to eventual extinction. To offer special protection to such groups merely prolonged the inevitable and violated natural law (Williams 1974). The 'ethnocide' of the Australian Aborigines was a product of such biological determinism. Although we tend to think of Social Darwinism as an outmoded and discredited discourse, its tenets are arguably alive and well in the philosophy of economic rationalism with its emphasis on efficiency, competition and utility and its slavish adherence to market forces—the economic analogue of survival of the fittest ethic (Feinberg 1975). The trouble is, while a meritocracy has some advantages over other methods of allocating positions of power and status, opportunity and reward, it is still deeply flawed in that the ambit of merit is narrowly defined and the system is not free, as its advocates suggest, of abuse or exploitation.

Given the way Australian society is currently structured, chances of economic success are limited. Similarly, given the way schooling is also structured, only a limited number can succeed academically. Much of this is related to the fact that education functions as a 'positional good' (Hirsch 1976; Hollis 1987; Marginson 1995) and that its advantages derive precisely from the fact that it has scarcity value and that its acquisition results in a measure of competitive advantage to *some* individuals. In order for this to be the case, some must be denied the opportunity for educational success, otherwise the positional advantage derived from its acquisition disappears and it has but marginal utility in terms of its value for social advancement. Hirsch's example of a stadium in which everyone stands on tiptoe bears this out: in the end, no one enjoys the height advantage gained from standing on tiptoe.

SCHOOLS AND CLASSROOMS

The experience of young Australians seeking tertiary admission at the conclusion of their secondary schooling provides some evidence of this: the economy of higher education is so organised that thousands of qualified and eager applicants are inevitably denied the positional advantage to be gained from higher education. Likewise, the youth job market is so constructed that 15–19-year-old school leavers face higher rates of unemployment, (which is now, when this book was being written, around the 30 per cent mark) than other sections of the Australian workforce, regardless of their abilities or qualifications.

Despite this, the rhetoric of equity (the term used in policy documents) was prominent in the decrees of education ministers until the advent of the Coalition government. In Australia, the Labor government from 1983–1996 implemented major equity reviews in its administration, a lead that was for a period followed in most state jurisdictions. Since Dawkins, the chief architect of these policies, Labor governments have been intent on lifting retention rates and expanding places in higher education—in spite of the fact that to do so lowers the positional advantage of a university education. It would appear though, that the main beneficiaries of these reformist policies were in fact the middle classes who continue to dominate the available places in higher education (Connell 1993). So, whether the structure of society has been made more equal by these developments is highly problematic: in many instances, the only change is that successful job applicants now need a university degree for what once required only a Year 10 certificate, an instance of what has been called 'diploma inflation' (Dore 1976).

Nevertheless, Australians appear to have come a long way in equity terms since before the Second World War, when higher education was the preserve of an elite and secondary education was undertaken only by a minority of the population. However, there remains an ever widening disparity between the resources and outcomes of certain private schools (the GPS league especially) and many government schools. According to McIntyre (1985), the high point in establishing an equitable education policy was from 1973 to 1975 when the then Prime Minister Gough Whitlam declared, 'Education should be the great instrument for the promotion of equality'.

At the time of writing, under the relevant Ministers, Senator Amanda Vanstone and Dr David Kemp (whose ideas on education we cited in an earlier chapter), a particularly austere and instrumentalist philosophy of education, combined with a more laissez-faire approach to funding favouring 'the strong' and 'the private', is asserting itself. Free market principles are also being applied to higher education. In all likelihood, these measures will subvert still further the critical functions of universities as well as their commitments to universal accessibility, which has only recently been achieved.

In the years since Whitlam, economic rationalists, following a global trend, have reshaped not only education but the national economy—one increasingly subject to market forces through deregulation and the privatisation of public facilities (Pusey 1991; Peters & Marshall 1996). At the same time, the rhetoric of equity is in vogue in public education policy, albeit in conjunction with 'efficiency' and 'outcomes', which are telling symbols of the current discourse that dominates public sector activity. The late 1980s and early 1990s have seen the announcement of social justice and equity strategy statements by Australian governments. However, the era of deregulation, market-driven excesses and higher rates of unemployment has left its mark on the whole of society, and especially the students (now, in the jargon of economic rationalism, often called clients) of our schools and universities.

Education now proceeds in a social environment dominated by policies and social practices, where people are more than ever inclined to think individually rather than collectively, and hence to act on the basis of personal freedom rather than in terms of social equality. In practice, this has led to an alteration in the discourse of education with renewed emphasis on competition rather than co-operation, efficiency rather than equality and performativity rather than scholarship. A pragmatic and utilitarian value has been placed on education by policy makers and embraced by administrators and the consumers of education so that choices in education are frequently motivated by extrinsic concerns alone. '*Where* (in job terms usually) will this course take me?' is the question often asked rather than 'What kind of *person* will this make me?' This is evident in the content of university advertising (another sign of the marketised times) directed at prospective students (Fairclough 1993; Wernick 1991), which makes much of the difficult employment situation and the fact that students from university X almost always gain high status jobs and more positional advantage from their degrees than those at university Y.

Noting these trends in the American context, Apple legitimately laments that the ultimate effect may be to eliminate from our collective memory the reasons why inequality in education, the economy and politics was once of public concern—as in the 1960s, when American governments and instrumentalities were so serious about racial equality that they embarked on the dramatic step of busing school children in and out of segregated communities (Apple 1986). Indeed, Apple's observations are even more apposite in the current context in which political correctness has been debased and there is a widespread populist racism that has been orchestrated by media figures and maverick politicians, and there has been generalised backlash against egalitarian policies.

The reasons for addressing the relationship between education and equality, then, remain more urgent than ever. They are various. For a start, the education system is a public institution. In Australia, governments provide more than 90 per cent of expenditure on education. Education is a public asset which should be addressing the public good. If the Australian people as a whole spend that amount, then it properly follows that we should address the question of distributive justice, that is, whether *all* Australians are benefiting to the value of this investment. Then there are questions about the fairness within the system relative to the expenditure of monies on particular parts of it. Connell (1993), for instance, makes the telling and provocative observation that more than twice as much money is spent on the educational provision of a university chemistry student doing an undergraduate degree (an inexpensive degree compared with that of medicine) as to that of the whole education of a student leaving high school at the end of Grade 9!

Moreover, there are disturbing signs that Australian society is more deeply divided than ever. The Burdekin Report of the Human Rights Commission (Australian Human Rights and Equal Opportunity Commission 1989) addressed the relationship between education and the homeless and abused children of Australian society, who now number a significant and growing minority. Burdekin indicates that tens of thousands of these children, many of whom would have left high school at the end of Grade 9, have no positive benefit from schooling at all. In the past, confronted by the cycle of poverty of which homeless youth is the latest expression, those who have worked politically for equity in education have generally adopted the 'standard basic provision' strategy. Claiming that education is a right for all, the aim is to spread it around so that everyone gets some, a basic provision.

As Connell (1993) suggests, there are problems with this view. For a start, it is becoming harder to sustain this view, 'as a citizen right', in the face of right-wing rhetoric which increasingly treats education as a commodity, a user-pays package. Also, in the technologically sophisticated society of the twenty-first century, the population needs a more advanced educational level than 'basic provision' if society is to be truly participatory and if its members are to survive in a society which is increasingly knowledge-based and dependent. The post-Fordist economy (about which we will talk later) is education reliant, and students lacking the requisite symbolic and epistemological background will be inevitably unemployed (Lingard 1994). Beyond that, the standard basic provision approach ignores the social patterns of stratification and inequality, in which a wealthy minority owns a high proportion of personal wealth, a situation that has been steadily deteriorating through the last two decades.[2] If governments merely fund basic provisions in such a context, nothing will be achieved to redress the larger imbalances within society.

There is a further problem: the 'basic standard provision' approach ignores the content of what is being distributed through education (i.e. the curriculum). As well as quantitative concerns to do with material resources, attention to the nature and quality of knowledge distribution is required. We have already noted in the previous chapter how the curriculum reproduces unequal social relations. If the 'standard basic provision' model is inadequate, then we must search for a different model.

The discourse of equality

The plethora of terms associated with the discourse of equality ('equity', 'affirmative action', 'equality of opportunity', 'social justice', 'warrantable discrimination', 'inclusiveness' and so on), is an indication that it is complex, confusing and not often well understood. As a result, educational policy goals aimed at equity can lead to conflicts of interest. (In practice, equity is the term under which goals of equality are applied to social policy.) Under equity provision, it becomes possible to advocate special programs for 'slow learners' and the 'non-academic', but at the same time this provides scope to argue for special provisions for those at the other end of the academic spectrum, namely, the so-called 'gifted' and 'talented'. We sometimes talk as if disadvantaged groups such as women, Aborigines, disabled or lower socio-economic groups should be admitted into educational institutions in proportion to their number, yet we also may argue that they be admitted into positions of superiority in hierarchical organisations without questioning the nature of hierarchy per se. This is often forgotten in the rhetoric of equal opportunity, that it is predicated on a redistribution of status positions rather than a questioning of status positions in themselves.

Such confusion leads a thoughtful critic like Warnock (1975) to contend that the concept of equality has distinct limitations when it comes to framing educational policy. Indeed, she maintains that as a principle, equality often confuses the discourse and is unable to settle vital policy questions such as, 'What is desirable to learn?' Warnock makes the obvious point that there is a very great difference between maintaining equal rights to education and rights to equal education. However, to make her point she introduces the confusing analogy of likening education to a piece of cake. When we talk of equality in education, are we doing anything more than slicing it into pieces as we do a cake? In effect, what is it we are distributing and, more to the point, what are the ingredients in this cake? Is there a more holistic approach to equality and education, one that looks not merely at resources, but at the whole curriculum, at philosophies of teaching as well as at socio-economic indicators, at education as a social good and not as a private possession? (Cohen 1981; Wringe 1984).

From an emancipatory perspective, the whole issue of equality cannot be separated from issues to do with power and empowerment, the questioning of organisational structures and the recognition of social conflict and oppression. It is not just a matter of dealing with issues of distribution (Young 1990). In effect, from this perspective, Warnock's educational cake is a mere slice of another cake, namely that of society. Indeed, in recognising the actuality of this more sizeable cake, we maintain that the discourse of justice cannot be impartial or disentangled from socio-economic issues of the kind that we have addressed in the first part of this chapter. In our view, an appropriate understanding of equality or equity must be linked to such an understanding of justice, which would also incorporate access to power and to ensuring that individuals and groups have an adequate democratic voice. Without such linkages, equality is open to misuse and misunderstanding. Indeed, if equality is not linked to an emancipatory form of justice, it may well degenerate into an unacceptable welfarism or a kind of inegalitarianism that Aristotle warned about—that is, the equal treatment of unequals which compounds inequality. Justice recognises 'difference' and 'inequality' and then seeks a remedy. In this sense, equality, mediated through justice, is intrinsically worthwhile. It can also be claimed, using a utilitarian argument, that equality so understood will benefit the *whole* community by enhancing its overall well-being, wealth and efficiency, and thereby increasing the general happiness of the greatest number.

Similarly, it may be claimed that justice should serve the common good and social solidarity. We argue that utilitarian considerations are not always adequate to make these judgments in a social policy area such as education. The common good and social solidarity are companion concepts, nurtured by the conviction that the interests of others deserve equal consideration with anyone's personal interest. Though the common good may flourish better in conditions of social democracy, it need not be equated with collectivism. Indeed, it is consistent with the common good to respect the autonomy of individuals and foster cultural diversity.

Justifying justice

Contemporary theorists of justice divide themselves between two major camps. On the one hand, there are the egalitarians who argue that the pursuit of equality in the distribution of public goods is a desirable end overriding all others and, on the other, libertarians who are suspicious of egalitarianism, believing that it encourages interventionist practices which constrain the freedom of individuals—the prime condition of happiness—to an unacceptable degree (see Sterba 1986; Hatton & Elliot 1994). The confusion and debate around concepts of justice and their application is compounded for egalitarians of a Marxist orientation. However they are not quite as sceptical as postmodernists, who dismiss all talk about equality as one of the perversions of the Enlightenment dream, as a grand narrative whose plot was flawed at its inception (Norris 1993).

Marxist theory has been sceptical of the language of justice and ethics generally, claiming that it deflects social reformers from the necessary goal of economic restructuring. In discussions of this debate, (Liston 1988; Neilsen 1989) it is claimed that if there is an ethical category that underpins Marxism, it is freedom and human emancipation rather than justice. Liston's analysis of radical theories of schooling, for instance, identifies a substantial issue for egalitarians, of whatever persuasion. However, as social theorists taking substantial inspiration from Marxism, we do not resile from ethical categories and the claims of justice.

With Walzer (1983) and others, we affirm that justice arises from the way we share culture as human beings: we are members one of another and respect for that constitutes the basis for justice. We therefore reject libertarian notions of justice, such as those promoted by Nozick (1974), which emphasise individual rights, deregulation and non-interference by the state, even to the extent of wishing to eliminate taxation and all welfare and public good provisions, including education, other than those, such as the police and the army, needed for the protection of property. Nozick's version of Utopia centres on a social formation based around a 'minimal state', an extremely attenuated form of government and public sector. The policy of the Howard government and that of the new right owes much to such thinking. Far from being emancipatory, as the word 'libertarian' might suggest, Nozick's position, which embraces authoritarian heartlessness with anarchistic freedom, only serves to protect the rights of the individual—in practice, the rights of wealthy and privileged individuals. In effect, there is a denial of the individual as a social being and an eschewal of all policies and practices which would serve to equalise the maxima and minima on the scale of advantage and disadvantage.

We acknowledge that justice and equality are difficult to achieve in social practice, and indeed might ultimately be illusory, but they are, nonetheless, worthy objectives. The objective is to go beyond mere equality of opportunity, which is a failed social measure, even though it is still advanced by social policy advocates of liberal and instrumentalist persuasion who, as we have seen, argue that marketplace conditions optimise educational achievement (Feinberg 1975). By contrast, our focus is on equal outcomes in social policy, on the attainment of a comparative justice, as far as possible. Contrary to the widespread impression that this leads to the homogenisation of the population, making every individual identical to every other individual, the focus is upon reducing the differentiations between social groups, of making, for instance, the educational position of migrant girls similar, so that they can thereby enjoy similar sets of opportunities, to that of dominant groups in Australian society.

An appeal to that most Australian of moral principles, giving everyone a 'fair go,' can be useful here, particularly when it is couched in terms of recognising that we are not often responsible for the advantages or disadvantages we possess. We have already referred in a previous chapter to natural lottery effects, to the contingencies of socio-economic circumstances, which from birth lock us into a situation of comparative advantage or disadvantage. None of us can control the parents that we have and the circumstances into which we are born; nor do we have any control over the allocation of natural endowments. Therefore, these lottery effects should be not held against us in the allocation of opportunities and welfare provision; nor should they be allowed (as they often are) to unduly benefit those with excess endowments and social advantage (Singer 1976).

On the contrary, our instinct for fairness would, in most instances, suggest that those most disadvantaged by these effects should be granted the kind of differential and favoured treatments that would enable them to compensate for their unfavourable initial circumstances. The trouble is, much-vaunted policies like equality of opportunity (as is often pointed out) (Wringe 1984) assume that initial circumstances are always uniform and that everyone starts off on the same footing—in other words, that there are no significant lottery effects that count against realising educational opportunities! Its failure in this regard means that equality of opportunity as a measure to mitigate disadvantage and to promote justice simply equalises access, nothing more, and leaves everything else up to the individual, to their will to learn and their tolerance of treatments that are often insensitive to the kinds of initial disadvantages that current school practices are unable to mitigate or redress.

Distributive justice

In a word, our interpretation of justice, and therefore of equality and equity, causes us to take the standpoint of the least advantaged in society, just as it causes us to evaluate the consequences of moral conduct in terms of placing oneself in the shoes of those for whom that conduct has consequences (Singer 1976). This means, in a nutshell, that in social policy generally, and in educational policy particularly, our philosophical commitment is to think through economic issues from the standpoint of the poor, not the rich, or race relations from the standpoint of the racially least powerful, or environmental questions from the standpoint of the most vulnerable species, and so on. In this view, the true test of decent society is how it treats its underprivileged members and how it treats their needs.

Such a view is supported by that most influential of theorists on justice, John Rawls (1972), whose work has been subject of widespread commentary and analysis (Claus 1981; Daniels 1975; Ryan 1985; Kukathas & Pettit, 1990; Theophanous 1994). We are by no means uncritical of Rawls; indeed, from the emancipatory viewpoint his theory is certainly deficient, but it provides a useful starting point for students and teachers thinking about equality. The basic question before Rawls is, 'What principles of social justice would free and rational persons accept if they chose such principles in a situation of genuine equality?' To address this question he creates a hypothetical 'situation of genuine equality' called 'the original position' in which the principles of justice may be discerned, and around which a type of social contract may be formed. The effect of such a scenario in testing the essentials of justice is to emphasise the following condition: whatever else is agreed to in the just society, one must make sure that an individual could accept being one of its weakest or least fortunate members. Rawls is seeking a contract which demonstrates justice as fairness.

Justice as fairness affirms both equal liberty and economic and social sharing as its constituent principles. The first principle grants everybody equal rights to the most extensive liberty, providing everybody else has equivalent liberties. The second principle allows for inequalities, but only where those inequalities advantage the least advantaged in society; it allows for inequality of position in cases where those positions are open to all. The modification of the equality principle is significant, as it allows *for* an unequal distribution of social resources where it favours the least advantaged. This means the construction of a social arrangement that also protects us from the possibility of gross misfortune and adversity, which alters our material circumstances and plunges us into unexpected poverty. This is the idea of social safety net, a welfare insurance scheme, that would guarantee certain minimal standards of living for all, including those in third world countries, and which involves radical redistributions of wealth and resources away from the rich nations such as the US and Australia, much of whose wealth and resources are squandered unnecessary wants and extravagance (Hatton & Elliot 1994).

In other words, Rawls' theory of justice supports affirmative action or warrantable discrimination (e.g. special education programs for the disadvantaged). This approach to justice affirms the importance of individual freedom, clearly a concern for our emancipatory perspective, but it insists that equity and social justice are prerequisites to liberty for all in our society. At this point, it is worth recalling Plato's *Republic* as discussed in the previous chapter. This was also a philosophical attempt to describe a just society, but unlike Rawls' society, in which fairness is seen as the means to justice, Plato believed that justice is more possible in a society where groups and classes fulfil their preordained positions and functions, which are absolute. Order and stability are the primary concerns of Plato's society which, in practice, is conservatively hierarchical with few attempts to remedy discrimination other than those which would interfere with individuals contributing to society what is fitting for them. Here we can see a view of social justice being outlined that is based on intellectual difference, that is to some extent meritocratic in that it is based upon the provision of differential forms of education that are matched to the innate capacities of the various groupings of society.

In contrast to Plato's view, justice as fairness has a redistributive function even though it is more properly described as a welfare concept of justice, because it pays scant attention to the need to transform socio-economic structures which may perpetuate unfairness. Despite its usefulness, Rawls' approach is weakened by an insufficient social theory. Supported by, and supportive of, a liberal analysis of society, Rawls' principles of justice apply to self-contained individuals who rationally keep faith with a contract in a society that has little or no social conflict. In truth, there is a 'veil of ignorance' operating here. The theory has only partial validity because it relies on a partial view of human nature and society. Despite its limitations, much can be drawn from Rawls' indisputable contribution in clarifying the concept 'justice' and the complexities which reconcile its key components: individual liberty and social equality. In particular, Rawls provides philosophical support for a standpoint on justice, the perspective of the least advantaged.

The criticisms Rawls has received from liberal and other theorists are an indication that he is perceived as being supportive of an emancipatory and socially critical interpretation of social policy. He certainly provides us with a starting point in the quest for an understanding of equality and equity based on justice. The deficiency in his view resides in his failure to acknowledge that equality of worth can only be guaranteed by equality of power, and power is rarely conceded without demand and conflict. Rawls' reliance on reason can only take us part of the way, because the cause of equality through justice often requires struggle and partisanship, which might necessitate the foregoing of individual liberties and special interests. Indeed, consensus is unlikely to produce justice: social justice is forged in the furnace of competing interests.

Other critics, particularly post-colonialist thinkers, see Rawls' perspective as indubitably Western, framed from principles of rationality and autonomy that are not universally shared (Young 1990). How can a Westerner, enjoying the fruits and luxuries of modern life, claim to appreciate the standpoint and perspective of the most disadvantaged?

As we have argued, equality through justice is not only difficult to articulate, it is also difficult to attain. Policies aimed at equality or justice will often contain ambiguities and contradictions. At this point, it is appropriate to pause and summarise the particular approach we are taking to social justice. It affirms the practice of freedom and equality, along with the need for provision to redistribute resources and redress inequalities. This view gives priority to the poor, the powerless, the disadvantaged in any society. It emphasises a concern for human rights at the individual level, while maintaining a parallel commitment to the human and non-human community as a whole, including future generations, together with responsibility for the entire environment, both natural and cultural. These latter considerations may, in particular historical contexts, qualify individual rights. However, a just society does not level down natural differences of talent and ability. It accepts such natural inequalities, but rates them as a common asset rather than an individual possession.

So private ownership of anything is a secondary privilege, not a fundamental right. Justice pursues mechanisms of socio-economic structural reform (rather than welfare) as the fundamental means to achieve justice in society. Justice has transcultural significance, such that it functions in any particular society as a continuing challenge to the betterment of that society. In the final analysis, justice is not calculating or based on envy or retribution; indeed, it is enriched when, within society, individuals act in ways that go beyond justice, such as dealing fairly, even forgivingly, with the unjust.

Justice and equality in schools and classrooms

What we are saying of justice in society generally can be applied to institutions or practices within society, such as education and schooling. Specifically, an understanding of education supported by this view of justice regards each human being as a knowing subject, precious, unique and fundamentally equal with others. It believes that each person has the right to find their voice, develop critical consciousness and become more fully human by knowing and changing the world. It therefore requires an education which awakens teacher and students alike to the possibilities for justice and the realities which prevent it; furthermore, it presumes that teachers and students will take a political stand for what they come to know to be justice, and against what they come to know to be injustice.

Thus education, concerned as it is with justice, must itself be just. The knowledge of justice and injustice is discovered by *acting* as much as by *thinking*—this is praxis knowledge. Finally, as an institution developed within the socio-economic structures of a society, education itself should be organised and educational resources distributed in ways that enhance social justice, especially by addressing the needs of the least advantaged through providing improved access and participation for these groups. In effect, this echoes the emancipatory approach of critical pedagogy. It is important that we attempt to interpret what this approach will mean to specific educational issues. What does equity through justice mean for the oft-repeated goals of education: efficiency, excellence and equal opportunity?

The rhetoric and regulation of efficiency are generally prominent in recent social policy. Wilenski (1986) has outlined how efficiency becomes the organising concept for public administration bureaucracies. An examination of recent educational policy documents shows an overwhelming pre-occupation with efficiency matters. Efficiency is not necessarily in conflict with justice and, by implication, equity. Rawls himself makes this case, claiming that in the perfect state, justice and efficiency are compatible (Wilenski 1986). He then concedes that this is not so 'if the basic structure is unjust'. The instrumentalists often argue in policy rationales that inequity (or injustice) breeds inefficiency and is therefore counter-productive to organisations and policies seeking efficiency. Indeed, this is usually the argument advanced by politicians and bureaucrats. It is one which has been echoed by Ken Davidson (1987), a journalist on economic affairs, who suggested that productivity is a product of equitably organised organisations and, further, that the life chances of all of us are threatened when empowering educational opportunities are denied to social groups.

To use his illustrative example: 'Someone who is illiterate in this society threatens me as well as diminishes his own chances' (Davidson 1987). Here, justice is valued primarily because of its instrumental potentiality. Equity is justified on the 'wastage principle'. For instance, women or other disadvantaged groups offer a 'pool of wasted talent' in that they have educational potential and skills which are under-utilised in the labour force. This appeal to the 'wastage principle' is reminiscent of the approach to the employment of women in wartime, or when there was a shortage of teachers. The principle is essentially instrumental, not valuing the just entitlement of women or other disadvantaged groups to the kind of education,

127

for reasons of its intrinsic worth, which would improve their social situation and enlarge their moral imaginations.

There are different concepts of efficiency and, in an era of technocratic-bureaucratic values, it becomes important to test what concept is being employed.[3] For instance, when efficiency is tethered to cost-cutting, as it often is under the practices of economic rationalism, equity can be sacrificed or conveniently overlooked. Furthermore, it becomes necessary to scrutinise systems such as schooling in order to determine how the ethos of efficiency has a subtle impact upon the fundamental rationale for the education system's existence. Despite the rhetoric about equity, the reality could be that in practice it is denied because of the prior agenda of efficiency. Certainly, in the instrumentalist approach to education, sensitivity to this concern may be dulled. In equity through justice terms, efficiency is not a sufficient end in itself: its justifications depend on other normative criteria—in Rawlsian terms, those related to the claims of the disadvantaged. More generally, in the emancipatory perspective, this would lead us to ask questions of the goal of efficiency, such as: Efficient to whom? Efficient about what? Who benefits? What are the costs? In all this, how are these answers reconciled with a critical understanding of education and justice?

Another imperative which is usually prominent in debates about education is the call for excellence or quality. Excellence in the sense of commitment to the craft, calling, outlook or processes one is studying is truly a virtue for education. In educational policy pronouncements (Commonwealth Schools Commission 1987), excellence generally means technological skill development which enables the national economy to be more productive and internationally competitive, such as that associated with Hawke's 'clever country' rhetoric. Such a slogan needs to be interrogated, for it raises more questions than it answers. For a start, what precisely is cleverness in this connection, and what is the relationship between cleverness and justice? The instrumentalist advocacy of cleverness, a current euphemism for excellence, may be equated with unfettered free enterprise in all sectors of the economy, starting with education. But the more traditional discourse of cleverness—often termed 'qualitarianism'—is related to an academic excellence which is not necessarily instrumental (although it can be) in character. Rather, it is about enabling individuals to realise potentialities in the tradition of a liberal and general education.

But are excellence and equality compatible educational policy goals? Is there some irreconcilable contradiction between the valuing of individual aspirations to success and the equal worth of all individuals, whoever they may be? As we have indicated earlier in this chapter, the philosophical quest for justice (especially as evident in the work of Rawls) attempts to reconcile the conflict between individual aspiration and the social good. In Rawlsian terms, the inequality which the pursuit of excellence may produce is only justified when, on balance, it promotes greater benefit to the least advantaged. If the same opportunity is available to all, policies for excellence in education must be subject to considerations of justice. The trouble is, the qualitarians often exploit this argument for their own ends, to preserve elite education on the grounds that its recipients eventually contribute to alleviating the plight of the disadvantaged through wealth creation and increase in national productivity. This is rather akin to the trickle down arguments used by economic rationalists: that unfettered wealth creation always has benefits for the lower levels of society, through employment. There is no need therefore to impose on its creators iniquitous taxation measures that would redistribute this wealth.

Rawls is, in some senses, sympathetic to these claims when he asserts about excellence that 'it is not in general to the advantage of the less fortunate to propose policies which reduce the talents of others' (Commonwealth Schools Commission 1987). Even so, Rawls' approach to excellence has been criticised for providing 'a basis for wasting both ordinary and exceptional minds and for indoctrinating students', and for being 'one sided' (Moline 1986). However, it is the understanding of excellence which is at fault here. In our terms, excellence in education is not about the production of an elite, but the creation of an egalitarian system of education which nurtures excellence in *all* pupils and over a range of domains, not a select few. This argument ultimately rests on what is meant by ability and talent in educational contexts, and whether these very problematic categories of human attribution are distributed on a universal or limited scale, as qualitarians would have us believe. Put simply, it is our belief that excellence in some form or other exists in all pupils.

Attempting to put this view into practice may confront the teacher with dilemmas. One dilemma confronting the egalitarian teacher is that of the so-called 'gifted' and 'talented' minority. The debate about this issue is complex to such a degree that the very categories must be called into question. Jonathan (1988), for instance, has argued, cogently we think, that gifted and talented children are not geniuses, but simply rather precocious products of extremely favourable home circumstances, i.e. rich in cultural capital, which the majority of children do not enjoy. According to her arguments, if favourable conditions produce favourable endowments, then it follows that improving the conditions of the unfavoured will also improve their endowments. In any case, it is our view that scarce educational resources should be allocated to enhancing the circumstances of the more obviously disadvantaged groups.

The importance of the argument about excellence is seen when it is related to the current Australian educational reforms. To argue for excellence or equality, apart from justice, may lead—wittingly or unwittingly—to the extreme of either a vocational–technical skills-based curriculum (instrumentalist) or an esoteric, academic curriculum (liberal) of the classical and traditional kind, both of which, admittedly, may result in a certain narrow excellence. In our view, programs based on the rhetoric of excellence from both liberal and instrumentalist sources have often been a cloak for maintaining inequities (Moline 1986).

The discussion of this point overlaps with, and anticipates, the question of equal educational opportunity. From the vantage point of our interpretation of social justice, there is a consensus that equality of educational opportunity is an insufficient social policy aim. Policies of equity require warrantable discrimination if there is to be equality of educational outcomes for, we repeat, there is nothing so unequal as the equal treatment of unequals. This is a matter to which Rawls pays considerable attention, by employing what he calls 'the difference principle'. The difference principle emerges in his exposition of the relationship between the second principle of justice (equality) and the first (freedom). In his theory of justice, Rawls explicitly declares that educational resources should be distributed according to how they enrich citizens' lives, including the less favoured (Moline 1986). This argument leads to a conclusion favouring warrantable (or positive or reverse) discrimination, which, for example, targets specific minority groups with special provisions for appointments and admissions, such as Aboriginal groups and rural and isolated students. Akin to this practice, and drawing from the same moral justification, is affirmative action, often expressed in special policy provisions which encourage equitable practices within organisations and institutions.

At the school face, the employment of the difference principle implies, for instance, that where non-English speaking background parents are not involved in school decision-making, there may be a need to provide greater resources for home/school liaison; or where some girls are absenting themselves from school sport activities there may be a need to rethink the school sport policy to provide more reasonable opportunities for girls; or, where poorer students are consistently performing badly in reading, increased human and material resources may need to be focused on this problem.

However, emancipatory analysts would regard Rawls as being too moderate in his approach to such affirmative action. Laudable as this welfare or compensatory view is, if we are to achieve just outcomes, we must understand that educational systems are located in socio-economic contexts. Equal opportunity alone cannot guarantee equity in terms of equal outcomes. The changes necessary for equity must be made on a number of socio-cultural and economic fronts: at best, educational institutions will only reflect and reinforce changes for equity in the wider society. Until policy makers develop programs sensitive to the structural origins of disadvantagement, equity policy will produce only incremental or illusory change. We are arguing that the intention to achieve equal outcomes from education depends on the pursuit of an emancipatory perspective; liberalism, instrumentalism and progressivism cannot sustain justice in this sense, because they have no critique of structural injustice—or at best have a limited appreciation of the social contexts in which schooling is located.

The need for a rigorous pursuit of equal outcomes rather than equal opportunity is borne out by an analysis of current policy. Certainly, the Department of Employment, Education, Training and Youth Affairs (DEETYA) has paid considerable heed to equity and social justice issues, but there is reason for concern, as expressed earlier, about the interpretation of equity arguments. Even if they are not peripheral, as might be suggested, there is still doubt that too much is being expected of education, compared with other sectors of society concerned in the struggle for equitable social policies.

Although the issues chosen to illustrate the relationship between education and equity are generally about the distribution of educational resources, it needs to be understood that we are arguing for much more than that. If it is no more than that, the debate will be seduced by the policy claims that social justice and economic growth can be promoted concurrently: seduced because the economic imperative (or the dominant ideology expressed as technocratic–bureaucratic consciousness) will demand sacrifices from the social justice imperative—as, for instance, in the drive for 'efficiency'.

What we are arguing for is such a coincidence between justice and education that concern for justice (and with it, human rights and responsibilities, and education for democracy) has a central place in the curriculum (Connell 1993). In order that such laudable objectives are not negated by it, the hidden curriculum also needs to be closely monitored. This coincidence is to be developed continuously in the engagement between education and society, a process which is of the essence in an emancipatory perspective. It is an engagement model, not a compensatory model, which seeks to make up for social injustices. Nor is it an oppositional model, which sets up alternatives for the disadvantaged (women's studies, technical schools or whatever), programs which can be marginalised or co-opted within the mainstream of education.

The emancipatory quest for justice in and through education may include such strategies, but it goes beyond them in an attempt to tackle questions of injustice within the mainstream and along with that, to empower the disadvantaged. What we are advocating has been dubbed a 'counter-hegemonic' approach, and we will examine it more fully in Chapter 11. Meanwhile, Connell et al. (1982) cite as an example of this approach that a goal of the Schools Commission's Disadvantaged Schools Project was to ensure 'that students have systematic access to programs which will equip them with economic and political understanding so that they can act individually or together to improve their circumstances'.

One final word about the relationship between equality in education and participation. Increasing participation rates among disadvantaged groups have been a major and justifiable objective for those pursuing policies of equity. Along with that, the language of participation and involvement has been extended to models of devolution in which decision making is referred back to the local levels. This type of participation creates dilemmas for our social justice approach. While involvement may be enhanced, this must not be at the expense of the provision of adequate resources to local communities. Justice and equity are diminished where devolutionary educational policy leaves disadvantaged communities to fend for themselves. This has been called the 'more for less thrust' approach to contemporary public policy (Lingard 1990).

Being equal to the task

In this chapter, we have argued for an approach to equity and equality as policy goals in education, based on a particular view of justice—one which gives priority to the standpoint of the least advantaged and which involves them in an empowering way in the design and implementation of curriculum and school decision making. We see this as being consistent with the emancipatory approach which emphasises that education is a public asset and educational policy should therefore be approached from the standpoint of the common good and the public interest.

Furthermore, we do not overlook the practical difficulties that teachers confront in schools when they try to achieve outcomes of equality; they are often confronting the more intractable elements of the socio-economic reality which, for the most part, remain beyond their control. However, we are not prepared to say that this means schools, teachers and educational communities are impotent in terms of effecting equitable changes. Schools may only be able to compensate for social inequities in a limited or partial way, but they can contribute substantially to the formation of individuals, who through a better understanding of the *real politik* of social life can collectively create greater social justice. The emancipatory perspective assumes the necessity of the link between justice and education. Both are normative terms and, in the socially critical sense, both derive from a similar vision for human society and the environment.

However, as has been illustrated in the discussion of specific issues, it is 'justice' which is normatively prior to 'education'. Education for injustice is education that is untrue to itself. Education, educational programs and policies, and educators themselves, need to be subject to a vision of justice if they are to be true to their vocation. Education floats on a sea of ethics with justice as the guiding current; indeed education is an inherently ethical enterprise, a theme to which we return in Chapters 11 and 12. To lose the vision of educational equality through justice would ensure that education degenerated into a charade, and would result in an uncritical acceptance of a state of affairs where the society was corrupted by the spiral of injustice.

NOTES

1. Data of the kind cited in this section are compiled by the Education and Evaluation Section of the Department of Employment, Education, Training and Youth Affairs (DEETYA), Canberra. For a recent summary of such evidence, see Williams (1988).
2. Andrew Dilnot's (1990) study into wealth in Australia showed that the wealthiest ten per cent of the population owned fifty-five per cent of wealth. ANU researcher, Bob Gregory, has produced evidence that in the 1990s Australian society has increasingly divided on economic lines. He refers to ghetto-isation, producing insulated suburbs of the very poor and very rich. These disparities are repeated to an even more profound degree

SCHOOLS AND CLASSROOMS

in the global economy, in the disparity between developed and less developed countries. To be specific, 80 per cent of the world's population has access to only 20 per cent of the world's resources, a situation which is likely to worsen rather than improve in the next century.

3 A fundamental question in a high-technology era is what concept of 'efficiency' we will choose: Western 'engineering-type efficiency' or a new type of 'integral efficiency'. In the latter, managers and designers of technology will need to explore ways of becoming integrally efficient, that is, of producing efficiency while optimising social and human values.

Keywords and phrases

- biological determinism
- equality
- equality of opportunity
- equity
- justice as fairness
- meritocracy
- minimal state
- natural lottery effects
- positional advantage
- positional good
- social Darwinism
- social formation or arrangement
- the difference principle
- utilitarianism
- warrantable discrimination

Tutorial and field activities

1 Examine the idea that education and social location (postal code) are strongly correlated with one another. This can be done by a variety of methods, but the simplest is to examine Australian Bureau Statistics of Information, available on a CD-ROM silver disc from your library. It is also probably available on a local area network. Take two dissimilar suburbs and examine the educational qualifications of their populations. What does this tell us about the distribution and location of education 'success' in the community?

2 Another observation in this chapter related to the differential funding of universities and the schooling system. Is it fair and just that so much more money should be allocated to university students (even though they are paying through the higher education contribution scheme for their education) than primary and secondary school students? What arguments, if any, can you formulate to justify the difference?

3 Analyse Rawls' ideas of distributive justice further. What mechanisms do we have in a contemporary society like our own which are Rawlsian in character and principle? Can these mechanisms be made to operate on a global scale; indeed, should they be made to do so?

4 Try and think of some other examples of 'positional goods'. Do they have absolute or relative scarcity? How are the respective values of positional goods protected? What is the role of the market in their allocation?

5 Find out if your state or territory has a social justice strategy focused on schools. If so, examine its contents and attempt to relate these contents to the theories of social justice discussed in this chapter.

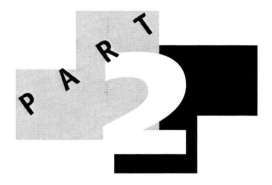

The disciplinary foundations of schooling

School to work, or learning to labour

School must seem strange at all times, it cannot be natural to go to school. It is no odder than the world outside, only more concentrated.

(Henry Green 1984)

Work, Consume, Die.

(Coronation Drive Bikeway, Brisbane 1997)

Beginning work

Work is one of the dominant categories of human experience, albeit one about which there is considerable ambivalence. The tendency to associate work with paid employment, with having a job or an occupation of some kind, with wage labour, tends to diminish the importance of forms of work to which no payment or position attach themselves. Housework is one such form of work; another is voluntary employment. Indeed, much of the necessary work that is done in society is of this kind, the kind that Illich (1981) has described, because it often supports and complements paid employment, as 'shadow work'.

Although many find the burdens of work distasteful and would do anything to give them up, we need to recognise that work is a necessary part of the survival process. Unless work is expended in the production of goods and services, be it in growing food, generating electricity, cooking meals, making clothes or rearing children, the life of human communities would soon disintegrate. Work is essential to the maintenance of the human habitat in all its complexity. As Marx (1981) suggested, being productive is part of the species condition, part of what defines human beings and humanises them. Having said that, though, work has changed its nature—and very profoundly—as the fabric of human society has become more complex and diverse, and more work dependent. In subsistence economies where work tends to be home-based and family-centred, there tends to be a more perfunctory attitude to work, with the main emphasis on producing those things which are immediately useful and essential for survival: hence the appositeness of the word 'subsistence'.

In modern societies, though, work has exchange value; it has become associated with the market economy, with the generation of surplus value, with profits and capital accumulation, and with workers selling their labour. Current assumptions about work with which we all are familiar include: (1) that it is associated with wage labour, (2) that it occupies the segment of life between school and retirement, (3) that it has positive moral virtues and so on, mostly having their origins in the exchange value notion of work. Like much else that we have discussed in this book thus far, these assumptions have their provenance in the industrialisation of Western society, which commenced in early parts of the modern age, having immense repercussions for our social order and the development of institutions like schools.

Notwithstanding the existence of high levels of unemployment in our society, the acceptance of early retirement as the norm, and considerable propaganda about the virtues of leisure, there is a general expectation that paid employment of some kind will result from education. Yet the reality of modern work, as it is organised in the post-industrial society, is that work patterns are more flexible and more inclined to be part time and transitory, based around contracts and involving regular retraining. Such conditions are symptomatic of so-called 'post-Fordism'. One of the features of post-Fordism is that the amount of work available in a society is concentrated among a core, labour force of an ever diminishing size (Roobeck 1990). This has led to the emergence of a dual society, split between those in work and those who are unemployed and are on welfare. In Australia, unemployment now hovers around the 8 per cent mark, and is much higher than this among young people. One of the consequences of this is poverty, which robs individuals of the opportunity to enjoy the fruits (dubious though these may be) of a consumer society, let alone its basic essentials. Thus there is a strong imperative to obtain paid employment in some kind.

But the desirability for paid employment transcends mere material security and gain, for much else is also tethered to being employed. Not only does paid employment provide an important social environment from which many of our friends and acquaintances come, but it is plain from the experience of retirees, or those who win the lottery and resign from their jobs, that life without work, in spite of work being a source of much discontent and alienation, is often intolerable and quickly loses its appeal. Further, as Hargreaves & Cooley have described it, work is one of the 'master categories of self-definition', one of those 'identity badges' which enable inferences to be drawn about a person (Hargreaves 1981; Cooley 1980). When we ask someone what they do, we expect them to mention their line of work not their hobbies or interests. Knowing that a person is a doctor or a hairdresser is more telling about their social and educational background than whether they listen to Percy Grainger's music and read the novels of Georges Perec. This is because the central divisions of society, those between the social classes, men and women and the spheres of the public and the private, are all closely related to the distribution of employment within our society.

A further adjunct of the value placed upon work is the stigmatisation of the unemployed. They are frequently depicted as dole-bludgers, as parasite-like, scrounging off the social security system in preference to working. The recent enthusiasm for working for the dole has its origins in this belief. Deeply embedded in these somewhat narrow-minded and bigoted attitudes is the Protestant work ethic, which fails to take account of the post-Fordist fact that jobs are in short supply and not always available to those who want them. As will be suggested later in this chapter, the work ethic has led to the suspicion that any forms of wilful idleness, of which unemployment is taken to be a modern manifestation, are sinful, tainted with the pernicious signs of the Devil! By contrast, work is pervaded with positive moral connotations, with the power to be ennobling and spiritually uplifting. Work, no matter how demeaning and undignified, is good for the soul and it is possible to gain innumerable joys and satisfactions from endless toil and labour. This view is best encapsulated in a powerful scene in Tolstoy's *Anna Karenin,* in which Constantin Levin works alongside the peasants gathering in the wheat harvest, experiencing the ennobling effects of work, both physical and spiritual.

In this chapter, we shall be concerned mainly with examining the relationship between schooling and work, and the part schooling plays in the reproduction of 'labour power'. We shall point out, among other things, that schools, since their inception in the nineteenth century, have played a prominent role in inculcating the work ethic, not only in terms of its moral profile, but also in terms of its material practices, in terms of respect for punctuality and attendance, for being deferent and for being able to tolerate boredom and monotony in the workplace. In other words, the school has been instrumental in programming the kind of subjectivity required in the modern workplace, in establishing the rightness and normality of the disciplinary regime which exists in most work situations. But we shall also point out that this function has been augmented and now encompasses not just instilling the work ethic in students, but also the knowledge ethic, for schools are increasingly concerned with sorting and sifting students along epistemological lines prior to employment. The new labour order associated with post-Fordism has, if anything, made this concern even more essential.

The capitalist divisions of labour

In spite of the widespread impression that education helps to create unity and social cohesiveness, it also sows divisions in society. As we saw in the first part of this book, as a technology of the self, the school is a mechanism for producing difference and, through its disciplinary regime, also deference. Although it is often suggested that this is because many students do not have the intellectual wherewithal to cope with more academic subjects, these differences also happen to replicate the differences which exist in the labour force.

The justifications for this have, in the main, tended to exhibit a 'structural functionalist' (Feinberg & Soltis 1985) character, as in Plato's *Republic*. As we noted in Chapter 5, when we discussed some of its sociological features, *Republic* was predicated on the assumption that an efficiently managed society was one in which each citizen had a particular role to play, allied to the specialised attributes with which they were born. Societies which took no cognisance of these attributes and which had their citizens play a multitude of roles for which they had no special aptitude or inclination were destined for chaos and ill-management. With the inclusion of education as a mechanism to determine these aptitudes and allocate individuals to appropriate positions in society, Plato was in effect supplying a blueprint for the sorts of 'dividing practices' exhibited in modern schools. Contrast this view of an ideal society with that of the early Marx, who conceived of a society in which skills and activities were broadly deployed throughout society, thus allowing greater free time for all, which meant more time for the enlargement of an individual's moral and ethical capacities via a broad range of cultural interests (Schmidt 1971).

SCHOOL TO WORK, OR LEARNING TO LABOUR

Work is far from being a monolithic concept. Within it, there are a multiplicity of divisions and sub-categories, not so much to do with types of work (e.g. with being a teacher, a computer programmer, a carpenter and so on), but with more generalised distinctions relating to the political economy of work as it has developed under capitalism. Work is now much more divided and is distributed more widely than it was in the past. Until the advent of the industrialised labour force, the main centre of work was an individual's place of residence, and skills tended to be kept within families from generation to generation. People did not, as they do today, go out to work; rather, they stayed at home, with everyone in the family unit, including children from a very young age, contributing to the work that needed to be done (Ariès 1962). Here again, we have an example of the way in which there was a continuity between childhood and adulthood as still tends to be the case in many Third World countries, with little cognisance taken of age and maturity. Moreover, families owned the means and matter of production, and tended not to sell their labour in exchange for wages, as happens now. Indeed, the whole concept of earning a livelihood through work is a comparatively recent one. When families were self-sufficient, producing the food and clothes they needed, the idea of earning money in connection with work was very foreign.

Contrary to its modern connotations, which are the exact opposite, in the Middle Ages, having a job and earning money were the badges of misery, for they signified that a person was homeless, was a vagrant, a beggar without family ties (Illich 1978). As society has evolved, newer and more sophisticated divisions in the workforce have emerged in which the means and conditions of production are no longer in the hands of families as they once were, but are held, instead, by large corporations, increasingly remote from the spheres of their influence and control. This has not happened overnight, but has occurred over the last two hundred years or so, leading to very different sets of working conditions than existed in the past, when more relaxed attitudes prevailed and adherence to the work ethic was less than strict (Watkins 1987).

Capitalism has led to a major restructuring of work in our society. In particular, it has brought about divisions within the workforce, and caused some categories of human beings to be excluded from it, children and older people being the most notable examples. It has also had ramifications for gender, leading to a distinction between productive and reproductive forms of labour. Reproductive labour, because it is associated with family life, with nurturing, with childrearing and with domestic responsibilities, has tended to be associated with women, whereas productive labour, which takes place outside the home, has been the domain of men's work, although this has changed over recent decades. Even sexuality itself was, at one stage, a target for control and regulation. In the generalised application of anatomo-politics, it was felt necessary that the supposedly excessive sexual appetites of the working classes be repressed in order that their energies were kept for the demands placed upon them in the factory (Foucault 1980).

Taking a holiday

A related distinction, which did not exist in the past, is that between work and leisure. These are now strongly demarcated, with clear and definite boundaries in terms of time and space. Nominally, leisure is time off work, either for an extended period as in the case of holidays, or for shorter durations like weekends and evenings, and it typically takes place in non-work environments, in specialised centres of leisure like tourist resorts. In one sense, leisure functions recuperatively, to reinvigorate the individual for work, and thus only has any meaning in terms of paid employment. Recreation, so to speak, re-creates the worker. Leisure is therefore a meaningless concept for the unemployed or for a person at home tied to domestic duties, for whom there are no holidays or specified times away from work. But even for those in work, leisure is not simply time off in which the individual is totally free to pursue his or her own interests and desires; leisure has been colonised by capitalism and become the domain of consumption, in which individuals no longer produce and create, but pursue planned distractions like video games, four-wheel driving, spectator sports and so forth, or consume what others produce (Biggins 1985).

Leisure in this sense has become big business, with whole economies (Queensland's is a good example) being linked to tourism and recreation. Indeed, Bourdieu has argued that paid employment, particularly for the new bourgeoisie, has become a way of embracing leisure; work is subservient to leisure, a way of funding trips overseas, a way of exploring new horizons and excitements (cited in Rojek 1989). Leisure is increasingly associated with consumption—an important facet of modern subjectivity. Like work, it is also associated with values and practices which have been produced by the discourses of modern society, such as advertising. We need to recognise the existence of a consumer ethic which complements the work ethic. Campbell (1989) who has written extensively about the generation of the consumer ethic, argues that it has its origins in the growth of cultural pastimes in the eighteenth century, those of the theatre, music and reading, and which made a measure of self-indulgence acceptable because they produced virtue and developed moral capacity. It was this background that eventually led to the emergence of a consumer society in which the consumption of goods and services has become as necessary to the health of the modern economy as their actual production.

It is important in this connection to differentiate leisure from mere idleness, which is unconstructive leisure, leisure without purpose and meaning. Such leisure is often seen negatively as leading to vice and bedevilment, to personal debasement and degradation, to illicit pleasure and wanton hedonism (Clarke & Critcher 1985). By contrast, properly exercised leisure, at the least in the traditional sense, involves constraint, is an opportunity for controlled and healthy activities, a time for moral improvement and self-education, a period in which to occupy one's time in constructive pursuits of self-development, a time of moderation rather than hedonism and excess (Cross 1993; Rojek 1985). Education, as was seen in Chapter 2, has always concerned itself with developing a healthy respect for leisure and its possibilities. Much of the curriculum, for instance, still centres around leisure rather than work activities. Think of subjects like physical education, art, drama, music, literature: their primary justification derives from their leisure rather than work utility, from their capacity to give individuals something constructive to do with their free time.

Unemployment (as it always does when its dimensions reach such a magnitude that it becomes a threat to social stability) has added a new dimension to this responsibility with some arguing that education should offer more in the way of leisure pursuits to enable the unemployed to wile away their time between jobs, at macramé and batik, in preference to being on the streets or in front of the television. The other option being canvassed is for education itself to become a form of leisure, an alternative to full-time and paid work, so that the unemployed would become permanently located within the school setting, productively engaged (Hargreaves 1981).

All such developments represent a departure from the traditional concept of leisure which was allied to reflection and contemplation. Leisure also tended to refer to a class rather than a set of activities occurring outside work, a class for whom society had made special provision to engage in activities that were more intellectual and material in character. The etymology of the word 'school' retains these connotations. The aristocracy and the priesthood were part of this class and they took on the role of moral guardianship of society, freed (liberated) from what were often regarded as the demeaning constraints of menial production. The abstention from productive work was accompanied by contempt for all forms of productivity, which were often portrayed as vulgar and crass and unlikely to ennoble the human spirit. Only through a life of leisure, freed from material care and the degradation of toil, could the maximisation of human dignity occur. The activities associated with this were generally of an artistic or scholarly kind, activities remote from the furtherance of human survival.[1]

In discussing the liberal orientation in the curriculum, mention was made of its advocates' frequent aversion to instrumentalism, which is regarded as defiling the proper course of education. An education which involves itself with something as contemptible as work, which attempts (as often occurs in socialist countries) to link learning with labour (Castles & Wüstenberg 1979), is regarded as being at odds with the true meaning and purpose of education. Of course, favourable pecuniary circumstances, like being of independent means or of possessing enough accumulated wealth to not have to work, must prevail if such education is to be viable, let alone have the consequences intended for it.

In any event, all versions of a liberal education, with their implied contempt for work and labour, tend to support versions of an elite-based society, centred either on an aristocracy or a plutocracy. And because of its unsavoury sociological connotations, there is sometimes a reluctance to adopt the phrase 'liberal education' in conjunction with certain educational recommendations. For instance, a committee at Harvard University, in thinking about the curriculum at the tertiary level, purposely avoided using the phrase, adopting instead the words 'general education' to describe what, in essence, was a liberal education, though intended not just for students of independent means but for everybody (Harvard Committee 1950). Yet, despite the arguments of its advocates, the truth is that there has always been a margin of vocationalism inherent in liberal education, for such education has always been presented as the ideal foundation for the priesthood, the public service and certain professions.

Returning to work

Although we have strayed away from the area of work, these observations about a leisure class and its consequences for education do have relevance, particularly in relation to a more apposite distinction in terms of modern society: that between theory and practice, which in the work situation reveals itself as a division between mental workers and manual workers. Although our species' name encapsulates notions of thinking and reflection—*sapiens*—as the key distinguishing feature of human as opposed to other natures, in truth human beings are as much associated with building and construction as they are with thinking and reflection. The fact that we tend to call ourselves *homo sapiens* rather than *homo faber* tends to perpetuate the thinking/doing hierarchy, which is further reinforced in the organisation of modern work. Central to this division are two classes of workers. One is a conceiver class, a technical intelligentsia, responsible for product development and marketing, as well as the organisation and management of industrial processes. They are the decision makers in the workplace. The second class of worker, responsible for the execution of the labour process, performs the menial tasks associated with production; it carries out the orders and instructions of the conceivers, rarely questioning or thinking about the consequences and impact of their decisions (Braverman 1974). They are *homo fabers*, as opposed to *homo sapiens*, in the work situation.

Yet this division between thinking and doing, conception and execution, between the domain of the head and the domain of the hand, which is at the core of modern work and its administration, was not always the case. The division between intellectual and physical work, which is often associated with some contempt for the latter, was once undifferentiated. The 'allergy to manual operation' had its origins in ancient Rome and Greece, and was consolidated initially in the Medieval monasteries and then in the universities of the time, with a refusal to teach the mechanical arts, which were regarded as empirical rather than theoretical (White 1975). This division eventually manifested itself in the division of labour. This began in Renaissance Florence with the building of its cathedral. For the first time, architects and artisans were separate classes of workers, the former overseeing the activities of the latter and prescribing for them particular tasks and operations.

Yet, as Cooley and others have pointed out, the reality is, that manual work is not devoid of thought or high order cognitive skills. On the contrary, in work in which there is a high degree of skill involved, there is a strong tacit component, which operates at the non-explicit level and which enables skilled craftspersons to make sophisticated judgements and decisions based around subtle and informed observations. Hence the opposition to deskilling through automation, which is seen as eliminating this knowledge base because it cannot be replicated by a computer program (Cooley 1980).

But the most forthright expression of this division between mental and manual labour came later with Adam Smith's descriptions of the pin manufacturing process, which he argued would be more efficient (and thereby more profitable) if the tasks involved were divided up and distributed among as many workers as possible in a way which foreshadows the procedures of the assembly line pioneered by Henry Ford. As Adam Smith argued, the division of labour saves time and increases the quantity of work that is possible (Smith 1986).

However, it is the theory of scientific management developed by Frederick Taylor in the United States in the first decade of the century which has done most to shape the nature of modern work. In helping to justify the division between the conceivers and the executants, Taylor argued that all 'brain work' should be removed from the shopfloor and that the production-line worker should, wherever possible, be a non-thinking being, a mere conduit for predetermined actions which have been timed and organised. When employers used to advertise outside their factories for hands, they were literally looking for that: mere appendages to machines, human levers to operate prescribed tasks, exercising few skills and no thought whatsoever (Herbst 1974; Wirth 1983). In this case, action is more important than reflection, which is regarded as an obstacle to productivity. As a consequence of this, the executants were denied access to decision making, and were prohibited from having an input into the management side of the work, which was the domain of the conceiver. Thus work tended to be organised in an authoritarian way, with anti-democratic features and with no sense of constructive interaction between the two classes of worker.

Another factor in the equation of modern work is time. Taylor's theories led to time and motion studies, in which the duration of workers' actions were measured against a stop-watch, and optimised in order to ensure that unnecessary effort was eliminated from the productive process. Modern work, then, tends to be—to use a distinction first developed by Marx—time-saving rather than time-absorbing, and is directed towards maximisation of output within the average working day (Jones 1982). Hence the appeal of automation and robots, which can 'work' twenty-four hours a day, without breaks, without becoming tired or alienated, and without going on strike or demanding wages, or superannuation and holidays.

The mechanisation of work, which has occurred in the shadow of Adam Smith and Frederick Taylor, has been condemned as a cause of widespread alienation in the workplace, particularly in the factory and on the assembly line. Much of Marx's (1981) condemnation of modern forms of work, for example, was directed towards the effects of industrialisation on human beings, that it made them mere slaves to the machine, and promoted estrangement, turning human beings into cretins and idiots. Even Adam Smith recognised these harmful effects—effects which, in his eyes, helped to justify the need for educating the worker as a way to offset the stupidity and torpor induced by machines (West 1963). One of the reasons why Ruskin and Morris wanted to preserve the craft traditions was that they, unlike machines, ennobled rather than demeaned the worker.

But not all work is organised in such a fashion as to induce a state of moronic powerlessness, to eradicate thought and skill, and to diminish autonomy and creative power. In recognition of this, Arendt (1959) argued that it was useful to differentiate work from labour. Labour she associated with toil, excessive physical exertion and the demeaning and boring work encountered in many modern workplaces, including the factory and the office. It leads to alienation and lack of personal fulfilment, the sort of thing Marx had in mind when he talked about the alienating effects of work. Coincidentally, although Arendt does not mention it, labour is also associated with hazards of various kinds, which are often life-threatening. One only has to think of the fate of the asbestos worker to realise this. Work, or what she preferred to call 'opus', by contrast, is intrinsically satisfying, unalienated and personally rewarding. It leads to the development and expansion, rather than the contraction and attenuation, of an individual's faculties. Moreover, work tends to be time-absorbing with concern for quality and excellence overriding that for quantity and productivity. In describing the characteristics of 'good work', Schumacher (1979) suggested that concern with permanence, health and beauty are its marked feature and, in this respect, it is the very obverse of labour. In addition, the worker has more autonomy. The clock-regulated structures of labour do not apply. The worker is able to determine the kinds of activities in which she wishes to engage, as well as the length of time spent on them. Artists, academics, writers and craftspersons enjoy such working conditions. They often have the freedom to construct their own work schedules and to choose the location where they work.

Post-Fordist or Taylor-made?

In some respects, this discussion of the manual and mental divide has been superseded across the labour force, but particularly so in high-tech industries like computing, bio-technology and business. Not only have there have been attempts to introduce more opus qualities to the workplace, but the division between manual and mental work is disappearing, as it is recognised that machines have usurped manual labour. With fewer and fewer tasks of a prescribed and predetermined kind, the competitive edge in industry is now centred around the smart or clever operator, who is more adept at solving problems than carrying out preset tasks. Thought-time has become a valuable resource in the workplace. Moreover, many workplaces are paying heed to more democratic arrangements, permitting most levels of the workforce to participate in the decision-making process. Particularly in Scandinavia, the industrial order has been shaped in terms of so-called 'socio-technical theory', in which the command structure of the workplace has been redefined, where management and workers often exchange roles, according to the exigencies of the task involved (Herbst 1974; Wirth 1983).

Earlier we mentioned some of the features of post-Fordism, a form of work organisation which, among other things, has attempted to redress some of the deficiencies inherent in the Taylorist and Fordist approaches to mass production that were pioneered in the assembly lines of the Ford Motor company. In the globalised economy, in fact, there has been a shift, because it does not facilitate enough market flexibility away from mass production. The successful economies and corporations are increasingly developing more specialised products that are niche-marketed, that are distinctive and customised, and in which quality and design as much as performance and quantity have become important hallmarks of market success (Bagguley 1991; Piore & Sabel 1984; Murray 1989). Benetton, the Italian clothing manufacture, is a good example of the post-Fordist company—one that has pioneered so-called 'flexible specialisation' and has employed computer technology at all levels of the production and distribution process. The labour force required for such specialisation is of different order and set of capacities than that required in a Fordist factory. In this regard post-Fordism has adopted some of the more salient features of socio-technical design. In particular, for example, it has challenged the Taylorist hierarchy and argues that all workers, irrespective of their positions in an organisation, need to be both conceivers and executants, thinkers and doers.

The pressure on schools has been to recognise these new developments in the way work is being reorganised, and to adapt to this socio-technical ethos. The Reports of Carmichael, Mayer and Finn that were discussed in Chapter 3, though they do not use the phrase, are post-Fordist in philosophy and ethos. They mention the need for workers to be problem solvers, to be multi-skilled and able to work in teams, and on the production of quality goods and services. Above all though, these Reports emphasise the need to create an education system in which the old, debilitating divide between mental and manual forms of knowing, which is at the heart of the education systems of all low ability nations (Brown & Lauder 1992), is overturned.

The origins of such thinking can be traced to the microeconomic reforms that the Hawke and Keating Labor governments introduced, and which followed the realisation that if Australia was to become a high-tech economy it needed to follow the patterns of labour and educational organisation apparent in successful economies like those of northern Europe, Sweden, Austria and Norway. These had been studied by the Australian Councils of Trade Unions (ACTU) and reported upon in *Australia Reconstructed* (ACTU/TDC 1987). Much of their success as economies was attributed to their education and training systems, and the degree to which their young people were participating in some form of post-compulsory education. Part of Australia's lamentable economic record stemmed from the fact that it was basically an under-skilled nation without a tradition of life-long learning (Ford 1984). Current education politics are designed to redress this, to provide a level of equality of opportunity and meaningful training opportunities that would increase the productive efficiency of the nation's economy.

While a post-Fordist approach has undoubted advantages over Taylorism, particularly if it is introduced properly into the schooling system, the post-Fordist labour force does not offer the same security as its predecessors. Indeed, some have argued, that the old Taylorist division is being replicated in the core and peripheral labour force, either replicated within a nation-state or, in a globalised economy, across nations, between the first and third worlds. The labour market in fact is increasingly organised on a global scale, with multinational corporations locating their activities in countries with low-cost labour and in economies where taxation regimes are conducive to investment (Lash & Urry 1994; Sivanandan 1989). It has also been argued that the same practices of economic deregulation that are also a significant feature of post-Fordism, are beginning to manifest themselves at the school level, with dire consequences for the equality of the educational system and the types of values that are taught therein (Ball 1990).

Nil sine labore: the work ethic

Throughout this book, we have suggested that the human subject is a protean form, whose final condition is produced from the discourses acting around it, which shape its desires, body, mentality and so forth. The so-called history of mentalities (Hutton 1981) attempts to chronicle the changing nature of the human consciousness as different cultural conditions emerge, placing new imperatives and demands upon the human subject. We have also pointed out the role knowledge, particularly that associated with the human sciences, plays in this process, providing new knowledges for acting on the human subject and for the human subject to enact. A clear instance of this is the way in which the Protestant work ethic was incorporated into the fabric of Western culture and gradually infiltrated itself into every individual's sensibility.

This ethic has been used to explain the emergence of capitalism in northern Europe. As can be inferred from the presence of the word 'Protestant', the Protestant work ethic had its beginnings in a fundamental shift in our religious tradition, namely, the Protestant Reformation, which eliminated much of the magic and ritual from religious observance, but also permeated itself throughout secular life generally (Weber 1958).

Before the Reformation, as we have seen, work was a much more *leisurely* affair, in which individuals conducted their business according to their own timetables and needs, without undue exertion or intensity. Work was fitted around life, rather than the other way around. The Reformation changed all this, and caused work to become part of the individual's religious duties, part of the process of spiritual accountability, a sign of salvation. This was due, in part, to the fact that the locus of responsibility for spiritual redemption was transferred from the church to individuals, and individuals became the auspices of their own salvation. Accompanying this change came a set of obligations relating to the secular and temporal life of the individual, such that any action in life had the potential to seal grace or sinfulness on their soul. Good work was seen as a way of attaining near-perfection, so that individuals' secular actions contributed to their spiritual well-being. It was this that created the theological framework in which capitalism was able to develop, permitting wealth creation to become what amounted to a redemptive act. And because wealth creation was associated with being ceaselessly productive, hard work came to be regarded as something likely to be looked upon favourably by God. Pictured thus, indolence was the enemy of profit, industry its friend. Poverty was the fault of the individual, a sign of godlessness, 'a comforting assurance that the unequal distribution of the goods of this world was the special dispensation of Divine Providence' (Weber 1958).

Thus the puritan outlook, the most rigorous formulation of which occurs in the theology of John Calvin, became associated with various forms of self-denial and abstinence, with strong disciplinary control. Wealth, though, was not to be flouted and advertised; all things were to be done in moderation, with an avoidance of excess and indulgence. The fruits of one's labour were not to be selfishly indulged, but were to be placed in the service of humanity generally, in charitable works. The Protestant work ethic was a complete moral package which led to the extension and fuller development of human resources, contributed to the maintenance of the social order and guaranteed that the individual gained 'an assured position in the eyes of God' (Anthony 1977). Notwithstanding this analysis, it is apparent that the Reformation revolutionised Western culture, providing a pathway for the development of universal education and free enquiry.

The trouble was that, at the time of its formulation, the work ethic was far from universally exercised. With the support of the Catholic church, which had encouraged the observance of countless feast-days during the calendar year, on which no work was done, Western society tended to be somewhat more indolent than it is today. In order to make society more productive, one of the first changes that occurred, following the Reformation, was the elimination of some 100 feast days from the Christian calendar. And in the intervening period, right up until the Industrial Revolution, Western society gradually underwent a period of progressive (some might say regressive) social engineering, which resulted in individuals coming to recognise the importance of work, of being productive, of not wasting time, and of using one's energies in resourceful and profitable ways. It did not matter whether the work was joyless or not, full of toil and backbreaking exertion, hazards and dangers; whatever form it took, work came to be regarded as an important antidote to sin, as a way of resisting temptations. Industry was conceived in moral and religious terms, as a dimension of virtue which had redemptive potential. Commensurate with this was the idea that time spent in anything other than work was mere self-indulgence and hedonism, and ought to be abstained from. Idleness was demonised. Even sleep was regarded as potentially dangerous to the condition of the soul. One of the other effects of this puritan discourse, then, was to introduce order and regularity into life, to ensure that time was used resourcefully as a contribution to being productive.

The coming of the work ethic was one of the first signs of the emergence of what we have called, following Foucault, the 'disciplinary society'. As a society, its primary concern was the development of various forms of technology, like prisons, asylums and (our concern) schools, which would enhance the productivity of its members. It is of note that these technologies, which emerged in the early modern period, were almost contemporaneous with the spread of the work ethic, thus providing, as we shall see, convenient locations for its inculcation. As they were originally conceived, even hospitals were supposed to participate in promoting the work ethic, as well as the moral and economic principles governing society! (Forty 1980).

Although this discussion might seem very remote from the classrooms of the 1990s, these attitudes persist, and they have shaped the purposes of schooling. In relation to issues like equity, for instance, there is a strong 'blaming the victim' mind-set which resists seeing the victim as being the outcome of systemic factors, those to do with an unjust social order produced and legitimated by capitalism and its legitimating ideologies like the Protestant work ethic. Similarly, success tends to be interpreted individualistically as simply a product of exertion and hard work, self-denial and industriousness, and not exceptional and favourable social circumstances. Frequently operating as isolated individuals, even teachers labour under the burden of the work ethic, blaming themselves for pedagogic failure and inadequate educational outcomes, not realising that these originate in a social order whose efficiency depends upon a winner and loser discourse, a sporting translation of Calvin's saved and unsaved.

Education and work

Rightly or wrongly, employment is often seen as the primary outcome of schooling, particularly among students who, in the main, see schooling as a preparation for employment. The curriculum is supposed to enhance the employability of students, by instilling them with basic skills and an appropriate set of attitudes commonly found in the workplace. In order to ensure that schools pay some heed to their requirements, employer groups are often represented, along with governments and higher education, on bodies concerned with curriculum planning and design (Wringe 1981). Given the centrality of work in people's lives, one could argue that this is understandable. By consulting with employer groups, schools are in a better position to ensure that their students obtain the credentials and skills required in order to maximise the possibility of employment. Moreover, with their frequent assertion that education should be tethered to the economy, governments around the world have become sympathetic to the view that schools should be more instrumental in outlook. Indeed, this view seems to have gathered apace in the last decade or so, with many countries in the Western world, including Australia, introducing various school-to-work transition programs designed to ensure that students understand what is expected of them as employees.

The perspective on education which is encouraging these practices and outcomes can be described as economic utilitarianism. In the past, and still in some quarters, this carries the label of a vocational approach to education in which school becomes, in large measure, a preparation for employment. However, economic utilitarianism in its latter-day technicist and managerial form may not be sufficient. Driven by what has been generally termed 'economic rationalism', this perspective has a long pedigree, being fathered by exponents of human capital theory, as discussed in a previous chapter. This perspective is uncomfortable with emancipatory attempts to challenge or critique the way society is ordered and constructed. This view is inclined to confuse education with socialisation and training, what was called 'small "e" education' in an earlier chapter.

'Vocational education' is not a fully satisfactory descriptor. Sometimes, it is packaged as 'life skills' education. It could also be described as 'education for economic competitiveness' or 'marketplace education' or 'education for technocratic proficiency'. It is education which accommodates technocratic values and, insofar as it uncritically accepts society's hierarchies, it may perpetuate injustice, elitism and class and gender inequities. Beck's (1989) survey of the British experience equates this model with the nineteenth-century industrial trainers. He identifies its call to get back to basics in education as the cloak for a hidden agenda: a reversal of traditional styles of education designed, above all else, to develop passive, uncritical, obedient, diligent, reliable operators for the workplace—a hidden agenda with undoubted political and industrial relations implications. Indeed, vocational education has been a way to prevent the development of working-class intellectuals (Feinberg 1983).

But among educational theorists, there has always been a degree of ambivalence about strong vocational tendencies in education. As we saw in the chapter on the curriculum, there have been those who have seen any form of vocationalist tendencies as a travesty of education, as a contradiction in terms (Oakeshott 1971). This argument claims that socialisation for the workforce is training, *not* education. On the other hand, some like John Dewey, though for reasons other than vocational preparation, have argued that occupations should be the centre of the curriculum, as through them many insights about the nature of society and the political economy of work can be taught. Ideally, schooling should be a blend of the practical and the theoretical, and occupations provide an ideal setting for their linkage (Archambault 1966; Dewey 1969; 1977). But in most cases, vocational education is a convenient way of achieving a de facto form of streaming, providing a place for the non-academic students and a range of subjects that allegedly appeal to their more practical proclivities.

However, these subjects often degenerate into mere skill formation, involving the inculcation of routines associated with the workplace, and an uncritical acceptance of the social relations which prevail in it. As we have seen, work is a central category in human existence and in the organisation of the political economy, yet few curricula actually treat the theme of work with the seriousness and intellectual rigour that it deserves. One exception here was the attempt in Victoria, under the aegis of the socially critical approach, to introduce studies of work and the workplace as a subject in the curriculum—in effect, a more authentic and critically informed type of careers education.

Those who espouse a closer relationship between work and schooling presumably do so in the belief that the skills and understanding provided by the classroom' have direct use-value in the workplace. Yet the evidence for the vast majority of occupations suggests that this is not the case. With the exception of some basic skills like literacy and numeracy, which are acquired in the early years of primary school, the knowledge-base provided by schools is not useful for most types of employment. As most students recognise, the curriculum has but a minimum of relevance for work and for life in general. Students in fact often recognise this, realising that what is learnt is less important than the symbols associated with learning, namely good marks, the attainment of diplomas and certificates, which are taken to be symbols of conscientiousness and industriousness (White with Brockington 1983).

In a study conducted of their expectations of school students, White (1987) found that employees expected them to be polite, well-dressed, punctual and deferent. Whether they were educated or not, seemed to be irrelevant. There are vestiges of the work ethic in these expectations. Indeed, for most occupations, the average school-leaver is over-qualified and over-knowledgeable, and what skills are required are better supplied by on-the-job training. With the exception of occupations requiring professional qualifications, or occupations which require specialist knowledge and expertise, the content of schooling is in actual fact superfluous to the needs of the workforce (Berg 1969; Livingstone 1987). All that is needed for most forms of work (labour) are the right attitudes, those associated with the work ethic. These are constituent elements of that 'economic self' which is important in securing and maintaining a job.

If there is a contingent relationship between school and work, it is not based around the curriculum. Thus some other explanation must be sought to explain the ongoing relationship between the two. One such explanation has been provided by so-called 'reproduction theory' which argues that there is a correspondence between the *processes* of schooling and work, and that these processes are more important, where the reproduction of labour power is concerned, than the *content* of schooling (Bowles & Gintis 1976). Thus, if we examine many of the material practices of schools, there are some strong structural parallels with those of the workplace.

The school day, and the school year (and we shall have more to say about these in Chapter 8) are scaled-down versions of the work day and the work year. They are also organised around basically the same binary structure, that between work (which corresponds to lesson time in the school) and break periods or recesses, times of temporary recuperation, when food and drink are taken and informal socialisation occurs. Inter-semester breaks correspond to holidays.

The social relations of the school are also homologous with those that prevail in the work situation. Even though the school is a rather unconventional worksite (its nearest parallels being the hospital or the prison), its structural organisation is nonetheless reminiscent of an orthodox worksite, particularly in terms of its administration structures. Although the homology can easily be over-exaggerated, disguising some the subtler relations between the two, the relationship between students and teachers, for instance, is analogous to that between executants and conceivers, which we argued earlier was central to the organisation of modern work.

Nonetheless, it needs to be borne in mind that students are not productive in the usual sense of the word, even though, under the terms of award restructuring, it is becoming fashionable to subject classroom work to the criteria of productivity. Teachers are part of the command structure of the school, part of its technical intelligentsia, whose knowledge and expertise determine the modes and matter of classroom production, and what work the students execute in the classroom. Moreover, they determine how this work is to be rewarded, for work in the school, like that of the capitalist workplace, is not only fragmented, but is also differentially rewarded and takes place in an atmosphere of competition rather than co-operation (Matthews 1980). The teacher also corresponds to the overseer (note the surveillance aspect of this word) in the workplace, monitoring the progress of students, ensuring that they keep 'on-task', to use a psychological term that is revealingly truthful about the processes of schooling. And, of course, this same homology tends to repeat itself within the social relations of the teaching hierarchy and the ancillary staff of the school, which students come to perceive as the natural order of work. Among other things, this has had particular consequences for gender relations, as women have tended not to occupy positions of power or responsibility within the school, thus creating the impression that such positions are generally reserved for men in society. This gender stereotyping is even more pronounced among the ancillary staff and the 'shadow workers' of the school, the 'tuck-shop ladies'.

Bowles & Gintis (1976) also pointed out that the ethos of the school is a critical dimension in the reproduction of labour power. They argued that working-class schools tend to be more authoritarian and rule-dominated, with a forceful and external locus of control which parallels the subjugated conditions of blue-collar work for which such schools are mainly preparing their students. By contrast, middle-class schools are less authoritarian, demanding from their students more initiative, self-discipline and the exercise of responsibility. This accords with the ethos of much white-collar work, that of the conceivers, which is the destiny of many students from such schools.

This aspect of Bowles & Gintis's work has been subject to considerable criticism. Their picture of working-class schooling, with students submitting to authority with a minimum of opposition, does not accord with the actual conditions of such schooling. In truth, the students of such schools are generally resistant to authority and are forever engaged in strategies designed to sabotage the teacher's will and intentions. They are anything but mere bearers of labour power. Not that this is of much assistance to them in the long run. For, as Willis (1977) and others have pointed out (Corrigan 1979; Everhart 1983), in being resistant to the processes of schooling, in not submitting to its dominant culture, such students merely consign themselves to the bottom of the occupational hierarchy and, increasingly, these days, to no occupation at all.

But wherever one ends up in this occupational hierarchy, there are expectations which pervade all forms of work and which must be observed if one is to retain a job and maintain employment. Time and time again throughout this book, we have argued that the cradle of modern schooling can be found in industrial Britain, at the beginning of the nineteenth century. We have suggested that before the Industrial Revolution and the emergence of modern capitalism, attitudes to work were somewhat laissez-faire and undisciplined, characterised by irregularity and informality. These were tolerable traits on the land, but in a factory where machines predominated and work was scheduled according to the clock, such attitudes were no longer appropriate and were, as the nineteenth century progressed, literally schooled out of existence. For as the early theorists of modern schooling recognised, the school was a powerful technology for inculcating the work ethic.[2]

Thus, if one examines the discursive practices of the school today, a high premium still tends to be placed upon habits like obedience, punctuality, constant attention, industriousness and so forth. For instance, absenteeism and punctuality, which will be examined in more detail in the next chapter, are subject to constant surveillance. Within lessons, students are constantly harangued to be attentive, to concentrate on their work, to avoid distractive behaviour. In fact, industriousness is one of the qualities which the school tends to venerate. We have already noted that mottoes are significant registers of underlying philosophy and ideology, as are statements of intent and purpose. Not all school mottoes pay heed to the work ethic, but many do. The frequent appearance of words like 'striving' and 'perseverance' are reminders of this. Indeed, the motto of one private school suggests that there is nothing without labour (nil sine labore)!

It is not surprising, then, given the value that is placed upon work, that when teachers report on their students they usually comment on their attitudes to work, and on whether they have been industrious and diligent during the year. Idleness and general indifference, along with non-productivity and failure to meet deadlines, are also objects of commentary. Even the wearing of a school uniform is often justified in school handbooks in terms of its utility in terms of cultivating the kinds of appearance and grooming standards which are required in working settings by employers. It has been claimed that even the boredom that lessons often induce is, in its own way, a preparation for the climate of work, which in most instances is repetitive and monotonous, tedious and uniform (Spring 1975). Interestingly, resistance theory often traces incidents of vandalism and mucking-up in school to the intense boredom that students feel in class and at school generally. Such students turn to a counter-school culture as a release mechanism, because it offers excitements and pleasures that the school's official culture does not. Those who tolerate this boredom without much opposition have, in effect, already submitted to the authority of the school, and its demand that they tacitly accept its regime without question or challenge.

Although learning is not a conventional labour process, it is nonetheless work in the sense that it consumes time and materials, and requires exertion and a certain amount of energy. Teachers certainly refer to it as such when they cajole and coerce their students to work with more conscientiousness. Their role in doing this closely parallels that of a production supervisor managing a group of human beings so they complete a series of tasks in an allotted time-span. School work takes a variety of forms, from writing assignments (a telling word in this connection) through to practicums of various kinds. The work is mostly 'privatised' rather than co-operative. As another evocative symbol of the degree to which an individualistic ethic pervades schooling, students are constantly enjoined to do their *own* work. Assisting others is regarded as an offence to the morality of classroom life. Yet in the post-Fordist world, working in teams and together on projects is a requirement in the workplace. School work is also time intensive and produced against the clock, with penalties being exacted for those who fail to observe deadlines and due dates.

Then there is *homework*, an important part of the educational process, as it is study in the absence of an overseer or supervisor. Homework is an exercise in self-control, whose completion signifies the degree to which disciplinary powers have been internalised and are self-enacted, have become part of the subject's normal everyday practices.

Yet, for the most part, notwithstanding occasional work experiences in the latter years of high school, *school* work is an *in vitro* rather than an *in situ* experience. Even those subjects like industrial arts and business (sometimes called commercial) studies, which are closest to the nature of real work, are pre-occupied with exercises, with practices and competencies in the absence of actual production. This is a somewhat indulgent form of apprenticeship, especially when compared with what happens in the workplace, where skills and practices are actually learnt while on the job, while being part of the labour process. On the other hand, it is quite common, especially for non-academic students, to be dragooned into the actual labour processes of the school, those which are needed for its day-to-day running, in what are almost simulated work situations. Students will often assist teachers with classroom tasks, helping them to tidy up textbook cupboards, distribute equipment and so forth. They will often help the office staff, assisting with reception and word processing. In some schools where banks and bookshops have been established, students will often play a prominent role in their organisation and management (Watts, Jamieson & Miller 1987).

Teachers' work itself is characterised by routines and repetitive tasks of a clerical and administrative kind which detract from the construction of their work as an essentially conceiver profession, with a strong reflective and intellectual dimension. In some respects, the teacher's position in the occupational hierarchy is ambiguous, causing many teachers to be unhappy about being labelled as workers, aspiring instead to the status of a professional, whose conditions of work they do not share (Connell 1985; Grace 1978; Harris 1982). More to the point, teachers rarely examine the ethos in which their work takes place, the issues that we have raised in this chapter always being taken for granted without consideration of their origins and their consequences, let alone the possibility for their reform. Frequently teachers do not have an opportunity, even in their student years, to review and amend their practices; instead, much of their time is taken up with 'busy work', a seemingly endless presentation of routine tasks for assessment, which too often are demanding of time, but not scholarly rigour.

Mental work and handiwork

Throughout this discussion of work, we have constantly alluded to the division between mental and manual forms of work, which could be described, given its pervasiveness and frequently uncontested nature, as an ergonomic version of dualism. In the chapter on the curriculum, we argued that this variety of dualism had its origins, beginning with Plato, in various versions of idealism which held that the embedded world, that of everyday experience and sensory perception, was saturated with distortion and spuriousness and needed to be transcended if the world of ideas and forms was to be apprehended. Such epistemology—for that is what it is—has normative repercussions for activities grounded in the material world, particularly those to do with the practices of everyday life, like manual labour.

But this distinction between the worlds of reflection and action, thinking and doing, which is a central theme in Western epistemology, also has economic origins in the distribution and organisation of work within our society. Following Braverman, we have argued that most work is divided between the processes of conception and execution. Nevertheless, we need to be aware that these Taylorist assumptions are now subject to questioning, and that post-Fordist reorganisations of work which stress the absence of hierarchies and the conjunction of thinking and doing are now in the ascendancy.

One of the most important functions of schooling in relation to work, then, is to replicate this distinction and to ensure that students are categorised as either one or the other (Browne 1981). This process of filtration, or what amounts to the ascription of an epistemological type to the student–subject, arises from what is an obvious occupational nightmare, that high-demand jobs—and these are usually ones to which status and prestige and high salary pertain—are in short supply.

One pervasive ideological feature of our culture is an 'individualistic logic', which encourages individuals to believe that anything, including the acquisition of a highly-paid job, can be accomplished by the simple exertion of tenacity and industriousness and a surfeit of the desire to succeed. According to this same logic, even the most unpropitious odds in the natural lottery can be overcome, providing the individual has enough will and determination. To support this argument, countless stories are cited of individuals who made it, who overcame the handicaps of home background, of starting with nothing, of rising to the pinnacles of the financial world with no education to speak of at all. Such stories only serve to reinforce the cogency of individualistic logic. Yet it is an axiom of societal life that not everyone can succeed, that is, if success is defined in terms of the acquisition of riches and a highly paid job. The dark side of individualistic logic, and it is not often that we hear about it, is that for every success there are countless failures. This is what Harris (1982) has called the 'interference elimination process'.

Because of the nature of the occupational market, which like every other market is one in which the forces of supply and demand operate, not everyone can realise their ambitions or make a reality of their aspirations. The efficacy of individualistic logic is such that many come to believe that this market operates without fear or favour, and that principles of justice really do operate when it comes to the allocation of reward and status within our society. If individuals do not attain success in society, then they only have themselves to blame. Either their attitudes were at fault: they did not exert themselves enough or take advantage of their natural talents; alternatively, they squandered their opportunities in wanton and unproductive ways. Indicative of this is the degree to which the unemployed often blame themselves for losing jobs or not obtaining them in the first place (Watson 1985). As we have suggested, the whole moral economy of schooling tends to reinforce the internalisation of blame, for it is concerned with attributing ill-success to personal inadequacy, be it of an innate kind in the case of intelligence, or of an attitudinal kind—the failure to be productive, to have acquired the work ethic. As we said earlier in our discussion of the work ethic, all this serves to take attention and blame away from the real culprit, which is a society structured in such a way as to require a few success stories and a large number of failures.

But even before the student reaches the workmart, ergonomic dualism has already set in. Although most states in Australia have abandoned the old division between technical and academic schools, which represented an institutional support system for the division between mental and manual labour within the broad front of comprehensive schooling that has replaced it, there are plenty of vestiges of this lingering tradition. For a start, there is a manual curriculum comprising, in addition to the basics, some practical areas of understanding like commercial and industrial arts. This is supposed to cater for the non-academic student—in effect, the future executant, the blue-collar worker. And it is not without coincidence that these subjects often actively discourage their students from thinking or acting with initiative, behaviour deemed inappropriate in the office or the factory. Taylor (1984), for instance, has pointed out how textbooks in office practice encourage would-be secretaries to defer to their boss, to be submissive and acquiescent and not to interfere with his work (and it usually is a he) unless called upon to assist.

Another aspect of this is that such students are often expected to be groomed in a way which echoes the demands of the office place. In addition, the manual curriculum is often attenuated, those following it leaving school at the earliest possible opportunity with a limited array of options and epistemological skills. This serves to entrap students within the ergonomic dualism. Leaving school prematurely means that their occupational opportunities are mainly confined to the manual sector, and the lack of a fuller epistemological repertoire means that they are also confined within this sector, with few opportunities to extricate themselves. This becomes of special concern because it is the manual sector which is most vulnerable to automation and job replacement, and without retraining the premature school leaver is disempowered indeed.

On the other hand, those following the other type of curriculum in the high school, namely the academic curriculum, are destined for a different occupational domain, one in which conceivers are dominant workers. Unlike the manual curriculum, which places a high emphasis on manual skills, on action and doing, the academic curriculum is almost exclusively theoretical, more concerned with thinking and reflection, and places a high premium upon symbolic manipulation, especially of the numerical and linguistic kinds. Students are expected to think for themselves, to develop critical skills and be able to present discursive arguments, the sorts of skills which will be required of them as conceivers. The academic curriculum is not designed to be a terminus, though it can be for some. Its primary function is to be a preparation for university and college, places which are demanding of mental knowledge, particularly of that sort relating to high-status professions such as law and medicine (Browne 1981).

In order to obviate this problem, there is a plain need for an inclusive curriculum and mixed ability grouping, which reduces the degree of vocationalism in the school setting, and permits *all* students to follow a more general education in the fashion advocated by emancipatory pedagogue. This is even more imperative, given that the traditional hierarchy between conceiver and executant is now being abandoned for more egalitarian forms of worker organisation—certainly the case in the Scandinavian examples alluded to earlier and also in post-Fordist approaches to education. Skill-specific vocationalism of the sort favoured by instrumentalists is not a good preparation for the kind of problem solving and imaginative thinking that the new kinds of post-Fordist work demand.

Conclusion

In spite of attempts to distance education from work, to prevent schooling from becoming nothing more than pre-employment training, we have tried to argue in this chapter that schooling, be it academic, technical or whatever, contains elements which lead to the 'vocationalisation of character' (Shor 1980). Although we have shied away from totally espousing the so-called 'correspondence principle'—namely, that the structures of the school are central to reproducing those of the workplace—the school nonetheless does have structural features in common with the workplace. However, we have also argued that, in addition to habituating students to the main parameters of work, its temporal dimensions and structures and the hierarchical distribution of its protagonists, the school also inculcates through its other micro-practices the work habits associated with the modern workplace. We have suggested that this was also the primary function of early-modern schooling, a function which has been carried on ever since, and which is registered in the content of the speech acts of teachers.

Among other things, teachers are always encouraging their students to be industrious and to strive, to put scholastic energies to good and purposeful usage. All students are subject to the same exhortation, suggesting that whatever work a students ends up doing, be it of the executant or the conceiver kind, the work ethic will still apply. In all its various senses, work is a central preoccupation of schooling, possibly the most central of all; we cannot, therefore, help but think about what happens in the classroom as a kind of labour process, one which is an embryo of that in the real world.

NOTES

1   The ideas here are mainly derived from Veblen (1970) which, although originally published in 1925, contains valuable insights into the way all societies and their elites, not just Western ones, operate. For instance, in

Polynesian societies, tribal chiefs would rather starve than do something as demeaning as feeding themselves.

2 Robert Owen was foremost among these. Contemporaneous with the Sunday school which we looked at in Chapter 2, for the working class there were those schools established by Owen alongside his factories at New Lanark. These were the industrial equivalents of the cathedral schools which had been built in the Middle Ages to train the clergy in scholarly and religious ways. Although Owen was deeply impressed by the importance of education as a medium of amelioration, one which could improve the overall character and potentiality of the human race, he was also of the conviction that schooling had the power to shape individuals and to mould their identity. Indeed, he called his first school the 'Institution for the formation of character'! Now what is interesting here is the kinds of habits that Owen saw as critical to the formation of character, namely obedience, order, regularity, industry and constant attention. These habits were not only accorded more importance than learning to read and write but they were broadly in line with the principles of the work ethic (see Castles & Wüstenberg 1979, Chapter 1).

Keywords and phrases

- consumer ethic
- core and periphery workforce
- Fordism
- labour power
- mental work
- post-Fordism
- Protestant work ethic
- reproduction theory
- Taylorism
- Weber

Tutorial and field activities

1 Investigate the degree to which the Protestant work ethic is an important part of the moral profile. Do individuals still believe in the importance of work in terms of its ennobling value? Or do most individuals have a more matter-of-fact attitude to work, and do not feel guilty or, in Christian terms, spiritually compromised if they idle the day away when they should be working? What do these investigations tell us about the persistence of the work ethic?

2 Reflect on your own experience of work. To what extent was it or is it post-Fordist in character? Is it true that by and large most organisations of work are Fordist in character, dominated by hierarchies and patterns of work in which those workers who are

the most poorly paid and have the lowest status have the least to think about?

3   If there is a close nexus between the character of work and schooling, then schools will, if this nexus is to be maintained, have to enact more post-Fordist approaches in their learning and teaching practices. Speculate as to what this would entail, and attempt to construct the profile of a post-Fordist classroom and school.

The chronology of schooling, or making subjects run on time

Stimpson (voice over): Perhaps I sound a little old fashioned. But, you know, we live in a world where time is becoming not less important but more so. Imagine a space-craft running late! It might miss its orbit completely, and find itself wandering off into the trackless depths of the universe.

(Michael Frayn 1986)

Starting time

Time shadows everything we do. Without wishing to dwell on its cosmic significance and the function it plays in the greater scheme of things, at the humbler level of day-to-day existence, the importance of time as a shaping force cannot be under-estimated. As the part of the backcloth of experience, time accompanies everything we do, providing a powerful reminder that life is limited in its duration, brought to an end by the simple if unpalatable fact of mortality. Yet there is a way in which the achievements of human beings, limited and trivial though they might be, live on from generation to generation, defying the extinguishing power of time. As we have portrayed them in this book, the structures of society are a kind of insurance scheme against the inescapable perishability of individuals, providing continuity between successive generations of human beings.

Our everyday social and material practices, be they in the kitchen or the classroom, are always referenced to the past, containing reminders of the inventiveness and ingenuity of anonymous human beings long since deceased. In this way, social and material practices are reproduced and regenerated; hence the importance of education in the broad sense, as an agent of cultural replication. Not that there is anything incorrigible about these practices, for as they are reproduced and regenerated, some of them are lost, never to be retrieved; many, as new problems emerge in society, are modified and redefined, extended and developed anew.

With monotonous regularity, time thus gives shape and form to the narrative of existence at all sorts of levels. Think of the way, for instance, in which time is an integral part of language, governing syntax, grammatical form and the inflexions of verbs. Tense—we even refer to it in terms of the present, the past and the future—is, after all, only a linguistic representation of the features of our temporal condition. Language though, through refracting experience through metaphors, can also distort our appreciation of time. Elias (1995), for instance, has noted how we talk about 'time passing'; but does time really pass or is such a notion a product of an artefactual sense of time, associated with clocks and other devices of 'timemeterage'? Yet surprisingly, given that it provides the framework within which existence and social life are located, time, like space (the theme of the next chapter), is an under-theorised domain in social theory (Carlstein, Parkes & Thrift 1978; Watkins 1986). In many of its dimensions, time—which, as we shall assert over and over again in this chapter, is a social construct with a distinctive social history and cultural etymology—has not received the same degree of attention as other aspects of social and cultural life. Right from the outset we need to be aware that knowing what time is, is a question of a very different order of nature than knowing what time it is (Adam 1995).

Until quite recently, the examination of time has been almost exclusively the domain of the philosopher and the physicist, who have posited various reasons for its special features, from the idea that time is an absolute measure to the possibility that it is a quality of mind, an intuitive construct around which experience is organised (Smart 1964; Quine 1960; Fraser 1987). Although we tend to think of it thus, ideas that time is linear, measurable, unidirectional, irreversible and progressive, that it is one continuous line of infinite duration, that it is another dimension of space, are products of contemporary philosophy and physics. In cultures where such philosophy and physics did not develop, it has been suggested that very different views of time prevailed, ones in which time was perceived as a cyclical and rhythmical process, in which events were expected to recur. Studies of the development of a temporal sense in young children suggest that they grow into our sense of time; they are not born with it; they tend to be present-centred, having little sense of the temporality or the progressiveness of time, or any idea that there might be a past or a future. Some young children even believe that time is reversible, and that it might be possible to grow smaller and become a baby again! (Orme 1986; Piaget 1969)

Time is a variable construct, which has a degree of cultural and (no pun intended) temporal specificity. In the previous chapter, we alluded to this when we discussed the evolution of work in modern society and noted how, among other things, attitudes to time and its usage have been radically reshaped and continue to be reshaped as post-industrialised forms of capitalism generate post-Fordist organisations of work. In this chapter, we shall extend this examination and argue that time is a central theme in the discourse of our moral economy, in the discourse of the disciplinary society of which it is a crucial element. In particular, we shall argue that the 'batch production model of education' (Hamilton 1980), in which, among other areas of concern, the use and organisation of time is a constant preoccupation of students and teachers alike, serves to promote not just a time-consciousness but a time conscience. It is through the practices of the timetable and its associated moral discourses, that our attitudes to time are framed and given form.

Time and the human condition

The technology of time is one of those ubiquitous features of contemporary life from which it is almost impossible to escape. Clocks of enormous variety and with ever-increasing degrees of precision, dominate every area of the urban environment, and the watch is an essential 'dress' item. Time-reminders are a regular feature of radio and television programs, providing an audio-calibration of the day (Johnson 1987). Calendars are also a ubiquitous feature of our environments, and many of us maintain diaries and electronic organisers, calibrated in quarter hour intervals of time, to provide more 'literal' reminders of looming engagements. That all forms and legal documents have date entries on them further emphasises the degree to which we are all expected to be conscious of the calendar, in order to carry out our basic duties as a citizen.

In consulting with businesses and government agencies, for instance, there is the general expectation that we will be able to cite, almost without thinking, basic biographical data like our date of birth, date of leaving school and commencing employment, age, number of years of residence at a particular address and so on. At the other extreme, as a further reminder of the depth of chronological consciousness in modern life, is the fact that we celebrate important anniversaries like birthdays, something which was not done in the past, when birthdays were not even recorded (Ariès 1962). Time, and its passage, thus permeates everyday consciousness in many diverse ways.

The effect of all this chronological intrusiveness is to remind us that the passage of time is continuous and, above all, measurable and of uniform duration. Yet we need to be aware that the time-meterage that is everywhere, literally ticking off the events of our lives, is but one form of clock, an external one, referenced to the movements of the solar system, utilising the Western units of time: minutes and seconds, days and months, years and centuries. But there are also internal clocks of a biological kind which control important physiological mechanisms like blood-sugar chemistry, pulse and heart rate, the menstrual cycle, and the very process of aging itself, and these are governed by complex diurnal and circadian rhythms (Young 1988).

There is another 'internal' clock which is of more relevance to our concerns, and that is the one connected with the actual experience of temporality, with the psychology and consciousness of duration. Contrary to the consistent and uniform measures of the clock, the experience of temporality is relative and variable. As Heller (1984) has argued, the chronometric regime—the regime of minutes and seconds—has caused the 'quantitative homogenisation of qualitative disparates'. In effect, Heller is highlighting what experience is always telling us about time, namely, that there is a difference between time as it is measured and time as it is experienced, between absolute and phenomenal time. From our day-to-day experiences, we all know that there are periods when time seems to pass by very slowly, when the hands of clock appear almost stationary and time seems to be abnormally prolonged. This often happens when we are bored; sad to say, it often happens in classrooms, when lessons appear to be monotonous and tedious. Forty minutes can often seem like an eternity.[1]

Illness is another time when the clock seems to slow down to almost intolerable proportions. On the other hand, there are periods when time seems to fly, when we have cause to wonder where the hours of the day have gone. Periods of great excitement and of intense activity, when every moment is filled with interest, seem to induce this sense of chronological compression, when hours seem like minutes. As Orme (1978) and Heller (1984) have pointed out, though their duration can be identical, 'filled time' often seems much shorter than 'unfilled time'. The subjective perception of time is related to the degree of its perceived plenitude or vacuity.

Another side to this aspect of temporality is the degree to which it is also extended through time and space. Via the facility of memory, the present is always haunted by the past, which punctuates the here and now with past experiences. Moreover, we can also project ourselves into the future and sequence our lives in such a way as to achieve certain objectives and realise certain aspirations. Such psychological time travel emphasises the degree to which the consciousness of time is not monolithic or restricted to a single plane of experience, but operates on a number of levels. Time consciousness is 'polychronic' (Hargreaves 1990), encapsulating 'many kinds of times that bear on our lives simultaneously' (Adam 1995).

In many cultures, particularly in the past, the absence of clocks has meant that the disparity between absolute and phenomenal time was less evident. Only in modern times (and fairly recently at that) have clocks and watches come to regulate the routines of everyday life, providing a measure against which to determine the duration of activities and creating a technology by which appointments can be kept, the length of the working day set and for transportation systems to be scheduled and synchronised. The technology involved is now freely available, almost on a universal scale, but this was not always the case. The first accurate clocks, ones which used a pendulum as a regulator, were not developed until the sixteenth century and their expense meant that their installation tended to be restricted to church towers. As an industry, though, that of clockmaking—the art of the horologist—was one of the most important in Europe right up until the eighteenth century. Even so, the possibility of owning a personal timepiece—in effect, a wristwatch—which enabled individuals to observe a strict time regimen was not really an affordable proposition until the early twentieth century (Landes 1983). Technologies such as the watch have redefined the temporal parameters of social life, generating whole new discourses and practices of time.

We can say, then, that our current time regime is of recent origin, dating back, like much else in the modern age, only to the Industrial Revolution. Across the world in the last hundred years or so, mainly as a result of international travel and communication, we have witnessed a globalisation of chronological measures, with most nations now using the European calendar and following Greenwich mean-time. In fact as systems of transportation and instantaneous communication have 'annihilated' the distances separating nations and continents, we have also witnessed a process of 'time/space compression' (Harvey 1990). However, in cultures where this regime is absent or has yet to gain widespread communal acceptance, different time regimes exist. In these cultures, the perception of time is anchored to the rhythms of nature, to the passage of the seasons, to the astronomical phases of the sun and the moon, and to the pressing demands of the agricultural year.

This tradition continues in the Australian bush and on properties, where more natural chronologies are more important then those of the city. Time, particularly in pre-modern societies, is seen as cyclical rather than linear; events are thought to repeat themselves, just like the phases of the moon and the tides of sea. The vast majority of cultures, in fact, have not developed 'abstract units of time such as the month or the year', referring instead to the incidence of events in terms of their proximity to natural phenomena, like snow or epidemics, floods and earthquakes (Doob 1978; Evans-Pritchard 1973). The idea of specifying the chronology of events in terms of a calendar and of pinpointing them to a particular time, of enumerating the passage of time in precise detail, is a product of a clock-regulated society. In cultures without instruments for measuring time, the perception of the past and of the future tends to be blurred and the passage of history is much less precisely delineated.

Western languages, in fact, are inadequately equipped to deal with such conceptions of time. An example close to home is the so-called 'Dreamtime' (jukurrpa) of traditional Aborigines and for which no accurate translation in English exists. In the Dreamtime, there is a psychological unity between events, people, nature, land and time. The past is in the present, and the future is in the now, the experience is characterised by a holistic continuity (very much as in our dreams) and it contains many immutable elements (Bell 1983; Christie 1985).

But the relativity of time-consciousness is also reflected in other discourses of time. The meaning of the word 'punctuality', for instance, only has significance when there are clocks to tell us whether someone is late for an appointment or not. As Bourdieu discovered in examining the time habits of the Kabyle peasants in Algeria, in a culture without clocks, attitudes to time are far more relaxed, with none of the pressures that prevail in societies that are subservient to the tyranny of the timetable. Refusing to be intimidated by its will and impositions, the Kabyle regarded the clock as the 'devil's mill'. Until French colonisation finally wore down their opposition to its tyranny, the Kabyle tended to live as they had always lived, eating when they felt like it, only working during the day, and having few concerns for being productive or increasing agricultural yield. Indeed, nothing was considered to show lack of decorum more than being overly concerned with haste and expediency, with being impatient, with completing tasks ahead of time, which was seen as 'diabolical ambition' at its most extreme (Bourdieu 1963).

As is very evident from many of our idioms, which serve to encode critical parts of our ideological formation, our culture, by contrast, is obsessed with time. We are forever talking about the pressure of time, of time being of the essence, of having not a minute to waste and so on. Moreover, we also place a moral value on not wasting or squandering time, on being habitually late and so on.

Not only are there differing attitudes towards time across cultures, but within cultures attitudes often differ, and can vary considerably. Some feminists have suggested that women's view of time, for instance, is different from that of men, tending much more to monumental and cyclical notions of time that contrast markedly with the linear and more scientific temporality of men (Adam 1995; Kristeva 1981). Attitudes towards the future also vary within cultures. There are those, for instance, who have a somewhat dismissive attitude towards the future and refuse to prepare for it, preferring to live forever in the present, in the here and now. Their perspectives on life tend to be short- rather than long-term. The idea of seizing the day, of making hay while the sun shines (it is to be noted that much of our proverbial wisdom is, in fact, centred on philosophising time), of enjoying yourself while you have the faculties and facilities to do so, of living for the day rather than tomorrow, is typical of the such perspective on life. Being future-oriented involves 'deferring gratification', sacrificing immediate pleasures in order to complete tasks and make investments, be they scholarly or monetary, for the sake of future security and prospects.

Much financial and career planning (a comparatively recent phenomenon) involves thinking about the future, about one's likely prospects, as do schooling and many other facets of modern life (e.g. taking out a superannuation policy or saving up for a deposit on a house). The 'lads' that Willis (1978) studied, for instance, spent most days subverting the chronological order imposed by the school. They failed to appreciate that in the bourgeois world of schooling, time was 'something you carefully husbanded and thoughtfully spent in the achievement of cherished objectives'. In this world of deferred gratification, individuals suppress spontaneous desires and project themselves into the future, planning their lives around goals and objectives.

These values do not come naturally to human beings, but are acquired at home and at school; they are not instinctual drives, but are products of particular social arrangements, conditioned by certain overriding imperatives within these arrangements. In our case, many of these imperatives derive from a particular form of capitalism, namely, industrial capitalism with its individualistic and commodified world-view and which has gradually come to be diffused across the globe (Thompson 1967).

Time is money

Modern time-consciousness, which tends to be linear and future-oriented, concerned with saving not wasting time, is a product of capitalism and the clock. As clocks and watches became more available, they came to regulate more and more aspects of existence, giving increased form and structure to the chronology of the day, the week and the year. This process did not occur overnight, but took place over some five centuries, those between the fourteenth and the nineteenth, and was also associated with the demise of feudalism and the rise of industrial capitalism (Thrift 1981). The process was only in part technological, associated as we have seen with the invention of reliable and portable timepieces; at the same time as this technology was becoming freely available, the whole discourse of time was also being reshaped and recast in the form in which we know it today, that of temporal adjunct of the work ethic. In this connection, there was a coalescence between this discourse and technology.

The first clocks appeared on churches, in villages and towns. The time regimen was imposed in a public way, in a way designed to secure obedience, with bells summoning the faithful to prayer, announcing the time at which work began and ended, and so on. The situation was somewhat analogous to the way in which power was administered in the pre-modern age, from the top downwards, from a conscious act of imposition on the part of the sovereign or the feudal lord. As the technology of time became more portable, and clocks and watches became part of the domestic environment, the time regime became more of a matter of self-administration, in which the individual has become accountable for scheduling their daily life (Landes 1983). The fact that so many of us carry diaries, to assist us with the organisation of our own time, is indicative of the degree which the management of time has become an individual responsibility. As a social practice, this is consistent with Foucault's notion of governmentality (1979), of a self-regulated population.

Modern time-consciousness, which is characterised by rigid segmentation, with times for work, for play, for eating and for sleeping, has its origins in the church and predates the Protestant work ethic. Monastic life was subject to a fairly severe time regimen, the day, like an early version of the school timetable, being divided into seven periods, each separated by the sound of a bell. In fact, the word 'clock' originally meant bell-tower (de Grazia 1964). As the main keepers of the time and the proprietors of clocks, the clergy tended to emphasise in their sermons the importance of saving time, of not squandering it on frivolous and materialist pre-occupations. Time was for prayer and the diligent practice of virtue, not indulgence and hedonism. The clocks of this period were even engraved with symbols like skulls, which emphasised mortality, and the preciousness of time in the face of the brevity of life (Landes 1983).

But it was the development of Protestantism which did most to alter the parameters of time-consciousness. As was noted in a previous chapter, one of the first initiatives taken by the leaders of the Protestant Reformation was the elimination of some 100 feast days from the church calendar. This led to a dramatic increase in the length of the working year, a year in which there had been almost as many holidays as work days. It is a misconception to think that our ancestors, prior to the nineteenth century, led particularly arduous lives, marked by long days and intense toil, with few holidays to speak of. On the contrary, their work regimen was considerably lighter than our own!

Even so, right through until the nineteenth and early twentieth centuries, the time habits of the population were never maintained with much rigour or conscientiousness. The work pattern of the year was irregular, still full of feast days, holidays, fairs and wakes. It was common, for example, for Monday to always be a de facto public holiday, a time of recovery from the heavy drinking and general hedonism of the weekend (Thompson 1967). Vestiges of 'Saint Monday', as it was known, persist today, in that most common of syndromes which often afflicts students and hung-over employees, known as Mondayitis; the Australian version of this syndrome is the 'sickie'.

Even the working day was different. Since most work was done at home in a cottage-industry situation, there was no one to oversee its completion, and workers had considerable autonomy over when and where they worked. As a result, cottage workers tended to have a much more perfunctory attitude to their labours, devoting themselves to work only when it was absolutely necessary. People worked long enough to ensure an income that kept their families fed, housed and clothed, and no more. Moreover, the work day tended to be punctuated with many intermissions and breaks, with much carousing at the local tavern. The time regime of work tended to be irregular, characterised by spurts of intense exertion when tasks needed to be executed in order to meet demand, followed by periods of comparative relaxation and idleness, when the pace of work was more flexible (Landes 1983; de Grazia 1964). Work was task- rather than time-driven, and more value was placed upon leisure than work. Puritanism changed this, creating a culture of timethrift. The Puritans' hatred of time wastage not only helped 'to concentrate effort, to focus attention on detail, but also to prepare for the rhythms of an industrial society, our society of the factory whistle and the alarm clock' (Hill 1964).

In the early modern period though, attitudes to time and work among the bulk of the population were far too ill-disciplined for the demands of industrial capitalism (Thompson 1967), particularly as they manifested themselves in the factory. In reshaping this situation and ensuring a more structured and organised time regime, the clock was a most important invention, possibly the key machine in establishing the social features of modern industrial age, far more important, suggests Mumford (1963) than the steam engine. It led to the progressive segmentation of time, forcing a strong demarcation between work and leisure. The clock provided a convenient and objective way of defining the length of the workday but, of more importance, it led to the pricing of time which meant it could be valued, bargained over, exchanged and given legal and moral status.

Exemplifying this is the degree to which many activities in modern life, from telephone calls, time on the Internet through to the hire of cars and videos, are priced according to various chronological rates, with fines and penalties being exacted for those who fail to return items of hire on time (Zerubravel 1981). Time has thus been built into the accountancy of trade, into the calculus of pricing the value of labour and the usage of services, including education. Four year degrees cost more than three year ones.

Time is now regarded as another resource, the ultimate non-renewable resource. In Benjamin Franklin's words, time is money, 'the bullion of the day', which extends to a time morality, in which credit is punctually paid and in which the wastage of time is derided and associated with lax discipline and personal control.[2] Also symptomatic of these new attitudes is the notion of 'free time' which, in signifying time in which we are not engaged in wage labour, also signifies time which is not priced and valued or commodified. But the whole spirit of this new discourse of time is towards saving time, with emphasis on time-thrift towards making work time one of intensive production, in which wasted time is regarded as the equivalent of throwing away money. Thus were born devices which monitored the chronological habits of workers, which kept tabs on their punctuality, on their absenteeism. The clocking on and off system, which was invented by Josiah Wedgewood and is a feature of many workplaces, is one such device.

The school register and the timebook that teachers sign when they arrive at school in the morning are its evolutionary offshoots. Failure to observe the basic time regime of work, of which punctuality and attendance are the most important features, was, and continues to remain, a punishable offence in the workplace which can result in the reduction of one's wages or, worse still, in dismissal.

Taylorism and Fordism had the effect of further intensifying this time regime. The time and motion studies of work with which Taylorism is associated involved precise chronometric observations, utilising stop-watches, observing actions of workers and determining the minimum time required to expedite an operation or task. Refining this Taylorist approach, Gilbreth developed a classification system of considerable precision and discrimination, such that a worker's actions and techniques could be broken down into separate movements called 'therbligs', measured in ten-thousandths of a minute!

This is the ultimate division of labour, which has its roots in the drill and dressage techniques of military training in the early modern period. Nor were these measures to improve worker efficiency restricted to capitalism. The piece-work movement, for instance, was pioneered in the Soviet Union with the Stakhanovite movement (Jones 1982). Not that these strategies for enhancing productivity by the minimisation of time wastage went unopposed.

As well as the struggle for better wages, unions have always been involved in ameliorating other conditions related to work, particularly those to do with its time parameters. The eight-hour day, which workers in Australia were the first in the world to obtain, is a product of this struggle and led the way in a general contraction of the number of hours and weeks of a year spent at work (Davison 1993). The emergence, under the impetus of post-Fordism, of job-sharing, flexi-time, flexible-rostering, short-term contracts and fractional-time employment are signs that the time-regime of work is undergoing reconstruction. The old Taylorist fixtures are being superseded by the regime of flexibility and deregulation to which reference was made in Chapter 6. One offshoot of these developments is that many employees now report that they are working longer hours not shorter, and often at weekends (Blyton 1989). The idea of a nine to five day, and five day week, for all workers, is almost a relic of the past.

School time

In the everyday practices of school life, time is always a conflict zone, as students contest the right of teachers to impose their chronological will on them. Teachers and educationalists have been slow to appreciate this, except in a strategic way, involving techniques to improve the delivery of this will. As studies of time-usage in the classroom have highlighted, the chronological efficiency of school time is far from impressive. Most students spend something like six thousand days in school but, in reality, when days off for sickness, excursions, sports carnivals and so on are subtracted, this figure soon decreases. And, where individual lessons are concerned, when time is taken out for arriving at a classroom and packing up at the end of a lesson, as well as the usual interruptions that occur during lesson times, like the giving out of messages and the constant badgering that goes on in order to keep students on task and attentive, most lessons turn out to be, at best, less than 20 per cent efficient (Denham & Lieberman 1980; Harris 1982a). In many lessons, the disruptions are of a magnitude and number to make even this figure look unimpressive.

The relationship between 'allocated time', the time actually given to a lesson on the timetable, and actual 'engaged time', the time in which some observable instruction and learning is actually occurring, is not a close one. But what these chronometric studies fail to reveal, of course, is the level of each student's real involvement in a lesson. For example, students tend to create 'back regions' in the school timetable when they engage in anything but school work. Incidentally, teachers do the same in their 'spares'—time set aside for lesson preparation (Hargreaves 1990). When factors like boredom and fatigue, not to mention the apathy and lack of interest in learning, are added to the chronometric aggregate, time wastage in the classroom is the norm rather than the exception. In calling for a radical reappraisal of the way in which time is allocated in schools, Harris (1982a) has pictured these dimensions of secondary school life in a way which highlights the contradictions inherent in the average school's time regime, and concluded that the school is a chronological absurdity.

Given these demonstrable inefficiencies, it is not surprising that much of the research that has been conducted on school time has been of a technicist kind, employing the instrumental rationality of scientific management. Following a dominant and influential trend in economic thought (Becker 1965; Holmes 1984), which has attempted to cost and place an economic value on time, the trend has been towards developing more efficient modes of allocating school-time. It is a domain in which the educational administration has felt particularly at home. Amongst its principal assumptions has been the theory that if time allocation and usage could be more efficient—if school time could be extended in some way, either by lengthening the school year or the school day or both—then learning outcomes (note the language of management) could be improved. In bolstering their arguments, the advocates of this view often assert that in economically successful countries, children spend a higher percentage of the year at school.[3]

Another area of interest for the school chronometrician is the timetable (and we will have more to say about it in the next section of this chapter). As the burden of new subject areas has been imposed upon it, new ways of structuring and organising educational time and its basic unit (i.e. the lesson or period) have been developed, from timetables which extend over ten days and fortnightly cycles through to vertical timetables which offer much more student choice and subject election.[4] Though these timetable innovations have various obvious advantages over their predecessors, they are only functional and tactical responses to the increased time-demand upon the curriculum caused by the emergence of new subject areas.

The trouble is that these formulae for increasing educational outcomes, which in places like the United States have had some government support, tend to disguise the fact that time (or the lack of it) is not the only critical factor in improving learning outcomes. In criticising the classroom efficiency movement, Levin (1986) has pointed out that it overlooks the 'situational variables' that impact on classroom learning. If these variables are not given due consideration, more time for learning will, in all likelihood, result in more time for boredom and alienation.

Nor do these examinations of time-usage contain any considerations as to the provenance of the time regime which governs schooling. Absent too is any appreciation of the ways in which schools are instrumental in the segmentation of time habits, something which we have suggested is all-pervasive in contemporary Western society. In this view, the efficient time organisation of the curriculum hinges not so much on its content, on its capacity to incorporate greater amounts of learning experience, as on its capacity to inculcate the right attitudes to time, to instil an organisation of time that accords with that in society at large. This comes from the time regime of the school and its associated routines and drills, rather than what is done with that time.

The phrase 'hidden curriculum' is often used to describe these effects, as if they operated invisibly and secretly, without conscious intent or awareness on the part of the subjects involved. Yet this is not so. The timetable is an act of conscious design and the discourse that supports its application and exercise is not hidden, and can be heard in any classroom. Thus we would prefer to talk about school time as part of the organisational culture of the school, as one of those visible and open discursive practices which is critical to the transmission of school learning, and which has arguably more important outcomes, namely those connected with the inculcation of important practices in everyday life.

The school and the clockwork sensibility

When children arrive at school and become students, one of the things they do is relinquish control over their time; they cede its ownership to the school administration, acting through its agents, the teachers. Their situation is not so different from that of teachers who, being employees of the state, have also relinquished control over their time, although they do receive wages in return for this sacrifice.

The time that teachers and students spend at school is not free time, time for which they are not expected to be accountable. Nor is school time unorganised time, devoid of any design, shape or predetermination. Even in preschools and kindergartens, where one might expect the use of time to be more easy-going and spontaneous, there are time 'scripts' in the background which are both subtle and intrusive in their impact (Sharp & Green 1975). In fact, as is the case with certain other institutions—the prison, the asylum (Goffman 1976), the hospital (Roth 1963), the army barracks, and religious communities like seminaries being the most notable exemplars—the time regime of the school is much more exaggerated than that governing normal life, in that it effects to prescribe the daily cycle of activities within an institution to an extreme degree. In fact, the ordinary principles of temporality are suspended and we allow ourselves to be governed by an organisation of time of a more calibrated and segmented kind than that encountered in other situations and organisations. Nowhere else, for instance, are our mental habits quite so severely regulated as they are in a high school, where at the sound of a bell, the audio declaration that the lesson hath endeth, students are expected to move from one mind-set to another, as if thinking in history and mathematics naturally comes in forty minute intervals (Harris 1982a).

In structural terms, school time is organised around durations of varying length and magnitude, though all take place within a framework of finitude, that at some point of time the process of institutionalised education ceases. For instance, the longer durations of school time, such as the number of years of compulsory schooling, and the ages at which schooling is to commence and finish, are all covered by government legislation and statute, and there is considerable variation between states. In Queensland, for instance, attendance at a high school only became mandatory in 1964 and children start primary school one year earlier than they do in New South Wales!

Yet, in spite of these local idiosyncrasies, another matter of states' rights, there tends to be a degree of 'durational rigidity' (Zerubavel 1981) within an educational system, which specifies the number of years of compulsory schooling, the ages at which it commences and ends, and the points at which transition between the various sectors of schooling occurs. The general trend throughout the world, though, is to prolong the number of years of schooling, and to encourage students to remain at school through to Grade 12, and for many more of them to proceed on to some form of post-compulsory education. The reason for this, according to the official discourse, is that we live in an increasingly complex and technological society, and a more educated citizenry is needed to cope with it. Abbreviated schooling, it is often said, is incompatible with the needs of the post-industrial society. This is yet another instance of the powerful discourse of instrumentalism asserting itself.

Such arguments need to be treated with a degree of circumspection, for they often serve more repugnant rationales, arising from a faltering economy, one devastated by automation and the destruction of the manufacturing sector and a generally contracting labour market for the young. For, as schooling expands, it does so at the expense of work, and in an economy where full employment is a thing of the past, the longer the entry into the workforce can be postponed, the less the pressure on a shrinking labour market.

THE CHRONOLOGY OF SCHOOLING

The time for schooling is distributed among the various sectors of education, and the transition from one sector to another generally constitutes a 'reporting point' in the overall cycle of education, when dossiers are compiled on students and some sort of public selection occurs, usually via mechanisms of assessment and examination (Dale 1972). These days, the transition between high school and university is the most significant of these reporting points. In the past, though, the transition from primary to secondary school was just as traumatic, also involving public examinations that determined to what type of secondary school students would proceed. In conjunction with the significance of these reporting points, the advent of universal schooling has tended to render uniform the rate of progress through school. The only account of differential intellectual development that is ever countenanced is streaming, and that is predicated on the assumption that capacity and ability are fixed irremediably. Thus all students (with the exception of a handful of repeats) are promoted at the conclusion of the school calendar year, irrespective of their stage of attainment within a subject or discipline.

Yet before the advent of universal schooling, age was an irrelevant factor in the organisation and distribution of the student population. There was no set age for beginning and finishing school, and students were admitted to university when they were ready. It is another one of its peculiar ironies that, in the evolution of education, the only sector to have preserved any modicum of this chronological flexibility is that of higher education, which permits students to exercise a modicum of freedom where the timing of their study is concerned. Deferment provisions, credit arrangements and generous prerequisites, not to mention flexible forms of timetabling, enable students to complete courses at a rate of their own determination, not the institution's.

Another one of the longer durations is that of the school calendar. We have already discussed some of the structural correspondences between work and schooling, and the school calendar is another of them. In one sense, the divisions between holidays and term times reflect the divisions of the work year, but in another they also reflect the continuing influences (anachronistic though they may be) of the agricultural year and the Christian calendar.

This is even more evident in some of the more traditional universities, which retain a term rather than a semester system, with terms called Michaelmas and Trinity. The placement of holidays bears a singular relationship to the highlights of the Christian year, to Christmas and Easter in particular. In fact, the academic year followed at Oxford and Cambridge, which began in the late Middle Ages, was designed to allow the scholars to escape to the countryside and thereby avoid the plague-ridden summer months (Young 1988). And when state schools came into existence in Britain in the nineteenth century, the long holiday in the summer was intended to assist rural communities, whose families needed the assistance of their children to gather in the harvest. This was a tacit recognition that the introduction of universal schooling placed time demands on communities, particularly rural communities, which interfered with traditional rhythms of living.

Even so, one of the issues most contended in the early years of universal schooling was its time regime, which was inflexible, preventing children from working when economic hardship demanded a contribution from them. An indication of this discontent was the degree to which school time was often a matter of conflict which provoked strikes, mass desertion from schools and widespread truancy, in spite of the statutory requirement that students attend school (Miller 1986; Humphries 1984).

As an indication of the degree to which new forces now shape the segmentation of the school calendar, it is worth pointing out how the various Australia states now stagger the allotment of school holidays to allow tourist areas to derive maximum benefit from them. It is leisure then, rather than work that is tending to shape the educational chronology of the late twentieth century. School holidays, in fact, represent the chronological 'other' of education. They are anticipated with relish and excitement, as long, uninterrupted 'periods' of time, freed from the authority of the 'clock discipline' that dominates the classroom (Cross 1993).

Of the shorter durations associated with education, that of the school day is a scaled-down version of the work day, and contains the same structural elements. Its organisation, like that of the school week, is represented in what amounts to the ultimate in the accounting of educational time-usage, namely the timetable. As a form, the timetable is another one of those Cartesian grids of specification which are characteristic of the modern age, in this case allocating teaching time called periods or lessons to particular domains of inquiry or knowledge.

The timetable is a temporal translation of the curriculum, packaged and partitioned via the school syllabus into thirty-five-minute lessons over a term or semester, with strong boundary features that discourages the abandonment of subject demarcations. The timetable is a type of epistemological clock, marking off the duration of the week in terms of various knowledge categories. The timetable also has the effect of activating the school as a school, of defining for how much of the day and the year it will be a venue of learning (Parkes & Thrift 1978).

It has its origins in the Benedictine monasteries of the Middle Ages, where the imposition of a timetable discouraged the idleness among the monks and freed them from a state of nature (Adam 1995). It was then transferred to the college sector in the sixteenth century, not as a rational basis for organising learning, but as a disciplinary measure to separate teachers from students—their relationships had become too intimate—and to prescribe for them both a daily regime. What eventuated, was a network of obligations and commitments which filled the whole day, from 4 am onwards, involving both religious and scholastic duties, as well as intervening times of recreation (Ariès 1962).[5]

Though that of the modern school is shorter in duration and less onerous in its demands than this timetable, it functions in much the same way, providing a hidden logic for organising and synchronising the activities school day, according to a symphony of bells and buzzers, sirens and hooters (Adam 1995).

It is easy to overlook the technology of the timetable, to see it as simply another one of those background phenomena, having few ramifications for schooling. But as we have constantly argued throughout this book, the apparently trivial and banal in the schooling process can, upon close scrutiny, reveal much about the nature of schooling and its underlying values. The timetable, for instance, is the medium through which the whole of school life is organised, controlling what students and teachers will be doing at various times during the week and where they will be doing it. For the timetable, as can be seen from the example in Figure 8.1 (see p. 187), is also (to coin what seems an appropriate word in this connection) a 'spacetable', specifying the various locations of lessons. The timetable defines the periodic nature of education.

Indeed, to be properly understood and decoded, the timetable needs to be read in conjunction with the school map or plan. In effect, the timetable is the school's navigational system, guiding its students and teachers through the day, telling them where to be and what sorts of mind-sets they need to don, even what garments to wear. This is what we mean by a grid of specification, something to which everyone within the school adheres and takes for granted, submitting to its authority with but a minimum of resistance and opposition. In effect, the timetable is part of the school's capillary system, through which its various practices and its power are circulated and reticulated.

The timetable is the ultimate reference point of school life, the first thing to be arranged out before the school year begins, and the first thing that is presented to students when they begin that year. Nothing proceeds without a timetable, and it provides a mechanism for placing and finding teachers and students; in other words, it is a system of indirect surveillance.

One characteristic of the timetable, be it in the workshop or the school, according to Foucault (1979), is that it 'eliminates the possibility of idleness', at least in theory. Thus the whole of the school week, including recess and lunch, is accounted for in terms of some activity or other. There is no free time at all. The student's daily routines are time budgeted. Moreover, as a strategy of domination, the school timetable impresses itself upon the student's whole body, dominating not its mental pre-occupations, but also physical ones, like bowel movements, which are supposed to occur only during recess.

The timetable is indeed a technology for making the subject regular, another instance of anatomo-politics in action. In sum, the timetable is, above all, symbolic of the degree to which the school is a 'finely calibrated disciplinary machine for the arrangement and classification of bodies, and the promotion and regulation of preferred activities' (Jones & Williamson 1979). It constitutes a diagrammatic representation of the various classifications and differentiating mechanisms inherent in the school: teachers, classes, subjects, lessons, rooms, streams, which divide and separate students from one another on a daily basis.

Yet, as a material practice, the timetable also contains ideological elements. Given that there is only so much time in the week and that the curriculum is always being expanded (rather than contracted) to encompass new educational experiences, the allocation of time tends to be an area of conflict in which the power and status of certain subjects can be at risk. Yet, in spite of this, the chronological allocations to subjects within the junior high school at least, aside from a few minor variations, appear to be same the world over; moreover, these allocations, along with the subjects themselves, were set at the commencement of the twentieth century and set by government statute, at least in Britain (Inglis 1985; Walton 1963). If we examine our specimen timetable (Figure 8.1), which is that of a Queensland high school student in the early 1990s, maximum time is given to mathematics and English, with proportionately less time allocated to other subjects, health being given least of all. This reflects the continuing importance that these two subjects have, and the comparative unimportance of subjects like health and typing. In fact, the timetable can be read in a variety of ways, apart from just chronometrically, as a device which encodes much information about the power and prestige of certain school subjects.

It is a useful exercise to compare a timetable of the 1990s with that of earlier periods. In the mid-nineteenth century, for instance, before the provision of universal education, the school timetable was not only of much longer duration, running most of the day, but also included a strong classical emphasis, involving the study and translation of Latin and Greek writers such as Juvenal and Thucydides. There were no instrumental subjects as such at all!

Figure 8.1	The timetable of Mental State High School				
Period	Mon.	Tues.	Wed.	Thurs.	Fri.
9.10–9.50	Maths	Music	History	Typing	English
	Ms Factor	Miss Beach	Ms Times	Ms Friday	Mr Keating
	D2	M1	D6	A6	A10
9.50–10.30	Science	Phys. Ed.	Music	Science	Maths
	Ms Curie	Mr Jogger	Miss Beach	Ms Curie	Ms Factor
	A17	Oval	B1	A17	D2
10.30–11.10	English	English	Typing	English	Geog.
	Mr Keating	Mr Keating	Ms Pitman	Mr Keating	Mrs Helios
	A10	Library	A6	B19	B8
Recess					
11.30–12.10	History	Science	Maths	Art	Typing
	Ms Times	Ms Curie	Ms Factor	Mr Symes	Ms Pitman
	A6	A15	B2	B16	A16
12.10–12.50	Music	Art	English	Science	Health
	Miss Beach	Mr Symes	Mr Keating	Ms Darwin	Mr Jogger
	B1	B16	A10	B1	D2
Lunch					
1.40–2.20	Art	Maths	Sport	Mrs Helios	Mr Symes
	Mr Symes	Ms Quang		Geog.	Art
	B16	B2		A3	B16
2.20–3.00	Typing	Cit. Ed.	Sport	Maths	Music
	Ms Pitman	Mr Preston		Ms Quang	Ms Beach
	A16	A1		B2	M1

The timetable of the twentieth century arises from a different educational culture altogether. Although there are some obvious differences, mainly relating to subjects having their names changed, as in changing from housewifery to home economics, the basic fabric of the timetable has remained almost identical, with many of the same subjects persisting, and with approximately the same allocations of time. Indeed the timetable, along with its supporting syllabus, constitutes a temporal translation of particular types of

knowledge, a construct for its transmission over a period of weeks or, in the case of university degrees, years.

Another part of the grid of specification is the lesson itself. One of the accompanying features of a technicist approach to teaching is the increasing tendency to plan for lessons. Student teachers, when they are on 'prac', are constantly enjoined to produce lesson plans, which generally conform to the same basic model, comprising aims and objectives, content and activities of a lesson. An important feature of these plans is the time breakdown of the lesson, the number of minutes to be allocated to the introduction, to exposition, to activities, to rounding off the lesson and so forth. Here again, there is stress on purposefulness, on not wasting time, on using it to achieve certain learning goals.

All this has the effect of fragmenting the pedagogic process, reducing it to ever smaller micro-intervals of times in which the strategies of the lesson are measured out in minutes in a sort of pedagogic version of a playscript. As yet another manifestation of the Taylorism that has embraced schooling, making lessons run literally like clockwork means that time usage in the school is not only more intensive, but also more accountable. As far as the students are concerned, this obsession with organising lessons in terms of finite amounts of time translates itself into activities being produced against the clock, a clear echo of the time-saving ethos of the factory. In fact, all school activities are dominated by the deadline, the examination and the classroom test being the culmination of this tendency. Yet if we accept the move towards a post-Fordist work ethic in which individuals are expected to account for their own use of time, to be able to organise their work independently of a scheduled set of activities, these industrial approaches to time that still dominate the school have passed their use by date!

Aside from the aforementioned vertical timetable, there are other more relevant ways of arranging school time such as the Dalton Plan, developed in the US during the 1930s, in which students negotiated with their teachers, who were seen as consultants rather than instructors, to complete programs of work at their own rate, budgeting their time accordingly (Brubacher 1947).

Time and the moral economy

Thus far we have only described the structural aspects of timetabling, the way in which time is allocated and organised during the school week. But we also need to recognise that within the school (as well as within society at large), time is associated with a complex moral economy, which reveals itself in a number of ways in the day-to-day happenings of the school.

On a number of occasions in this book, we have suggested, following Foucault, that the school is an important technology associated with the establishment and preservation of the disciplinary society. Among other things, the use of time is of paramount concern in such societies, and schools have become important sites for promoting disciplined time-usage, wherein we become conscious of time and its value in the moral scheme of Western society. As was indicated in a previous chapter, the issue of cultivating appropriate time habits was certainly of concern in the initial phases of universal schooling in the UK and Australia. In the 1870s, for instance, the superintendent of a teacher training institute in Victoria characterised the ideal school as one displaying 'Punctuality, Order, Discipline, Method', and in which the children were reared on the virtues of regularity and time-thrift (Davison 1993).

But time discipline begins much earlier than at school, as Berger & Luckmann (1973) have pointed out. When the child is born, she is soon socialised into habits of the clock regime, being fed and encouraged not on biological demand but in terms of the chronological agenda of the society of adults. Schooling simply reinforces this agenda, but of more importance is the fact that it gives it a moral force and rationality to the routines of adult society. For surrounding the quantitative dimensions of the timetable are a whole array of qualitative features, to do with not deviating from the school's time regime, which tends to take a similar form wherever schools exist. A special value, reinforced by legal statute, is placed upon being in attendance at school in the first place, of being punctual, of not missing lessons: hence the need for the school register to keep track of attendance. Absence from school is expected to be reported. As one school handbook, in outlining the procedures for such reportage, puts it, 'Regular attendance and punctuality are of the highest importance'. In specifying the conditions of punctuality, the same handbook remarks, with a considerable degree of detail and precision, that students 'are expected to be at school and ready for work (with books out and port away) before the first bell at 8.25 am'. Those who either wilfully, or through no fault of their own, transgress these requirements, are issued with a late slip, issued from the Main Office, usually by the deputy principal.

This keeping track of the daily movements of students in and around the school is partly in the interests of their security; but it also has the effect of reinforcing the importance of punctuality as part of a repertoire of desirable time habits. More serious transgressions of these habits, like truancy, which is against the law, are of a more significant order altogether, emphasising the degree to which schooling is a form of civil conscription from which parental obligation cannot escape, at least, as homeschoolers have discovered (Holt 1982), not without considerable legal difficulty.

One of the important side-effects of this is to reinforce the monopoly that schools have over *education* (the word is italicised to emphasise that it is being used in its institutional rather than normative sense (see Chapter 2). It also has the effect of elevating the importance of lessons as the time for learning. As Harris's clever little syllogism about these matters demonstrates, there is an inexorable logic to the timetable, namely, that 'educational goodies are to be had in lessons' and absence from them, either mentally or physically, means that these goodies are not being acquired (Harris 1982a; and also Middleton 1982). Hence, if lessons are missed, so too is an important source of educational wisdom.

But it does not end there. Within these same lessons, which are the source of all educational goodies, students are constantly being harangued about the virtues of better time management. A considerable percentage of teacher discourse is punctuated with policing time and asserting moral injunctions connected with it ('Who has not finished?'; 'How many of you have reached Question 9?'), with references to the importance of time in the learning process (Ball, Hull, Skelton & Tudor 1984). Thus students are always being urged not to waste time or to fritter away their opportunities to learn in class, either within lessons or in school generally.

Many of the 'infra-penalties' (Foucault 1979) that are imposed on students relate to chronological infractions and transgressions. Students who waste time in lessons are often told that they will have to make up for it in their own time, at home or during recess. Nor does the control and ownership of the student's time cease with the end of the school day, for students are expected to use some of their own time completing homework. To cite once again from our school handbook: one of the provisions that parents are expected to assist with is the arrangement of 'a regular time in a suitable atmosphere, away from major distractions such as television' for the completion of homework. In another handbook the amount of time, 'as a rough guide', to be allotted to homework is prescribed ('Year 8: 15 minutes per period taught ... Year 12: 30 minutes per period taught)'. Moreover, the whole discourse of schooling is saturated with chronological homilies of various kinds, of stories about students who wasted their time at school and ended up regretting it.

Many of these stories are often cast in terms of deferred gratification, of sacrificing immediate goals and pleasurable activities for the sake of investing in the future. Time-thrift, or the resourceful use of time, is constructed constantly as a significant factor in the calculus of educational success.

Finishing time

In this chapter, we have argued that schools have played a central role in the construction of the new time-consciousness, which emerged at the beginning of the modern age (Thrift 1981; Watkins 1986). We have suggested that this consciousness places great emphasis on time-thrift and on treating time as both a moral and economic commodity. The emergence of this consciousness, we have argued, cannot be separated from the emergence of industrial capitalism, which demanded a more disciplined workforce, particularly where time attitudes were concerned.

We have argued that the time regime of the school, although somewhat more exaggerated than that which exists within the workplace, stresses values central to the organisation of modern work, such as punctuality and attendance. In addition, though, it also reinforces the temporal dimensions of the work ethic, those to do with using time resourcefully, with not wasting it. Altogether these temporal practices reinforce the disciplinary approach to schooling spoken of in earlier chapters, and they substantially underline the degree to which these practices complement the instrumental functions of schooling. None of these things referred to are a matter of overt or intentional design; they are part and parcel of teacher education and professional preparation. But they do not have to be, because they are part of the inherited practice in the administration of schooling, which most teachers accept as part of the natural (not the constructed) regime of the school. Clearly an emancipatory approach to education must address this administrative culture if it is to 'free up' school time for a more ethical and socially critical climate for learning.

SCHOOLS AND CLASSROOMS

NOTES

1. It is also useful to consult student commentary on the experience of school life. Not too many of these have been published (and some of them are quite dated now) but in those that have, one of the most frequent bones of contention is the fact that the time seems to 'drag' in school and that many of its activities are boring and tedious. Among other things, pupils would prefer more flexible timetabling arrangements. See Newcombe & Humphries (1975); Blishen (1975); White with Brockington (1983).
2. Weber (1958) sees Franklin's writings as central to the 'spirit of capitalism', though to them one could add also the self-help philosophy of Samuel Smiles, whose book (1968) on this subject, first published in 1868, was often given as a school prize.
3. Japanese children spend 243 days at school whereas their American counterparts spend only 180 days (Smark 1990). The figures for Australia vary between states (194 days in Victoria, 197 in Queensland) and also between state and private schools, with private schools usually having a shorter school year than state schools.
4. Much of the literature on school time is in fact about timetabling, about how to do it and to jostle the time demands of subjects with the limited time available (Walton 1963). The vertical timetable is a significant departure from the traditional timetable, in that it tends to be set by the students rather than the teacher, and in this respect shares characteristics in common with the timetable of a tertiary student (Middleton 1982).
5. Hoskin (1990) has argued recently that in fact its origins can be found earlier than this, in the pre-Christian era in Greece and Rome.

Keywords and phrases

- absolute time
- grid of specificiation
- phenomenal time
- time consciousness
- timetable
- timethrift

Tutorial and field activities

1. Examine a high school timetable and calculate the percentage of time devoted to each subject. What does this tell us about the status of certain school subjects? You might also like to compare the timetable of arts students at university with that of an engineering or medicine student. What does this tell us about these areas of study?
2. Think about the subjective perception of time. Does time seem to go faster in tutorial or lectures? Why is this the case, do you

think? Remove your watch or cover the clock in your tutorial room. Make an estimate as to when you think forty-five minutes has past. Is estimating time akin to estimating weight? Is the clock the equivalent of a milestone?

3   Harvey (1990) has noted how time/space compression is one of the significant features of the postmodern condition. He associates this with modern communication systems and transportation systems Arguably, the Internet adds another, more accessible dimension to time/space compression. Discuss.

4   Why are there no bells and sirens to mark the end of lectures and tutorials at university?

5   List some of the commoner idioms and proverbs relating to our time habits and behaviour ['less haste, more speed', 'a stitch in time saves nine' 'quality time'], particularly those used by teachers. What do these tell us about our attitudes towards time?

6   Hargreaves has suggested that teachers create 'back regions' during their time at school in which they conduct activities that are outside of teaching duties. Ask teachers what they do in during such 'back region' times? Alternatively, you might like to think of the 'back region' times in relation to your part-time job.

7   In spite of the fact that we live in an age when the clock rules our activities, especially in the school, a great deal of time is wasted in schools. Using Kevin Harris' (1982a) article as a model, calculate the amount of time that is wasted in a typical lesson, in typical school day, school week and school year.

The character-building building: the architecture of the school

... manners, morals, habits of order, cleanliness, and punctuality, temper, love of study and of the school, cannot fail to be in considerable degree affected by the attractive or repulsive situation, appearance, outdoor convenience, indoor comfort of the place where they (children) are to spend a large part of the most impressionable period of their lives.

(E. R. Robson 1972)

Entrance

Following on from an examination of time, it seems quite natural to turn to the issue of space and its significance as an important dimension of educational life. Since the advent of relativity theory, the two have been treated together as continuous physical constructs. Time is an extension of space, whose equivalents of up and down, right and left are hence and ago (Quine 1990). Indeed, many of the observations that were made about time in the previous chapter—namely, that it is anthropocentric, subject to cultural construction and so on—apply equally to space. The tension between the objective measures of space and its perception at the subjective and phenomenological levels are as pronounced as it is with time.

Among other things, we had cause in the chapter on time to examine the way in which language reveals much about the way a particular culture constructs its time. The same is true with space. Words which qualify distance, such as 'far' and 'close', are context dependent. The notion of something being far away is different in a culture where the principal mode of mobility is walking, as distinct from driving a car. One of the impacts of 'time/space compression' (an idea discussed in a previous chapter) is that it has transformed the perception of space into time (Harvey 1990). When we are asked how far it is to drive to a place, we invariably say that it is ten minutes or half-an-hour. Spatial perceptions have become temporal perceptions. However spatial values of a sort have been preserved in the language of relationships, a clear reminder that intimacy, among other things, has much to do with the maintenance of distance, with controlling the parameters of personal and social space. Distance etiquette varies from one social situation to another, with closeness of contact varying according to the formality of the situation. Moreover, these etiquettes also vary between cultures (Hall 1959) and cause confusion and embarrassment when they are transgressed.

Value connotations are also embedded in our basic spatial orientations. As Heller (1984) has argued, upwardness, perhaps because of its celestial connections, has favourable moral connotations and is associated with positive mental states. The use of the word 'heavenly' exemplifies this, as does the drug induced state of being high. Downwardness, on the other hand, has rather different connotations associated with depression, melancholia, depravity. These stem from the idea that hell is located in a region below us. Spatial metaphors also permeate much of our thinking about the nature of society and the movements and processes within it (Bourdieu 1985). We talk, for instance, about knowing one's place in society, of people being down and out, about social climbers, social mobility and social movements, when referring to groups of artists or activists committed to revolutionary change.

Yet, in spite of its obvious importance in the domain of human affairs, space, like time, is an area which most social theory has tended to overlook or under-estimate in the power equations of social life. One reason for this, so it has been asserted, is that much social theory, having been influenced by Marx and the Enlightenment tradition, has tended to eschew the importance of the spatial dimension in societies, in favour of treating their temporal dimension. The claim is that, by analysing the cyclical and teleological nature of history and chronicling the lives of the disadvantaged and the oppressed, social life is produced historically and is therefore subject to intervention and change. In short, individuals can intervene in their history to the extent that they cannot in their geography. Thus there has been a tendency to subordinate the spatial dimension of social theory to that of time, to concentrate on historical accounts of social development and change, which are politically more actionable than space (Bourdieu 1985; Soja 1989).

In the last decade or so, though, there have been some signs that this subordination is being redressed, as more and more social theorists, particularly of those working within a post-structuralist paradigm, venture in a more concerted way into the territory of space. The literature on sociology and culture of space is now quite extensive and ranges over a large number of spatial phenomena including tourism, shopping malls, theme parks and architecture (Dunlop 1996; Gottdiener 1995; Reekie 1992; Shields 1991; Urry 1990; Zukin 1995). Indeed, some trepidation has been expressed when this spatialisation of theory has resulted in an elision of history, which is seen as a reassertion of bourgeois and reactionary thought, reducing the potential for political and revolutionary change (Gross 1981–82; Callinicos 1989).

For the theorist of space, Foucault's work has been especially influential; moreover, it is work which does not display any tendency towards historical elision. His writings placed great emphasis upon the importance of the space/power nexus as it manifests itself in the architectural fabric of institutions like prisons and asylums. As Foucault's work in this area demonstrates consistently, history is not being left behind in this investigation of space; rather, it is being incorporated as part and parcel of a more general understanding of social practices of everyday life, of which the organisation and arrangement of space within buildings is a critical part. Indeed, as time and space are recognised as indispensable co-ordinates of their respective domains of interest, the overall tendency has been for history to become more geographical and geography more historical. In the case of the latter, Hägerstrand's studies of city usage, which he calls 'time geography', have shown how space is regionalised and zoned differently at different times during the day, week or year, or even lifetimes. Hägerstrand sees life as a form of choreography, in which individuals weave a complex dance through time and space, with significant events occurring at points he calls 'stations' (see Pred 1972; 1981; Giddens 1984).

In this chapter we shall argue, after an examination of architectural meaning, that space manifests itself in various ways within the school setting. The first and most obvious of these is the architecture of the school which, like everything else discussed in this book, has a long and complex cultural etymology. We shall trace this etymology and suggest that the technology of modern schooling, which developed in the early modern age and which is primarily associated with the invention of the classroom as a regulated form of educational space, not only facilitates the surveillance of the student body, but is also instrumental in creating difference and deference among that body. However, the architecture of the school, notwithstanding any modifications and additions to it which often occur during the life of a school, is a relatively fixed and stable part of school space. Increasingly, it is common to talk about 'built environment' rather than architecture to describe the fluid and flexible nature of spatial life, in which classrooms, for instance, are used in multiple ways, in which furnishings and their rearrangement, notices, educational artefacts, pictures, even graffiti and vandalism, recreate the architecture of the school in line with the changing demands of students and teachers. To these we must add the dress of teachers and students and the 'choreography' of their movements around school, which are all subject to strict regulation and control, and all part of spatialisation of an educational environment which is extremely theatrical, like a costume drama.

Much of the literature on school space and architecture tends to be of a technical rather than analytical kind (Peters 1996; Sultana 1995), written for the benefit of other architects or teachers attempting to produce open rather than closed classrooms, in which the barriers of learning are not restricted by furnishings or other material inconveniences.[1] In seeing educational space simply in terms of its pedagogic possibilities, this literature rarely unmasks its power and social dimensions, which we shall argue are a critical element in the distribution and enactment of school power, another dimension of the school's anatomo-politics. Far from being a benign element in the schooling process, then, space is a significant force in the structuration of the school's everyday life, part of its capillary network, through which the social relations and the divisions which are a central part of that life are constantly recreated and via which corporate control over the school population is established. For we are asserting that the partition and segmentation of space that occurs in the school environment, and which is used to make the school population tractable and manipulable, assists the establishment of a disciplinary society.

Meaningful architecture

Buildings are a central element in the spatial dimension of life, fulfilling, in modern societies, a whole array of functions apart from that of shelter and protection from the elements generally. In all human settlements, be they small or large, cities or villages, there are two main categories of architecture. The first is the domestic, comprising those built environments like houses and apartment blocks in which human beings live their private and intimate lives, where they spend much of their leisure and indulge in family life. The second category of architecture is that of the public domain, the buildings where more communal activities are conducted. Within this broad category there are various specialised categories of built environment which contain activities such as those associated with work and maintaining the civil facets of communal life. The factory and the office are typical examples of the former, the courthouse and the parliament of the latter. The internal structures of these buildings reflect their functions.

Another important sector in the category of public architecture is that group of buildings associated with the organisation of cultural experience and with socialisation. It is to this category which buildings like schools, theatres, concert halls, sporting stadia, libraries and museums belong (see Bennett 1990; Walsh 1992). Their various internal organisation and structures constitute a form of epistemological spatialisation, with different spaces, rooms and areas set aside for different categories of cultural activity and phenomena. Think of the way, for instance, an art gallery 'spatialises' the history of art in terms of particular groupings of artists, either geographically or chronologically, or within art movements. All these groupings are cultural constructs. In the same way, the school is an architectural representation of Western culture, its specialist rooms, like laboratories and music rooms, reflecting a material exemplification of a certain view of knowledge, in which science and music are seen as dominant and important cultural categories worthy of having rooms to themselves to house the specialist equipment and facilities, also epistemologically specific, involved in their teaching. The architecture of the school is a 'living document', revealing much about the 'conceptualisation of the pedagogic project' (Sultana 1995).

Buildings, then, can be analysed in a variety of ways, not just architecturally. Architecture, in one sense, is concerned with engineering, with technical matters to do with the construction of buildings. In another sense, though, it is also concerned with their design, with their overall aesthetic. Indeed, architecture is as much a branch of aesthetics as it is engineering, and the subjective reception of buildings can be treated in much the same way as the reception of other forms of art, as appealing to deeply embedded grammars of judgement and taste that transcend the vagaries of history and geography, which are of universal appeal (Scruton 1979). There are other traditions in aesthetics, though, which see judgement and taste as social constructs rather than universals (Bourdieu 1984).

But buildings also have social meanings, which transcend their aesthetic effects and which can be read and decoded just like any other non-natural language with which we are familiar. These meanings are multiple rather than singular in character, relating to the properties of a building in various value domains. Baudrillard, who has developed a special interest in the visual and spatial aspects of late twentieth-century society, has argued (merging Marxism with semiotics) that a building can be analysed in terms of its use value, its exchange value, its sign value and its symbolic value. The first relates to its practical function as a shelter or place of containment for goods and services or pieces of machinery and tools; the second to its value as a commodity, not just as an asset but as the embodiment of labour and capital; the third to its capacity to generate difference and status, to provoke desirability and acquisitiveness; last of all, the building has value in terms of its appeal to pre-logical thought, of the sort associated with its aesthetic or historical appeal, and in terms of its capacity to generate feelings of sentiment and nostalgia, and to epitomise traditional or contemporary values (see Goss 1988).

Baudrillard's analysis is useful in that it provides the basis for a social semiotics of buildings and their environments. Such environments are not neutral, and the dispersal of buildings within them reflects the value attendant on certain areas and suburbs, which are rated not just functionally in terms of closeness to important services and facilities, but also in terms of their prestige and status. The class division of cities reflects this, in that neighbourhoods and suburbs are differentiated in terms of their socio-economic status, their capacities to attract people of certain outlooks and interests, even of sexual preference (Modjeska 1989; Raban 1988). The architecture of public buildings also reflects their symbolic status, creating convenient and readily visible reminders of the dominant and pervasive ideologies operating a particular time of history. The cathedral, for instance, dominated the Medieval city in much the same way skyscrapers and shopping complexes (symbols of the power of capital) dominate the city of today, as an architectural affirmation of the authority of God.

In the same way, school architecture has been used to assert traditionalism, to reinforce conservative educational philosophies, to give a visual reminder that the school reflects traditional rather than modern educational values. Thus the typical private grammar school (even those built in the 1930s when more modernist forms of architecture were being adopted) resembled a barn with 'ecclesiastical trimmings' (Godfrey & Castle 1953), such as bell-towers, mullioned windows, arched roofs and doors. Such ornamentations were outward manifestations of the school's commitment to traditionalism. Even the layout of such schools, with their quadrangles and cloistered areas, not to mention the presence of chapels and refectories, suggested how closely these schools were modelled on the Medieval university, which in turn owed much to the monastery (Seaborne & Lowe 1977).

Indeed, age and tradition, particularly as it is expressed in school buildings, have acquired a special cachet in the current educational environment, which has been thoroughly marketised and where 'image' has become a selling point, even for educational institutions. Older schools, in which traditional architecture predominates, have a particular competitive market advantage in this regard and make most of their photogenic buildings and the years of their establishment in their advertising and promotional materials. Schools which do not have these traditions tend to invent them (Hobsbawm & Ranger 1984), creating a pastless past for themselves!

By contrast, government schools (particularly in Australia), which have always had a more functional and technicist educational approach—one more aligned to the needs of the workforce and the economy—tended to have had a more functionalist architecture, one which followed the more modernist (Bauhaus) forms being widely employed in factories and office. There were none of the neo-Gothic and Georgian flourishes characteristic of the more traditional schools. Indicative of this is the fact that such schools tended to have canteens rather than refectories, a clear reminder that their main clientele tended to be working class, and as such, were destined for the trades rather than the professions. In the nineteenth century, though—and this again serves to corroborate our thesis that during this period schooling was invested with moral rather than economic intent—school architecture was supposed to ennoble the spirit, exhibiting the kind of architectural proportions calculated to inspire children to high moral ideals and practice. In fact, it is instructive to examine the writings of school architects of this period. Alongside their detailed plans of schools, which included descriptions of furniture and didactic apparatus, there were frequent homilies about the purposes of instruction and pedagogy, which emphasised the importance of establishing chaste and clean habits, good manners and punctual behaviour (Barnard 1970; Robson 1972). Indeed, learning almost seemed to be secondary to these other purposes.

ARCHITECTURE OF THE SCHOOL

As a form of technology, buildings have changed their character to encompass the new demands that have been placed upon them. Like any other forms of technology, they were not spontaneously created, but were invented and have gone through processes of evolution and development, with new styles and types of habitat being developed and others becoming extinct to coincide with the emergence of new social practices. The houses in which we live are prime examples of the sorts of changes which have occurred in architecture. In the past, houses were much more communal than they are now, with little privacy and few separate rooms to which members of the household could retreat when they wished to enjoy privacy. Individuals tended to live in general-purpose rooms, where they ate, slept, received visitors, danced, dressed and worked (Ariès 1962). People tend to live much more collectively than they do today. Even the furnishings of such rooms, like beds, were large enough to permit communal activities and it was not uncommon for families and friends to sleep together. There were no specialist rooms like kitchens and bathrooms, as there are in the modern house, and individuals did not expect to have rooms to themselves.

This highlights an important function of space: the degree to which it conditions behaviour and social practices. As is clear from the way space is zoned and regionalised in the modern house, certain areas become active and are engaged at different points during the day. In time-geography terms, the choreography of house-space is linked to the chronology of daily life. Bedrooms tend to be used at night, kitchens at meal times, the lounge during the evening. Some rooms, such as toilets and bedrooms, sites of intimacy, are more private than others. In houses with double storeys, this segmentation contains a vertical dimension, with upper parts of the house tending to be the sleeping quarters, the lower the living quarters (see Bourdieu 1973). Spatial organisation and utilisation always have a strong temporal dimension to them, something which is especially apparent—as we shall see—in institutions like schools, where movement and location are a matter of predetermination, where the timetable constitutes a choreography of the school day.

Spatial usage is far from being arbitrary, and there is an element of behavioural control within buildings which prescribes where we will be located within them and what conducts will be expected from us in their various spaces and settings. Goffman (1975) has written in some detail about these controls, particularly in relation to the framing effects of certain buildings. The example he cites is the theatre, a space in which there is a strong demarcation between the performers and the

201

audience, which defines the character of participation permissible on either side of the point of demarcation, between the stage and the auditorium. There is also a temporal dimension to this participation, which is engaged when the curtain rises and falls, and which marks the onset and 'the wiping away of make believe' and which defines what is expected of audience and actors alike.

Fronting up to the school

Buildings, in other words, act like different sets of parentheses in the normal prose of experience, bracketing it off and containing a specialised set of conducts that are not normally exercised or observed elsewhere in unbracketed experience, that come into being when the building's institutional functions are engaged or 'keyed', to use Goffman's word. The school is a good example of such a framed environment, one in which there are frames within frames. The school's physical setting, which is a bounded one marked by some of fencing or nature strip, tends to emphasise the degree to which the 'physical plant' of the school is set apart from its surrounds, acting, as in other 'total institutions', as a form of structured exclusion which is deterrent to more 'natural' forms of social interaction (Goffman 1976; Evans 1979). The increase presence of security signs in and around schools tend to further emphasise this 'spatial apartheid', reminding visitors that they must report to the office and that the school buildings are under constant electronic surveillance.

To use our theatrical metaphor, when the curtain rises on the school day, the actors in the school play proceed to certain, preassigned spaces, even to the extent of wearing different dress, particularly where the students are concerned. The teachers, after parking their cars in an area allotted to staff, proceed to staffrooms, where they have their own desks, a space they can call their own. While these days teachers are more or less free to choose their own styles of dress, this was not always the case and is still not the case in more conservative and traditional schools, where teachers are sometimes expected to wear academic gowns or, in the case of men, to wear suits and ties. Indeed some schools like their business counterparts have begun to introduce forms of corporate wear for teaching staff.[2]

But whatever their raiment, teachers plainly stand out from the students, who are expected, except on rare occasions such as free dress days, to wear some form of school uniform, even in primary schools. This is of a prescribed type and form, relating to such things as the length of a girl's dress, often expressed to the nearest centimetre and the type of clothes and shoes to be worn at various times of the year and by what age groups. School prospectuses and handbooks contain pages on such matters, on specifying what in the way of dress is tolerated within a school and what is not. Hair-styles and jewellery are given special attention in these manuals of prescription, and students are informed that these are to be a matter of conservative expression, with many schools prohibiting punk styles and forms of jewellery that are excessive and which allegedly draw attention to the student. One school prospectus, for instance, mentions that students can wear religious medals (and even these have to be hidden behind a collar) but not zodiac chains, which are presumably regarded as un-christian. When it deals with hairstyles, the same prospectus specifies that 'fringes should clear the eyebrows and hair must be worn above the collars and above the lobes of the ears for boys'. It goes without saying, of course, that make-up is strictly forbidden. Moreover, in order to ensure that the school's dress regulations are being observed with due respect and conscientiousness, many schools have days on which particular aspects of raiment like shoes and hemlines are inspected to ensure compliance.

Policy on school dress and appearance is, in fact, often extremely conservative and prescriptive, and has become more so in the last few years. It is often the cause of much unnecessary conflict within schools, as students seek ways to circumvent a school's sartorial regulations. Many students have been suspended for wearing too many nose-studs, having their hair too long or too short, or the wrong colour and so on. Some of these conflicts have even gone to litigation, and have been subject of legal settlement in the supreme court!

The context of the market is, in part, responsible for the revival of concern about uniform, as are parents who typically see the so-called 'uniform' school as one in which disciplinary and educational standards are high. Appearance has become a benchmark of education quality and the character of a school, rightly or wrongly, is judged to be immanent, as it is elsewhere in the community (Finkelstein 1989), in the dress and grooming standards of its students. But aside from being a mark of educational quality, the form of body inscription known as the uniform, is also a panopticon device, facilitating surveillance, enabling the movements of students from a particular school to be monitored in and around the community. The school badge immediately discloses the origins of a group of recalcitrant students to their onlookers! Hence schools stress in their handbooks the need for students not bring to dishonour to their uniform when they wear it outside school.

As a frame within the overall frame of the school, the classroom is a another example of behavioural parenthesis. As in Goffman's theatre, there is a point of demarcation between the teacher and the students, which means that at the commencement of a lesson the teacher situates herself in one area of the classroom, usually at the front and at a desk which is larger and more imposing than those of the students, while the students situate themselves in front of her, at desks organised in various configurations, according to the preferred pedagogic style of the teacher.[3] In older schools, the teacher's desk was often raised on a platform—in one sense, a symbolic reminder of his or her authority in the classroom and in another, a convenient surveillance point from which to monitor the conduct of the class. The teacher also enjoys mobility rights within the classroom, which students are denied and have to seek permission to exercise. No one tells the students or teachers to locate themselves thus; they do it automatically, without thinking; if they do not, they are soon reminded of their positional obligations and are put back in their place. This indicates the degree to which they have internalised and are able to enact the basic choreography of the classroom 'ballet', one in which they are constituted as students with an assigned position in the classrooms. The school bell provides an auditory cue marking the onset and the closure of a lesson, and thus corresponds in this respect to the function of the curtain in the theatre, though not always having the same silencing effect!

Another useful concept from Goffman's (1971; 1975) writings on space is that of 'front regions' and 'back regions'. In many social settings, but especially those of work, there is a tendency to zone off regions, to privatise them and to place them beyond surveillance and supervision, so that they can become sites where activities and behaviours of a subversive and non-productive kind can occur. These sites Goffman calls 'back regions', and they are very different from 'front regions' where work and behaviour is always disclosed, always open to inspection and monitoring, where the supervisor or overseer is always operating. Back regions are one of the counter-disciplinary sites within an institution, places where private or collective resistance is practised, where illicit and tabooed activities are conducted. Among other things, sexual activity, particularly when it involves genital contact, tends to be a back region phenomenon, although it has not always been thus closeted. Ariès (1962) and Elias (1978) have noted that in the past it was often conducted in disclosed areas, without apparent embarrassment or shame.

In thinking about schools and classrooms, students are masters at zoning off back regions, permitting them to do things in secret, to remove themselves from the teacher's line of vision, to put themselves beyond surveillance. Within lessons, they are forever devising strategies which will enable them to conduct conversations with their friends, to continue with activities outside the ambit of the lesson and so on. Toilets, because they are zones which are least open to surveillance, are, of course, major centres of back region activity, where smoking and drug-taking may occur.

The panopticon or society's gaze machine

The first schools in the Western world were attached to monasteries and cathedrals, and their architecture, as we have already noted, contained ecclesiastical features. But these church schools, which tend to be associated with a liberal educational tradition, represent a different tradition from the state school in terms of their architectural origin. The first plans for the state school have their origins in the early modern age, when other forms of public architecture like those of the asylum, the prison and the hospital were also being planned. As institutions, they were all intended to have a strong moral impact and to solve problems in the community, which went above and beyond their primary function, and their architecture reflected this.

Asylums and hospitals are a case in point. As the workforce became more mobile and less home-based, the family and community structures which were able to support the ill and the elderly began to vanish, and institutions were needed to take them out of the community, so that they were longer a direct burden on its more productive members. The segregation of the mad and the sick which occurred in early parts of the nineteenth century was in part a response to the 'commercialisation of society', to its increased subservience to the market and its demands (Scull 1980). Hospitals were not only supposed to treat persons, but also to school them in the economic and moral principles of modern society, and to deter undeserving cases from their midst. Hence the architecture of hospitals was not only palatial and graceful, designed to celebrate their philanthropic origins; at the same time, it also exhibited penal elements, designed to deter malingers and hypochondriacs, who were trying to avoid work (Forty 1980). So too with prisons, which were also intended to be places which inculcated respect for being productive and useful.

Another important features of these institutions, reflected in their architectural structures, was that they were often internally segregated, with partitioned areas and 'cellular' elements, as in hospital wards. In conjunction with these structures, their inmates were subject to classification and ordering, either along the lines of their disability or their crime. Spatial distribution within an institution was never arbitrary, but reflected complex human taxonomies accessible to penologists and doctors which served to quarantine and group those of similar disability and mentality. The architecture of these institutions was part and parcel of the task of governmentality and reflected the need to isolate abnormality, be it of a mental, physical or criminal kind. In the case of schools, the focus was somewhat different, the object being to produce normality and virtue within its quarantined population.

Schools played, as we have argued, an important role in 'population control'. One of their overriding concerns in the early modern period was to develop forms of instruction involving the greatest number of students for the least possible cost, particularly as it was the public purse which was involved (Jones & Williamson 1979). As we have said before, the motive for this was the formation not of an erudite and learned population, but simply one that practised productive habits, that was immersed in the work ethic, was honest and respected property, that avoided hedonistic and promiscuous behaviour, and that contributed generally to national efficiency and productivity. The moral tone of the early schools was set by the Sunday Schools, which were their immediate predecessors, and which were pledged to eradicate the anti-social activities that were perceived to be endemic among the working classes. Their pedagogic design was largely influenced by the ideas of Joseph Lancaster and Andrew Bell, among others, who solved the numbers problem by inventing the monitorial method, in which an able pupil-teacher, under the supervision of a master, instructed a group of students. Lancaster thought that such an invention would enable one schoolmaster to be able to responsible for the education of a thousand students in the one area (Robson 1972; Hamilton 1989).

The architecture of schools has always tended to stress the need to be able to watch students, and to take in their activities at a single glance or gaze. One writer on school architecture in the nineteenth century described the teacher's eye as the 'great instrument of moral discipline' (Barnard in McClintock 1970). As we have already indicated, the positioning of the teacher's desk in the classroom in conjunction with their roving practices tends to symbolise the teacher's overseeing functions. Certainly, students are often the first to be aware of the carceral features of their environment, often perceiving themselves to be the prisoners and their teachers their warders. Indeed, when the program Colditz (a German prisoner of war camp) was popular on television in the UK, a study of one English school found that the students had called the staff after the German guards in the series and even named certain exits from the schools after escape routes from Colditz Castle (March, Rosser & Harré 1978).

The panopticon (which literally means 'all seeing'), Jeremy Bentham's design for an ideal prison, represents the most forthright expression of this desire to be able to monitor and observe completely each inmate's activities without them knowing whether they were being actually watched or not—seeing without being seen. This design, which was an elaboration of a Russian factory that Bentham visited, shows a circular building, with cells located on its circumference, each being visible and observable from a central inspection point, the site where panopticism is exercised, the observation point for the eye of power.[4] Bentham (1984) who supported monitorial methods of instruction, believing them to be a most efficient way of generating learning, felt that panopticism could also be the basis of school construction, as well as chicken coops and taverns. In his rather extensive treatise on education, entitled *Chrestomathia*, meaning 'conducive to useful learning', he outlines a complete curriculum in great taxonomic detail and prescription, and also provides some observations about a suitable environment for this education. Among other things, he remarks that one schoolmaster could teach some 600 students, the number he believed was the maximum possible for 'constant inspection of one and the same Master'. Moreover, the inspection tended to be pyramidical, an example of hierarchical observation with the students being surveyed by monitors, monitors being surveyed by teachers, teachers by head teachers, and so on upwards through the chains of command in the educational bureaucracy. Vestiges of these procedures continue today, although they tend to be more subtly practised. Teachers continue to watch students, but their activities are in turn surveyed via the submission of their workbooks to inspectors and subject masters. The post-Fordist variant of this surveillance is the regular appraisal of teachers and the application of performance indicators which is part of the regime of award restructuring and quality assurance; in effect, however, it is a surveillance mechanism for ensuring ever more classroom efficiency and productivity.

Like his contemporaries, Bentham also believed that the best conditions for learning were those in which students were graded according to ability, and competed for rewards and places of honour. This added another important invention where the technology of the early modern school was concerned, and one which still remains with us today, namely that of the classroom, the operative part of this word being its stem, 'class', which was the word gained acceptance over its synonyms such 'draft', 'division' and 'section' (Hamilton 1989). This is the equivalent of the cell in the prison, or the ward in the hospital, the structural basis for segmentation and segregation within the school. Before the invention of the classroom, which became a standard part of school architecture in the 1850s, the education of students mostly occurred in an unsegregated way, without due recognition taken of their age or ability, in form- (which referred to the item of furniture on which students sat) rather than class-rooms. Accomplishment rather than chronology was the basis for student classification (Ariès, 1962; Seaborne 1971). Cohorts of students were formed around the stages of progress through a course rather than along lines of ability or age; they were not class-ified.

With the invention of the classroom came the multi-room school, and with it more refined systems of scholastic calibration which served to systematise the school and unify its overall disciplinary character within the framework of 'simultaneous instruction' (Hamilton 1989). Forthwith, the panopticon elements of school tended to be classroom- rather than school-based. One of the givens of the modern classroom situation, for instance, is that all students are located in front of the teacher, sitting at desks, themselves a product of the calibrated environment.

But this was not always the case. For a start, desks—along with blackboards—are a recent addition to the suite of classroom furnishings. And the idea that students should sit in front of the teacher, instead of at the side of the room as occurred in the pre-modern classroom, is one of Lancaster's innovations, along with some modifications made by David Stow, who thought that structuring students in rows and within smaller groups would enable them to be positioned more effectively for the purposes of scrutiny and surveillance (Hunter 1988).

Australian school architecture of this period (as it has been ever since) tended to follow the English model, including the practices of monitorialism and the kinds of furnishings, in spite of the inappropriateness of this for the climatic conditions. There were some local variants, however. For instance, the schools of the goldfields were of the portable variety, made of canvas and iron, to cater for the mobile population. School accommodation was often poor, and in many cases churches duplicated as schools during the week. State governments tended not to give schools the priority that they gave to other public services like railways and the mail, and their architecture, towards the end of the nineteenth century, tended to be devoid of ornament and the architectural symbolism through which their authority and presence was asserted (Burchell 1980).

Above all, though, the incorporation of the classroom into the early modern school brought about a major transition in the disciplinary apparatus of schooling. For, accompanying the invention of the classroom, were the other elements associated with contemporary schooling: timetabling, grading, subjects, specialist teachers, lessons and streaming (Hamilton 1989). In facilitating what amounted to the general segregation of students and divisions within the curriculum, the existence of classrooms also helped to facilitate the prevalent economy of schooling; namely, that divided groups tend to compete with one another, and that such competition tends to nurture striving and achievement. Indeed, as school architecture has evolved—admittedly at the prompting of a general expansion of the curriculum to include new subject and discipline areas requiring specialist learning environments—the school environment has become increasingly a grid of segmentation, of spatial specification, parallelling that of the timetable, with its strong frames.

The classroom, the basic cell of school life, facilitates the divisions and demarcations between groups of students, who are allocated to different areas and rooms within the school according to their subject preferences, their abilities and their capacities, and also to their age. The time/spacetable (see Figure 8.1) thus allots students within the planned space of the school. It is a matrix, a Cartesian grid, which represents a chronological and topographical distribution of bodies synchronised to the school's epistemological regime, and it regulates the spatial conduct and habits of teachers and students, as well as the other personnel associated with the school, such as the janitors and tuck shop ladies. Its decoding depends on the ability of the school population to absorb the plan of the school and decode its legends in terms of its notational system, its room numbering system and the orientation of these in terms of the school's principal landmarks and buildings such as the oval, playgrounds, the administration block, assembly hall and gymnasium.

Along with these specifications are others, concerned with the kinds of clothing to be worn in certain classrooms like laboratories and workshops, and other places of learning within the boundaries of the school (e.g. the oval). In a sense, the architectural arrangement of the school, which centres on classrooms, be they of a generalist or specialist kind, is yet another mechanism for manufacturing differences between students, literally a concrete symbol of the various student types, and a way of zoning certain epistemological practices. This is particularly true in the high school, and even more so in the university. In fact, from their locations within the school and the kinds of classroom to which they most often gravitate, it is possible to construct an academic profile of students, much as one can from glancing at their timetables. We should add a qualification here, one which relates to the situation in the primary and early childhood sector. There students tend to remain in their own space, rather than being distributed around the school according to the curriculum. By contrast with this, in high schools, the subtle message to students is that the space/timetable has greater priority than their need for a sense of belonging, for a home room. Even so, the home room of the early childhood and primary school, while it might give the impression of being a freer space, is still one which is subject to regulation and control (Tyler 1993).

The design of the modern school is subject to government regulations and bureaucratic statutes, with specifications relating to such things as the area of space required within a classroom for each student, lighting and ventilation, fire exits from buildings and so on—all of which are subject to government statute. These have led to the dispersal of the panopticon features throughout the schooling system (Gordon 1980). Although pedagogic styles have played a role in determining classroom and school design, particularly in the primary school where open classrooms have become the norm, in the past these have tended to be subsumed by more overriding concerns such as those to do with safety and prudence, especially in the area of health, rather than pedagogic sense and understanding. For instance, at the turn of the century, schools became subjects of special concern for the medical profession and students were studied as the victims of poverty, of privation and neglect. Hygiene and the control of infection became issues of real concern for school architects, as were issues to do with temperature and lighting. The design of schools was influenced accordingly, particularly by the hygiene movement, which, among other things, believed in the so-called miasmic theory of infection, that poison gases, as they were called, not only spread diseases in the classrooms, but made students tired and lethargic. It led to the demise of school designs, common in the nineteenth century, based around central halls and communal areas, and their replacement with pavilion and open air schools which were sunny and well-ventilated. Their design was supposed to disperse any germ-bearing air but often proved icily cold in winter (Horvath 1987; MacLure 1984; Rodwell 1995; Seaborne & Lowe 1977).

Thus the school architecture of the early twentieth century both in Australia and overseas was dominated by health discourses in which building specifications centred around designs that would serve to inhibit the spread of diseases. Measures to facilitate the spread of knowledge and learning were of secondary concern and did not become an issue of architectural concern until the postwar period, when schools become more child-friendly, when their furnishings were designed with children in mind. Indeed, the program of postwar school architecture with its use of modern materials and industrial designs represented a concrete exemplification of progressive social thinking and urban planning which was prevalent at the time, which was intent on creating a more equitable and fairer society (Saint 1987). It is with regret that, with the adoption of market-oriented policies by governments of all persuasions in the 1990s, we have seen an eclipse of such enlightened approaches. Indeed, the school buildings of the 1990s, like much other late twentieth-century design, are characterised by retro-style elements that look backward to the buildings of the past and symbolise a retreat to more conservative values.

Sexuality was also a matter of architectural concern, and not just in boarding schools where the discourse on this matter revealed itself in the structuring of dormitories, along with the strict regulation of sleeping hours (Foucault 1980). In Henry Barnard's writings on school architecture to which we have already referred, along with the need for well ventilated and well-lit classrooms, there are regular allusions to the need for a thoroughly clean school-house, free of what he calls 'profane and libidinous marks', by which he presumably means the sort of graffiti which will 'corrupt the heart and excite unholy and forbidden appetites' (McClintock 1970).

The power of school buildings

The architecture and buildings of the school provide the basic design of school life. But as elements in that design, their function is always fluid and subject to alteration, providing than the structural background in which the various furbishings associated with the educationworld such as desks and blackboards are located and against which the day-to-day activities of the school take place. Indeed, we need to examine these more fluid elements of the school's built environment. Notices, flags, badges, pennants, documents and pamphlets, exhibition spaces and boards of various kinds, around the school are as much a part of the school's space as its actual buildings and setting (Corrigan 1987), containing telling symbols of how space is to be used and is used. But these furbishings, that define the character and ethos of a particular school, can also be object lessons, providing much that is telling and insightful about its organisational culture. In fact these furbishings, following Arendt (cited in Csikszentmihalyi & Rochberg-Halton 1981) can be divided into two main types.

First, there are the educational tools of trade, those 'objects of action' and specialised furnishings which relate directly to the school's instrumental order, to its educational functions, such as desks and computers, sporting equipment and musical instruments. Second, there are other sets of furnishings which represents 'objects of contemplation' and veneration, and which are not necessarily functional but are, nonetheless, important in terms of defining the ethos of a school, in contributing to its 'expressive' and symbolic order, to its semiotic economy.

School architecture is another instance of governmentality, one that is instrumental in reproducing the social relations that supervise modern life, particularly in the domain of work. We can see this in the spatial division which exists between the executants and the conceivers in the schooling process, which results in a differential allocation of spatial privileges. As with everything else within the school, the power relationship where space is concerned is asymmetrical. The most obvious manifestation of this is that teachers have staffrooms to themselves, to which they retreat during recesses and at lunch time. As is clear from the notices that always appear on staffroom doors, teachers guard these refuge areas with considerable vigilance, as if they had the status of a sanctuary. Students are informed that they cannot walk into them without first being invited, without knocking and seeking permission to cross the boundary that separates them from normal and unregulated school space.

The staffroom is not a free enclosure like a classroom or the playground, to which all members of the school community are granted automatic access. As a restricted area separated from the general body of the school plant, the position of the staffroom is somewhat analogous to the relationship existing between the administration area in the school and its teaching spaces, which in turn echoes the relationship between the management and production areas in a factory.

Thus the administration space in schools is removed from its teaching spaces, located in an area to itself, comprising a suite of offices occupied by the school's principal and deputy principal, and an administrative section where the school's office staff work with their administrative technologies: telephones, computers, fax-machines, facilities, waiting rooms and so on. Because this area tends to act as an interface between the school and the outside world, and to be the place which visitors to the school encounter first, it is an area of special significance in the physical plant of the school. Receptions and vestibules, as the emergent literature on educational marketing emphasises (Davies & Ellison 1991; 1992), are frequently places where first and telling impressions are made which can influence significantly the way a school is perceived and apprehended. Thus in a context in which schools are increasingly image conscious they have begun to attend to these interface areas both in terms of communication strategies, such as answering the telephone, and their appearance in terms of the presentation which must be immaculate if the right impression is to be created! In these areas, too, are found a variety of 'objects of contemplation' relating to the various aspects of school's 'expressive order' (Bernstein, Elvin & Peters 1966), to its achievements, particularly of a sporting and academic kind. Thus cabinets of sporting trophies and pennants tend to adorn the walls, along with rolls of honour and lists of the school dux.

Such iconographies of excellence provides a structural and objective representation of the meritocracy in action (Seaborne & Rowe 1977). They also exemplify the degree to which the ethos of individuality dominates the moral economy of schooling; those who succeed in schools, be it in an academic or sporting way, deserve to have their names writ large and in gold leaf in the school's vestibule.

Another noteworthy feature of the administrative space is that the principal and deputy principal have offices to themselves and enjoy a degree of privacy denied to other members of the school community, who occupy more disclosed environments. This spatial arrangement also means that they are not freely accessible, that speaking with them is not automatic but a matter of appointment or secretarial intervention. Counterpose this with the mode of communication to students, which is mostly public, occurring via the airwaves of the school loudspeaker, which punctuates every school space with announcements and commands—for example, for students to present themselves at the office, the site of school governance.

On the symbolic level, the effect of this segmentation is to assert the authority of the school's major officers, and to provide a spatial rationalisation for more deferent forms of behaviour and conduct in their presence. As Goss (1988) has noted, in all buildings, 'the segmentation of space manifests and at the same time creates the separation of inhabitants', providing important behavioural cues for their inhabitants, according to the positions, be they of a vocational or hierarchical kind, they occupy in buildings. As a general rule, those occupying the highest positions in an organisation tend to occupy the most enclosed spaces, the lowest the most disclosed (Harris & Lipman 1980). Open areas, be they in offices, factories or schools, are always the place where executants are to be found, another instance of panopticism. Thus the school's topography, which is saturated with power dimensions, echoing those in other public buildings, becomes another dimension of the school's structured imposition, another way of asserting that the divisions between the school population are natural and logical, and follow those which exist in the society outside school, where the conclaves of management are also separate from the general body of workers, enjoying more comfortable and luxurious conditions. Nor should the role of furniture be discounted in these spatial equations of power distribution. Particularly in public service environments, the allocation of furniture like tables and chairs to offices, specifically in relation to their size and—in the case of chairs—their degree of comfort, has always depended upon the position that an 'officer' occupies in the hierarchy of the public service (Joiner 1971).

In the case of students, the spatial asymmetry of power is particularly noticeable. The only space that they can truly call their own in a school is maybe a locker, and that hardly constitutes a space to which they can retreat when they wish to have privacy or time to themselves! The only space which facilitates a modicum of privacy for the student is a cubicle in the toilet, which is hardly the most prepossessing of environments; moreover, it is one which is only accessible at certain periods during the day, namely recess, when it tends to be much in demand. Playgrounds and oval areas offer students somewhat more autonomy and spatial freedom than they enjoy in the classroom, more opportunity to find 'back regions' but their activities within these areas are constantly subject to surveillance from teachers on playground duty. Indeed, as it was originally conceived by David Stow in the early modern period of schooling the playground was to be an 'uncovered classroom', an important domain of moral training in which a student's true character and disposition could be observed in its natural state (Hunter 1988).

In any case, the freedom of the playground is only relative, limits being placed on the repertoire of possible conducts there and the range of areas that are accessible to the students during recesses and lunch hours. For not only are certain areas placed out of bounds—another factor of spatial control—but the struggles for space which occur within the prescribed play areas during recesses and lunchtimes are another important aspect of the production of subjectivity, particularly where gender is concerned. Boys, for instance, tend to be more assertive and demanding where the occupation of playground space is concerned, and it is their games and sports which dominate the playground, leaving girls to occupy its perimeters.

With the exception of the 'back regions' that they create for themselves, which place them beyond the scrutiny of teachers, students are always disclosed within the boundaries of the school, always subject to its gaze machinery. Even their movements within and around the school are subject to prescription and regulation. School rules often include sections on how students are expected to move between lessons. Speed of movement is stressed, although running is prohibited, and students are told not to loiter, especially around toilets and verandahs. Yellow lines on the playground often indicate the preferred 'thoroughfares' around the school to prevent pedestrian congestion between lessons. Entrance to classrooms is also subject to regulation and only occurs under the supervision of a teacher, with students being expected to line up, usually in two columns, girls on one side, boys on the other. Spatial supervision even continues out into the vicinity of the school, where students are expected—as one school prospectus puts it—'to stand to one side on pathways' and 'to allow the free passage of the general public'. Students who wish to leave the school grounds during school time must gain official approval. Infraction of any of these spatial regulations can incur various micro-penalties.

Even the moral discourse of teachers contains frequent references to movement matters, as when students are told to hurry themselves along and not waste time in idle chatter, although much of this discourse on physical deportment tends to concentrate on posture matters, as in encouraging students to sit or stand up straight and not to hunch themselves over their desks. Such posture control is an important feature of the school's anatomo-politics, more stressed in the nineteenth century than it is today, when desks were carefully designed and measured to optimise standing and sitting, and to facilitate the closure of desks with a minimum of noise. Indeed, vestiges of the quasi-militaristic approach to student movement and comportment, educational versions of dressage and drill, persist at morning parade and at the beginning and end of many lessons, when students are told to stand, to sit, to take out their books, to prepare for writing and so forth. Such pedagogic drill is a remnant of the Victorian era, when it was felt that such micro-structuring of movement through repeated actions and drill was the best way to secure obedience and submission, initially in the school and then generally within society (Hurt 1977). The objective was to make the body like a machine, activated by the will of the teacher, with actions being co-ordinated via numbers.

But within the school curriculum generally, anatomo-politics has now been transferred to physical education, where posture and physical movements, admittedly in relation to the various sporting areas, are subject to discipline and precise regulation in ways which are constructed and designed to support particular definitions of subjectivity. As was suggested in a earlier chapter, our physical comportments are also matters of construction and social invention. For instance, in physical education, there is a tendency for the mesomorph—the svelte, athletic, almost anorexic and more male shape—to be regarded as the desirable norm, with other more normal body shapes being regarded as unfit, indicative of an ill-disciplined fitness regime (Colquhuon 1990).

But the classic case of anatomo-politics in action is the activity of throwing, particularly its overarm variety, which involves the use of lateral space. It is has often been alleged that girls cannot throw in this way because of anatomical reasons. Yet the real reason is not biological at all. To the contrary, it originates from cultural conditions in which women are expected to limit their physical potential, to under-utilise space and motility and to generally hamper and inhibit their movements in the interests of appearing more tentative and more vulnerable than men. Physical movement and comportment is part of the production of gendered subjectivity, in which women are expected to play the role of the other (Young 1980).

It is within the classroom itself that spatial control is most pronounced. Some of the controls are self-imposed, perhaps deriving from some kind of territorial atavism, the impact of some form of ancestral memory, such as the tendency to always sit in the same seat in a lecture theatre, week in week out, and to be mildly irritated when another student is occupying *our* seat (Dale 1974). But it might also be a reflection of the fact that early on in our school careers, our placement within the classroom was frequently a matter of teacher prescription, one which created displeasure if this prescription was broken. As an aid to memorising the names of their students, teachers often compile little plans of the spatial dispositions of their students within the classroom and that is one reason why students are encouraged to remain in the same position from lesson to lesson.

But location is also used as a form of behavioural control, with students being rotated around the room, generally from the back to the front, to permit closer surveillance and supervision, when they 'muck up' or otherwise subvert a lesson's progress. It was also common practice to use the layout of desks in the classroom as a 'dividing practice' as a way of positioning and ranking students according to their academic abilities, with the so-called brighter ones sitting in one quarter of the room and the duller ones in another. The most forceful expression of this spatial regulation, though, tends to occur during times of examination and testing, when the layout of examination rooms and the distance between desks is a matter of precise specification, as much a part of the regulation of examinations as the times set for their completion.

Exit

In this chapter, we have attempted to demonstrate that the school's architecture is far from being a neutral and passive element in the schooling process. On the contrary, it is an extension of the power processes which pervade the everyday life of the school, facilitating such things as the separation and segregation of students, and the maintenance of distance between teachers and students. More than this, the architecture of schools is an example of the eye-of-power in action, with not only the buildings themselves, but also the furnishings and the organisation of students within classrooms, facilitating surveillance. Indeed, the whole school environment is a specialist space, a region requiring codes of behaviour and habits of conduct not encountered elsewhere, at least not to the same intensity and degree of organisation.

In thinking about these processes, which are central to school life and its practices, we need to think about whether their logic and justification are defensible in terms of ameliorating the processes of learning. It is obvious, for instance, that the space in schools is used as a way of keeping students from teachers, as a way of helping students to know their place within the school, and subsequently within the world, according to their placement within the school. In mainstream schooling, space is used as a way of asserting power over students, rather than as a way of empowering them. In these ways, the disciplinary mode is reinforced. It is notable that some radical experiments in education such as the Philadelphia Parkway Program (Bremer & van Moschzisker 1971) have attempted to remove learning from the setting of the school, to place it within the community, where the segmentation of space that occurs in the school environment can be transcended. In a generalised way, the school setting tends to separate school from community, removing it from society's problems and concerns and setting up a spatial disjunction between them. An emancipatory approach would minimise this disjunction by attempting to create structures which would encourage communication between the school and community and give society's problems a central focus in the classroom.

NOTES

1. A good example of purely technical analysis of school architecture, one lacking any critical insights into the controlling nature of school space, is a special issue devoted to school architecture of the *Harvard Educational Review*, 1969.
2. Tertiary students were also once subject to such prescription, particularly those involved in more conservative courses like teaching. In one of its previous incarnations, the university where the authors teach, was a place where dress regulation, even twenty years ago, was strictly adhered to and students were often chastised for wearing such unteacherly garments as dungarees, which were seen as the clothing of plumbers, not would-be teachers.
3. Much of the literature on pedagogic space has examined the effects of desk layout on lesson participation, it being generally recognised that more informal layouts encourage greater participation and involvement, although not necessarily more learning (Sommer 1967).
4. This design is reproduced in Foucault (1979). For a discussion of the panopticon's origins and the impact it had on prison architecture in the nineteenth century, see Evans (1982).

Keywords and phrases

- appearance discourses
- back regions
- dividing practices
- expressive order
- frame theory
- front regions
- instrumental order
- objects of action
- objects of contemplation
- panopticon
- semiotic economy
- surveillance
- symbolic architecture

Tutorial and field activities

1. What are the major differences between the architecture and spatialisation of the university as compared with that of a school? Is it just a matter of the larger scale and magnitude of the former or are their more significant differences in terms of the epistemological organisation of their space and physical plant? Does the more luxurious layout and luxuriant landscape of the university suggest something about funding levels of universities when compared with schools? Are these funding disparities fair and justified? Of what significance is the fact that the lecturers have offices to themselves? What does it indicate about the conduct of teaching and learning within universities when compared with that of schools?

2. Since Bentham originally conceived of the idea, societies have increasingly resorted to panopticism, no more so than in the last decade or so. The widespread use of video cameras in public places and in commercial buildings such as shopping complexes is an example of electronic panopticism. What other forms of postmodern panopticism are there? Is this form of intrusion into our public and private lives justified? Should we worry about the threat to our civil liberties that this invasive technology poses?

3. Examine a range of school handbooks and prospectuses and sections therein dealing with uniform and dress matters. Note the degree of prescription appertaining to these matters, particularly in relation to skirt length and body ornamentation. Are private schools more prescriptive in dress regimes than state schools? If so, to what do you attribute this difference? Discuss the whole issue of dress and schooling. Is the uniform simply a means of regimenting the school population, of encouraging students to monitor their own dress habits? Or is character really immanent in appearance, and can we judge institutions by the various images they present to the outside world? Or should we, as Plato suggested, be cautious about drawing moral inferences from the surface appearance of the world, from such inscriptions on the body as the uniform?

4. Examine the entrance areas such as their signage and office areas of educational institutions, including universities. What kinds of 'objects of contemplation' typically appear, in addition to those mentioned in the chapter, in such areas? What do these

objects tell us about the organisational and symbolic economy of the school?

5   Reflect on the 'back region' utilisation of space. Do students at universities engage in back region activity, say, in lectures? What form does it take? Discuss some back region activities of students at schools? Can backroom activity ever be stopped? Will it always occur? Think what smokers have to do in order to satisfy their addiction now they have been stopped from smoking in most public buildings. Indeed, should back region activity be stopped? Does it, for example, act as a kind social safety valve, allowing members of an educational community to conduct 'illicit' activities for which they might otherwise find more dramatic outlets?

Assessment and examination: getting a measure of the subject

We have no class examinations in the school (Summerhill), but sometimes I set an exam for fun. The following questions appeared in one such paper: Where are the following: Madrid, Thursday Island, yesterday, love, democracy, hate, my pocket screw driver?

(A. S. Neill 1974)

On your marks!

Among the many tasks confronting the teacher, none is more wide-ranging in its significance and impact than assessment, and none presents more problems for the teacher with an ethical and emancipatory perspective. The tasks associated with assessment, which are varied and many, are constant and unremitting. They involve, among other matters, the devising and construction of assessment items and an array of associated clerical tasks, marking scripts and tests, compiling assessment statistics and entering marks, and writing reports on students.

These task are also ones whose cumulative impact have the potential to influence the life-chances of students. As occupational and educational opportunities are often linked to classroom performance, to scores entered on record cards and résumés, to results gained in examinations, there is a sense in which the results of assessment can mark a person for life. Parental interest in schooling is invariably concerned with test and examination results, almost to the exclusion of everything else. Efficacious or not, employing bodies and tertiary institutions invest a great deal of significance in these results, regarding them as the touchstones of talent and future performance, as if their veracity were infallible and beyond reproach.

Therefore it is not surprising that students come to regard good examination results as the only benchmarks of success at school. This is also true of employers who see such results, at least according to the perceptions of students (White with Brockington 1983), as reflecting capacity for hard work and industriousness. Those students who fail to appreciate the correlation between good school results and the acquisition of employment drop out or become members of an anti-school culture, which compounds their difficulty.

As Hextall (1976) has pointed out, school assessment systems are always political in character; they play a significant role in determining a person's eventual position in society the labour market. That is not to say that some individuals do not achieve considerable economic and social, and even academic standing, success in spite of poor performance at school. There are cases of such individuals (many of them quite famous) but they tend to be the exceptions rather than rule. For it is the trends and patterns among educational outcomes not the anomalies that provide the more instructive indictments of the schooling system. For, at a most general level, the aggregate effects of assessment are bound up with the structure of society, with sustaining the illusions of a meritocracy, a system dependent on considerable faith in the instruments and measures of assessment, as determinants of human potential and capacity.

At another level, assessment is often used to coerce students into action, to increase their productivity, to impress upon them the virtues of industriousness and the risks involved from squandering opportunities and not making enough of one's aptitudes. The moral economy of schooling is, in large measure, sustained through the need to attain good marks, to avoid the stigma of failure and to maximise opportunities for success. One consequence of this is that students, even at university, tend only to work if there is some form of assessment involved. Fixing grades to students is also frequently accompanied with judgements about their moral calibre, about their capacity to apply themselves and to exhibit appropriate scholarly attitudes—those the school expects of its *good* students, namely being passive, docile, conscientious and co-operative rather than disruptive (Bowles & Gintis 1976).

Thus there is no disjuncture between the measures of cognitive and moral worth, as school success is as much tethered to moral calibre as it is to mental calibre. Assessment is used as a mechanism of censure, through which behaviour—both moral and cognitive—is regulated, and around which the basic parameters of contemporary social life are framed. The idea that there are winners and losers, and that ability and capacity are legitimate differentia when it comes to the just allocation of reward and status in society, flows directly from classroom assessment, as does much of the ideology of individualism rampant in a capitalist and postmodern society. Not only does school assessment create the conditions in which the competitive ethos of our society ripens and flourishes, but it also serves to construct ideas about capacity and talent, the most powerful and prevalent being that these are in short supply, that they are normally not universally distributed, and that they are restricted to particular areas of epistemological endeavour.

As we saw in Chapter 6, where we dealt in some depth with educational inequality, a number of regrettable consequences flow from this. One is that it helps to justify limiting access to education, especially beyond the compulsory years. This means that the circulation of important knowledge and epistemological capacities needed for a powerful critique of society at a popular level tends to be restricted to cultural and privileged elites (Hannan 1982). In effect, it provides a powerful rationalisation for the intellectual disenfranchisement of a large proportion of the population. Another consequence is that the power to acquire and retain classroom knowledge is regarded (often quite without foundation) as an excellent barometer of other powers, like those to do with communication, with possessing the capacity to understand others, especially their problems and dilemmas, which are indispensable skills in the human service industry and which are not necessarily products of an academic background. But these consequences are only one outcome of an assessment regime which encompasses many other concerns apart from cognitive and intellectual issues.

From the moment of birth, children are constantly being assessed, measured and quantified, as part and parcel of a societal regime in which individuals, at many times during their lives, are objects of mandatory study and objectification, targets of tests and examinations which the modern state demands of its individuals in order to satisfy health, economic, citizenship or educational requirements. Much of this 'technology of subjectivity', as it has been called, is an extension of the 'normalising gaze', to which we have already referred, and which centres on ensuring that individual exhibits normal patterns of development and behaviour, be they cognitive, physical, economic or whatever. It represents another example of social regulation, population control, to ascertain deviancy and treat its incidence (Rose 1990), another example of the mechanism through society is rendered transparent and visible. For the majority who lie within the accepted parameters of normality, what follows is a regime of assessment designed to identify difference, to measure capacity and potential, and to organise courses of learning coincident with these measures.

Such technologies have, as their end, the need to enhance the productivity and moral worthiness of individuals. The principal venue for the exercise of this regime is the school, and its main disciplinary ally in this respect has been psychology which, in the twentieth century, has provided a whole of series tests and procedures designed to objectify the child's internal mental state and to individuate it. Classroom assessment—the subject of this chapter—is but one form of this regime. Its quasi-scientific status (which some have argued should be challenged) has helped to increase its legitimacy as a vehicle for 'governing the soul' (Meadmore 1995; Rose 1990; Walkerdine 1990).

The terms of assessment

Assessment is an offshoot of those general processes of evaluation whose genealogy stems from that most common of activities, namely judgement. There is hardly a domain in everyday life in which we do not exercise judgement of one kind or another, in which we do not appraise and express preferences and which involves the attachment of value or worth. The notion of 'weighing up', which is embodied in the etymology of the word 'examination'—the concept of making a decision between competing interests and rivals—is central to the judgement process. Films, books, rock music, clothes and food are all domains in which we make and pass judgements, in which we express a dislike or liking, a loathing or passion for something. Typically, evaluative judgements occur in domains which have an aesthetic or moral character, as when we judge a person's conduct to be good or bad or when we say that a film was to our liking or not. There are also specialists in the area of judgement who make a profession from adjudicating in matters to do with judgement and taste. This involves a degree of so-called connoisseurship, which arises from long experience with the objects being judged, be they bottles of wine, paintings, blends of tea, poems, gymnasts or whatever. Indeed Eisner (1979) has argued that the techniques of connoisseurship could be used to evaluate the effectiveness of the curriculum.

A central element in the judgement process is the application of standards and criteria against which judgements are measured; that is, the process is normative in character. For all judgements involve a degree of comparison, of establishing whether something compares favourably or unfavourably with something else of a similar kind, with the norm. There is also a set of terms associated with these judgements, that are employed in assessing something's virtue (e.g. good, excellent, mediocre, original, indifferent, satisfactory). In addition, there is another range of terms that enables comparative judgements to be made, for things and persons to be ranked against one another, as when we say Person A is better at mathematics than Person B. These terms form a natural scale of judgement.

Comparative judgements often involve grading of some kind, a setting of standards against which performance or magnitude is measured. For instance, eggs and apples are graded according to size, as are people, when we say that they are short, of medium build, tall, etc.

In the complex ethnography of the educationworld, the domain in which the passing of judgements has its most powerful impact is in the area of educational capacity. The notion that some people have more ability and capacity than others is commonly held, is embedded in the everyday assessment of individuality. In the language of individuation, for instance, it is common to characterise a person as clever, bright, articulate, able, intelligent, talented, average, gifted, slow, dumb, stupid or thick. We also use slang terms to do the same thing, such as vegie, dummy, spastic, etc. Many of these terms are products of the discourse of psychologism and are attributed in terms of certain academic capacities, serving to shape the way a particular student's identity is regarded.

It is commoner, for instance, to use words like 'bright' and 'clever' in association with mathematical capacity than that of home economics. The alleged intellectual demands of particular subjects is seen as a critical factor in the attribution of brightness and cleverness. In effect, as Edelman (1977) has argued, the language of attribution is powerful in its impact within educational institutions, especially when reinforced with the authority of psychology, serving to create categories and classes of individuals, determining their eventual status and powers of influence. But this language is also part of a more generalised moral economy relating to what counts as esteem worthy ethical capacities in human subjects, capacities which are often rewarded and made the subject of adulation. In the past, for instance, children were often identified in terms of whether they displayed these capacities or not, and were labelled accordingly.

There is also degree parallelism or isomorphism existing within the various semiotic scales of grading systems, be they numerical, alphabetical, verbal or statistical. Grading systems are not neutral, but connote a variety of attributes about the potential and the intellectual disposition of their subjects. They are not just rewards for work done—they also constitute the ways in which an academic profile of a student is outlined and delineated, so that by charting the high and lows, in effect, the contours of a student's grades, their academic career can be mapped out, and allegedly predicted (Cherryholmes 1988). Assessment systems are also an important source of biographical reportage, providing databases from which dossiers are compiled on individuals, which they are expected to retain and, these days, to update, making them available, should they be requested, to prospective employers and tertiary institutions. This in another aspect of the information society that operates increasingly through the lives of individuals. It is another facet of governmentality, in which individuals are not only enacted upon but are also expected to enact on themselves, though monitoring and keeping a record of their conducts and activities.

Thus the student, after so many years of schooling of being the subject and object of pedagogic observation, is gradually translated into a 'web of texts'. This comprises scores on psychological and personality tests and results for end-of-semester examinations, as well as more non-discursive and impressionistic forms of observations about character and moral standing made by their teachers, which are also part of the assessment and evaluation regime. This is all part of the dossier-construction process, in which a profile of a particular student is gradually drawn, comprising all manner of observations on them, everything from examination marks and psychological tests to medical examinations and behavioural evaluations. The result is a kind of inventory of human traits, a record of achievements (or, in many cases, non-achievements) based around standardised criteria and descriptors, sometimes called 'comment banks'.[1] Thus, as Foucault (1979) suggested, the mechanisms of assessment has meant that the individual can be introduced into a 'field of documentation', in which their behaviour is codified and notated according to the complex nomenclature of individuality and difference that has developed in the modern period. In the reference proforma shown in Figure 10.1, based on one from a Queensland high school, the calibrations in these fields are evident, and are closely related to the value dimensions of the work ethic, as in the comments about punctuality, industry, dress and grooming.

Moreover, it is not just students who are being assessed. These days the procedures and techniques of assessment extend to schools themselves and the whole educational system. The ideology of 'performativity' that we have discussed previously as a characteristic of instrumentalism is being employed, under the urging of governments and businesses, to assess and amend educational programs, to render them more efficient and accountable. Under the policies which were developed by Dawkins (1988), mechanisms such as institutional profiles were put into place so that educational programs could be placed under constant assessment and scrutiny.

Figure 10.1 Mental State High School: State High School reference				
Student's Full Name: Georges Perec Year Level: 12				
Personal characteristics	**Very Good**	**Good**	**Satisfactory**	**Need for improvement**
Grooming and dress				x
Manners and courtesy		x		
Industry			x	
Co-operation			x	
Punctuality			x	
Reliability				x
Initiative				
Readiness to accept				
Guidance				x
Leadership			x	
Sociability		x		

It is not that individuals have become subject to panopticism but also whole systems of education. It is quite common, for instance, particularly in the UK and increasingly in Australia, for the educational performance levels of educational institutions, including primary schools and universities to be published in league tables, in which institutions are ranked according to their performance in public examinations. At the same time, consumer criteria are increasingly being applied to educational institutions, particularly at the tertiary level. This has led to a spate of publications, consumer guides (Ashenden & Milligan 1996), published annually and sponsored by national newspapers, which rank institutions in terms of affordability criteria and the degree of value for money that their courses offer. This leads to competition (and of course economic rationalists argue that competition leads to better results and more efficient institutions) between schools and an increased concentration on outcome measures at the expense of more laudable educational concerns. Nor are such assessment regimes confined to the educationworld. Increasingly, large corporations and bureaucracies, including Departments of Education, are appraising their employees, including teachers, on a yearly basis, requiring them to participate in performance evaluation schemes, assessing their productivity and efficiency and applying psychological tests to determine their suitability for employment.

As Holt (1985) has suggested, the classroom is a 'test-ridden' environment in which students are constantly being assessed, principally in the areas of behaviour and cognitive achievement. These processes of assessment, especially where examinations are concerned, can induce considerable anxiety and trauma, that can result in under-performance. As a genus, that of assessment is one with diverse species, ranging from psychometric instruments like intelligence and creativity tests through to classroom forms of assessment, such as essays and projects, to public examinations set by universities and testing services provided by bodies such as the Australian Council of Educational Research.

Some of the assessment is of the self-evaluative kind and is of a non-intimidatory kind, particularly when it involves computer-assisted learning. The instruments themselves can also take a variety of forms, from objective tests with one-word answers to be completed in a short interval of time through to research activities, which, in the case of some higher degrees like a PhD, have a much longer duration (three years and longer) and involves the production of a book-length thesis. Sometimes the assessment is terminal, at other times continuous. In the case of the latter, the assessment centres on the production of assignments, the giving of presentations or demonstrations of one sort or another, according to the nature of the subject matter being studied. Assessment instruments also vary from subject to subject. In the more practical subjects, a student's capacity to perform an action or operation is likely to be of more significance than a capacity to write and prepare papers; where assessment centres on symbolic manipulation, there is an emphasis on the capacity to articulate a point of view, to develop a discursive argument in a paper or an essay. And of course there are some disciplines, some courses, in which there is a marriage of both types of assessment, as in the case of medicine or teacher education, both of which involve practicum components.

Indeed, with the adoption of competency approaches to assessment, another reflection of the spread of educational instrumentalism, in the education systems of the UK and Australia (Hyland 1991; Marginson 1993; Norris 1991), the practicum has undergone something of a renaissance in the last few years, and most learning, even in very abstract and theoretical domains, is expected to be demonstrable in terms of explicit criteria and performance outcomes. While there are some virtues in encouraging educationalists to think about the performance implications of their teaching and relating much more of their curriculum to the real world and to reducing the divide between theory and practice, there are some possible dangers in making education too competency-based. The most notable of these is that the complete capitulation to competency measures stemming from the workplace could lead to the marginalisation of non-instrumental forms of knowing, which transcend performativity and which require wider understandings than those possible under the reductionist dictates of the competency movement (Carr 1993; Usher & Edwards 1995).

An examination of examinations

In Europe, at least, the industry associated with assessment began in the nineteenth century, with public examinations for the public service and the military, and entrance into professions like architecture and pharmacy.[2] The reasons for developing such systems of examinations were in part prompted by the Utilitarians such as John Stuart Mill, who argued that they provided an alternative to the patronage system, which was notorious for its nepotism and corruption and offered no guarantees that competent individuals from a broader or more representative cross-section of society would be recruited into the ranks of the public service and the professions. With the similar kinds of reasoning, parallel developments also took place at universities like Oxford and Cambridge, and subsequently spread to the schools (Gordon & Lawton 1978). Examinations developed in conjunction with the emergence of the meritocracy, but they also coincided with a commodified view of knowledge which emerged much earlier, in the Middle Ages, with the introduction of print technology which had a considerable impact on the way in which knowledge was organised and spatialised (Ong 1958). As a result, knowledge gradually came to be seen as something which could be acquired and possessed and, more to the point, tested and examined.

But the modern examination which was invented in the nineteenth century for the purposes controlling entry into universities and the professions was very different from its Medieval predecessors in that it was written rather than oral. With its implied suspicion of the authority of the written word and its capacity to convey the integrity of knowledge and understanding, the regime of the viva voce (the live voice) dominated education, and still does so at its highest levels. For instance, in many of the more traditional universities of Europe and the United States, doctoral candidates are expected, for the final part of their examination, to defend their dissertations in the face of a panel of relevant experts. Indeed, when examinations were first trialed in universities, the opposition to them was so forceful that they had to be withdrawn, albeit only temporarily (Hoskin & Macve 1986).

Another innovation associated with the introduction of the modern examination was that it was marked and assessed; there was an attempt to quantify and enumerate, and subsequently scale, the results achieved by students in their various exams. Along with examinations, we tend to think that schooling has always been associated with the bestowal of marks and grades, part of the taken-for-granted realm of pedagogic history, but these are recent inventions where pedagogic practice is concerned, reflecting a particular phase in the development of education when the imperatives of accountability began to show themselves. It was felt, for instance, that the great virtue of the written examination was that it had the capacity not only to encourage the more conscientious application of scholarship, prompting higher levels of achievement, but that it was also fairer, impartial, less susceptible to corruption and more economical than the oral examination, a form of educational confession par excellence; moreover, it afforded the opportunity to control the university syllabus, restricting its survey to only that knowledge which was good and true. But, above all—and here again the gaze machine reasserts itself—it was felt, according to one of its apologists, that the written examination provided a 'daugerrotype' or photography of the student's mind (see MacLeod 1982). Moreover, the technology meant that the different attainments of students could be compared with one another, and be placed on a cardinal scale, one on which they were ranked according to their results.

Yet the alleged gains of the examination over previous modes of selection were, and continue to remain, largely illusory. The reality of examinations is that they tend to reinforce the status quo far more forcefully than perhaps any other educational invention. Far from facilitating a meritocratic reordering of society, the public examination, by its very nature and character, has tended to favour students of a middle class background; in other words, it has tended to perpetuate the same old success stories. One reason for this is that examinations, especially of the public and state type, tend to reinforce a narrow view of culture and knowledge, one which is aggressively middle class, male, white and Anglo-Saxon. Because much learning and teaching, particularly at the upper ends of high school, is centred on examination preparation, this tends to diminish the opportunity for local variations to the syllabus, which would more adequately reflect the interests and needs of the local student community. In an interesting analysis of English examinations in the United Kingdom, at the GCE and CSE levels, Barnes & Seed (1984) discovered, much to their dismay, that not only was the literary culture being examined mostly English, with a decided preference for the traditional canon (e.g. Thomas Hardy and Jane Austen), but that the language register demanded took no account of local and dialect variants of English. And this in a subject which was about communication! As if this were not enough, these same examinations are still used in some of Britain's ex-colonies (e.g. the Caribbean) as the primary vehicles of selection into higher education.

Another worrying aspect of examinations is that they tend to foster a certain view of knowledge and understanding. Not only do they constrain the curriculum, discouraging forms of educational exploration that are not exam-related, but they also encourage 'banking' forms of pedagogy, of the kind which are teacher- and answer-oriented. As a result, students can be left with a spurious epistemology, with the notion that all matters to do with knowledge and understanding have single and right answers, that they are essentially uncomplicated, with nothing to contest or debate. All epistemological subtlety tends to be obscured by the imperious demands of the examination, which tend to reduce issues to thirty-minute blocks of prose, as if all that needs to be written about the rise of Fascism in Europe during the 1930s and the role Picasso played in the establishment of Cubism can be said in such blocks. There is a tendency to eschew questioning and extended argument; students try to 'cue' into what the examiners regard as the ideal answer.

Yet the true condition of knowledge, as we saw in Chapters 1 & 5, is that nothing is less certain than knowledge, particularly in the humanities and the social sciences, where debate and controversy, polemicism and argument are the essential conditions of epistemological activity. These effects tend to be compounded by the fact that examinations place a high premium on memory, which requires that all issues and understanding be distilled into memorable proportions, into dimensions which can be transported into the examination room. Ong (1971) has suggested, in fact, that the three-hour examination is the last vestige of an oral culture, when the verbalisation of knowledge was indicative of learning, when mnemonic techniques were developed which enabled scholars to recall with ease and efficiency large bodies of prose and poetry without the assistance of the printed word. But the 'noetic abundance' of the book and the printed word, and now the electronic database, has transformed the processes of knowledge retrieval, reducing the importance of memory to almost trivial proportions. Indeed, these days it is the skills of a librarian and information technologist rather than a mnemonicist that are required for its retrieval.

Quantifying natural lottery effects

More or less contemporaneous with the invention of the examination was the emergence of psychometry, systems of psychological testing which provided general measures of a person's intellectual capacity and ability in selected areas. Throughout the latter part of the nineteenth century, there was intense interest in the basis of mental attributes, not just of genius, but also such alleged pathologies as criminality and prostitution, which were thought to have neurological origins. The popularity of psuedo-sciences such as phrenology (the nineteenth century's version of astrology) which attempted to establish links between the contours of the skull, particularly that of criminals and deviants, were the antecedents of modern-day psychometry (Gould 1991). Such investigations eventually led to the development of more sophisticated types of mental mensuration such as intelligence tests, which served to confirm the intellectual differences between human beings, and—more to the point—the degree of their distribution.

Hence such knowledge provided grounds for supposing that traits like intelligence were not in limitless supply but were restricted, at least in their uppermost categories, to a small percentage of the population. Thus it became imperative that the state, if it was to benefit from their potential contributions, needed to identify and isolate its most intelligent members for specialised educational treatment. Adding to the already large 'avalanche of numbers' (Hacking 1990) in modern society, an era began of widespread educational testing which encompassed not just intelligence, but also creativity, personality, reading and so on. It enabled students to be placed on various grids of specification, to be translated into quotients, scores, numbers and profiles of various kinds which augmented their school marks, serving to explain and corroborate them. Through these 'portable inscriptions of individuality' as they have been called (Latour 1986), the mentality of a student can be precisely calibrated and calculated and, above all, differentiated from others.

At the same time, there was interest in optimum development in areas of morality and cognition, which stressed that these followed phases and stages which every normal (with the accent on the word 'normal') child could be expected to pass through. Thus as the result of studies of child development by Piaget and Kohlberg, there was a heightened awareness of normal patterns of development. The overall effect of these psychological filtering systems—which were always in the hands of experts who, through their knowledge, had power to distribute individuals to different kinds of institutions—provided mechanisms for separating the normal from the abnormal, the deviant from the conformist. They also provided additional lenses for teachers which informed their 'normalising gaze', focusing its attention on forms of cognitive abnormality and social disadvantage.

But whatever form it takes, assessment—at least within the institutional setting of a school or a university—is results-oriented, tailored to produce an inscription of educational capacity and potential. The measures associated with it provide an indication of a person's cumulative achievements within the schooling system, and they figure prominently in such autobiographical statements as the curriculum vitae (c.v.), more commonly known in the school setting as a résumés. These have superseded the report and represent, in Foucault's terms, documents of confession, which incorporate important 'facts of life' and provides a 'detailed inventory of self', highlighting items, such as educational credentials, which have most 'exchange value' (Metcalfe 1992).

Assessment measures and scores, provide an autobiography of numbers, a text through which a person can be read, a convenient summary, in quantitative form, of their scholastic profile. Typically, these assessment measures are obtained at the various nodal points within the schooling system (i.e. the transition from primary to high school, from the junior to senior parts of high school, from high school to college or university), at points within the system where selection and differentiation of student population occurs. The principal function of assessment is that of sorting and sifting, and facilitating the creation of a meritocratic system, marked by the progressive elimination of larger and larger numbers of students from the schooling system. Assessment exists to limit the number of successes within the system; it is a form of population control within the system, designed to ensure that large numbers of educational careers terminate at those points beyond which they cannot all be accommodated. In other words, there is a close correlation between educational achievement and the number of places that exist for students at university and college.

Foucault regards assessment, or what he prefers to call the 'examination', as a central part of the schooling process, one which combines the observing hierarchy with the normalising judgement (Latour 1986). Examinations constitute a mechanism for observing and recording educational behaviour. In fact, Foucault sees a continuum between the medical examination and the educational examination. The teacher, along with the educational psychologist, practises a form of anatomo-politics, specialising in a mental anatomy that depends for its results on tests and examinations. But whether, in the end, these results constitute a real advance on phrenology is a moot point.

Schooling, in other words, has formalised the processes of human grading, of intellectual quality control, processes necessary if the allocation of scarce academic rewards (namely, university places) is to occur with a degree of efficiency, and with the full complicity of those participating in the process. It is a process designed to demonstrate that 'universal educability' is a myth—designed, in other words, to prove that capacity and potential are differentially distributed in every school population. While teachers can exert moral pressures on some to succeed and can intervene in the cognitive fates of others to ensure that they overcome temporary learning difficulties, the numbers game is such that a large proportion of students, along with their parents, must be convinced that their scholastic capacities are limited and unworthy of further development. Assessment procedures, along with psychometric tests, provide the pedagogic technology to do this.

A number of things follow from this.

First, it means that school work must be organised in such a way so as to improve or maintain the capacities of some students, while progressively diminishing or even exacerbating the capacities of others. As the system cannot tolerate a 100 per cent success rate, grading instruments must be devised that convince some of those to whom they are administered that they lack the relevant educability to pass beyond a certain point of schooling. Norm-referenced forms of assessment, which are still used widely and have staged something of a come back (Meadmore 1995), do this very effectively, for they are predicated on the assumption that, in every generation of students, capacity is distributed in approximately in the same way, along a normal or Gaussian curve (just as height and weight are), and that in every population sample of students there are approximately the same numbers capable of educational success.

In fact, the normal curve is a statistical ideal developed in the nineteenth century by Francis Galton, the father of modern-day psychometrics. According to its representation of ability distribution, no amount of effort or good and imaginative teaching will increase the number of successful students in a given sample. Yet why should intelligence and ability be normally distributed like other physical traits? As it is currently practised in many pedagogic situations, assessment is simply a mechanism for identifying successful students, for placing them on the bell-shaped ability curve, for corroborating a pre-ordained distribution.

Second, it means that, because we are interested in measuring the potential of students, and in differentiating such potential from that of others, when assessment is involved, students—as teachers constantly stress—are expected to work on their own, in private, without the assistance of others; indeed, when this occurs, students are penalised, and in some instances disqualified. The alternative, namely criterion-based forms of assessment, makes no so such assumptions about the educability of the school population, and assesses students in terms of their capacity to achieve certain pre-established objectives within a continuous program of learning. Theoretically, at least, a result sheet does not have to conform to any statistical ideal whatsoever. Yet the reality is that in circumstances where university admission is concerned, the results of such assessment are always subject to moderation via the normal curve.

More crosses than ticks: marking as a sign system

In that it does not contribute to any productive processes or economic system, classroom work has a special quality, different in character from most other forms of work. The long hours, both in and out of the classroom, that students spend completing projects or writing assignments is an extreme form of surplus labour, with few benefits or rewards other than those the teacher chooses to confer upon them, or that accumulate from the longitudinal processes of schooling. Its transient nature, its separation from real productive processes, epitomises the artificiality of much schooling, as well as how dissimilar learning in school is from the acquisition of learning that occurs on the job, in an officeplace or on the shopfloor, where the 'student' learns through participating in the 'productive' process and is assessed, not in terms of their performance in assignments or classroom tests, but in practising acquired skills and competencies.

As Lave (1988) has pointed out, there is, in fact, a world of difference between learning in school and learning in the real world and, as she discovered in her studies of supermarket arithmetic, there is no statistical relationship between classroom to the real world learning. Part of this has to do with the fact that learning is a whole body experience, involving much more that the mind, including the setting in which it is located. Practical intelligence is different from academic intelligence. In turn, the teacher's role in assessing the students' work is itself time-consuming and burdensome, involving the reading of and commenting upon, countless scripts, of staggering uniformity and unoriginality (Hextall 1976).

As examples of educational discourse, the objects of assessment constitute a distinctive genre, with special authorial properties and functions. The genre, as we have seen, also takes a variety of textual forms, ranging from public examinations through to objective tests, from essays through to practicums, and have a degree of co-authorship involved. The students, in most instances at least, are 'commissioned' to write an assignment on a topic the teacher sets, to complete a test the teacher has designed. After the text has been marked by the teacher, it is returned to the student: the marking constituting the full realisation of the genre. The genre is one which symbolises a literate culture in action, in which the written word in all its forms represents the transaction of learning, its material realisation, in which texts about texts, writing about writing, and words about words have become the ultimate yardsticks of capacity and competency. The essay epitomises this all pervasive mechanism for assaying of ability.

The genre is also associated with elaborate conventions and ceremonies, as well as a strict moral code. Most forms of assessment, for instance, take place against the clock or the calendar, requiring that a test or an assignment be completed in a specified period of time, with micro-penalties being exacted for those who fail to meet these deadlines. The public examination is a complex piece of educational theatre, surrounded with ritual and secrecy provisions, in which the examined are spatialised, according to preset parameters determining the distance that must separate the candidates. In this way their conduct in the examination room can be monitored and surveyed by so-called invigilators (a telling word in this connection), lest the moral code controlling the conduct of examinations be transgressed or violated. This code outlaws copying, plagiarism and other forms of cheating, for assessment is as much a test of morality as it is 'mentality'. Even the exam paper itself is full of 'terse commands' and imperious typography ('THIS EXAMINATION PAPER MUST NOT BE REMOVED FROM THE EXAMINATION ROOM'; 'CALCULATORS ARE NOT PERMITTED'), designed to reinforce the seriousness and forbidding nature of the occasion (Inglis 1985). The fact that examinations also take place in silence, in an era when silence exists in few other environments, adds to the atmosphere of intimidation. Indeed arguments could be mounted that the introduction of muzak into examination rooms might assist rather than aggravate students (who are now used to working with noise in the background) powers of concentration.

We have already noted that the production associated with assessment is exceedingly privatised, prohibiting forms of co-operation designed to assist the individual, that would detract from the assessment being a true measure of the individual's mentality. Interestingly, many working-class students resist the ethos of examination, refusing to co-operate with its 'secrecy' provisions, often copying from one another and deliberately cheating. Working class children, along with their families, have always tended to have an outlook on life characterised by co-operation and sharing, one which is dissonant with the 'bourgeois ethic of rational and methodical striving for personal achievement and advancement' (Humphries 1984; Miller 1986). Moreover, students would often deliberately fail school examinations in order not to extend their education in a way which might threaten the economic survival of their families.

The assessment regime also has a distinctive textual order. In the previous chapter, we discussed frame theory in conjunction with the architecture of schools, but it can also be applied to various textual and aesthetic forms (Uspensky 1973; Lotman 1977; Turner 1991). The most obvious example, and the one from which the theory derives its name, is a painting whose frame delineates the point at which a painting begins and the remainder of the world ends, so to speak, separating art from life. Analogously, the covers of a book and its title pages act as a kind of frame for literary texts. As within institutions, these frames act as a behavioural key, defining the range of what is possible within the frame and providing a an interpretive schema that predetermines, to some extent, the reader's expectations. Where aesthetic forms are concerned, the frame also renders the text or the artefact involved inviolable, so that its contents or form cannot be modified without authorial permission.

Assessment texts are also framed, though with somewhat different behavioural keys involved. Think of the way in which items of assessment are structured in terms of certain textual conventions.

Students, on their title pages, are asked to write their names, the class to which they belong and the name and subject of the item for which they are being assessed, to date and to number the questions they are answering, and so on. The item is set within specified margins, room enough for the teacher to comment or sub-editorialise the work involved. For, unlike most other textual forms, those of the assessment are not inviolable and sacred. From the teacher's point of view, the assessment genre is a complex semiotic, demanding distinctive forms of reading and writing. Examination scripts, essays and test papers are 'read' with a different modality and intent than those appertaining to other texts. They are not read in the way that short stories or magazine articles are—for the purposes of being entertained or informed—even though many assessment 'texts' can be informative and entertaining.

On the contrary, the modality of reading is much more judgemental than that prevailing elsewhere, and its closest analogue is to that of the editing and proofreading. The text is often received as an object of deviance, to be normalised, to be surveyed as an object of correction. Marking is another instance of the normalising gaze in action. The whole focus of the 'reading' is on whether an assignment topic has been answered, and whether the mode of answering displays the symbolic properties of good educational prose. The assessment gaze is normatively engaged, is ever alert to what is absent as much as to what is present; it focuses on manner rather than matter, with the way something is said rather than what is said. The reading is one in which the perception of errors and mistakes predominates, students being held to account for them. Fallacious lines of reasoning, non-sequiturs, solecism, sophistry and other deviations from rationality become the focus of negative commentary, a symbolic reminder that the thought and language patterns of students are being regulated and formed, another instance of the school's disciplinary regime in action. Lucidity and rigour in argument, as well as a responsive literary style, one marked with appropriate rhetorical flourish, seem to impress examiners and teachers (Markus 1974; Ozolins 1981).

The assayed text is thus always being measured up against a perfect answer, a 'pre-text', an imaginary exposition covering all facets of the topic, which the teacher as examiner has created and imagined, one which conforms to the patterns of Western thought, which obeys the laws of argument and conforms to the grammar and register of 'education speak'. This 'pre-text' exists in the teacher's mind as a vague mental image, an immanent text, more chimerical than actual, more ideal than real, that always shadows the assessment process, and which only reveals itself in the marking process, in the textual annotations and in the admonitions that the teacher appends to the work. Unlike most other kinds of 'reading', that of assessment is always accompanied by a pen: it is an activity in which the teacher is involved in a re-inscription process, in which he makes marks on, makes remarks on, and sometimes remakes, the text. The whole procedure of assessment has correctional overtones and admonitory features, and is yet another manifestation of the micro-penalty system which characterises much of school life (Pudwell 1989).

This 'over-writing' or metatext consists of a complex set of textual conventions, involving stock comments and ciphers, grading scales and abbreviations, designed to communicate to students the merits and demerits of their work. This metatext is often referred to, quite inappropriately, as 'feedback'.[3] It is an admixture of evaluative terms, exhortatory phrases and various 'diacritical' marks and strokes of the pen, a veritable shorthand of marks signifying praise and criticism. Other signifiers ensure that this shorthand is not taken to be part of the student's text, one being the colour of the teacher's ink (usually red), which is designed to stand out (Goffman 1975). The metatext consists of ticks and crosses, wavy lines of varying levels of intensity, questions and exclamation marks, through to full-scale explanatory accounts, usually in the form of an 'epilogue' to the paper, providing a page-by-page 'breakdown' of the work being assessed.

The 'fundamental particles' of the processes of marking are the tick and cross, whose signifying properties encompass the pass/fail opposition which is at the heart of all assessment systems, be they of a qualitative or quantitative kind. Everything else in the process is an elaboration of this opposition, designed to indicate the quality of the pass or the degree of the failure. The tick and cross, then, are the binary arithmetic of assessment, the basis of its calibration system. As a sign without words, a cross can convey a multitude of sins, everything from a spelling mistake to a passage of complete and utter irrelevance or unacceptable English. And the use of dashes and lines of various states of linearity and curvilinearity, not to mention question and exclamation marks, serve to locate more specifically the region of error and degree of inadequacy involved, major or minor. The tick, on the other hand, is a sign of general satisfaction, a response to an absence of errors, a mark of approbation, indicating that the text is more or less satisfactory, and that no major errors or weaknesses are apparent.

The commentary that these diacritical marks provide is mostly inferential. In using them to accent certain passages, the teacher assumes that the student (rightly or wrongly) is able to decode their significance, that she has, at some stage, learnt to translate them into meanings of various kinds. For of course the teachers cannot control the way their remarks at the end of an assignment are 'read' and received; much of the impact of this is felt, initially at least, at the psychological level, in raised or diminished self-esteem.

The language of assessment is extremely impactful, if only because much of it is imbued with moral colourations; indeed, many of the words used are employed in the evaluation of moral personality, causing an overflow effect (Urmson 1961). The language also tends to be broken and discursive, laconic and aphoristic, resorting to the idioms and cliches of assessment: the verbal equivalents of ticks and crosses. The communication is sporadic; it occurs in the margins and at the conclusion of the work, a correctional discourse that lays siege upon the textual territory created by the student. This siege occurs in manifold ways, usually (though not always) to demonstrate the inadequacy of a passage, either by putting a heavily scored line through it or rendering its opacity lucid, simplifying its convoluted constructions, respelling the misspelt, repunctuating the mispunctuated and so on. Much of the focus is on correcting, on eliminating deviance from the linguistic and rational norms. The commentary can be constructive and helpful, though mostly it uses the standard evaluative terms, terms which, as we indicated earlier, are the semantic equivalents of the symbols used in grading systems.

There is, in other words, a clear analogue between lexical and numerical registers used in grading systems, such that the evaluative words like 'good', 'bad' and 'indifferent' readily translate themselves into numeric or symbolic grades, and vice versa. The assessment calibration system, which can take a numerical or verbal form, is thus largely metonymical: numbers substituting for words and vice versa. A good piece work is the numerical equivalent of 7 out of a 10. The words of qualitative discourse, in other words, can be readily converted into quantitative forms. This, along with the belief that ability is differentially (to be precise, normally) distributed, is deeply embedded in the whole ideology of assessment.

It is not that these micro-practices associated with assessment are wrong in themselves; it is when they are allied to the disciplinary ethos of schooling generally, with its tendency to disempower, that their negative aspects are displayed. Too often, the nexus between learning and assessment is ruptured, and assessment becomes an end point rather than a catalyst for learning. The challenge is to make assessment part of the empowering process, so that correction and modification are creative and constructive, leading to the extension rather than the attenuation of learning.

The aesthetics of assessment

With the development of assessment techniques in which objectives and criteria are specified in advance, and achievement and learning are measured against them, the process has become increasingly fragmented, and part- rather than whole-oriented. This fact helps to further the cause of mechanising the process of mental development—the great false idol of contemporary education. Even subjects like art have not been able to resist this trend. Indeed, in order to defend their place in the curriculum, they have been pressed into employing supposedly more 'objective' approaches to assessment (Apple 1981; Aspin 1986). Such educational reductionism—and it is rampant in much pedagogic theory these days, and becoming more so as the competency movement gathers apace—is grounded in a false assumption, namely that the judgements involved in the assessment process can be totally objectified, that the subjective elements inherent in them can be removed altogether; in effect, that the processes of valuation can be rendered entirely objective and made part of the realm of instrumental rationality.

But, as with other epistemological processes, the examiner's inclinations and intellectual tastes cannot be discounted in the process of assessment, for they influence how the examined is perceived and apprehended, and finally judged. If an apparently neutral and very scientific process like measuring the wavelength of the colour blue is beset with subjective elements (Polanyi 1972), then the possibility of removing these from a much more subjective process like assessment are remote, to say the least. Of course, the move to criteria-based forms of assessment has cajoled teachers into specifying more clearly what they are hoping to observe in what they assess, but setting the criteria and judging whether they have been realised or not is a region in which a great deal of subjectivity can still be expressed. Particularly when a text of some kind is involved, the teacher's own rhetorical preferences and linguistic standards, as we have seen, are likely to be significant contributors in how an assessment item is assayed and eventually judged. There might or might not be some objective elements whose realisation can be attested to, but these are always offset by others whose merits and demerits reflect the values of the assessor as much as anything else. It is in this area that the assessor intrudes upon the assessed, in which judgements are fluid and open to personal modification, in which the scrutiny of the assessor is deeply embedded with her own values and predispositions, which affect how a work is perceived and ultimately assessed.

In fact, the whole assessment endeavour, particularly when it focuses upon work in which symbolic manipulation is involved, is closer to aesthetic valuation than anything else, and many of the responses involved are aesthetic in character and rely on a considerable degree of ethical intuitionism. These days it is common to assert that the features of aesthetic response are socially constructed, are products of particular historical and social formation. This response, which usually induces pleasure, tends to be engaged in contexts wherever there is elegance, coherence, structure, erudite asides, novelty, formal simplicity, wit and irony, pleasure and satisfaction, and work displaying these features is more likely to receive a judgement of approval than that which does not. So it is with classroom work: the attention of the assessor is more likely to be sympathetically engaged when the work being assessed displays aesthetic properties, and disengaged when it does not, even in subjects and disciplines like science and mathematics which are not generally associated with aesthetic presentation of a linguistic kind at least.

But this dimension has particular importance in essay and assignment work, where facility and skill with language is a form of aesthetic presentation. In emphasising this point, Bourdieu & Passeron (1977) have pointed out that the 'axes of differentiation' between students focus, much of the time, on the ability to apply rhetorical skills as much as they do on epistemological skills. In discriminating between two pieces of work, both of which adequately cover an assignment topic, the one displaying more linguistic finesse and grace, more aesthetic properties, is likely to be judged superior to the other. As such, the assessment process favours the adept wordsmith, those with an aptitude for the rhetorical flourish and the telling turn of phrase.

A final comment

In this chapter we have attempted to indicate that the processes of assessment are much more complex than many teachers and educationalists have acknowledged. The considerable effort to improve these processes, to render them more scientific and objective, is misplaced in that it fails to recognise that all processes of assessment are grounded in subjective judgements, judgements which are often more to do with measuring linguistic facility than content mastery. We have also argued that assessment involves a complex semiotic, depending for its effectiveness on particular 'modes' of reading and the interpretation of various assessment ciphers. The trouble is, much assessment is concerned with grading and ranking students, with facilitating the sorting and sifting mechanism that enables them to be more easily placed within society's occupational and educational hierarchy. The era of psychologism has tended to render these differences visible and demonstrable. Assessment is the place within the school, as we have said, where hierarchical surveillance meets normative judgement, where the school's spatial and temporal regime is married to making determinations about an individual's mentality and locating on a grid of human capacity and potential. For, above all else, it is through assessment and examination that we come to know our educational subjects, come to affix numbers and scores to them, so that their mentality is calculable, visible and recordable.

In effect, all assessment is directed to demonstrating that some students have a limited capacity for learning, with proving that their cognitive capacities are attenuated, thereby removing the need for the teacher to attempt to remedy the situation. While this remains the prime purpose of the assessment process, its use as a mechanism to diagnose learning deficiencies in order to overcome them, rather than to prove that they cannot be overcome, will always be limited. What we need in the classroom are modes of assessment that maximise success and minimise failure, that concentrate on qualifying rather than selecting students, that grade students in such a way as to upgrade rather than to downgrade them (Broadfoot 1979). As far as the previously described educational perspectives are concerned, assessment of the kind outlined in this chapter is highly unproblematic. The exception is the emancipatory perspective. The teacher committed to liberatory pedagogy and a critical curriculum would inevitably find assessment a troublesome and potentially contradictory area of practice, one whose precepts appear to undermine the aspirations of the emancipatory approach and are riven with manifold ethical difficulties.

NOTES

1. One recent innovation in school assessment is profiling, which at least permits pupils a measure of input into their profile, though Hargreaves has suggested such 'records of achievement', as they are called, do open the possibility for trimming and tailoring of pupils 'to the requirements of efficient employer selection and systematic social control'. See Hargreaves (1986).
2. The first examinations were in fact developed in Imperial China, in the fifth century BC, for admittance into its civil service. See Broadfoot (1979).
3. 'Feedback' is one of the modern clichés of the assessment lexicon. Appropriated from that of electronics, the word is in fact misused, for in electronics feedback signifies 'noise' or sound without information, which is precisely what feedback should not be!

Keywords and phrases

- aesthetic evaluation
- bell-shaped curve
- competency
- criterion-based assessment
- meritocracy
- natural lottery effects
- normal curve
- normalising gaze
- phrenology
- psychometry

Tutorial and field activities

1. As has been indicated in this chapter, assessment and evaluation are everyday activities, which we employ in a range of domains when we make judgements about films, music, clothes, books and individuals. Take one such domain and discuss the criteria that are used to differentiate the good from the bad, the exceptional from the mediocre in the domain.

2. Given that the processes of assessment are fraught with problems and that it is extremely difficult to produce reliable and objective criteria for measuring and ranking institutions against one another, particularly schools, should we be wary of the steps towards establishing educational league tables in which the educational performance of schools are ranked in terms of their capacity to produce students with high OP and TER scores? What are the possible dangers inherent in such ranking?

3. Examine some of the work that you did at school or have done at university, and look at the way it has been marked and

evaluated. Look at the marks in the margins and the comments that have been made on the work and about it. Are there some phrases and marks which are regularly used? Are the comments useful? Do you ever attempt to amend your work accordingly? Or is the 'feedback' of no use whatsoever? Identify some forms of assessment from which you have learnt something.

4   Discuss alternative assessment schemes and approaches to evaluation. Are there different ways of establishing whether someone has learnt something rather than writing an assignment or doing a series of exercises?

Education and 'The Risk Society': teaching with an ecological time bomb

... poverty is hierarchic, smog is democratic.

(Ulrick Beck 1992)

Booting up

Human culture has always been built around technology, satisfying basic needs such as food and shelter as well as higher needs such as art, transmission of knowledge and understandings. On balance, human beings have acquired considerable material security through the development of technology: it is generally perceived as 'progress'. However, in recent decades—the era of high technology, computer technology, space technology and nuclear technology—the peril of technology for human beings is becoming as apparent as its promise. The idea that technology necessarily leads to progress is one which should be treated with caution and circumspection. During its long association with human beings, technology has qualitatively changed. Yet there is a continuity between its initial manifestations in prehistory and those of the late twentieth century, with which technology is usually associated—the high-tech artefact such as the personal computer and the microwave oven. If by technology we mean an artefact which offers a measure of control over the forces of nature, then there is a continuum of sorts between the flint axe and the silicon chip. It is the divisions within this continuum that differentiate the technology of prehistory from that of the postmodern society (Kemmis 1987).

The functions of technology are best understood as extensions of the human anatomy, for extending its corporeal power and the versatility of its actions. Thus we can think of the spear (a relatively primitive form of technology) as an extension of the arm, as a form of prothesis, enabling its natural reach to be extended. The same applies to the lever and to more sophisticated forms of technology such as the wheel, which acts as an artificial leg, facilitating more efficient modes of locomotion and mobility. Analogously, information technology (and here we are thinking not just of the computer but also the book and 'primitive' calculators such as the abacus) is an extension of the powers of memory, permitting massive amounts of information to be stored and retrieved, across the generations of humanity (McLuhan 1974; Young 1988).

In this chapter, we examine the link between technology and education, which in some senses is a contingent one. After all, the maintenance and development of technology depends on certain types of knowledge and understandings being passed on from generation to generation, which is where education (which, as we saw in earlier chapter, helps to secure intergenerational continuity) enters the scene. But this relationship needs to be seen in other than functional terms. We shall argue in this chapter, particularly in its initial sections, that humankind's relationship with the technology is at a 'turning point' (Capra 1982) and the way forward for this relationship may be both qualitatively and quantitatively very different from that of the present. In recognising this, we need to see education as adopting less of a slavish relationship to technology, one where it is a handmaiden to educational needs, and more of a critical one in which the dangers of unregulated technological development are at the forefront of social concern. In short, education, we shall argue, will need to place technology in an ethical and moral context, at the broadest level possible—namely the global—in which the appreciation of the consequences of technological change are profound rather than superficial and in which every innovation is judged in terms of negative and positive contributions to the well-being of all species and the ecological health of the planet.

'The Risk Society'

Whatever the type of technology involved, be it the flint axe or the latest generation computer, the same attitude of mind, the same ideology, has led to its invention and production. We shall have more to say about this ideology later. For the moment, it is enough to say that this ideology, now all powerful, has produced forms of technology that now threaten the natural environment and its all too fragile biosphere. As we move into the next millennium this threat presents us all, especially teachers, with a major ethical challenge (see Chapters 7 & 9, Preston 1996).

At a less dramatic level, artificial intelligence and the amassing of huge databases on human populations, the 'mode of information' as Poster (1990) has called it, threaten to outwit human beings and pose threats for their civil liberties. Machines are doubling their intelligence every decade, while people are not, although the word 'intelligence' in conjunction with computers needs qualification. Computers do not think in the human sense of the word; they are only glorified filing cabinets, with an infinite capacity for storing and classifying information. Their capacities for thinking about that information are limited indeed (Roszak 1986). The discourse of ethics is being radically transformed by the world of biotechnology, raising issues to do with what constitutes life and death, paternity and maternity (Hepburn 1996; Rowland 1984; Wells & Singer 1984; Singer 1994).

To every technological innovation, it seems there is a dark side. The more technology dominates and manipulates nature and human beings, the more we are free from material burdens, but the more enslaved we become to the processes that free us. Despite this alarming outlook, we cannot overlook the benefits of technology. They are apparent when we visit the medical practitioner, use a personal computer to write an assignment or travel overseas. However, the point is that technology cannot be accepted uncritically and we should not confuse efficiency with progress or local and personal benefits with global and collective costs.

Nor should we be oblivious to the equity issues involved in the access to technology. Its main beneficiaries tend to be the inhabitants of the Western democracies rather than the nations of the underdeveloped world whose resources tend to be plundered and ravaged for the sake of maintaining the excessive and indulgent lifestyles of Westerners, and an increasing minority of them at that. As is increasingly clear, transplanting this lifestyle to the whole planet, as appears to be happening at the moment, particularly in countries like China, which have embraced Western-style capitalism hook, line and portable phone, will result in a 'culture of scarcity' which will inevitably endanger economic and social stability (Beck 1992). There are already signs that this culture, a legacy of colonialism, already exists, particularly in disease ridden and strife torn central Africa, which could be blueprint for the future.

EDUCATION AND THE 'RISK SOCIETY'

Whether we like it or not, the current lifestyle of the West (now being mimicked by the rest of the world) is edging the planet towards an environmental catastrophe of massive proportions, produced by an overuse of resources and a slow poisoning of the biosphere. This prospect, which seems more real than ever, has been caused through excessive pollution and the unmitigated development of natural resources; this, despite attempts to marry economic development with a sustainable economy and to render it benign in terms of its impact on the ecology of the planet. In effect, we are faced with developing a regressive, negative-growth economy, one which will place less of an ecological burden on the finite resources of the planet and its frail life-support system, and which will once again allow its natural capital to re-accumulate.[1] One of the positive offshoots of globalisation is that it has led to the establishment of world bodies with statutory powers to control the environment and to monitor any significant degradation in its health.

If all this seems unduly alarmist, we need to recognise that the Western view of technology is comparatively new, born of a link between a globalised capitalism and an anthropocentric view of nature. In Western societies, this view derives from an certain attitude of mind, which is central to the Enlightenment project, but in fact has its origins in the Judaeo-Christian tradition, in the myth of the Fall. In contrast to his prelapsarian situation, when man (and we emphasise man in this connection, for reasons that will be explained later) lived in harmony with nature, his subsequent nature was disconcertingly predatory, with a generally despotic attitude towards nature. In this tradition, the planet and its resources, in all their apparent bountifulness, exist for the benefit of humankind. On one reading the Bible gives authority for the human race to pillage the planet of its resources for the improvement of their material well-being (Birch 1975; 1990; Passmore 1974). The Puritan tradition reinforced this belief, with John Calvin arguing that God 'created all things for man's sake'. Further, as we indicated in a previous chapter, in the Western tradition there has been a tendency to be ambivalent in attitude towards nature, which has been contrasted with the more civilised and rational creations of human beings. Nature in this tradition was despised, regarded as primitive and undeveloped, something to be subdued and civilised, regulated and controlled, even exterminated. According to the seventeenth-century philosopher, John Locke, land, meaning wilderness, only became property when it was developed and turned into farmland.[2]

Thus has grown up in Western societies an anthropocentric view of the Earth and its biosphere, in which man has sovereignty over the planet, which is his natural dominion. With the development of science and natural philosophy in the sixteenth and seventeenth centuries, a secular foundation for this ideology was provided. Bacon, one of the first philosophers of science, summed up the power and direction of the new ideology when he suggested that nature, in order to be commanded, had first to be obeyed, meaning that its laws and conduct needed to be understood and decoded before its utility could be fully exploited. The importance of this insight in relation to technology cannot be over-estimated, for it recognised that in order for technology to advance, it needed to be tethered to science, the discipline most able to understand the laws of nature. Thus developed the techno-empiricism from which modern technology is derived, for modern technology, unlike its previous forms, is based around scientific insights and employ its laws and theories, and it is this which has given it unrivalled power over nature.

Bacon, along with other natural philosophers, also helped to further legitimate a predatory attitude towards nature, which went further than anything alluded to in the Bible. Before the emergence of techno-empiricism, the outlook towards nature was somewhat circumspect, characterised by a notion of stewardship: nature needed to be conserved and protected for the benefit of future generations in order that it could continue to provide us with our needs. When we talk of mother nature, it is this view of nature that is being alluded to—a nature that, like a mother, provides her children (in this case humanity) with their day-to-day needs. Such a view of nature, it has been argued, imposed a morality of restraint on the uses to which nature was put, to the extent, for example, that in the Middle Ages there was a reluctance to mine and quarry unless it was absolutely essential, on the grounds (no pun intended) that such practices actually violated mother nature and risked threatening her generosity and largesse. With Bacon and other seventeenth-century philosophers, this view tended to change and their writings display a wanton disregard for mother nature and her body, encouraging unrestricted use of the planet's resources. The Earth is depicted, using feminine metaphors, as a planet to be 'bound into service' and 'made a slave' of man (Easlea 1981; Merchant 1982). An added incentive to the Baconian outlook was the development of capitalism, especially in its most recent phases, wherein its continued expansion is predicated on the ever more bountiful production of material goods, using more and more resources, consumed in ever greater numbers, by more and more inhabitants of the planet.

The so-called conservation movement, in all its various forms, has begun to question these techno-empiricist discourses which have led to degradation of the quality of life on this planet, even to the extent of threatening its long-term survival. This movement bases its claims upon certain empirical facts in relation to environmental degradation caused by technology: that countless species are being rendered extinct; that important components of the biosphere, like the ozone layer, are being destroyed; that the destruction of rainforests is leading to an unacceptable accumulation of carbon dioxide in the atmosphere, the so-called 'green house effect', which is causing a general warming of the planet, and so on. These inescapable facts have led conservationists to the conclusion that the momentum of the technological juggernaut must be slowed down, perhaps even turned around, if the planet is to have any worthwhile future at all.

Because they have been widely canvassed in the media, these arguments have almost become clichés in late twentieth-century thinking, although this ought not to detract from their importance. But there is another way of treating our environmental obligations and duties, and that is via the moral and ethical claims of the natural environment. These have been studied by environmental philosophers who have suggested that, independent of any empirical arguments that might justify a conservationist (or as it is often called, a 'biocentric' or 'ecocentric') outlook, other inhabitants of the planet, such as animals and trees, have the same entitlements, the same rights to existence and the resources required for their support, as do human beings. The so-called Gaia principle is sometimes invoked, suggesting that the Earth as a whole is an organism in which every living unit is symbiotically related, indicating the need for a more holistic world view. Environmental philosophers are attempting, in effect, to restore a more organic view of the planet, one which places nature, the biosphere—not man—at the centre of things. This decentering is correlated with a set of duties and obligations to the natural world, which revolves around respect for all its organisms including cockroaches and crocodiles, not a select few like human beings, cuddly pandas and koalas (Elliot 1995; Elliot & Gare 1983; Taylor 1986).

Interestingly, one of the notable blind spots of both critical and postmodernist thinkers is any sustained appreciation of the environmental difficulties that face contemporary society. Their interest in technology has tended to centre on analysing the more generalised impact of technology, particularly information technology, on the cultural industries (Featherstone 1993), of which, as we mentioned in the previous chapter, education is an example. In its earliest phase, al theory took a special interest in the impact of radio on societies, it as a possible mode of indoctrination that made possible the ...se of Fascism and other totalitarian ideologies. T. W. Adorno (1976) was the consistent advocate of this view, even seeing within the rhythms of popular music and jazz the seeds of the authoritarian state.

This view has now been thoroughly discredited, though it lingers on in frequent assertions that the electronic media have led to the contraction of reasoning abilities and the willingness to engage in sustained argument. It is alleged that the electronic media, which place a special premium on keeping individuals attentive, on ensuring that they never lose interest in the narrative, have produced an audience of accelerated sensibilities, who are easily frustrated by more demanding activities like argument, reading, thinking or reflection. In short, not just television, but also rock music, and film, have made it difficult for teachers to cultivate the kind of reflectiveness that is central to the educational process (Aronowitz 1977; Shor 1980). It is also a view that is prevalent among more conservative critics (Bloom 1987), who have blamed the fragmentation of society on proliferation of popular culture.

Among postmodernist thinkers, Baudrillard (1985; 1989) has developed a special interest in the newer forms of electronic technology, television and videos and now the Internet, which he argues constitute the technology of the 'simulacra'. In his view, this technology has become the medium of the real—the 'irreal' and the 'hyperreal'—eclipsing ordinary, unmediated experience and replacing it with electronically processed reality, one which always appears to us through a screen of some kind. This has had the effect of creating a new cultural condition, in which reductionism and rational referentiality have collapsed, in which sovereignty has passed from the subject to the object (Baudrillard 1989). The coverage of the 1991 Gulf War was an interesting instance of the way the electronic media increasingly interpolates experience. It placed us in direct and immediate contact with missiles, with the war as it was happening, but the live coverage was screened in a depersonalised way, without victims; it was something akin to a video game, only the ammunition was live and the deaths real. The simulacra we were offered provided a reality of sorts, but it was falsified reality, one without pain and human suffering, one which ironically, in being so close to the war, placed it at a distance, making it just another spectacle, alongside the spectacle of one day cricket and the latest Hollywood blockbuster.

This also highlights the degree to which the cultural industries have created the 'global village', a one world culture, mostly emanating from the US. Indeed, Bauman (1992) makes the interesting distinction between the universal and the global. He suggests that the universal linked peoples, at least those of the West, through Enlightenment values such as rationality and autonomy, and the belief in freedom and equality; globalisation produces universality through a commodity base; it links the peoples of the world together, not through Kant and Shakespeare, but Coca Cola and Melrose Place, a dubious virtue to say the least!

In earlier chapters (especially Chapter 2), we noted the analyses of technocratic culture by scholars such as Lyotard and Habermas. Lyotard claims that the new information technologies are bringing about a transmutation in the nature of knowledge, while Habermas identifies the dominance of what he calls 'technical interest' in the political and social life of advanced capitalist societies, a dominance which reshapes popular moral values. If claims such as these are accurate—and we believe they are—then they are critically significant for every topic discussed in this book. Indeed, they indicate a revolutionary cultural context for the task of education, in which we must anticipate futures where, according to Roszak (1986), 'our children will be thinking in ways that we can't even imagine at the moment'.

Before we attempt to unravel further the impact of technology, it is worth noting that there is a long history linking education and technology. The emergence of mass schooling in the aftermath of the Industrial Revolution is one major chapter in the story which we have already told, as we think it is a crucial one in the development of the disciplinary practices associated with the modern school. Political and general community interest in education is often provoked by some perceived need to harness national resources for a leap forward technologically. So the alarm in the United States when the Soviet Union launched its Sputnik spacecraft in the late 1950s was felt in the classrooms of the nation: a renewed educational effort was demanded to 'catch up' technologically (Noble 1988). A similar concern is transparent in the current interventions into education by Australian governments, begun by Dawkins and now being continued in a somewhat more conservative vein by the Coalition. These initiatives require education and training to address the low skill base of the Australian economy, to make it more competitive technologically, as part of the general process of microeconomic reform needed if Australia is to participate in a globalised economy increasingly driven by the cultural industries (Lash & Urry 1994). These industries are education-dependent industries. Indeed the whole current economy is increasingly dependent on not just highly educated producers but also consumers as well, who are more likely to invest their surplus incomes in extending their lifestyle opportunities. This might occur through aestheticising their everyday lives, restoring houses and making them more comfortable with designer label furnishings, or through travel and cultural experiences, be they of a hedonistic or artistic kind (Featherstone 1990). The post-Fordist economy which is centred on niche-marketed products, in which design and look, and above all, symbol, have become as important as function and performance, reflects this emphasis on lifestyle profile, on the self as commodity.

These examples illustrate the political potency of technology: it fuels economies, and governs our lives to a point where the sophisticated mystery of high-tech may evoke an almost religious allegiance and veneration, altogether a pervasive and consuming culture. Yet this god-like eminence is not usually recognised by its devotees as a 'problematic force'; the demon within the god is often ignored. Indeed, technocratic consciousness generally and blindly addresses problems by seeking yet another 'technical fix' rather than questioning the idolatory of technology. Thus the problems of environmental degradation become problems for technology to solve, without ever contemplating lifestyle changes, aimed at focusing on the causes of this degradation such as reducing consumer demand. Instead, the focus is on further technological innovation in order to expand economic growth. The consumption of ever new and more novel commodities is the way in which the economy grows. Although most Western households have everything they need in order to survive and sustain themselves, the post-industrial economy requires the kind of originality that produces new forms of household gadgetry and new commodities, new artefacts that every household will eventually come to consider a necessity.

In the last two decades, there have been countless instances of such commodities that did not exist thirty years or so ago, that were not at all crucial in terms of the quality of life available to most people. The existence of videos, home theatre, compact disc players, personal computers, cellular phones and so on has not really promoted palpable improvements in lifestyle or increased the calculus of happiness in the community. These artefacts are not really needed; they are wants which the consumer economy has generated. And these days, most companies and corporations have large research and development sections given over to product innovation, to the marketing of new 'wants', that most individuals will come to 'need'. This is a new kind of technical intelligentsia, the mandarins of consumption, upon which capital increasingly depends for its survival and continued expansion (Gorz 1978). It is little wonder that, according to the dictates of economic rationalism, answers to social and ecological problems can only ever be conceived in technological terms, in making economies more productive and consumer-oriented.

The critical and emancipatory perspective undergirding this book refuses such an approach. Technology and its effects are problematic, of the severest and most alarming kind, and are not just material. As we have been discussing in the preceding chapters, technology has repeatedly been applied to measure, restrict, coerce and control human needs for space, work and use of time. Human technologies have been organised into networks of power by institutions such as schooling to 'domesticate' the lives of individuals, rather than to liberate them or, as Rose (1990) characterises the process, to 'govern the soul'. Hence we have made no apology for describing the school in this book as a form of technology, one for producing certain kinds of subjectivities and mentalities.

Out of work

In the era of 'high tech' or 'advanced tech', the stakes for human emancipation are even higher. The alternatives are sharp. Technology could reduce us to 'a sort of bee-like behaviour', routinely reacting to imposed systems and equipment; on the other hand, armed with political, ethical and technological knowledge and ability, human communities could choose to be architects of cultural forms which shape technological development to enhance human creativity and maximise human choice within the parameters of ecological responsibility. In other words, the choice is 'whether we intend to act as architects or behave like bees' (Cooley 1989). In particular, technology could liberate human beings from much of the drudgery and toil that demeans life, renders it machine-like and leaves many human beings with latent and dormant talents unchallenged and unrealised.

We believe, along with Marx, that technology should be directed towards enabling people to 'work less, live more'. As Gorz (1982) has argued in exploring this possibility, for the first time in the history of humankind, the advent of computer technology makes this dream realisable. For the fact is, this technology can produce everything we need and more: it is potentially many times more productive than any group of human beings could ever hope to be. Yet human beings continue to work longer hours and more weeks of the year in jobs which produce more frustration and alienation than satisfaction and fulfilment. The tyranny of the workplace under the combined regime of the desktop computer and the fax and the mobile phone has become more autocratic and dictatorial than ever it was under the worst excesses of Taylorism.

The fundamental conviction of our critical and emancipatory perspective is that technology is fashioned historically by men and women. We reject technological determinism, while recognising that technological processes can at times assume a self-generating dynamic. Fashioned within historical and cultural contexts as it is, technology is not ideologically neutral. It comes within a package of values and ideological norms, though it may of course influence and reshape those norms and values. By and large, certainly in the experience of societies like ours, technology has flourished in ideological and cultural contexts which may be described as capitalist and consumerist. Fundamental to capitalism and its consumerism is the maximisation of profits and the maintenance of an hierarchically structured society. In this context, technology exacerbates inequalities of power in society, instantiates competition as natural, as conducive to bringing out the best in individuals. What we are arguing is that, although contemporary technological systems impact powerfully on people and societies in the late twentieth century, power lies not in the technology as such, but in the alignment between the cultural values that are implied by these technologies (values such as efficiency, competitiveness, performativity and utility) and the supporting culture, which in the case of capitalism emphasises values such as acquisitiveness, growth, individualism and private property (Ellul 1964; Hill 1988; Jones 1982; Winner 1977).

This potent mix has ramifications for education. One obvious implication of technological developments is the change in the labour market occasioned by the structural adjustments necessitated by certain technological developments. It is often argued that though the employment profile of a society will be altered through technological developments, new jobs will be created to compensate for jobs that are lost. However, there are many studies which cast doubt on this prognosis (Apple 1988). Bluntly stated, the new technology has eliminated many more jobs than it has ever created; in fact, the figures of job elimination are staggering in their magnitude. In the United Kingdom alone, as a result of the word-processing revolution that the invention of the desktop computer facilitated, some four million office jobs have been destroyed, never to be replaced. Car manufacturing, once a labour-intensive operation, is now so efficient that assembly lines in Japan and the United States can produce 1300 cars a day with a mere 67 workers! As industries and businesses become more computer efficient, they can bypass the need for large labour forces, and have been doing so for the last three decades.

As the era of full employment fades into the prospect of some golden age, it seems likely that post-industrial societies are moving to a more complex stratification of the workforce in which there are even more potential losers. In the post-Fordist era, as we saw in the chapter on work, a new regime of flexible production and consumption contrasts with the relatively stable mass production and consumption of Fordism, characteristic of capitalism since the Industrial Revolution. Post-Fordist work and the fast capitalism with which it is associated, now requires a different kind of labour force, one which is flexible and multiskilled, devoted to the core values of the corporation (Gee, Hull & Lankshear 1996). In a British report, Leadbeatter describes a five-fold segmentation of the labour market in the wake of late twentieth-century technological changes: the long-term unemployed; those who suffer short-term unemployment; the peripheral workforce, a growing army of part-timers, temporary workers, home workers and the self-employed who are suspended in the grey area between unemployment and full-time employment; unskilled and semi-skilled workers; and, finally, genuinely core workers, permanent skilled workers with stable employment prospects—the aristocrats of the labour force (Leadbeatter 1987).

In practical effect, in certain national economies, particularly 'fourth world economies' such as Britain under Thatcher and Australia under Howard (Castles & Mitchell 1992), the result of post-Fordism is a workforce where roughly two-thirds do quite well and one-third are consigned to a perpetual insecurity of contracts, of part-time jobs and, in many cases, no jobs at all. What is emerging is a two-tiered labour force in which there is an 'aristocracy of tenured workers' and a growing mass of permanently unemployed, with a fluid group of temporary workers in between, who are required to be mobile and willing to move to localities where companies are hiring labour (Gorz 1982). As was argued earlier, the same patterns of labour mobility are operating on a global scale, with migration from third world countries to the West in order to satisfy the labour requirements (Waters 1995).

If social conflict and tension (which create the conditions for the emergence of the authoritarian state) are to be avoided, what is required is some radical redistribution of work, perhaps even the elimination of work as we have known it since the Industrial Revolution. Again Gorz is instructive here, suggesting that the working week should be contracted to twenty hours, which he suggests is plausible by the end of the century given the new technology, without any correlative reduction in productivity or even loss of wages. This would mean that everyone would work, producing the material necessities of life, and everyone would also have more free time to participate in the spheres of work that gave them genuine satisfaction, the work of the opus type described in Chapter 6 and over which they had autonomy and ownership of the means of production (Gorz 1985). In effect, this would mean a resurrection of the pre-capitalist mode of production, in which there was more free time than work time and in which social and non-economic activities predominated. But Gorz's paradise is also a post-industrial and anti-productivist world that has moved away from the debilitating 'ideology of perpetual growth', which in any case, as we have argued, cannot be extended on a planetary scale without posing catastrophic consequences for the biosphere. In other words, Gorz's paradise might seem like paradise, but in the circumstances of increased environmental and ecological degradation it really is the only viable option that guarantees any future for the planet whatsoever.

Further effects

Inasmuch as schooling is seen as preparation for this world of work or worklessness, the consequences of all this for educators are enormous. Technology has further profound effects with significant implications for the classroom. Technological developments have extended the range of human choices greatly and, with that, opened up many moral dilemmas, which an emancipatory approach would confront in the classroom. Because of technology, we can 'parent' children through a surrogate mother, but ought we to do so? Because of technology, we can travel into space, but ought we spend billions on such programs while millions of people starve on Earth? Because of technology, we can strip our forests for a range of convenience products, but ought we for the sake of future generations? And so on. Technological advances require of human communities more sophisticated levels of moral and ethical sensitivity.

Yet the disturbing paradox is that technology has resulted in a diminution of our moral sensitivity. We do what we can, not because we ought to, but because we can, and because we believe that some technology will fix up our mistakes if there are any. Technology creates choices, but not necessarily the freedom or ability to exercise those choices in terms of values which might generally be considered as ethical priorities, values like justice, equity, co-operation or care for the weak. Such values, as we have seen, are not high on the list of capitalist or technocratic norms. It is not surprising, therefore, that the more developed and technologically dominated society becomes, the more it is demoralised or amoralised. We might well ask whether schools have a role to play in responding to this consequence of technological development. The moral and ethical crises emerging in post-industrial, high-tech societies are surely another challenge for educators. This is one of the reasons we promote the case for ethics education in the next chapter.

An even more subtle and insidious outcome of technocratic rationality is 'technocratic mindedness', as opposed to 'critical mindedness'. 'Technocratic mindedness' threatens that critical, autonomous thinking capacity we have regarded as a necessary attribute of an educated, not just a clever, society. 'Technocratic mindedness' is characterised by an uncritical acceptance of the technological view of knowledge and hence progress. The question of the limits of economic growth is dismissed, as are equity questions related to this growth. There is a pre-occupation with measurement, prediction, control, efficiency and government by experts, and an undue veneration for the gadgetry and wizardry of technology of the sort we have already mentioned. Value issues—those in the realms of the political, the social, the educational and the ethical—get reduced to technical questions. The question becomes not whether A ought be done, but how A can be done. The minority who wield technocratic power, as well as the majority who are to be the passive consumers of the goods produced in the technocratic culture, are too often caught together in a mass of unconscious and uncritical apprehension of their reality, knowing no other way to understand it, for they are surrounded by a variety of anti-critical forces. Popular consciousness becomes false consciousness, desensitised and deficient in critical powers.

That is not to say there is not a latent discontent with the technocratic culture, sometimes evidenced in resistance to, and inversion of, consumerist values at a popular level, and even low-level subversion like stealing from shops, refusing to buy certain products, computer-hacking, developing counter-hegemonic forms of fashion and so on. These are characteristics of a rebellious consciousness, to use Freire's term, the embryonic expressions of counter-hegemonic practice.

SCHOOLS AND CLASSROOMS

Biting into information technology

So far we have talked about technology in general terms. Because the business of teachers includes storing and disseminating knowledge, they interface directly with information technology, from the book and the calculator through to its latest manifestation, the personal computer. The range of information technologies which impact on learning and teaching in society is vast, extending from the print media to CD-ROMs and from delivery systems now taken for granted, such as video cassette players, to international satellite-mediated teleconferences. However, it is the computer, commonplace in homes and offices, which has created particular opportunities and demands in schools and universities (Lanham 1993; Luke 1996). From the outset, we need to realise that the computer is only a mechanism for the storage of information. It is the latest manifestation of other mechanisms that have augmented our memory capacity, namely, the numeric and alphabetic system, the book and the printing press, which are the computer's immediate ancestors in terms of facilitating information storage in excess of the capacity of human memory.

We are not intending to report on or analyse at length the pedagogical or economic impact of computers. Luke (1996) provides an accounts of these, particularly in terms of the impact that the advent of cyberculture, the information highway and edutainment are likely to have on the schooling process. However, it is useful to give a brief assessment of the impact computers are making upon education. There is not a lot of evidence that computing has had a significant impact on students' learning, or indeed that it has actually altered the pedagogical environment. However, the potential for the computer-oriented classroom and lesson to alter teachers' work has been well documented. Harris (1982) and Apple (1998) have anticipated a product-oriented relationship between teacher and student in which pre-packaged units and computers seriously threaten the very basis of teaching itself. This might seem like the view of an educational Luddite but we can already see signs of this in the degree to which textbooks are technocratically evaluated for their capacity to teach competencies. Even the design and format of textbooks has taken on the character of computer graphicacy with button-style icons and window formats. Indeed, an American report of a Californian 'classroom of the future', actually in operation, describes the change of the teacher's role from 'information-giver' to 'information facilitator'. In this classroom, a high-tech teacher station replaces the teacher's desk; from it the teacher utilises network systems, to manipulate information, and to send individualised learning material to each student's desk, as well as to monitor progress and provide immediate feedback' (Larick & Fischer 1986).

Some might prefer to regard this as a re-skilling of the teaching role, but given that computerised knowledge packages are likely to lessen the importance of the individual teacher in preparation of materials, the overall impact for the average teacher is likely to be deskilling or, as Harris (1982) calls it, 'proletarianization', an alienating experience. In effect, to use an earlier concept, high-tech is turning the classroom into a Taylorised environment in which teachers are the mere 'executants' of a pedagogic process, whose skills and abilities have been relegated to those of the textbook writers and software programmers whose 'instructions' they increasingly operationalise.

The exacerbation of socio-economic, gender and race differences in schooling is another consequence of computer education (Luke 1996). A number of studies, including an Australian report, demonstrate that wealthier schools and boys have been the beneficiaries of increased computer facilities in schools (Atweh, Hickling-Hudson & Preston 1990). Apple's observations concerning the comparative lack of computer facilities in disadvantaged school in the late 1980s remain a concern. He reported that in the US two out of every three students currently learning about computers were boys and while over two thirds of schools in affluent areas had computers, only approximately 41 per cent of poorer public schools had them (Apple 1988). Of course, much more significant than the possession and mere usage of computers in schools is the way they are used. Again there is evidence that private schools and schools in more advantaged areas have more comprehensive and enlightened information technology programs, whereas a working-class school typically employs low-level, mechanistic and rote techniques in whatever programs are implemented. There is also evidence to suggest that boys, rather than girls, are the more consistent users of computers, which follows on from the fact that mathematics and science were the first subjects to embrace this technology, but also from the fact that girls have tended to find it difficult to find stations in computer laboratories, as they were usually dominated by boys (Collis 1987).

Another feature of the introduction of computers into schools has been the way in which the computer industry has tended to promote its wares at cut rates to schools and higher education institutions in an effort to corner the market for future sales of its products (Roszak

1987). The extent to which the computer and the computer industry can distort or transform the educational process is illustrated by an advertisement in a New South Wales promotion, 'In Touch with Secondary Education'. Under the banner 'Toshiba Supports Technology High School', we learn that Toshiba (Aust.) Information Systems Division sponsors (yes, that is the precise term!) Muirfield Technology High School (a public school) at North Rocks in Sydney (Connell 1993). The company uses the school's name and photographs of the school's students using its products in its corporate advertising. As the corporate agenda and the school agenda become interlocked, computerisation and privatisation go hand in glove, illustrating how the entrepreneurial and utilitarian approach to education is fostered by the technological imperative embodied in computers.

While the proliferation of computers in schools in this decade has been quite rapid and promises, with many governments committed to installing more information technology in schools, to be more so in the future, it has not generally been able to keep pace with the overall computerisation of society. Often, computer hardware has been virtually thrown at schools by educational systems without adequate preparation of teachers or any coherent curriculum policy to accompany the equipment. According to the Australian study (referred to above), this ad hoc policy development has resulted in a bias in computer education, so that computer competence becomes an end in itself rather than a tool to assist conceptual learning. In addition, the use of the computer tends to be concentrated on mathematics or business education courses, rather being transferred to the social sciences or other humanities. As a result, according to the same Australian study, it is less likely that the usage of the computer will be contextualised within a study that examines the social and ethical implications of technology (Preston 1992).

In our view, this is unsatisfactory, because questions of the technical correctness of what can be done with computers are not the most important issues for educators to address: rather, ideological and ethical questions concerning the purposes of education in an advanced technological society transformed by the information revolution are the fundamental ones.

From the emancipatory perspective, it is imperative that the curriculum ensures that students understand how information technology emerges from the military-industrial complex (increasingly organised on a global scale) of the most powerful nations. The Internet, it needs to be stressed, was a product of star wars technology, when the cold war was at its nastiest. Instead of contextualising information technology in this way, there is a tendency to reduce it to a set of mechanical skills to be mastered. When, for example, it is argued (as it often is) that students of the 1990s need to emerge from schools computer literate, this tends to mean that they should be familiar with keyboard skills and some programs, which are always undergoing revision and simplification. The era of user-friendliness means that computer skills can be self-taught anyway. The trouble is, the channelling of energies and ever-diminishing resources into what is a capital-intensive area is often at the expense of developing, even displacing, more important cultural literacies. The computer, after all, is only a tool, a complex filing system, a giant library catalogue, a memo-writing device, a super typewriter and calculator, nothing more. In the end, this tool is only as good as its user's skills, in writing, mathematics, history, art and so on; what do they say—'garbage in, garbage out'.

In our view, to be computer literate is to understand the full context in which this technology has evolved and the impact it has had on the political economy, on work, on the information and knowledge industry (Shor 1986). Anything short of this is computer illiteracy! In other words, we need to inform students that the educational applications of information technology are but a by-product of an industry which has a host of other facets—military, leisure, domestic and business. Furthermore, the curriculum needs to locate the computer, facsimile, the videotext, Internet and e-mail in an understanding of the social and industrial conditions in which actual production takes place. The vision of information technology as clean and scientific, providing unlimited access to information and information transfer facilities, glosses over the private control of such technology, as well as its use by secret intelligence agencies and financial institutions like banks to conduct surveillance of our financial habits. That vision ignores not only the often-unhealthy or exploitative conditions of its production in poorer Third World countries, where computer chips are made using cheap labour, but also the multinational corporations struggle for control of the industry, leading to information monopolies with massive centralisations of power causing social injustices, particularly within the cultural industries. Rupert Murdoch's manoeuvres on the global stage are particularly instructive in this regard.

There is another potentially insidious aspect of information technology to be addressed if we are to adopt a critical use of the computer in the classroom. By processing and packaging knowledge as information, the nature of knowledge is distorted, for knowledge is more than information. Computers are good at storing and retrieving data, but more data does not necessarily mean greater understanding. Information technology is just that, information and data: it is not a knowledge technology. As Roszak (1987)[3] reminds us, 'the mind thinks with ideas, not with information'; and it is ideas which are crucial in the knowledge-generation process. Information may inform or embellish ideas, but it does not create them. Ideas have priority in the evolution and maintenance of cultures. They are the core of cultural wisdom and keys to the extension of understanding. The data processing of information remains important, but the consequence of an excess of information or data may be to immobilise, distract or confuse, if there are no guiding and discriminating ideas. Roszak concludes that the principal task of education is to teach us how to deal with ideas: 'how to evaluate them, extend them, adapt them to new uses'. Even fifth-generation computers, which signal the prospect of artificial intelligence, remain a subset of information technology, rather than wisdom technology, a coupling which sounds rather strange. Wisdom cannot be commodified, as can information, which is then able to be bought, possessed, sold and acquired.

By reifying information, distorted pre-packages of meaning are applied to particular social contexts. Thereby, as we noted earlier, multinational corporate meaning suffuses the global village, producing an homogeneous international culture centred on technocratic values. Standardised information threatens to subvert cultural difference and diversity.

A further hidden aspect of information technology, and computers in particular, warrants exploration by educators. Weizenbaum (1981) has analysed other limitations of computerisation in a controversial book, which parallels many of the arguments explored by Roszak and to which we have already alluded. In Weizenbaum's opinion (and it is not a view shared by all those writing in the field of artificial intelligence (see Boden 1977)) humans can care and choose; computers, however, can decide but not choose, and they do not care. Arguably, education ought to give shape to the caring and choosing capacities of human beings. This could involve ethics education. As computers enter the education equation, it is worthwhile to remind ourselves of that. Not that computers necessarily dull compassion, but they are, as we have already said, part of a technocratic package with values oriented towards efficiency rather than compassion. A more important debate may be whether computers diminish our capacity to be critical thinkers.

Though the overall impact of technocratic consciousness in society may be to limit critical forces (Shor 1980), it is not at all apparent that this fault can be attributed to computer technology per se. Indeed, as Turkle (1984; 1985) has shown, as an 'object-to-think-with', the computer stirs up fundamental philosophical questions if we approach it critically, and can even aid in the formation of a reflective citizenry. The advent of the Internet and the World Wide Web, with their almost enormous resources of information, make the possibility of genuinely reflective citizenry more possible than ever.

Though it may be a popularly held belief that technocratic culture is antithetical to the pursuit of philosophy, we regard that view as highly contestable. Granted, those who promote technocratic processes (including some who are involved in computer education) may have a limited interest in, or commitment to, the pursuit of social ethics and philosophical analysis in any significant sense. Nonetheless, in the human community generally, there are signs that the cybernetic age, the post-industrial era, the silicon chip phenomenon, are all accompanied by reflections about the kind of society that we are constructing under the technological imperative. The growth in green consciousness is part of the evidence of a more reflective response in certain quarters. Technocratic culture is called upon to justify itself not only in relation to human beings, but also in relation to being itself.

At the centre of the new interface between technology and philosophising are old issues: What is it to be human?; What is mind?; What is intelligence?; What is consciousness? Questions of epistemological and ethical inquiry join the metaphysical interrogatives: What is the relationship of information to knowledge and, for that matter, to wisdom?; What is 'the good', the morally defensible, in all this? The ethical concern centres on wider and more profound questions than merely adopting a code of ethics for the computer profession. Though the controlling interests of technocratic culture might be reluctant to finance the pursuit of these questions in formal educational environments, the questions will not only not go away, they will become more urgent and more insistent, consciously and unconsciously, within the human community.

There are other positive assessments of information technology to be noted. As we argued in Chapter 1, analysts of the information revolution, such as Lyotard, remind us that, notwithstanding critiques of information technology such as we have just cited, the information revolution has undeniably altered human cultures. Lyotard prefers to emphasise the emancipatory possibilities of information technology. Its transmission through a transnational culture and its potential for individuals to access all sorts of information unlock a process which postmodernists in the Lyotard mould would say challenges state bureaucracies hell-bent on blocking the flow of information by reversing tendencies to centralisation. It may be that cultural shifts are taking place which will limit the controlling and coercive features of technology, but for our part, we cannot be as optimistic or as uncritical as some might be. Despite transitions in capitalism and the abandonment of totalitarian 'socialist' systems, it is clear to us that the dominant mode or packaging guise in which information technology is presented remains an hierarchical, aggressively competitive system dedicated to the accumulation of capital through the maximisation of profit. While contradictions will emerge and communications will raise the level of expectations of the underclass in various societies, such a system is unlikely to deliver technology which is liberating to the vast masses of human society as long as their access to capital remains at levels of relative poverty within their societies.

Altogether, information technology presents us with a strange mixture, a potion which is arguably both toxic and curative. Educators are confronted by an unavoidable but teasing dilemma: how are we to appropriate the benefits that computers and other information technologies offer to enhance the development of autonomous and critical thinkers while at the same time resisting its accompanying bias towards privatisation and individualisation, and its apparent bias against the social justice and social solidarity priorities, which our emancipatory and socially-critical perspective has declared?

Educational perspectives on technology

In our view, a satisfactory accommodation between technology and education is, at the same time, necessary, possible and difficult. The crucial ingredient in that accommodation is the way in which technocratic culture (the bearer of technology) is mediated into educational institutions and policy. It is our contention that this requires a focus on the emancipatory and socially critical approaches if we are to minimise the damaging consequences of technology in education. It is not a question of dismissing technocratic rationality and scientific cultures; rather, it is a matter of submitting these phenomena to 'the dialectical interrogation they deserve' (Aronowitz & Giroux 1985). Exploration of this claim is the task of this section.

There are those who resort to simplistic, conservative arguments based upon the vocational or economic instrumentalist view in their quest for an approach to education driven by technological developments. By and large, this instrumentalism is misplaced, not only because of its misunderstanding of education, but because it misunderstands the needs of the workplace and the effects of technology in the workplace (Watkins 1989). Computers have begun to occupy a high profile in most workplaces. There are few jobs or domestic activities in which some version of a computer is not required. But the point is, the skills required are elementary and unsophisticated, and can be quickly acquired. There is, therefore, no need for massive amounts of educational time to be devoted to computer training.

Given this scenario, it would be a distinctly mistaken view to endorse narrowly vocational or instrumentalist approaches to technology education which emphasise a training approach, or call for a concentration of 'hands-on' experience in schooling. Such an approach is unlikely to lay the foundation for what, arguably is of much more importance, namely, the careful scrutiny of technology, its options and the critically thoughtful approach to retraining and re-education throughout life which the advanced technological society actually requires.

On the other hand, the therapeutic or humanistic perspective outlined in Chapter 3 is no adequate response to the technological imperative either. Its focus on personal growth may, at best, help individuals to cope with change in much the same way that aspirin helps the individual cope with a brain tumour. What is required is an educational approach that confronts rather than avoids the issues of technological development, in a way that enhances the human capacity to shape these developments, and places them in the service of the community rather than the corporation. Historically, the liberal argument has been offered as the alternative to instrumentalism (Marchello 1987). However, its pre-occupation with the preparation of students to move into society to strive for the preservation of what is essentially human and humane now appears as a shallow and inadequate response in the face of technological rationality and the evident impact of post-industrialism superstructures.

While the general education of the liberal tradition opposes the extremes of technocratic culture and jealously guards the freedom of individuals under threat in a bureaucratic technocracy, it may not of itself provide the social analysis which specifically engages technocratic culture. Indeed, liberalism's penchant for individualism may reinforce the individualistic ethos associated with technology in a capitalist society. On the other hand, the contrast between technocracy and liberal views may be so sharp that it prevents liberal education from appropriating the benefits of technology; more likely, liberal views will be experienced by the student as lacking relevance to their cultural experience, so setting up either a type of cognitive dissonance or an outright rejection of liberal and culturally transforming values. One may conclude that the liberal orientation is not an adequate perspective within which to address and incorporate technology in education. The civilisation and civilising ideas of the Enlightenment, once defended by liberalism, are now subsumed in, and are even challenged by a technocratic consciousness. Technology and technique are offered as the basis for social, political and ethical choices, and indeed, for rationality itself. So powerful is this agenda that to question it seems absurd or incredible.

Quitting

Clearly any approach to education which fails to accept or seriously engage the impact of particular technologies and the technocratic culture is bound to be ineffective and redundant. On the other hand, we believe it is possible to design and implement policy, curriculum and pedagogical practice based on the dialectical view that schools are both the products and producers of society, and that education does not only reflect society and its values, but also shapes the knowledge, values, social relationships and practices that constitute a society. This view is consistent with the emancipatory perspective or socially critical perspective advocated throughout this text. We grant that, in the face of technological imperatives, this cannot be any soft or naively Utopian emancipatory view.

In the final chapter, we will make specific reference to pedagogical strategies for a socially critical use of information technology in the classroom. Teachers and educational administrators informed by this view will take particular care for the way in which technocratic culture is incorporated into educational institutions. Such an approach will address the fundamental social and ethical questions emerging in contemporary, technological society: the future of work, equity and justice considerations, the widening of concepts of literacy to social and political literacy, the encouragements of ecological sensitivity, the recognition of the limits to growth argument, as well as the general critique of technology outlined in this chapter. Above all else, they will bring critical-mindedness to bear on technocratic-mindedness because critical-mindedness, cultivated through questioning, dialogue, analyses and action, may restore the reflective and communicative modes of human interaction threatened by the impact of technocratic culture (Bullough, Goldstein & Holt 1984). Nothing less will equip students for the changes of the imminent millennium.

NOTES

1. Underlying this view is the 'limits to growth' thesis which was first canvassed by the Club of Rome in the late 1960s and discussed in Schell (1982). Although its computer models were discredited, the basic thesis that the planet can only support a finite number of human beings and that untrammelled development can continue only so long still stands. Indeed, in the past decade the thesis has been resurrected, with greater urgency than ever. David Suzuki has been the most ardent exponent of negative growth economics, although his views have been foreshadowed by Illich (1979), Heilbroner (1965) and Boulding (1965). Ted Trainer (1985) has attempted to discuss the educational implications of such thinking.
2. This is one of reasons why the Australian Aborigines' claims to land rights were treated with contempt. Because there was no evidence of agriculture in Australia, the continent was regarded as a *terra nullius*, and therefore no one owned it (Reynolds 1989). Hence its invasion could proceed without any necessary negotiation with the owners of the land, because legally the Aborigines had no property! This has been a core issue in the High Court decision to recognise native title.
3. Roszak discusses the notion of 'the master ideas' which, in the end, do not depend on information, yet they are critical to the formation of cultural movements and the evolution of human society. He cites as an example of a master idea: 'all men [sic] are created equal'. In his view, the cult of information may obscure the great ideas.

Keywords and phrases

- anthropocentric
- biotechnology
- consumerism
- fast capitalism
- techno-empiricism
- technocrat
- technocratic
- technocratic-mindedness

Tutorial and field activities

1. Compare the computer and information technology facilities of schools in the government and non-government sectors. Either survey your tutorial group or telephone a sample of schools in each sector. Establish the numbers of computers per student in the school. Try and find out whether the school requires (many in the non-government sector do) that their students possess a laptop computer as a condition of enrolment. Should there be wide disparities between the computer resources of schools, what are the likely consequences of this on educational outcomes, particularly in a world where computer facility and literacy are likely to be mandatory prerequisites for work in the near future.

2. In the light of the impending ecological crisis, how should schools become more environmentally conscious? What practices have you observed in schools (include universities as well) which suggest that they are? Could we imagine an eco-school, a school which recycles its waste and is self-sufficient in resources and energy? (see the Tvind school as an example, which is discussed by Castles & Wüstenberg 1979). Develop an environmental policy for such a school. This should also involve a transport policy, covering the transport of students to and from the school.

3. Find out more about some recent catastrophes, e.g. Chernobyl nuclear fire, Exxon Valdez oil spillage. Consider how these illustrate the dangers of unregulated technology and the responsibility to the planet and its future generations. What implications do these awesome events have for us and teachers and citizens?

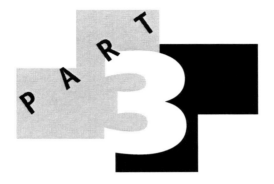

From discipline to emancipation

Education for a change: some reflections for practice

> ... social reconstruction does not just happen, but rather social practice and social transformation are the products of human agency.
>
> (Kevin Harris 1996)

A recapitulation

Over the last eleven chapters, we have traversed a large amount of educational territory. Our intent has been to demonstrate that the everyday practice of schooling is imbued with a cultural etymology, one that has a long history and is complex in meaning. We have done this purposely to show that schooling is neither an asocial nor an ahistorical phenomenon, but is one with a complex genealogy, which is steeped in allusions and references to the past, to our cultural inheritance, to the deep subconscious of the Western tradition, and to the structures of society.

We have also attempted to demonstrate the continuity that exists between school practices and those of other important spheres of human endeavour, like work. We have tried to show that it is impossible to isolate schooling from its context, from its contact with other institutions in the complex fabric of modern society. In essence, we have suggested that schooling as a moral technology, as a technology of the self, has been instrumental in generating a disciplinary society, a society of subjugated subjects who enact their own subjugation in their daily practices. But the production of this society has also been accompanied by the production of difference for, particularly in its most recent phase, schooling has been, in large measure, a technology concerned with the selection and categorisation of human beings, with the ascertainment of their abilities and their allocation to appropriate forms of education. Difference, in effect, means not just a different social position, but also a different epistemological background. The goal of difference with deference, which is the underlying motivation governing modern schooling, has been supported by the sciences of pedagogy. These have provided ascientific basis for classifying and categorising, normalising and treating students, for segmenting the school population in terms of its intelligence and degrees of normality—be it of a moral or mental kind.

Throughout this book, however, we have counterposed this disciplinary regime of school with a regime we have called 'emancipatory'. In marked contrast to the former regime, the latter is concerned with releasing rather than attenuating the potential of human beings and the transformation of society according to a vision of social justice. We have argued that the oppressive regime of schooling, which reflects the oppressive nature of society, needs to be confronted, unravelled and deconstructed, and replaced with a regime like that of the emancipatory one which acknowledges each individual's authenticity and right to a fair and just repertoire of educational experiences. Moreover, the emancipatory approach recognises that schooling is a political act which cannot be separated from its social functions without presenting a false impression for all those involved. As an instrument of social advancement, schooling is deeply flawed, dominated as it is by a meritocratic system which rewards the children of the already successful, leaving the unsuccessful untouched by the opportunities that the schooling system affords. In this sense, the modernisation of society to its most radical degree, meaning one broadly based on egalitarian principles, which school is supposed to have assisted has failed and failed to a degree of magnitude that is disappointing in the extreme. Maybe, as it has been argued, most notably by Hunter (1995), such 'principled accounts of schooling' are romantic and idealist, and fail to analyse the degree to which schools are an 'improvised reality from the available and governmental technologies' as a means of coping with immediate and dire contingencies.

The chapter on the 'risk society' is different from earlier chapters in that it tries to sketch a scenario of the future rather than that of the past. It is plain that this scenario, with its dark and sepulchral backdrop, requires a radically different kind of human being, a new kind of human subject. As we place our feet on the doorstep of the twenty first century, at the beginning of a new millennium, the profile of the future is pessimistic, to say the least. With the prospect of an ecological catastrophe, the collapse of the Third World and the urgent need for a sustainable economy grounded in an ecology that builds rather than destroys natural capital, there is, more than ever, a need for social critique, of the kind that we believe the emancipatory perspective is most able to generate.

If this chapter is briefer than the rest and has adopted a more sermonising—some might say evangelical—tone, it is partly because we believe that summing-up chapters should be brief and to the point, minus the qualifications and caveats that tend to occur when more didactic objectives are uppermost. It is also our view that the action for pedagogical change which our approach invites cannot be simplistically itemised or spelled out like a menu or a recipe: to that extent, we can point in action-implying directions, but in large measure teachers, in conjunction with each other and the educational community, must experiment and make their own practical paths forward.

Setting guidelines for practice

Having reached this point in the book with some detailed analyses of what schooling is like and why it is that way, it behoves us now to examine what schooling could or ought to be like, if we took the emancipatory perspective seriously and deployed it as a general pedagogic and societal practice. Insights discussed in Chapters 3, 4 and 6 are especially relevant here, as they describe ways to overcome the problems in the disciplinary approach outlined in Part 2. But a word of caution: we need to recognise that education, of all pursuits, is trapped, as Usher & Edwards (1995) have suggested, in its own logic and agendas, practices and ideals. By definition, education always involves a considerable degree of control and constraint, government and governmentality, discipline and deference. On the surface, this makes the call for the application of more utopian ideals based on emancipatory logics free of the disciplinary imperatives seem somewhat contradictory, not to say impossible. In short, education, of whatever kind, will always be in danger of hoisting itself on its own petard: emancipatory objectives will always be inhibited by disciplinary ones, and vice versa. The point is to recognise the limitations that are inherent in the very idea of something called education, and to work around and through them.

In Chapter 6 we outlined a normative basis for evaluating school practices and educational policies. We spoke of justice as fairness, which sometimes needs to apply the principles of affirmative action or warrantable discrimination on behalf of the most disadvantaged in society. As a fundamental premise, social justice is critical for emancipatory pedagogists. When other goals, such as efficiency, excellence or even equal opportunity, are posed for school development plans or macro-educational policy—and, in effect, for classroom practice—emancipatory pedagogists would use the benchmark of social justice to evaluate these goals and plans. They ask of every practice and policy, 'Who will benefit?' and 'Who will be disadvantaged?', and they select their options according to a view of justice which will reallocate resources (in every sense of the word) for the benefit of society as a whole, with particular concern for the poor and the disadvantaged. In this ongoing task, emancipatory educators insist that the burden for greater justice in society should not be placed too directly on educational institutions; governments and citizen groups must initiate wide ranging policies to create social justice in the community. So whatever program of reforms we point to in this chapter, and whatever the reader is inspired to attempt in a school or community setting, it is our view that justice as fairness is an important touchstone for making choices.

In an important text which should be read alongside this chapter, McLaren (1989)[1] indicates other touchstone criteria for emancipatory educators. We would agree with him that all programs and practices developed from this perspective should take the problems and needs of the students themselves as the initial starting point of a curriculum program. The emancipatory approach is not primarily concerned with the ideological or political correctness of the teacher's point of view. Indeed, the correctness or otherwise of this point of view might have to be modified in the light of student experience. Though this concern may create conflict in most school systems, an emancipatory school agenda is responsive to the agenda of students, whose lives and values have been, in large measure, framed by popular culture, by videos and rock music, commercial television and the Internet, American sport and fast food. Knowledge must be meaningful to students before it can be critical. If this is one test teachers can apply to measure their effectiveness as critical educators, the complementary measure is whether their teaching is empowering, sharing authority with students, experiencing the 'we' of learning rather than the 'us and them' mode of interaction prevalent in disciplinary schooling.

The emancipatory teacher's fundamental role is to empower students to become their own teachers, by revealing to them the questions and problems which beg interpretation in their own experience and to engage in critical dialogue between self and society.

This is what we mean by being counter-hegemonic. None of this means abandoning the classroom to anarchy or abrogating a commitment to the traditional curriculum; on the contrary, it implies negotiated order and purpose, a discipline springing from within the classroom community; to be empowered is to be responsible, and irresponsible behaviour is counterproductive in the emancipatory classroom, although it must be analysed and understood (Freire & Shor 1987).

So we are offering these guiding questions for any teacher who adopts our preferred perspective:

- Are we being fair and just, especially to those who are often excluded—namely those students who drop out or miss out?
- Are we taking account of the students' point of view and experience?
- Are we adopting empowering measures or power-coercive measures?

There are other supplementary questions those faithful to the emancipatory agenda might pose. One to which critical teachers must be sensitive is, 'How does my teaching or this policy respond to the need to protect the environment and cultivate an ecologically sustainable society?' More and more, such a question deserves priority.[2]

Critical pedagogy

Mainstream schooling, as we have argued, has been dominated by a disciplinary orientation, one dedicated to the disempowerment rather than the empowerment of students. But alongside mainstream schooling, there has always been a radical tradition which has seriously questioned orthodox pedagogy, drawing attention to its inhumane treatment of children and its failure to recognise the preconditions of efficacious learning. Some of the celebrated names of educational theory: Vives, Erasmus, Comenius, Locke, Rousseau and Dewey are part and parcel of this tradition. Its modern representatives are figures like A. S. Neill, Dora Russell, Sylvia Ashton-Warner, R. F. Mackenzie, John Holt, Ivan Illich, all of whom sought to overturn conventional school practice, highlighting, among other things, its irrelevancy and its tendency to violate the natural desires and instincts of children. The emancipatory perspective has inherited this tradition, sharing with it a general concern to ameliorate the conditions of schooling and the experience of being a student in the late twentieth century.

But, unlike some previous exponents of the radical tradition, the critical pedagogues confront the political dimension of schooling, recognising the role it plays in the generation of an oppressive society, and that pedagogical transformation necessarily takes place in the mainstream. It also has a more collective than individualistic viewpoint, eschewing the do-your-own-thing perspective that is characteristic of much radical education and which, in effect, reinforces the logic of individualism that runs rampant in modern society (Cagan 1978). Nonetheless, we would want to preserve from this tradition the need for a more 'convivial' type of schooling, as defined by Illich (1978), one which is marked by a more caring and thorough-going humanity than is characteristic of the 'manipulative', highly bureaucratised and anti-democratic environments that many large schools now exhibit. We find some of Starratt's (1994) ideas on the constitution of an ethical school also compelling. Starratt argues that an ethical education should be underpinned by a multidimensional framework combining an ethic of care, an ethic of justice and an ethic of critique.

We have argued that much of the oppression that pervades the modern school originates in the hidden curriculum, in its spatio-temporal regime, which was intended to produce a specific kind of subject who, in the face of postmodernism, has outlived its usefulness. We need to expose this power dimension, to bring its capillary network to the surface, and to contest its assumptions and lay bare its contradictions. For this network is only a construct, and if it restricts the consummation of the learning process, it should be modified—maybe even abandoned—so that the episodes of learning are freer and more natural. Learning does not have to occur in a school, especially when schooling inhibits its acquisition. There have been schools without walls, where learning has been situated in the community, away from a disciplinary institution, where learning has involved travelling, studying cultures and work directly, and being self-sufficient while at the same time being responsible for a group's well-being (Bremer & van Moschzisker 1971; Castles & Wüstenberg 1979). The computer also offers the possibility of adding new, non-institutionally based dimensions to the educational process.

Where time is concerned, the same criticisms apply. Like school space, the timetable can also be disabling rather than enabling, particularly for students not used to working against the clock. For instance, Shor (1980) has argued that the timetable is often at loggerheads with the attainment of real education, not allowing enough time to generate the kind of argument and debate which is central to the acquisition of a critical disposition, particularly for students who are not used to concentrating their mental energies on such things. The clockwork approach to schooling needs overhaul where working-class students are concerned.

There can be no arguments against this, because the system is being subverted and sabotaged by these same students anyway. The timetable might as well be officially abandoned given it has already been abandoned by these students in practical terms. The whole form of schooling thus needs close scrutiny, to determine whether it is really conducive to learning in a postmodern age. The whole texture and textuality of the classroom may need attention, with reform being directed towards the practices of teachers modifying them in such a way as to reduce their 'didactic, lecturing tones' in favour of more conversational and idiomatic approaches that are more aligned to studentspeak (Freire & Shor 1987).

Nor can the content of schooling escape the purview of reform. For critical pedagogues also recognise the social and cultural conditions in which late twentieth-century schooling is located; these are very different from the nineteenth-century ethos which still permeates the curriculum and its content, as well as its extra-curriculum. To be specific, they recognise that the modern student is immersed, virtually from the moment of birth, in popular culture, in rock music, in soap operas, in fashion and in consumerism, in a culture which is more powerful in its impact than that of education. Teachers need to deal sensitively with this culture, to show that its elements can be deconstructed and re-envisaged in a way which can lead to the reform of social relations, can be a catalyst for radical re-imagining.

Popular culture, from soap operas through to rock music, can be used as a way of entering into the hearts and minds of students, and way of thinking about gender roles and their renegotiation (Gilbert & Taylor 1991). It can be 'problem-posed', connecting with the unpopular culture of schooling. In the long run this is a more empowering process. What is needed is a pedagogy which is situated in the lives and culture of our students, which problematises the everyday, and which addresses their world in a meaningful and significant way. This need not mean a capitulation to presentism, to the world of the here and now, for in addressing situated themes, the critical pedagogue can move to their historical and social underpinnings, as a prelude to a more critical perspective on them, one which addresses the praxis dimensions of learning.[3] This is the very obverse of the liberal perspective, heavily indebted to Plato's idealism, which eschews the everyday on the grounds of its transient nature, and it is also different from the instrumental perspective which tends to accept the everyday uncritically and to ground the curriculum in terms of human capital needs of the economy.

Assessment is a critical area for the pedagogue to address since so much in the student's life is dependent upon it. Drawing on Freire's theories, Broadfoot (1979) has suggested giving the responsibility for the content and method of learning and its evaluation to the pupil. By doing so, we would establish praxis in the learning, allowing the student to define issues and learning tasks through the interpretation mediated by his or her own culture, to retain the essential creativity of all kinds of work in using a range of skills at his or her own discretion. We would thus not alienate the learner from the products of her labour by putting an external (commodity) value on them in the form of marks and grades based in dominant cultural standards.

By allowing the learners themselves to create rather than receive knowledge, they will develop their own critical consciousness and a valuation system based on a dynamic relationship between their own experience and the wider reality of history. In contrast to other approaches which see assessment as the end point of learning, critical pedagogy seeks forms of assessment which are integral to learning.

Feminist pedagogy can also provide many lessons for the critical pedagogue. As with the emancipatory perspective, it tends to emphasise the importance of basing classroom learning around the immediate propensities of the learners rather than the teachers, in allowing the curriculum to be generated from, rather than imposed on, the learners. In line with this, it also has a commitment to non-competitive forms of assessment, to co-operative forms of learning which encourage achievement in the whole constituency of learners, not just a few. Feminist pedagogy is also committed to non-hierarchical classrooms of the cultural circle kind, based on democracy and parity of esteem, where the teacher tends to wither away as the circle gains confidence in its learning powers and its capacity to execute control over its own education.

In addition, feminist pedagogy tends to be committed to more holistic approaches to learning, where there is none of the fragmentary epistemology characteristic of male-stream tradition, where reason and feeling, body and mind are dichotomised (Gore 1993; Schneidewind 1987). A further insight of feminist pedagogy identified by Taylor (1989) which can be translated into the teaching of all disempowered groups, is the development of a sense of collective identity—rather than the cultivation of individual identity that is characteristic of educational perspectives other than the emancipatory.

In an area like computer education, a pedagogy based on the critical and emancipatory perspective (Atweh et al. 1990; Bigum 1987) would double-check to ensure in any class using computers that:

1. students are becoming aware of the social effects of computers on individuals and society
2. as a means to learning, not an end in itself, the computer is an empowering tool for students
3. the benefits of computer education are presented as a social good not an individual possession
4. questions of equity are addressed in school organisation, and
5. there are closer links between computer education and the social sciences and humanities rather than simply the mathematical or commercial subjects, as is widespread current practice.

Altogether, the critique of technology would be a higher education priority than technological competence in an emancipatory pedagogy, though it would not rule out the latter. Computer technology can also be a valuable aid in the fostering of supportive networks between emancipatory teachers, for instance, enabling them to exchange and develop software packages alternative to those supplied by corporate interests. This is even more possible with electronic mail systems and web-site pages, which all schools should develop.

That is not to say that there are not worthwhile innovations generated from other perspectives happening in mainstream schooling. Indeed, innovation has become the norm rather than the exception in the schooling system, and 'making it new' has become a kind of panacea. Yet much of this innovation is dominated by vocationalism, as in the Senior College movement in Queensland, which is part of the TAFE system. We are not opposed to vocationalism as such, particularly as we have argued that there is a strong link between schooling and work. It is fatuous to pretend that students do not expect employment as one of the outcomes of schooling, particularly in a decade where jobs are becoming scarcer.

However, it is possible to engage the discourse of vocationalism dialectically, as when business education—an area which has expanded considerably in the ethos of economic rationalism—is re-imagined in the light of different kinds of practices, in non-capitalist forms which are not dominated by profit or the market. This is what we mean by extending the limits of possibility within the frameworks of the prescribed curriculum. The curriculum is both disabling and enabling, and the emancipatory teacher exploits the latter.

On the other hand, vocationalism is no substitute for a good general education, even a liberal education, for the trouble with vocationalism is that its outcomes are always of limited duration and value, particularly in an era of technological innovation and change when skills are prone to go out of date very quickly. It is better to be generally rather than specifically prepared for the world, and we agree with defenders of the liberal perspective that the contents of such education provide the kinds of epistemological foundations required for all types of employment and situation. The best kind of vocational education is, in fact, a liberal/general education, along the lines advocated in the Myer Report (AEC 1992), which stresses the importance of a convergency between theoretical and vocational forms of knowing.

Moreover, we certainly cannot abandon the traditional subjects or academic goals. We are going to need, in spite of some misplaced postmodernists who argue the contrary, scientists and technologists in the future if we are to overcome our problems. But we need new sorts of scientists and technologists, whose outlook is located in a strong moral and ethical frame, who recognise the limits of science and technology (Toulmin 1990). The same is true of economists and social scientists, who need to understand the context in which their practices are located and applied. In short, Lyotard's performativity needs to be displaced by a strong ethical sense, by an awareness of the public good.

The fostering of this strong ethical sense presents a formidable challenge and opportunity for radical teachers. We believe that higher priority should be given to moral or ethics education in school curricula and teacher education. However, the implementation of this is fraught with the possibility of distortion and damage. It is a controversial area requiring care in the classroom. The challenge to emancipatory teachers is to develop ethics education within a socially critical framework; otherwise it will easily degenerate into the moralistic and disciplinary—something which will do little to contribute to the construction of a fairer world (Beck 1990; Preston 1994; 1996; Stradling, Noctor & Baines 1984; Strike & Soltis 1985).

The transformative teacher

It may be time to reconceptualise the profession of teaching as a 'vocation' or, better still, a 'moral trade' (Connell 1993) rather than simply as a career. This is because teaching is one of those social practices which involves an intrinsic commitment to the public good, characterised by ethical responsibility. Of course, if teaching is so valuable in our society then it is necessary for society to value the practice and to demonstrate this through employment conditions that are commensurate with this role. Nonetheless, it behoves teachers to reflect on their role in ethical terms.

There are teachers and teachers. The kind of teachers we are profiling are dedicated to a transformative agenda, in which the conditions of educational oppression are reformed progressively. They also recognise that schooling is political and political action is needed for its reform. Such teachers, in the words of Giroux & McLaren (1987), have a 'social conscience' and a 'social consciousness'. Thus, the transformative teacher will involve himself in many domains and attempt to intervene in many sites, not all of them necessarily pedagogical or educational. The most local site of all is, of course, the teacher's own classroom, which will be a venue of fairness and social justice, of collective responsibility and democracy, of mutual accountability and respect, of moral and ethical integrity, where the limits of possibility are exploited to the maximum and to the advantage of the disadvantaged, to those who are earmarked to lose in the educational system.

But it also important for such teachers to assert the transformative agenda in other forums: in syllabus committees, in staff meetings, in curriculum associations, in those venues where change to practice is legitimated and encouraged. It is also important for teachers to involve themselves in trade unionism, in order to enhance and optimise their working conditions. Unions are important institutions, in spite of recent legislation to minimise their presence and impact, in the fabric of the modern state and it seems that their role in the future, with award restructuring and enterprise bargaining as parts of their new agenda, is likely to impinge more on the classroom and not just in terms of wages and salaries. In this situation, where the performance of teachers is ever more subject to scrutiny, it is important that unions define and articulate what adequate performance actually entails, so teachers' performance comes to encompass matters to do with social justice and equity.

The transformative teacher is also one able to bring the skills of education to bear on civic and moral issues. Something as trivial as writing to a local newspaper constitutes the kind of action we have in mind. At a more significant level, though, such a teacher would involve him/herself in local political action, in protest activity such as preventing a threat to a local environment, where their skills and intellectual accomplishments can be used to assist other members of the community to promote causes and instigate political action.

Teachers also need to establish solidarity with other 'progressive workers' in the community, with social workers, with librarians (their nearest allies in terms of promoting knowledge acquisition) with the medical profession, with public servants—with whom they share interests in common, particularly where establishing a transformative agenda is concerned (Giroux 1981; Freire & Shor 1987). Just as there are disadvantaged schools, so too there are disadvantaged hospitals, often in the same locality; in this respect, teachers share a community of interest with nurses and doctors, and also with the community at large. The teacher's responsibilities, then, do not cease at the classroom door or at the school gate.

In effect, what we are talking about is the teacher as one of Gramsci's 'organic intellectuals', working alongside students and parents, mobilising political action in the community, raising its consciousness about inequitable practices. Aronowitz & Giroux (1985) have taken Gramsci's category and typified the 'transformative intellectual'. They identify four categories of intellectual within the educative environment. First, they speak of 'accommodating intellectuals' who, in effect, support the dominant society and its ruling groups, and often have access to the mainstream media. Talkback radio hosts, who nurture reactionary views in the community, are a good example. Second they speak of 'critical intellectuals' who have an alternative ideology and critique of society, and who adopt a self-consciously apolitical posture, which avoids activity to change society.

Many academics at universities, who occupy positions of privilege and potential influence, and who have multifarious skills, fall into this category. They then identify 'hegemonic intellectuals' who intervene and provide leadership on behalf of dominant groups and classes. Those who occupy positions in right wing think-tanks and advise conservative governments are typical examples. Fifth, they speak of 'transformative intellectuals' who advocate and actively work for emancipatory change and cultural transformation; the contradictions and tensions such intellectuals or teachers experience within the formal educational institutions in which they generally work require a counter-hegemonic outlook and strategy. The lot of the transformative intellectual is to engage in the kinds of struggle and resistance which are the forerunners of reform and renewal. They are sustained by a sense of Utopia, not as an unrealistic nowhere, but as the necessary hope referred to in Chapter 4.

Thinkers like Gramsci, and later Giroux, call for intellectuals who consciously work with an oppressed minority group (e.g. an isolated, rural group) or class to improve their situation and plight, to extend the arms of justice and fairness to embrace them. This means not just working within the framework of the school, but also in the community at large, adjusting the reins and horizons of its consciousness, to embrace the vision of a better and fairer world. In this sense, being an intellectual means having a strong commitment to ideas and their distribution, a function that is doubly necessary within small towns and the bush, far from the metropolitan centres of thinking and cultural activity. Teachers are often the only trained 'intellectuals' in such places, so that they need to extend the services of themselves as educators of students to the community at large.

In this connection it is appropriate that we indicate how teachers are to maintain themselves as intellectuals—to keep themselves in the peak of mental condition, to use an aerobic analogy. It goes without saying that teachers must keep themselves informed, and not just about their teaching subjects. After graduating, unless they engage in further study, the chances are that they will never examine another text of this kind, which deals with critical and social theory, and which shows the links between education and the broader society and culture. We believe this is sad for a number of reasons.

For a start, this theory is always evolving and changing, undergoing paradigmatic transformation and extension, not all of them necessarily for the better. So how are teachers to keep themselves in touch with developments in theories and ideas which enlighten the practices of education? One obvious way is to enrol in a postgraduate program of some kind. But that is a fairly dramatic step, and one which is fairly demanding in terms of time and effort. We would point out that at a time of 'diploma inflation' (Dore 1976), perhaps diploma hyper-inflation, which depresses the long-term exchange value of credentials such as undergraduate degrees, most teachers will be required to undertake some form of postgraduate study, if only for career advancement purposes.

In the meanwhile, the better solution is simply to read and listen, which is what most study amounts to anyway. But read and listen to what exactly? Aside from the research literature, which is not always readily accessible to teachers in remote locations, far away from university libraries, the simplest thing to do is to read magazines and journals of the literary and socio-cultural kind, of which there are a number in Australia. Then there is the Internet, which offers a veritable cornocopia of sources. In addition, there are often radio and television documentaries which critically analyse societal as well as educational issues; the emancipatory teacher will aim to be informed through these media discussions.[4]

Furthermore, involvement in various social-change agencies and in environmental and political movements can help teachers stay informed and retain a critical sensitivity, to contextualise their work as educators. Participation in social action through community groups, as well as trade unions and subject associations, facilitates praxis knowledge which is crucial to the emancipatory approach.

Some lessons for teacher education

There are some lessons here for teacher education. Teacher education faces a crisis in the 1990s under the impact of economic rationalist reforms, such as those initiated in Australia in higher education by the Labor government and which have continued under the blitzkrieg policies of the Coalition government. There are those like Sharp (1990) who see little reason to defend academic faculties of education, and then there are those whose technical interest in reorganising university education is putting an even greater strain on schools of education, ensuring that they are confined to the lowest status amongst tertiary studies. We believe that the resistance and counter-hegemonic mode of the emancipatory perspective outlined in this chapter—especially pertinent if teacher education is to make its mark as it serves both schools and society (Ginsburg 1988).

The arguments canvassed in this chapter, and throughout this book, are not much in favour at the moment in teacher education, which is increasingly becoming more performance-oriented, more instrumentalist in character. There is a tendency to remove courses in philosophy, sociology and history (which we regard as central to teacher education) from undergraduate programs, in favour of concentrating on teaching techniques and curriculum design. This has its place and value but not if it is conducted in the absence of contextual studies.

In praxis terms, the concentration on the action polarity of the dialectic is at the expense of the reflection polarity, at the expense of considering questions to do with power, discourse and culture. In practice, this is manifested in teacher education courses which are, for the most part, crammed full of busy work projects, developing materials with no conscious attention to the theoretical considerations underpinning them. In the long run, such approaches only lead to the 'proletarianisation of teacher's work', to its deskilling, to a reduction in its status (Giroux 1988).

Without even discussing the methodological flaws in this tendency, which are legion and grounded in questionable epistemological assumptions (Cherryholmes 1988), such educational reductionism, popular though it might be with the technocrats, removes the consideration of classroom issues from a contextual base. To appeal to technocratic rhetoric, such approaches are shortsighted on the grounds of efficiency alone. As it is the contextual texture of schooling which interferes with efficient learning, a lack of appreciation of this texture will lead to greater school inefficiency, not less.

Further, such approaches to teacher education lead to an intellectual deskilling of the teaching profession which, on any grounds apart from that of political neutering (which some of course favour), cannot be justified in terms of what is required of teachers in the late twentieth century and beyond into the new millennium, even by conservatives. But if we accept the emancipatory agenda of this book, then teachers need an intellectual education of the broadest sort, embracing sociology, ethics, philosophy and history, which places them in contact with the social origins of education, with the range of ideologies and discourses that have governed and are governing, and will likely govern, Western society and its institutions like education. Teaching and the values of education to which it is finally accountable, in other words, requires a synthesis between action and reflection; as a profession, teaching is praxis incarnate.

A coda

In this chapter, we have argued for an emancipatory approach to schooling. We have suggested that more than ever—given the problems, both social and ecological, which are more likely to become commonplace in the twenty-first century—we need citizens with a critical outlook, who are able to combine technological skills with political and ethical responsibility. Hence our faith in critical theory which, unlike postmodernism, retains a faith in the possibilities of history, in the agenda of the Enlightenment. This means more education, not less; moreover, it means education for more people, not less, and it means a more intellectual education for these people, including teachers. Deference with difference is no longer enough.

The benefits of education need to be distributed in a more egalitarian fashion, and used in ways that are not for the purposes of self-advancement alone. Moreover, the disciplinary society is redundant in troubled times. Compliance and deference in the face of global problems are no longer appropriate. We need individuals who will demand alternative social and economic orders, who will have the imagination and the skill to turn their intellectual energies to a sustainable future.

The problems of the twenty-first century have a social and technological character, and require a merging of the emancipatory interests of philosophy with that of science. But they remain fundamentally the problems of the human species in our relentless quest to make lives that are more satisfying, to make a more worthwhile culture and to rid it of its most alienating features. Our technological and social constructions mean that this quest is even more problematic for the 'risk society' of the twenty-first century. This realisation contains the fundamental challenge for teachers. Unless they take up this challenge, we are doomed, and the end of history and society will be somewhat more than a mere paragraph in a postmodern text.

NOTES

1. McLaren's discussion is particularly illuminating because it contains extensive journal entries from his actual teaching experience with young people from the underclass in an inner-city Toronto school. It is worth noting that most discussions of actual classroom practice from critical pedagogues focuses on the teaching of the disadvantaged. There is a need for fuller detailed discussions of counter-hegemonic teaching in mainstream schools.
2. For an excellent discussion of classroom environmental education, see *Education Links,* 37, Summer 1989/90.
3. In the critical pedagogic tradition, Freire's work is central and the idea of problematising the everyday, of starting with the concrete reality of the learner, is pivotal to his approach. See Freire (1985). See also Giroux, Simon et al. (1989). But a most concerted attempt to discuss critical pedagogy in the arena of the classroom is Shor (1980) which should be mandatory reading for all teachers.
4. Instances of literary and media resources include *Meanjin* and *Overland*. To them one could add *Arena Magazine* which is a more politically engaged magazine, with a genuinely 'left' editorial policy. *Education Links* does something similar where schools are concerned. In terms of the emancipatory approach, the *Critical Pedagogy Networker,* from the School of Education, Deakin University, is an essential resource. We suggest that a subscription to *The New Internationalist* would be relevant. It also useful to establish an account with a good bookseller, one who issues regular catalogues of recent releases, with annotated titles to provide an idea of

the contents of books. We also have great faith in the informative power of ABC radio and television, yet another important public institution under the threat of the Sword of Damoclese, massive budget cuts, but whose programs provide oodles of nourishment for the culturally famished. The great virtue of these programs is that they traverse so much territory, from science through to education, art to politics, and everything in between. The Open Learning programs are an obvious source of enlightenment for teachers, but might we also suggest Robyn Williams' incomparable *Science Show* as a starter, and the book review programs on the ABC like *Books and Writing* and *Book Talk*. And, as a way of finishing the day, nothing quite rivals Phillip Adam's *Late Night Live*, which always has challenging interviews with avid thinkers from around the world. From time to time, Australian progressive thinkers publish readable works which chart alternative futures for Australian society. Such books can stimulate the classroom teacher's vision beyond the present and the particular. Recent instances of such publications are Camilleri (1989); Gollan (1990).

Glossary

Ancien régime   a period of European history immediately preceding the French revolution.

Capitalism   the description of an economic order (our economic order) dominated by the imperative of profit and capital accumulation, in which the law of the market prevails, and which is characterised by a set of exploitative social relations based around class and gender.

Conscientisation   a term used by Freire to indicate the process of awareness raising which results from learning in a praxis mode. Freire postulated four levels of human consciousness: magical consciousness, naive consciousness, rebellious consciousness and, in the advanced stage of awareness, critical consciousness. The process of moving between these stages is described as conscientisation.

Deconstruction   an oft-practised activity these days, it refers to attempts to analyse the human subject, discourse (q.v.), to highlight its protean and contradictory character, to show the disunity in its apparent unity, to show multiple voices in texts, multiple dimensions of human subjectivity, etc.

Dialectic   a word which has special significance in Marxism, especially in conjunction with 'materialism', which expresses the notion that everything is in a state of continuous transformation, arising from opposing and contradictory forces.

Discourse   a term from linguistics and post-structuralism, referring to what is said and thought in the exchange of ideas, from the trivial remark to the prepared oration, from the memo to the academic paper. Discourse is guided and shaped by rules which help shape what are called 'discursive practices', and these are regulated differently at different times and places. Discourse analysis is concerned with analysing such things. Discourses are also the range practices which produce modern subjectivity.

Enlightenment   refers to a period of European intellectual history, beginning in the early part of the seventeenth century and ending in the nineteenth century, when there was a belief that reason should be the absolute ruler of human life.

Epistemology   is one of the sub-disciplines of philosophy which is concerned with establishing the conditions and foundations of truth and knowledge, with establishing the conditions under which we claim to know something is the case.

Ethnography an approach in sociological research concerned with recording and analysing in the field the nature of institutional life, and the experience of the 'actors' within it, through interview—in other words, through special attention to their interpretations of the way that life is perceived.

Globalisation describes the processes of cultural unification which are occurring across the planet at the moment, particularly in terms of culture and the media. It also describes much of the political unification which is also occurring, leading to larger and larger political groupings, centred around economic activity.

Hegemony refers to those processes by which the ruling class establishes and maintains its rule with the consent and compliance of the subjugated class, the working class.

Hermeneutics is an important part of critical theory, and refers to a style of critique centred on the unravelling of meaning, particularly in the basic forms and categories of everyday life. It is a sort of phenomenology (q.v.) applied to words.

Historiography is the art and method of recording history.

Humanism is a tradition of Western thinking which has been dominant since the Renaissance and which has given a prominent place to rationality in its epistemology, to the recognition that culture in the multiplicity of its forms can lead to human perfectibility.

Marketisation describes the processes by which public sector activity such as that associated with schooling is increasingly subject to market processes and critieria. This is manifested in advertising and concern about image.

Meta- as in meta-theory and meta-narrative, denotes a theoretical analysis of theory, narrative.

Metaphysics is the branch of philosophy which deals with the nature of things, with their first causes.

Patriarchy a term much used in feminist theory, it refers to social arrangements like our own, in which men dominate women, in which power relationships always favour men, delivering higher status and position to them.

Phenomenology is the name of an approach to philosophy which focuses on the phenomena which flood consciousness in a way which suspends preconceptions and predispositions about them.

Polity is the word which gives us 'politics', referring to the complex of institutions within the state responsible for law and order, government and bureaucracy.

Positivism is one of the earliest forms of social theory which believed that social life could be understood empirically and, once this was so, societies could be organised on a more rational and scientific basis. Partly because it eliminates the need for critique and reflection, positivism is now a term with pejorative overtones.

Post-Fordism refers to a type of work practice currently being adopted across technological societies. It needs to be seen in conjunction with Fordism, which was developed on the Ford assembly lines in the 1920s and was associated with a job for life. Under post-Fordism the workforce will experience a range of jobs and responsibilities in their lifetimes and is required to be flexible, mobile, better educated and multi-skilled.

Praxis a term common in Marxist discourse, which refers to activity of a theoretical and active kind which leads to the reformation of practice and society.

Semiotics originally a branch of linguistics, semiotics, or the science of signs, deals with representations and codifications of meaning in sign systems, especially in the media and literature.

Teleological refers to doctrines like Marxism and Christianity, in which ends and purposes pre-dominate, in which the movement of human societies is towards some evolutionary goal or other.

Utopia literally 'no place', refers to the depictions of idealised societies like those described by Plato, Thomas More and William Morris.

References

Abercrombie, M. L. J. 1974, *The Anatomy of Judgment*, Penguin, Harmondsworth.
ACTU/TDC 1987, *Australia Reconstructed*, AGPS, Canberra.
Adam, B. 1995,*Timewatch: the Social Analysis of Time*, Polity, Cambridge.
Adams, H. 1995, *The Education of Henry Adams*, Penguin, Harmondsworth.
Adelstein, D. 1972, 'The Philosophy of Education or the Wit and Wisdom of R. S. Peters', in T. Pateman (ed.) *Countercourse: a Handbook for Course Criticism*, Penguin, Harmondsworth.
Adler, M. 1982, *The Paidea Proposal: an Educational Manifesto*, Collier, New York.
Adorno, T. W. 1976, *Introduction to the Sociology of Music*, Seabury Press, New York.
Anderson, D. & Vervoorn, A. 1983, *Access to Privilege: Patterns of Participation in Australian Post-Secondary Education*, Australian National University Press, Canberra.
Anthony, P. D. 1977, *The Ideology of Work*, Tavistock, London.
Apple, M. 1981, 'Curriculum Form and the Logic of Technical Control', *Economic and Industrial Democracy*, vol. 2, no. 3, August.
—— 1982, *Education and Power*, Routledge & Kegan Paul, London.
—— 1985, *Education and Power*, Ark, Boston.
—— 1986, 'National Reports and the Construction of Inequality', *British Journal of Sociology of Education*, vol. 7, no. 2, pp. 171–90.
—— 1988, *Teachers and Texts: A Political Economy of Class and Gender Relations in Education*, Routledge, New York.
Archambault, R. G. 1966, *Lectures in the Philosophy of Education 1899 by John Dewey*, Random House, New York.
Arcilla, R. N. 1995, *For the Love of Perfection: Richard Rorty and Liberal Education*, Routledge, New York.
Arendt, H. 1959, *The Human Condition*, Anchor Books, New York.
Ariès, P. 1962, *Centuries of Childhood: A Social History of Family Life*, Vintage, New York.
Arnold, M. 1973, 'Culture and Anarchy', in G. Sutherland (ed.) *Matthew Arnold on Education*, Penguin, Harmondsworth.
Aronowitz, S. 1977, 'Mass Culture and the Eclipse of Reason: The Implications for Pedagogy', *College English*, vol. 38, no. 8, April, pp. 768–74.
—— 1988, *Science as Power: Discourse and Ideology in Modern Society*, Macmillan, London.
Aronowitz, S. & Giroux, H. 1985, *Education Under Siege*, Bergin & Garvey, Boston.
Ashenden, D. & Milligan, S. 1996, *Good Universities Guide*, Mandarin Books, Port Melbourne.

Aspin, D. 1986, 'Objectivity and Assessment in the Arts: The Problems of Aesthetic Education', in M. Ross (ed.) *Assessment in Arts Education: A Necessary Discipline or a Loss of Happiness*, Pergamon Press, Oxford.

Atweh, W., Hickling-Hudson, A. & Preston, N. 1990, *Social Ethical and Practical Implications of the Innovation of Commuter Education in Queensland Secondary Schools: A Research Report*, Queensland University of Technology, Brisbane.

Australian Education Council (AEC) 1991, *Young People's Participation: Post-Compulsory Education and Training (Finn Report)*, AGPS, Canberra.

Australian Education Council (AEC) 1992, *Putting General Education to Work: the Key Competencies Report (Mayer Report)*, Australian Education Council and Minister for Vocation Education, Employment and Training, Canberra.

Australian Human Rights and Equal Opportunity Commission 1989, *Our Homeless Children: Report of the National Inquiry into Homeless Children*, AGPS, Canberra.

Bagguley, P. 1991, 'Post-fordism and Enterprise Culture: Flexibility, Autonomy and Changes in Economic Organization', in R. Keat & N. Abercrombie (ed.) *Enterprise Culture*, Routledge, London.

Bailey, C. H. 1984, *Beyond the Present and the Particular: a Theory of Liberal Education*, Routledge & Kegan Paul, London.

Ball, S. 1990, 'Management as Moral Technology: A Luddite Analysis', in S. Ball (ed.) 1990, *Foucault and Education: Disciplines and Knowledge*, Routledge, London.

—— 1993, 'Education, Markets, Choice and Social Class: the Market as a Class Strategy in the UK and the USA', *The British Journal of Sociology of Education*, vol. 14, no. 1, pp. 3–19.

Ball, S., Hull, R., Skelton, M. & Tudor, R. 1984, 'The Tyranny of the Devil's Mill: Time and Task at School' in S. Delamont (ed.) *Readings on Interaction in the Classroom*, Methuen, London.

Bantock, G. H. 1980, *Dilemmas of the Curriculum*, Martin Robertson, Oxford.

Barcan, A. 1980, *A History of Australian Education*, Melbourne University Press, Melbourne.

Barnes, D. & Seed, J. 1971, *Rhetoric, Romance and Technology*, Cornell University Press, Ithaca, New York.

Barrow, R. 1976, *Common Sense and the Curriculum*, George Allen & Unwin, London.

Barrow, R. & White, P. (eds) 1993, *Beyond Lberal Education: Essays in Honour of Paul H. Hirst*, Routledge, London.

Baudrillard, J. 1985, 'The Ecstacy of Communication', in H. Foster (ed.) *Postmodern Culture*, Pluto Press, London.

—— 1988, *Selected Writings*, Stanford University Press, Stanford.

—— 1989, 'Symbolic Exchange and Death' and 'Simulacra and Simulations', in M. Poster (ed.) *Jean Baudrillard: Selected Writings*, Polity Press, Cambridge.

Bauman, Z. 1992, *Intimations of Postmodernity*, Routledge, London.
Beck, C. 1990, *Better Schools: A Values Perspective*, Falmer Press, New York.
Beck, J. 1989, 'Education, Industry and the Needs of the Economy', *Cambridge Journal of Education*, vol. 11, no. 2, pp. 82–106.
Beck, U. 1992, *Risk Society: Towards a New Modernity*, Sage, London.
Becker, G. S. 1965, 'A Theory of the Allocation of Time', *Economic Journal*, vol. 75, pp. 493–517.
Becker, H. 1982, *Art Worlds*, University of California Press, Berkeley, CA.
Bell, D. 1976, *The Coming of Post-Industrial Society: a Venture in Social Forecasting*, Penguin, Harmondsworth.
—— 1983, *Daughters of the Dreaming*, McPhee Gribble, Melbourne.
Ben-David, J. 1971, *The Scientist's Role in Society: A Comparative Study*, Prentice-Hall, Englewood Cliffs, NJ.
Bennett, T. 1990, 'The Political Rationality of the Museum', *Continuum*, vol. 3, no. 1.
Bentham, J. 1984, *The Collected Works of Jeremy Bentham*, in M. J. Smith & W. H. Burston (eds) Clarendon Press, Oxford.
Berg, L. 1969, *Education and Jobs: The Great Training Robbery*, Penguin, Harmondsworth.
Berger, P. & Luckman, T. 1973, *The Social Construction of Reality*, Penguin, Harmondsworth.
Bernstein, B., Elvin, H. L. & Peters, R. S. 1966, 'Ritual in Education', *Philosophical Transactions of the Royal Society of London*, 251, Series B, pp. 429–36.
Bernstein, B. 1972, 'On the Classification and Framing of Educational Knowledge', in M. F. D. Young (ed.) *Knowledge and Control: New Directions for the Sociology of Education*, Collier Macmillan, London.
Biggins, D. 1985, 'The Image of a Socialist Society', *Social Alternatives*, vol. 4, no. 4.
Bigum, C. et al. 1987, *Coming to Terms with Computers in Schools*, Deakin Institute for Studies in Education, Geelong.
Birch, C. 1975, *Confronting the Future: Australia and the World: The Next Hundred Years*, Penguin, Harmondsworth.
—— 1990, *On Purpose*, University of New South Wales Press, Sydney.
Birch, I. & Smart, D. 1989, 'Economic Rationalism and the Politics of Education in Australia', *Politics of Education Association Yearbook*, 1989, pp. 137–51.
Bishop, S. 1986, 'Education for Political Freedom', *Liberal Education*, vol. 72, no. 4, pp. 323–26.
Blishen, E. 1975, *The School That I'd Like*, Penguin, Harmondsworth.
Bloom, A. 1987, *Closing of the American Mind*, Simon & Schuster, New York.
Blyton, P. 1989, 'Time and Labour Relations', in P. Blyton, J. Hassard, S. Hill & K. Starkey (eds) *Time, Work and Organization*, Routledge, London.
Boden, M. 1977, *Artificial Intelligence and Natural Man*, Harvester Press, Hassocks.

Bottomore, T. 1984, *The Frankfurt School*, Tavistock, London.
Boulding, K. 1965, *The Meaning of the Twentieth Century*, George Allen & Unwin, London.
Bourdieu, P. 1963, 'The Attitude of the Algerian Peasant Toward Time', in J. Pitt-Rivers (ed.) *Mediterranean Countrymen: Essays in the Social Anthropology of the Mediterranean*, Mouton, Paris.
—— 1973, 'The Berber House', in M. Douglas (ed.) *Rules and Meanings: The Anthropology of Everyday Knowledge*, Penguin, Harmondsworth.
—— 1984, *Distinction: a Social Critique of the Judgment of Taste*, Harvard University Press, Cambridge, Mass.
—— 1985, 'The Social Space and the Genesis of Groups', *Theory and Society*, vol. 14, pp. 723–744.
—— 1988, *Homo Academicus*, Polity Press, Cambridge.
Bourdieu, P. & Passeron, J. C. 1977, *Reproduction in Education, Society and Culture*, Sage, London.
Bowen, J. & Hobson, P. R. 1974, *Theories of Education: Studies of Significant Innovation in Western Educational Thought*, John Wiley, Brisbane.
Bowers, C. A. 1982, 'The Reproduction of Technological Consciousness: Locating the Ideological Foundations of a Radical Pedagogy', *Teachers College Record*, vol. 83, no. 4, pp. 529–57.
—— 1987, *Elements of a Post-Liberal Theory of Education*, Teachers College Press, New York.
Bowles, S. & Gintis, H. 1976, *Schooling and Capitalist America*, Routledge & Kegan Paul, London.
Branson, J. & Miller, D. 1979, *Class, Sex and Education in Capitalist Society*, Sorrett, Melbourne.
Braverman, H. 1974, *Labor and Monopoly Capital*, Monthly Review Press, New York.
Bremer, J. & Moschzisker, M. van 1971, *The School without Walls: Philadelphia's Parkway Program*, Holt, Rinehart & Winston Inc., New York.
Brent, A. 1978. *Philosophical foundations for the Curriculum*, George Allen & Unwin, London.
Broadfoot, P. 1979, *Assessment, Schools and Society*, Methuen, London.
Brown, P. & Lauder, H. 1992, 'Education, Economy and Society: an Introduction to a New Agenda, in P. Brown & H. Lauder (eds) *Education for Economic Survival: from Fordism to Post-Fordism?* Routledge, London.
Browne, K. 1981, 'Schooling, Capitalism and the Mental/Manual Division of Labour', *Sociological Review*, vol. 29, no. 3.
Brubacher, J. S. 1947, *A History of the Problems of Education*, McGraw Hill, New York.
Buckley, J. H. 1974, *Season of Youth: the Bildüngsroman from Dickens to Golding*, Harvard University Press, Cambridge, Mass.
Bullough, R., Goldstein, S. & Holt, L. 1984, *Human Interests in the Curriculum: Teaching and Learning in a Technological Society*, Teachers College Press, New York.

Burchell, L. 1980, *Victorian Schools: A Study in Colonial Government Architecture 1837–1900*, Melbourne University Press, Melbourne.

Cadogan, M. & Craig, P. 1976, *You're a Brick, Angela! A New Look at Girls' Fiction from 1839–1975*, Victor Gollancz, London.

Cagan, E. 1978, 'Individualism, Collectivism and Radical Educational Reform', *Harvard Educational Review*, vol. 48, no. 2.

Callinicos, A. 1989, *Against Post-Modernism: A Marxist Critique*, Polity Press, Cambridge.

Camilleri, J. et al. 1989, *New Economic Directions for Australia*, Centre for Australian Social Policy Analysis, Phillip Institute of Technology, Coburg, Victoria.

Campbell, C. 1989, *The Romantic Ethic and the Spirit of Modern Consumerism*, Blackwell, Oxford.

Capra, F. 1982, *The Turning Point: Science, Society and the Rising Culture*, Fontana, London.

Carlstein, T., Parkes, D. & Thrift, N. 1978, 'Introduction', in T. Carlstein, D. Parkes & N. Thrift (eds) *Timing Space and Spacing Time, vol. 1: Making Sense of Time*, Edward Arnold, London.

Carr, D. 1993, 'Questions of Competence', *British Journal of Educational Studies*, vol. 41, no. 3, pp. 253–71.

Castles, F. & Mitchell, D. 1992, 'Identifying Welfare State Regimes: the Link between Politics, Instruments and Outcomes', *Governance*, vol. 5, no. 1, pp. 12–18.

Castles, S. & Wüstenberg, W. 1979, *The Education of the Future: An Introduction to the Theory and Practice of Socialist Education*, Pluto Press, London.

Cavell, S. 1984, *Themes Out of School: Effect and Causes*, North Point Press, San Francisco.

Cherryholmes, C. 1988, *Power and Criticism: Post-Structural Investigations in Education*, Teachers College Press, New York.

Christie, M. J. 1985, *Aboriginal Perspectives on Experience and Learning: The Role of Language in Aboriginal Education*, Deakin University Press, Victoria.

Clarke, J. & Critcher, C. 1985, *The Devil Makes Work: Leisure in Capitalist Britain*, Macmillan, London.

Claus, J. F. 1981, 'Radical Reform Within a Liberal and Democratic Framework: Rawls and the Radical Critique of Schooling', *Educational Theory*, vol. 31, no. 2, Spring, pp. 153–65.

Cohen, B. 1981, *Education and the Individual*, George Allen & Unwin, London.

—— 1982, 'Return to the Cave: New Directions for Philosophy of Education', *Education Analysis*, vol. 4, no. 1.

Collis, B. 1987, 'Adolescent Females and Computers: Real and Perceived Barriers', in J. Gaskell, & A. McLaren (eds) *Women and Education: A Canadian Perspective*, Detsely Enterprises, Calgary, Alberta.

Colquhuon, D. 1990, 'Images of Healthism in Health-Based Physical Education', in D. Kirk & R. Tinning (eds) *Physical Education,*

Curriculum and Culture: Critical Issues in the Contemporary Crisis, Falmer Press, London.
Commonwealth Schools Commission, 1987, *In the National Interest*, AGPS, Canberra.
Connell, R. W. 1983, 'Democratising Culture', *Meanjin*, vol. 42.
—— 1985, *Teachers' Work*, George Allen & Unwin, Sydney.
—— 1991, 'The Money Measure: Social Inequality of Wealth and Income', in O'Leary & R. Sharp (eds) *Inequality in Australia: Slicing the Cake*, Heinemann, Port Melbourne.
—— 1993, *Schools and Social Justice*, Pluto Press, Leichhardt, NSW.
Connell, R. W., Ashenden, D. J., Kessler, S. & Dowsett, G. W. 1982, *Making the Difference*, George Allen & Unwin, Sydney.
Cooley, M. 1980, *Architect or Bee? The Human/Technology Relationship*, TransNational Co-operative Limited, Sydney.
Cooper, B. 1984, 'On Explaining Change in School Subjects', in I. Goodson, & S. Ball (eds) *Defining the Curriculum: Histories and Ethnographies*, Falmer Press, London.
Corrigan, P. 1979, *Schooling the Smash Street Kids*, Macmillan, London.
—— 1987, 'In/forming Schooling', in Livingstone, D. et al. *Critical Pedagogy and Cultural Power*, Macmillan, London.
Craig, P. (ed.) 1995, *The Oxford Book of Schooldays*, Oxford University Press, Oxford.
Crane, D. 1972, *Invisible Colleges: A Diffusion of Knowledge in Scientific Communities*, University of Chicago Press, Chicago.
Cross, G. 1993, *Time and Money: the Making of Consumer Culture*, Routledge Kegan & Paul, London.
Csikszentmihalyi, M. & Rochberg-Halton, E. 1981, *The Meaning of Things: Domestic Symbols and the Self*, Cambridge University Press, Cambridge.
Dale, R. 1972, 'The Use of Time in the School', in G. Esland, R. Dale & J. Sadler (eds) *The Social Organization of Teaching and Learning*, Open University Press, Milton Keynes, Bucks. pp. 93–123.
Dale, R. 1974, *The Culture of the School*, Open University Press, Milton Keynes, Bucks.
Daniels, N. (ed.) 1975, *Reading Rawls*, Blackwell, Oxford.
Davidson, K. 1987, 'Equity and Efficiency', *The Victorian Teacher*, vol. 4.
Davies, B. 1989, 'Education for Sexism: A Theoretical Analysis of the Sex/Gender Bias in Education', *Educational Philosophy and Theory*, vol. 21, no. 1.
Davies, B. & Ellison, L. 1991, *Marketing the Secondary School*, Longman, Harlow, Middx.
—— 1992, 'Developing a Marketing Culture in a School', *Studies in Educational Administration*, no. 57, pp. 13–18.
Davidson, A. 1990, *Blazers, Badges and Boaters: a Pictorial History of School Uniforms*, Scope Books, Horndean.
Davison, G. 1993, *The Unforgiving Minute: How Australia Learned to Tell the Time*, Oxford University Press, Melbourne
Dawkins, J. S. 1988, *Strengthening Australia's Schools*, AGPS, Canberra.

de Castell, S. & Luke, A. 1986, 'Models of Literacy in North American Schools: Social and Historical Conditions and Consequences', in S. de Castell, A. Luke & K. Egan (eds) *Literacy, Society and Schooling: a Reader*, Cambridge University Press, Cambridge.

de Certeau, M. 1984, *The Politics of Everyday Life*, University of California Press, Berkeley, CA.

de Grazia, S. 1964, *Of Time, Work and Leisure*, Anchor Books, New York.

Denham, C. & Lieberman, A. (eds) 1980, *Time to Learn*, National Institute of Education, Washington, D.C.

Department of Employment Education and Training 1989, *The Hobart Declaration on Schooling*, AGPS, Canberra.

—— 1989, *A Fair Chance for All*, AGPS, Canberra.

Derrida, J. 1976, *Of Grammatology*, Johns Hopkins University, Baltimore.

Dewey, J. 1937, *Democracy and Education*, Macmillan, London.

—— 1969, *Interest and Effort*, Library Association, New York.

—— 1977, 'On Industrial Education', *Curriculum Inquiry*, vol. 7, no. 1, pp. 53–60.

Dilnot, A. 1990, 'Wealth: From Least to Most', *Australian Society*, July, pp. 14–17.

Donzelot, J. 1979, *The Policing of Families*, Pantheon Books, New York.

Doob, L. W. 1978, 'Time: Cultural and Social-Anthropological Aspects', in T. Carlstein, D. Parkes & N. Thrift (eds) *Timing Space and Spacing Time, vol. 1: Making Sense of Time*, Edward Arnold, London.

Dore, R. 1976, *The Diploma Disease*, George Allen & Unwin, London.

Dretske, F. I. 1969, *Seeing and Knowing*, Routledge & Kegan Paul, London.

Dunlop, B. 1996, *Building a Dream: the Art of Disney Architecture*, Harry N. Abrams, New York.

Easlea, B. 1981, *Science and Sexual Oppression: Patriarchy's Confrontation with Woman and Nature*, Weidenfeld & Nicolson, London.

Eco, U. 1983, *The Name of the Rose*, Harcourt, Brace, Jovanovich, San Diego, CA.

Edelman, M. 1977, *Political Language: Words That Succeed and Policies That Fail*, Academic Press, New York.

Eisner, E. 1979, *The Educational Imagination: On The Design and Evaluation of School Programs*, Macmillan, New York.

Eisner, E. 1985, *The Art of Educational Evaluation: A Personal View*, Falmer Press, London.

—— 1985, *The Educational Imagination: On the Design and Evaluation of School Programs*, Macmillan, New York.

Elias, N. 1978, *The Civilising Process: The History of Manners*, Blackwell, Oxford.

—— 1995, *Time: an Essay*, Blackwell, Oxford.

Elliot, R. (ed.) 1995, *Environmental Ethics*, Oxford University Press, New York.

Elliot, R. & Gare, A. (eds) 1983, *Environmental Philosophy: A Collection of Readings*, University of Queensland Press, St Lucia.

Ellsworth, E. 1989, 'Why Doesn't This Feel Empowering? Working

Through the Repressive Myths of Critical Pedagogy', *Harvard Educational Review*, vol. 59, no. 3, pp. 297–325.

Ellul, J. 1964, *The Technological Society*, Vintage Books, New York.

Employment, Education and Training 1990, *Priorities for Reform in Higher Education*, AGPS, Canberra.

Evans, K. 1979, 'The Physical Form of the School', *British Journal of Educational Studies*, vol. 27, no. 1, February, pp. 29–41.

Evans, R. 1982, *The Fabrication of Virtue: English Prison Architecture, 1750–1840*, Cambridge University Press, Cambridge.

Evans-Pritchard, E. 1973, 'Time is not a Continuum', in M. Douglas (ed.) *Rules and Meanings: The Anthropology of Everyday Knowledge*, Penguin, Harmondsworth.

Everhart, R. B. 1983, *Reading, Writing and Resistance: Adolescence and Labor in a Junior High School*, Routledge & Kegan Paul, Boston.

Fairclough, N. 1993, 'Critical Discourse and the Marketization of Public Discourse: the Universities', *Discourse and Language*, vol. 4, no. 2, pp. 133–168.

Featherstone, M. 1991, *Consumer Culture and Postmodernism*, Sage, London.

Feifer, M. 1985, *Going Places: the Ways of the Tourist from Imperial Rome to the Present Day*, Macmillan, London.

Feinberg, W. 1975, *Reason and Rhetoric: The Intellectual Foundations of Twentieth Century Liberal Educational Policy*, John Wiley, New York.

—— 1983, *Understanding Education: Towards a Reconstruction of Educational Inquiry*, Cambridge University Press, Cambridge.

Feinberg, W. & Soltis, J. F. 1985, *Schools and Society*, Teachers College Press, New York.

Fenstermacher, G. D. & Soltis, J. E. 1986, *Approaches to Teaching*, Teachers College Press, New York.

Feyerabend, P. 1975, *Against Method*, NLB, London.

Finch, L. (ed.) 1996, *Young in a Warm Climate: Essays in Queensland Childhood*, Queensland Review/University of Queensland Press, St. Lucia.

Finkelstein, J. 1991, *The Fashioned Self*, Polity Press, Cambridge.

Ford, G. W. 1984, 'Australia at Risk: an Underskilled and Vulnerable Society', in J. Eastwood, J. Reeves & J. Ryan (eds) *Labor Essays*, Drummond, Blackburn, Vic.

Forty, A. 1980, 'The Modern Hospital in England and France: The Social and Medical Uses of Architecture', in A. D. King (ed.) *Buildings and Society: Essays on the Social Development of the Built Environment*, Routledge & Kegan Paul, London.

Foucault, M. 1970, *The Order of Things: An Archaeology of Human Sciences*, Tavistock, London.

—— 1975, *Madness and Civilization: an Archaeology of Medical Perception*, Vintage Books, New York.

—— 1979, 'Governmentality', *Ideology and Consciousness*, vol. 6, pp. 5–21.

—— 1979, *Discipline and Punish: The Birth of the Prison*, Penguin, Harmondsworth.

—— 1980, *Power/Knowledge: Selected Interviews and Other Writings*, C. Gordon (ed.) Pantheon, New York.
—— 1980, *The History of Sexuality, Volume 1: An Introduction*, Vintage Books, New York.
—— *The Care of the Self*, Penguin, Harmondsworth.
—— 1988, *The Uses of Pleasure*, Penguin, Harmondsworth.
Fraser, J. J. 1987, *Time: The Familiar Stranger*, University of Mass. Press, Amherst.
Fraser, N. 1989, *Unruly Practices: Power, Discourse and Gender in Contemporary Social Theory*, Polity Press, Cambridge.
Frayn, M. 1996, *Clockwise: a screen play*, Methuen, London.
Freire, P. 1972, *Cultural Action for Freedom*, Penguin, Harmondsworth.
—— 1974, *Pedagogy of the Oppressed*, Penguin, Harmondsworth.
—— 1985, *The Politics of Education: Culture, Power and Liberation*, Macmillan, London.
Freire, P. & Shor, I. 1987, *A Pedagogy for Liberation: Dialogues on Transforming Education*, Macmillan, London.
Frow, J. 1990, *The Social Production of Knowledge and the Discipline of English*, University of Queensland Press, St Lucia.
Gee, J. 1993, 'Quality, Science and the Lifeworld: the Alignment of Business and Education', *Critical Forum*, vol. 2, pp. 3–13.
Gee, J., Hull, G. & Lankshear, C. 1996, *The New Work Order: Behind the Language of the New Capitalism*, Allen & Unwin, St. Leonards, NSW.
Geuss, R. 1982, *The Idea of Critical Theory: Habermas and the Frankfurt School*, Cambridge University Press, Cambridge.
Gibson, R. 1984, *Structuralism and Education*, Hodder & Stoughton, London.
—— 1986, *Critical Theory and Education*, Hodder & Stoughton, London.
Giddens, A. 1984, *The Constitution of Society*, Polity Press, Cambridge.
—— 1985, 'Jürgen Habermas', in Q. Skinner (ed.) *The Return of Grand Theory in the Human Sciences*, Cambridge University Press, Cambridge.
—— 1990, *The Consequences of Modernity*, Polity Press, Cambridge.
Gilbert, P. & Taylor, S. 1991, *Fashioning the Feminine: Girls, Popular Culture and Schooling*, Allen & Unwin, North Sydney, NSW.
Ginsburg, M. 1988, *Contradictions in Teacher Education and Society: A Critical Analysis*, Falmer Press, London.
Giroux, H. 1981a, 'Hegemony, Resistance and the Paradox of Educational Reform', *Interchange*, vol. 12, no. 2/3, pp. 3–26.
—— 1981, *Ideology, Culture and the Process of Schooling*, Falmer Press, London.
—— 1983a, 'Critical Theory and Schooling: Implications for the Development of Radical Pedagogy', *Discourse*, vol. 3, no. 2, April, pp. 1–14.
—— 1983, *Critical Theory and Educational Practice*, Deakin University Press, Geelong.
—— 1988, *Teachers as Intellectuals: Toward a Critical Pedagogy of Learning*, Bergin & Garvey, Granby, Mass., p. 122.

Giroux, H. & Aronowitz, S. 1985, *Education Under Siege*, Routledge & Kegan Paul, London.

Giroux, H. & McLaren, P. 1987, 'Teacher Education as a Counterpublic Sphere', in T. S. Popkewitz (ed.) *Critical Studies in Teacher Education: Its Folklore, Theory and Practice*, Falmer Press, London.

Giroux, H. & Simon, R. 1988, 'Schooling, Popular Culture, and a Pedagogy of Possibility', *Journal of Education*, vol. 170, no. 1, pp. 9–26.

Gleick, J. 1987, *Chaos: Making a New Science*, Heinemann, London.

Godfrey, J. A. & Castle, C. R. 1953, *School Design and Construction*, Architectural Press, London.

Goffman, E. 1971, *The Presentation of Self in Everyday Life*, Allen Lane, London.

—— 1975, *Frame Analysis*, Penguin, Harmondsworth.

—— 1976, *Asylums: Essays on the Social Situations of Mental Patients and Other Inmates*, Penguin, Harmondsworth.

Goldstrom, J. M. 1977, 'The Content of Education and the Socialisation of the Working-Class Child 1830–1860', in P. McCann (ed.) *Popular Education and Socialization in the Nineteenth Century*, Methuen, London, pp. 93–109.

Gollan, A. (ed.) 1990 *Questions for the Nineties*, Left Book Club Co-operative, Sutherland, New South Wales.

Gooding, D. 1992, 'The Procedural Turn; or, Why Do Thought Experiments Work', in R. N. Giere (ed.) *Cognitive Modes of Science*, University of Minnesota Press, Minn.

Goodson, I. F. 1988, *The Making of the Curriculum*, Falmer Press, Brighton.

Goodson, I. F. & Ball, S. J. (eds) 1984, *Defining the Curriculum: Histories and Ethnographies*, Falmer Press, London.

Gordon, C. (ed.) 1980, *Power/Knowledge: Selected Interviews and Other Writings 1972–1977 Michel Foucault*, Pantheon Books, New York.

Gordon, P. & Lawton, D. 1978, *Curriculum Change in the Nineteenth and Twentieth Century*, Hodder & Stoughton, London, pp. 120–21.

Gore, J. 1993, *The Struggle for Pedagogies: Critical and Feminist Discourses as Regimes of Truth*, Routledge, New York.

Gorz, A. 1978, 'Technical Intelligentsia and the Capitalist Division of Labour', in M. Young & G. Whitty (eds) *Society, State and Schooling*, Falmer Press, Lewes, pp. 131–50.

—— 1982, *Farewell to the Working Class: An Essay on Post-Industrial Socialism*, Pluto Press, London.

—— 1985, *Paths to Paradise: On the Liberation from Work*, Pluto Press, London.

Goss, J. 1988, 'The Built Environment and Social Theory: Towards An Architectural Geography', *Professional Geography*, vol. 4, no. 4.

Gottdiener, M. 1995, *Postmodern Semiotics: Material Culture and the Forms of Postmodern Life*, Blackwell, Oxford.

Gould, S. J. 1991, *The Mismeasure of Man*, Norton, New York.

Grace, G. 1978, *Teachers, Ideology and Control*, Routledge & Kegan Paul, London.
Green, H. 1984, *Pack My Bag*, Oxford University Press, Oxford.
Gross, D. 1981–2, 'Space, Time and Modern Culture', *Telos*, vol. 50, pp. 59–78.
Grundy, S. 1987, *Curriculum: Product or Praxis*, Falmer Press, London.
—— 1990, 'Praxis Traps: Changing the Discourse for Education for Educational Praxis', paper presented to the Queensland Curriculum Conference held at Griffith University, Brisbane, June.
Gutek, G. L. 1988, *Philosophical and Ideological Perspectives on Education*, Prentice-Hall, Englewood Cliffs, NJ.
Habermas, J. 1972, *Knowledge and Human Interests*, Heinemann, London.
—— 1974, *Theory and Practice*, Heinemann, London.
—— 1984, *The Theory of Communicative Action, vol. 1: Reasons and the Rationalization of Society*, Heinemann, London.
—— 1987, *The Philosophical Discourse of Modernity: Twelve Lectures*, Polity Press, Cambridge.
Hacking, I. 1990, *The Taming of Chance*, Cambridge University Press, Cambridge.
Hall, E. J. 1959, *The Silent Language*, Doubleday, New York.
Halliwell, G. 1990, 'Infusing Critical Pedagogy into Early Childhood Teacher Education', *Unicorn*, vol. 16, no. 1, pp. 47–52.
Hamilton, D. 1989, *Towards a Theory of Schooling*, Falmer Press, London.
Hannan, B. 1982, 'Assessment Reporting and Evaluation in Democratic Education', *VISE News*, no. 31, July/August, pp. 24–31.
Hanson, N. R. 1969, *Perception and Discovery*, Freeman, Cooper & Company, San Francisco, CA.
Hargreaves, A. 1986, 'Record Breakers?', in P. Broadfoot (ed.) *Profiles and Records of Achievement: A Review of Issues and Practice*, Rinehart & Winston, London.
—— 1990, 'Politics of Time and Space', *International Journal of Qualitative Studies in Education*, vol. 3, no. 4, pp. 303–320.
Hargreaves, D. H. 1981, 'Unemployment, Leisure and Education', *Oxford Review of Education*, vol. 7, no. 3, pp. 197–210.
Harley, J. B. 1988, 'Maps, Knowledge and Power', in D. Cosgrove & S. Daniels (eds) *The Iconography of Landscapes: Essays on the Symbolic Representation, Design and Use of Past Environments*, Cambridge University Press, Cambridge.
Harris, H. & Lipman, A. 1980, 'Social Symbolism and Space Usage in Daily Life', *Sociological Review*, vol. 28, no. 2, pp. 415–28.
Harris, K. 1979, *Education and Knowledge: the Structured Misrepresentation of Reality*, Routledge & Kegan Paul, London.
—— 1982a, 'The Secondary School: Administrative Wonder and Educational Absurdity', *Social Alternatives*, vol. 2, no. 4, pp. 31–41.
—— 1982b, *Teachers and Classes: A Marxist Analysis*, Routledge & Kegan Paul, London.

—— 1996, 'The Hard Cold Task Ahead', *Education Links*, vol. 52, Winter, pp. 4–9.

Hartnett, A. & Naish, M. 1986, *Education and Society Today*, Falmer Press, London.

Harvard Committee 1950, *General Education in a Free Society*, Harvard University Press, Cambridge, Mass.

Harvard Educational Review, 1969, vol. 39, no. 4.

Harvey, D. 1990, *The Condition of Postmodernity: An Enquiry into the Origins of Cultural Change*, Blackwell, Oxford.

Hatton, E. 1994, 'Social and Cultural Influences on Teaching', in E. Hatton (ed.) *Understanding Teaching: Curriculum and the Social Context of Schooling*, Harcourt Brace, Sydney.

Hatton, E. & Elliot, R. 1994, 'Social Justice and the Provision of Education', in E. Hatton (ed.) *Understanding Teaching: Curriculum and the Social Context of Schooling*, Harcourt Brace, Sydney.

Hay, A. 1988, 'A Market Approach to Education', *Professional Administrator*, vol. 40, May/June, pp. 4–8.

Hebdige, D. 1988, *Hiding in the Light: on Images and Things*, Routledge, London.

Heilbroner, R.L. 1965, *An Inquiry into the Human Prospect*, Calder & Boyars, London.

Held, D. 1980, *Introduction to Critical Theory: from Horkheimer to Habermas*, Hutchinson, London.

Heller, A. 1984, *Everyday Life*, Routledge & Kegan Paul, London.

Hempel, C. G. 1966, *Philosophy and Natural Science*, Prentice-Hall, Englewood Cliffs, NJ.

Henry, M., Knight, J., Lingard, R. & Taylor, S. 1988, *Understanding Schooling: An Introductory Sociology of Australian Education*, Routledge & Kegan Paul, London.

Hepburn, E. 1996, *Of Life and Death*, Dove, Melbourne.

Herbst, P. B. 1974, *Socio-Technical Design: Strategies in Multidisciplinary Research*, Tavistock, London.

Hesse, H. 1977, *The Glass Bead Game*, Penguin, Harmondsworth.

Hextall, I. 1976, 'Marking Work', in G. Whitty & M. Young (ed.) *Explorations in the Politics of School Knowledge*, Nafferton Books, Driffield.

Hextall, I. & Sarup, M. 1978, 'School Knowledge, Evaluation and Alienation', in M. Young & G. Whitty (eds) *Society, State and Schooling*, Falmer Press, London.

Heyck, T.W. 1982, *The Transformation of Intellectual Life in Victorian England*, Croom Helm, London.

Hill, C. 1964, *Society and Puritanism in Pre-Revolutionary England*, Secker & Warburg, London.

Hill, S. 1988, *The Tragedy of Technology: Alignments Between Cultural and Technological Change*, Pluto Press, London.

Hirsch, E. D. 1987, *Cultural Literacy: What Every American Needs to Know*, Houghton-Mifflin, Boston.

Hirsch, F. 1976, *Social Limits to Growth*, Harvard University Press, Cambridge, Mass.
Hirst, P. 1974, *Knowledge and the Curriculum: A Collection of Philosophical Papers*, Routledge & Kegan Paul, London.
—— 1987, *Educational Theory and its Foundation Disciplines*, Routledge & Kegan Paul, London.
Hollis, M. 1987, 'Educational as a Positional Good', in Straughan, R. & Wilson, J. (ed.) *Philosophers on Education*, Macmillan, London.
Holmes, M. 1984, 'The School Schedule or Mistress', *The Canadian Administrator*, vol. 23, no. 5, February, pp. 1–6.
Holt, J. 1982, *Teach Your Own*, Delta, New York.
—— 1985, *How Children Fail*, Penguin, Harmondsworth.
Holt, M. (ed.) 1987, *Skills and Vocationalism: The Easy Answer*, Open University Press, Milton Keynes, Bucks.
Hooton, J. 1990, *Stories of Herself When Young: Autobiographies of Childhood by Australian Women*, Oxford University Press, Melbourne.
Horvath, A. 1987, 'The Effects of Compulsory Education on School Architecture', *History of Education Society Bulletin*, vol. 40, Autumn, pp. 13–17.
Hoskin, K. W. 1990, 'Foucault under Examination: the Crypto-Educationalist Unmasked', in Ball, S. (ed.) *Foucault and Education: Disciplines and Knowledge*, Routledge, London.
Hoskin, K. W. & Macve, R. 1986, 'Accounting and the Examination: A Genealogy of Disciplinary Power', *Accounting, Organizations and Society*, vol. 11, no. 2, pp. 105–36.
Howie, G. 1969, *Educational Theory and Practice in Saint Augustine*, Routledge & Kegan Paul, London.
Hobsbawm, E. & Ranger, T. (ed.) 1984, *The Invention of Tradition*, Cambridge University Press, Cambridge.
Humphries, S. 1984, *Hooligans or Rebels? An Oral History of Working-Class Childhood and Youth 1889–1939*, Blackwell, Oxford.
Hunter, I. et al. 1991, *Accounting for the Humanities*, ICPS, Brisbane.
Hunter, I. 1988, *Culture and Government: The Emergence of Literary Education*, Macmillan, London.
—— 1995, *Rethinking the School: Subjectivity, Bureaucracy, Criticism*, Allen & Unwin, St. Leonards, NSW.
Hurt, J. S. 1971, *Education in Evolution: Church, State, Society and Popular Education 1800–1870*, Rupert Hart Davies, London.
—— 1977, 'Drill, Disciplinary and the Elementary School Ethos', in McCann, P. (ed.) *Popular Education in the Nineteenth Century*, Methuen, London, pp. 167–91.
Hutton, P. 1981, 'The History of Mentalities: The New Map of Cultural History', *History and Theory*, vol. 20, no. 3, pp. 237–59.
Hyams, B. K. & Bessant, B. 1972, *Schools for the People: An Introduction to the History of State Education in Australia*, Longman, Melbourne.
Hyland, T. 1991, 'Taking Care of Business: Vocationalism, Competence and Enterprise Culture', *Educational Studies*, vol. 17, no. 1, pp. 77–87.

Illich, I. 1971, *Deschooling Society*, Penguin, Harmondsworth.
—— 1979, *Tools for Conviviality*, Fontana, London.
—— 1981, *Shadow Work*, Marion Boyars, London.
Inglis, F. 1981, *The Promise of Happiness: Value and Meaning in Children's Fiction*, Cambridge University Press, Cambridge.
—— 1985, *The Management of the Ignorance: A Political Theory of the Curriculum*, Blackwell, Oxford.
Jenks, C. 1996, 'The Postmodern Child', in J. Brannan & M. O'Brien (eds) *Children in Families: Research and Policy*, Falmer Press, London.
Johnson, L. 1987, *The Unseen Voice: a Cultural Study of Australian Radio*, Methuen, London.
Joiner, D. 1971, 'Office Territory', *New Society*, 7 October.
Jonathan, R. 1985, 'Education, Philosophy of Education and Context', *Journal of Philosophy of Education*, vol. 19, no. 1, pp. 13–25.
—— 1988, 'The Notion of Giftedness—or, How Long is a Piece of String?', *British Journal of Educational Studies*, vol. 26, no. 2, July, pp. 111–25.
Jones, B. 1982, *Sleepers Wake!: Technology and the Future of Work*, Oxford University Press, Melbourne.
—— 1986, 'Teaching Basic Skills for the Information Age', *Unicorn*, vol. 12, no. 2.
Jones, K. & Williamson, K. 1979, 'The Birth of the Schoolroom: A Study of the Transformation in the Discursive Conditions of English Popular Education in the First Half of the Nineteenth Century', *Ideology and Consciousness*, vol. 6, pp. 59–110.
Junor, A. 1991, 'Education: Producing or Challenging Inequality', in J. O'Leary & R. Sharp (eds) *Inequality in Australia: Slicing the Cake*, Heinneman, Port Melbourne.
Kemmis, S. & Carr, W. 1986, *Becoming Critical: Education, Knowledge and Action Research*, Falmer Press, London.
Kemmis, S., Cole, P. & Suggett, D. 1983, *Orientations to Curriculum and Transition: Towards the Socially-Critical School, Victorian Institute of Secondary Education*, Victorian Institute of Secondary Education, Clifton Hill, Victoria.
Kemp, D. 1986, 'Education and Values', *IPA Review*, Winter, pp. 52–55.
Kenway, J. with Bigum, C. & Fitzclarence, L. 1993, 'Marketing Education in the Postmodern Age', *Journal of Education Policy*, vol. 8, no. 2, pp. 105–122.
Kirk, D. & Tinning, R. 1990, 'Introduction: Physical Education, Curriculum and Culture', in D. Kirk & R. Tinning (eds) *Physical Education, Curriculum and Culture: Critical Issues in the Contemporary Crisis*, Falmer Press, London.
Kirschenbaum, H. & Simon, S. B. (eds) 1973, *Reading in Values Clarification*, Winston Press, Minn.
Kleinig, J. 1982, *Philosophical Issues in Education*, Croom Helm, London.
Kline, S. 1993, *Out of the Garden: Toys, TV and Children's Culture in the Age of Marketing*, Verso, London.

Kociumbas, J. 1997, *Australian Childhood: a History*, Allen & Unwin, St. Leonards, NSW.

—— 1988, 'The Best Years?', in V. Burgmann & J. Lee (eds) *Making a Life: A People's History of Australia Since 1788*, Penguin, Ringwood, Victoria.

Kramer, L. 1987–1988, 'Education; Failing Future Generations', *Institute of Public Affairs: FACTS*, vol. 36, no. 3, December 1987–February 1988.

Kristeva, J. 1981, 'Women's Time', *Signs: Journal of Women in Culture and Society*, vol. 7, no. 1.

Kritzman, L. D. 1988, *Politics, Philosophy, Culture: Interviews and Other Writings, 1977–1984*, Routledge, London.

Kuhn, T. S. 1973, *Structure of Scientific Revolutions*, University of Chicago Press, Chicago.

—— 1974, 'Second Thoughts on Paradigms', in F. Suppe (ed.) *The Structure of Scientific Theories*, University of Illinois Press, Urbana, Ill.

Kukathus, C. & Pettit, P. 1990, *Rawls: a Theory of Justice and its Critics*, Polity Press, Cambridge.

Landes, D. S. 1983, *Revolution in Time: Clocks and the Making of the Modern World*, Harvard University Press, Cambridge, Mass.

Lanham, R. A. 1993, *The Electronic Word: Democracy, Technology and the Arts*, Univeristy of Chicago Press, Chicago.

Laqueur, T. 1976, *Religion and Respectability: Sunday Schools and Working Class Culture 1780–1850*, Yale University Press, New Haven. CT.

Larick, K. T. & Fischer, J. 1986, 'Classroom of the Future: Introducing Technology to Schools', *The Futurist*, May–June.

Lash, S. & Urry, J. 1994, *Economies of Sign and Space*, Sage, London.

Latour, B. 1986, 'Visualisation and Cognition: Thinking with Hands and Eyes', in H. Kushlick (ed.) *Knowledge and Society*, vol. 6, JAI Press, Greenwich, CT.

Lave, J. 1988, *Cognition in Practice: Mind, Mathematics and Culture in Everyday Life*, Cambridge University Press, Cambridge.

Lawrence, D. H. 1975, 'The Novel and Feelings', in Williams, J. & Williams, R. (ed.) *Lawrence on Education*, Penguin, Harmondsworth.

Lawton, D. 1975, *Class, Culture and the Curriculum*, Routledge & Kegan Paul, London.

Leadbeatter, C. 1987, 'In the Land of the Dispossessed', *Marxism Today*, April, pp. 18–25.

Levin, H. 1986, 'About time for educational reform', in P. Watkins (ed.) *Time, Organization and the Administration of Education*, Deakin University Press, Geelong, Victoria.

Lingard, B. 1994, 'The Struggle for More Socially Just Schooling', *Queensland Teachers' Union Profession Magazine*, vol. 12, no. 1 November 24, pp. 1–5.

—— 1983, 'Education and Radical Change: The Philosophy and Practice of Paulo Freire', in W. Haines (ed.) *Reader in Philosophy of Education*, BCAE, Brisbane.

——1990, 'Teachers and Equity: Definitional and Policy Considerations', *Unicorn*, vol. 16, no. 3, August, pp. 156–62.

Liston, D. P. 1988, *Capitalist Schools: Explanation and Ethics in Radical Studies of Schooling*, Routledge, New York.

Livingstone, D. W. 1987, 'Upgrading and Opportunities', in D. Livingstone, et al. *Critical Pedagogy and Cultural Power*, Macmillan, London.

Lloyd, G. 1984, *The Man of Reason: 'Male' and 'Female' in Western Philosophy*, University of Minnesota Press, Minn.

Lodge, D. 1978, *Changing Places*, Penguin, Harmondsworth.

—— 1985, *Small World*, Penguin, Harmondsworth.

Lotman, J. 1977, *The Structure of the Artistic Text*, University of Michigan Press, Ann Arbor, MI.

Luke, C. 1996, 'ekstasis@cyberia', *Discourse: Studies in the Cultural Politics of Education*, vol. 17, no. 2, pp. 187–207.

—— 1989, *Pedagogy, Printing and Protestantism: The Discourse on Childhood*, State University of New York Press, Albany, New York.

Lunn, E. 1982, *Marxism and Modernism: An Historical Study of Lukacs, Brecht, Benjamin and Adorno*, University of California Press, Berkeley, CA.

Lyon, D. 1994, *The Electronic Eye: the Rise of Surveillance Society*, Polity Press, Cambridge

Lyotard, J. F. 1984, 'Defining the Post-Modern', in G. Bennington, et al. *Post-Modernism*, ICA Documents 4, ICA, London, pp. 6–7.

——1984, *The Postmodern Condition: a Report on Knowledge*, Manchester University Press, Manchester.

MacIntyre, A. 1987, *After Virtue: A Study in Moral Theory*, Duckworth, London.

MacLeod, R. 1982, 'Introduction: Science and Examinations in Victorian England', in R. MacLeod (ed.) *Days of Judgment: Science, Examinations and the Organization of Knowledge in Late Victorian England*, Nafferton Books, Driffield.

MacLure, S. 1984, *Educational Development and School Buildings: Aspects of Public Policy 1945–73*, Longman, Harlow, Middx.

Mangan, J. A. 1981, *Athleticism in the Victorian and Edwardian Public School: the Emergence and Consolidation of an Educational Ideology*, Cambridge University Press, Cambridge.

Marchello, J. 1987, 'Education for a Technological Age', *Futures*, vol. 19, no. 5, pp. 555–65.

Marginson, S. 1993, *Education and Public Policy in Australia*, Cambridge University Press, Melbourne.

—— 1995, 'Markets in Education: A Theoretical Note', *Australian Journal of Education*, vol. 39, no. 3, pp. 294–312.

Markus, R. 1974, 'Principles of Marking', *Times Higher Educational Supplement*, 1 March.

Marsh, P., Rosser, E. & Harré, R. 1978, *The Rules of Disorder*, Routledge & Kegan Paul, London.

Marshall, J. 1996, 'Personal Autonomy and Liberal Education: A Foucauldean Critique', in M. Peters, W. Hope, J. Marshall & S. Webster (eds) *Critical Theory, Poststructuralism and the Social Context*, Dunmore Press, Palmerston North.

Martin, J. R. 1985, 'Becoming Educated: A Journey of Alienation or Integration?' *Journal of Education*, vol. 167, no. 3, pp. 71–84.
—— 1993, 'Curriculum and the Mirror of Knowledge', in R. Barrow & P. White (eds) *Beyond Liberal Education: Essays in Honour of Paul H. Hirst*, Routledge, London.
Marx, K. 1981, 'Economic and Philosophical Manuscripts', *Early Writings*, Penguin, Harmondsworth.
Matthews, M. 1980, *The Marxist Theory of Schooling: A Study of Epistemology and Education*, Harvester Press, Brighton, Sussex.
Mauss, M. 1973, 'Techniques of the Body', *Economy and Society*, vol. 2, no. 1, February, pp. 70–88.
McCarthy, C. 1995, 'Imperial Fictions: School Music and the Production of Adolescent Identity in the Postcolony', *Discourse: Studies in the Cultural Politics of Education*, vol. 16, no. 3, pp. 331–45.
McClintock, J. & R. (eds) 1970, *Henry Barnard's School Architecture*, Teachers College Press, New York.
McIntyre, S. 1985, *Winners and Losers: The Pursuit of Social Justice in Australian History*, Allen & Unwin, Sydney.
McLaren, P. 1986, 'Death of Politics: A Brazilian Reprieve', *Educational Theory*, vol. 36, no. 4, pp. 389–401.
—— 1986, 'Post-Modernity and the Death of Politics: A Brazilian Reprieve', *Educational Theory*, vol. 36, no. 4, pp. 389–401.
—— 1989, *Life in Schools: An Introduction to Critical Pedagogy in the Foundations of Education*, Longman, White Plains, New York.
McLuhan, M. 1974, *Understanding Media: The Extension of Man*, Abacus, London.
McPeck, J. F. 1981, *Critical Thinking and Education*, Martin Robertson, Oxford.
McWilliam, E. 1994, *In Broken Images: Feminist Tales for a Different Teacher Education*, Teachers College Press, New York.
Mead, M. 1980, 'Our Educational Emphases in Primitive Perspective', in N. Keddie (ed.) *Tinker, Tailor ... the Myth of Cultural Deprivation*, Penguin, Harmondsworth, pp. 96–107.
Meadmore, D. 1995, 'Linking Goals of Governmentality and Politics of Assessment', *Assessment in Education*, vol. 2, no. 1, pp. 9–22.
Merchant, C. 1982, *The Death of Nature: Women, Ecology and the Scientific ReVolution*, Wildwood House, London.
Meredyth, D. & Tyler, D. (eds) 1993, *Child and Citizen: Genealogies of Schooling and Subjectivity*, ICPS, Brisbane.
Metcalfe, A. W. 1992, 'The Curriculum Vitae: Confessions of a Wage Labourer', *Work, Employment and Society*, vol. 6, no. 4, December, pp. 619–641.
Meyrowitz, J. 1985, *No Sense of Place: the Impact of Electronic Media on Social Behaviour*, Oxford University Press, London.
Middleton, M. 1982, *Marking Time: Alternatives in Australian Schooling*, Methuen, Melbourne.
Middleton, M. et al. 1986, *Making the Future: The Role of Secondary Education in Australia*, Commonwealth Schools Commission, Canberra.

Mill, J. S. 1971, 'Inaugural Address at the University of St Andrews', in F. W. Garforth (ed.) *John Stuart Mill on Education*, Teachers College Press, New York.

Miller, P. 1986, *Long Division: State Schooling in South Australian Society*, Wakefield Press, Netley, South Australia.

Modjeska, D. (ed.) 1989, *Inner Cities: Australian Women's Memory of Place*, Penguin, Ringwood, Victoria.

Moline, J. N. 1986, 'Justice and Liberal Education', *Liberal Education*, vol. 72, no. 4, pp. 281–99.

Moore, T. W. 1977, *Educational Theory: An Introduction*, Routledge & Kegan Paul, London.

Moretti, F. 1987, *The Way of the World: the Bildüngsroman in European Culture*, Verso, London.

Mumford, L. 1963, *Technics and Civilization*, Harcourt, Brace, New York.

Murray, R. 1989, 'Fordism and Post-Fordism', in S. Hall & M. Jacques (eds) *New Times: the Changing Face of Politics in the1990s*, Lawrence & Wishart, London.

Musgrave, P. W. 1985, *From Brown to Bunter: the Life and Death of the School Story*, Routledge & Kegan Paul, London.

National Board of Employment, Education and Training (NBEET) 1992, *Australian Vocational Certificate Training System (Carmichael Report)*, NBEET, Canberra.

National Commission for Employment Policy 1986, *Computers in the Workplace: Selected Issues*, NCEP, Washington.

Neill, A. S. 1974, *Summerhill*, Penguin, Harmondsworth.

—— 1992, *The New Summerhill*, Penguin, Harmondsworth.

Neilsen, K. 1989, *Marxism and the Moral Point of View: Morality, Ideology and Historical Materialism*, Westview Press, London.

Newcombe, B. & Humphries, D. 1975, *Schools Out!*, Penguin, Ringwood, Victoria.

Newman, J. H. 1927, *The Idea of a University*, Longman, London.

Nicholson, C. 1989, 'Post-Modernism, Feminism and Education: The Need for Solidarity', *Educational Theory*, vol. 39, no. 3, pp. 197–205.

Nidditch, P. H. 1973, 'Philosophy of Education and the Place of Science in the Curriculum', in G. Langford & D. J. O'Connor (eds) *New Essays in the Philosophy of Education*, Routledge & Kegan Paul, London.

Noble, P. D. 1988, 'Education, Technology and the Military', in L. E. Beyer & M. W. Apple (eds) *The Curriculum: Problems, Politics and Possibilities*, State University of New York Press, Albany, New York.

Norris, C. 1984, *The Deconstructive Turn: Essays in the Rhetoric of Philosophy*, Methuen, London.

—— 1993, *The Truth about Postmodernism*, Blackwell, Oxford.

Norris, N. 1991, 'The Trouble with Competence', *Cambridge Journal of Education*, vol. 21, no. 3, pp. 331–41.

Nozick, R. 1974, *Anarchy, State and Utopia*, Basic Books, New York.

NSW Department of Education 1990, *Equity and Excellence*.

Nyberg, D. 1981, *Power over Power: What Power Means in Ordinary Life, How it is Related to Acting Freely, and What it Can Contribute to a Renovated Ethics of Education*, Cornell University Press, Ithaca.

Nyberg, E. & Egan, K. 1981, *The Erosion of Education: Socialisation and the School*, Teachers College Press, New York.

O'Brien, M. 1981, *The Politics of Reproduction*, Routledge & Kegan Paul, London.

O'Connor, D. J. 1973, 'The Nature and Scope of Educational Theory', in G. Langford & D. J. O'Connor (eds) *New Essays in the Philosophy of Education*, Routledge & Kegan Paul, London, pp. 47–65.

Oakeshott, M. 1967, *Rationalism in Politics and Other Essays*, Methuen, London.

—— 1971, 'Education: The Engagement and Its Frustration', *Proceedings of Philosophy of Education Society of Great Britain*, vol. 5, no. 1, January.

Oakley, A. 1988, *The Men's Room*, Flamingo, London.

Okin, S. M. 1980, *Women in Western Political Thought*, Virago, London.

Olson, D. 1977, 'From Utterance to Text: the Bias of Language in Speech and Writing', *Harvard Educational Review*, vol. 47.

Ong, W. J. 1958, *Ramus: Method and the Decay of Dialogue*, Harvard University Press, Cambridge, Mass.

—— 1971, *Rhetoric, Romance and Technology*, Cornell University Press, Ithaca.

—— 1982, *Oralcy and Literacy: The Technologising of the Word*, Methuen, London.

Opie, I. & Opie, P. 1959, *The Lore and Language of Schoolchildren*, Oxford University Press, Oxford.

Orme, J. 1978, 'Time: Psychological Aspects', in T. Carlstein, D. Parkes & N. Thrift (eds) *Timing Space and Spacing Time, vol. 1: Making Sense of Time*, Edward Arnold, London.

Orwell, G. 1954, *Nineteen Eighty Four*, Penguin, Harmondsworth.

Ozolins, U. 1981, 'Victorian HSC Examiners' Reports: A Study of Cultural Capital', *Melbourne Working Papers*, pp. 142–83.

Parkes, D. & Thrift, N. 1978, 'Putting Time in its Place', in T. Carlstein, D. Parkes, & N. Thrift (eds) *Timing Space and Spacing Time, vol. 1: Making Sense of Time*, Edward Arnold, London.

Parkinson, G. H. R. 1967, 'Humanistic Education: Some Philosophical Considerations', in R. Straughan & J. Wilson (eds) *Philosophers on Education*, Macmillan, London.

Passmore, J. 1974, *Man's Responsibility for Nature*, Duckworth, London, especially Chapter 1.

——1980, *The Philosophy of Teaching*, Duckworth, London.

Peters, M. 1995, 'Introduction: Lyotard, Education and the Postmodern Condition', in M. Peters (ed.) *Education and the Postmodern Condition*, Bergin & Garvey, Boston.

—— 1996, *Poststructuralism, Politics and Education*, Bergin and Garvey, Boston

Peters, R. S. 1961, *Authority, Responsibility and Education*, George Allen & Unwin, London.
—— 1966, *Ethics and Education*, George Allen & Unwin, London.
—— 1972, 'Education and the Educated Man', in R. F. Dearden, P. H. Hirst & R. S. Peters (eds), *Education and the Development of Reason*, Routledge & Kegan Paul, London.
—— 1973, 'The Justification of Education', in R. S. Peters (ed.) *The Philosophy of Education*, Oxford University Press, London.
Peters, T. 1992, *Liberation Management: Necessary Disorganization for the Nanosecond Nineties*, Fawcett, New York.
Phenix, P. 1964, *Realms of Meaning: A Philosophy of the Curriculum for General Education*, McGraw–Hill, New York.
Piaget, M. 1969, *The Child's Conception of Time*, Basic Books, New York.
Piore, M. J. & Sabel, C. F. 1984, *The Second Industrial Divide: Possibilities for Prosperity*, Basic Books, New York.
Plato, 1972, *The Republic*, trans. H. D. P. Lee, Penguin, Harmondsworth.
Polanyi, M. 1972, *Personal Knowledge*, Routledge & Kegan Paul, London.
Pollock, L. 1983, *Forgotten Children: Parent–Child Relations from 1500 to 1900*, Cambridge University Press, Cambridge.
Popper, K. 1972, *The Logic of Scientific Discovery*, Hutchinson, London.
—— 1973, *Objective Knowledge*, Oxford University Press, London.
Poster, M. 1989, *Jean Baudrillard: Selected Writings*, Polity Press, Cambridge.
Postman, N. 1982, *The Disappearance of Childhood*, Delacorte Press, New York.
Poynton, K. 1996, 'Giving Voice', in E. McWilliam & P. Taylor (eds) *Pedagogy, Technology and the Body*, Peter Lang, New York.
Pred, A. (ed.) 1981, *Space and Time in Geography: Essays Dedicated to Torsten Hägerstrand*, CWK Gleerup, Lund.
Pred, A. 1972, 'The Choreography of Existence: Comments on Hägerstrand's Time-Geography and Its Usefulness', *Economic Geography*, vol. 53, pp. 207–21.
Preston, N. 1988, *The Dawkins New Education Initiative: A Philosophical Analysis*, M.Ed thesis, University of New England.
—— 1990, 'The Fitzgerald Report and Education: A Case Study of Ideology, the State and Education Policy', *Unicorn*, vol. 16, no. 1, pp. 8–14.
—— 1992, 'Computing and Teaching: a Socially-Critical Review', *Journal of Computer Assisted Learning*, vol. 8, pp. 49–56.
—— 1994, 'Ethics Education: a Comprehensive Approach', *New Horizons*, December, pp. 31–40.
—— 1996, *Understanding Ethics*, Federation Press, Sydney.
Pudwell, C. F. 1989, 'Marking Children's Work: Some Reflections', *Curriculum*, vol. 8, no. 1, Spring.
Purpel, D. 1989, *The Moral and Spiritual Crisis in Education*, Bergin & Garvey, Westport, Conn.
Purvis, J. 1984, 'The Experience of Schooling for Working Class Boys and Girls in Nineteenth-Century England', in I. F. Goodson & S. J. Ball

(eds) *Defining the Curriculum: Histories and Ethnographies*, Falmer Press, London, pp. 89–115.

Pusey, M. 1991, *Economic Rationalism in Canberra*, Cambridge University Press, Canberra.

Quine, W. V. 1960, *Word and Object*, MIT Press, Cambridge, Mass.

—— 1990, *Quiddities: An Intermittently Philosophical Dictionary*, Penguin, Harmondsworth.

Raban, J. 1988, *Soft City*, Collins Harvill, London.

Raper, M. 1982, 'Schools Perpetuate, Aggravate and Legitimise Inequality', *Independent Education*, vol. 12, no. 3, pp. 12–17.

—— 1984, *Schools, Girls and Tomorrow: The Challenge for Schools*, Schools Commission, Canberra.

Rawls, J. 1972, *A Theory of Justice*, Oxford University Press, London.

Reekie, G. 1992, 'Changes in the Adamless Eden: the Spatia and Sexual Transformation of a Brisbane Department Store 1939–1990', in R. Shields (ed.) *Lifestyle: the Subject of Consumption*, Routledge, London.

Reich, R. B. 1991, *The Work of Nations: Preparing Ourselves for 21st Century Capitalism*, Alfred A. Knopf, New York.

Reiger, K. M. 1986, *The Disenchantment of the Home: Modernising the Australian Family 1880–1940*, Oxford University Press, Melbourne.

Reimer, E. 1971, *School is Dead*, Penguin, Harmondsworth.

Reynolds, H. 1989, *Dispossession: Black Australians and White Invaders*, Allen & Unwin, Sydney.

Rich, P. J. 1989, *Elixir of Empire: the English Public Schools, Ritualism, Freemasonry, and Imperialism*, Regency, London.

Richmond, W. K. 1975, *Education and Schooling*, Methuen, London,

Robson, E. R. 1972, *School Architecture*, Humanities Press, New York.

Rodwell, G. 1995, 'Australian Open-air School Architecture', *History of Education Review*, vol. 24, no. 2, pp. 21–41.

Rogers, C. 1983, *Freedom to Learn in the 80s*, C. E. Merrill, Columbus, Ohio.

Rojek, C. 1985, *Capitalism and Leisure Theory*, Tavistock, London.

—— 1989, 'Leisure and "The Ruins of the Bourgeois World" ', in C. Rojek (ed.) *Leisure for Leisure: Critical Essays*, Macmillan, London.

Roobeck, A. J. M. 1990, 'The Crisis in Fordism and the Rise of a New Technological Paradigm', *Futures*, vol. 19, no. 2.

Rorty, R. 1977, *Philosophy and the Mirror of Nature*, Princeton University Press, Princeton, NJ.

—— 1983, *Consequences of Pragmatism*, University of Minnesota Press, Minn.

—— 1984, 'Habermas and Lyotard on Post-Modernism', *Praxis International*, vol. 4, no. 1, April, pp. 32–44.

Rose, M. 1991, *The Post-Modern and the Post-Industrial: A Critical Analysis*, Cambridge University Press, Cambridge.

—— 1990, *Governing the Soul: The Shaping of the Private Self*, Routledge, London.

Roszak, T. 1986, *The Cult of Information: the Folklore of Computers and the True Art of Thinking*, Pantheon, New York.

—— 1987, 'Computers: A Solution in Search of a Problem', *Australian Society*, April.

Roth, J. 1963, *Timetables: Structuring the Passage of Time in Hospital and Other Careers*, Bobbs-Merrill, Indianapolis, NY.

Rowland, R. 1984, *Woman Herself: A Women's Studies Perspective on Self-Identity*, Oxford University Press, Melbourne.

Russell, D. 1980, *Tamarisk Tree: vol. 2—My School and the Years of War*, Virago, London.

Rux, M. 1988, 'Truth, Power, Self: an Interview with Michel Foucault', in L. H. Luther, H. Gutman & P. Hutton (eds) *Technologies of the Self: a Seminar with Michel Foucault*, University of Mass. Press, Amherst.

Ryan, A. 1985, 'Reinventing Ethics in the Return of Grand Theory IV, John Rawls', *Australian Society*, April, pp. 15–17.

Saint, A. 1987, *Towards a Social Architecture: The Role of School Building in Post-War England*, Yale University Press, New Haven, CT.

Sarup, M. 1978, *Marxism and Education*, Routledge & Kegan Paul, London.

Sarup, M. 1988, *An Introductory Guide to Post-Structuralism and Post-Modernism*, Harvester Wheatsheaf, New York.

Schell, J. *The Future of the Earth*, Picador, London.

Schmidt, A. 1971, *The Concept of Nature in Marx*, NLB, London.

Schneidewind, N. 1987, 'Feminist Values: Guidelines for Teaching Methodologies in Women's Studies', in I. Shor & P. Freire (eds) *Freire for the Classroom: A Sourcebook for Liberatory Teaching*, Heinemann, Portsmouth, NH.

Schultz, T. W. 1977, 'Investment in Human Capital', in J. Karabel & A. Halsey (eds) *Power and Ideology in Education*, Oxford University Press, New York.

Schumacher, E. F. 1973, *Small is Beautiful*, Blond & Briggs, London.

—— 1977, *A Guide for the Perplexed*, Jonathan Cape, London.

—— 1979, *Good Work*, Harper & Row, New York.

Scruton, R. 1979, *Aesthetics of Architecture*, Methuen, London.

Scull, A. 1980, 'A Convenient Place to Get Rid of Inconvenient People: The Victorian Lunatic Asylum', in A. D. King (ed.) *Buildings and Society: Essays on the Social Development of the Built Environment*, Routledge & Kegan Paul, London, pp. 37–60.

Seaborne, M. 1971, *The English School: Its Architecture and Organization 1370–1870*, Routledge & Kegan Paul, London.

Seaborne, M. & Lowe, R. 1977, *The English School: Its Architecture and Organization, vol. 11, 1870–1970*, Routledge & Kegan Paul, London.

Senate Standing Committe on Employment, Education and Training 1990, *Priorities for Reform in Higher Education*, AGPS, Canberra.

Sharp, R. 1990, 'Rescuing a Socialist Practice of Education', *Education Links*, 38, pp. 14–20.

Sharp, R. & Green, A. 1975, *Education and Social Control: A Study in Progressive Education*, Routledge & Kegan Paul, London.
Sherwin, M. 'The Law in Relation to the Wishes and Feelings of the Child', in R. Davie, G. Upton & V. Varma (eds) *The Voice of the Child: a Handbook for Professionals*, Falmer Press, London.
Shields, R. 1991, *Places On the Margin: Alternative Geographies of Modernity*, Routledge, London.
Shilling, C. 1993, *The Body and Social Theory*, Sage, London.
Shor, I. 1980, *Critical Teaching and Everyday Life*, South End Press, Boston.
—— 1986, *Culture Wars: School and Society in the Conservative Restoration 1969–1984*, Routledge & Kegan Paul, London.
—— 1987, *Freire in the Classroom: A Sourcebook for Liberatory Teaching*, Heinemann, Portsmouth, NH.
Simon, R. 1985, 'Critical Pedagogy', *International Encyclopedia of Education*, Pergamon, Oxford, pp. 1118–20.
Singer, P. 1976, *Practical Ethics*, Cambridge University Press, Cambridge.
Singer, P. 1994, *Rethinking Life and Death*, Text Publishing, Melbourne.
Sivanandan, A. 1989, 'New Circuits of Imperialism', *Race and Class: A Journal for Black and Third World Liberation*, vol. 39, no. 4, pp. 1–19.
Smark, P. 1990, 'Longer School of Thought', *Sydney Morning Herald*, 27 October.
Smart, J. J. C. 1964, *Problems of Space and Time*, Macmillan, New York.
Smiles, S. 1968, *Self-help: the Art of Achievement Illustrated by the Lives of Great Men*, Sphere, London.
Smith, A. 1986, *The Wealth of Nations Books I–III*, Penguin, Harmondsworth.
Snook, I. 1986, 'The Concept of Conscientization: Paulo Freire's Philosophy of Education', *New Education*, vol. 72, no. 4, pp. 304–14.
Soja, E. W. 1989, *Post-Modern Geographies: the Reassertion of Space in Critical Social Theory*, Verso, London.
Sommer, R. 1967, 'Classroom Ecology', *Journal of Applied Behavioral Science*, vol. 3, no. 4.
Spring, J. 1975, *A Primer of Libertarian Education*, Free Life Editions, New York.
Starrett, R. J. 1994, *Building an Ethical School*, Falmer Press, London.
Sterba, J. P. 1986, 'Recent Work on Alternative Conceptions of Justice', *American Philosophical Quarterly*, vol. 23, no. 1, January, pp. 1–22.
Stoppard, T. 1993, *Arcadia*, Faber & Faber, London.
Stradling, R., Noctor, M. & Baines, B. 1984, *Teaching Controversial Issues*, Arnold, London.
Strike, K. & Soltis, J. S. 1987, *The Ethics of Teaching*, Teachers College Press, New York.
Sultana, R. G. 1995, 'The Architecture of Pedagogical Encounters', *Education: Journal of the Faculty of Education, University of Malta*, vol. 5, no. 3, pp. 2–6

Taylor, P. W. 1986, 'The Ethics of Respect for Nature', in D. Van De Veer & C. Pierce (eds) *People, Penguins and Plastic Trees: Basic Issues*, Wadsworth, Belmont, CA.

Taylor, S. 1984, 'Reproduction and Contradictions in Schooling: The Case of Commercial Studies', *British Journal of Sociology of Education*, vol. 5, no. 1.

—— 1989, 'Empowering Girls and Young Women: The Challenge of the Gender-Inclusive Curriculum', *Journal of Curriculum Studies*, vol. 21, no. 5, pp. 441–56.

Taylor, S., Rivzi, F., Lingard, B. & Henry, M. 1997, *Education Policy and the Politics of Change*, Routledge, London.

Thagard, P. 1988, *Computational Philosophy of Science*, MIT Press, Cambridge, Mass.

Theile, B. 1986, 'Vanishing Acts in Social and Political Thought: Tricks of the Trade', in C. Pateman & E. Gross (eds) *Feminist Challenges: Social and Political Theory*, George Allen & Unwin, Sydney.

Theophanous, A. 1994, *Understanding Social Justice*, Elika Books, Melbourne.

Thompson, E.P. 1967, 'Time, Work-Discipline and Industrial Capitalism', *Past and Present*, vol. 38, pp. 56–97.

Thrift, N. 1981, 'Owners', Time and Own Time: The Making of a Capitalist Time Consciousness, 1300–1800', in A. Pred (ed.) *Space and Time in Geography: Essays Dedicated to Torsten Hägerstrand*, CWK Gleerup, Lund, pp. 56–84.

Tolstoy, L. 1973, *Anna Karenin*, Penguin, Harmondsworth.

Toulmin, S. 1972, *Human Understanding*, vol. 1, Clarendon Press, Oxford.

—— 1990, *Cosmopolis: the Hidden Agenda of Modernity*, Free Press, New York.

Toulmin, S. 1982, *Return to Cosmology: Postmodern Science and the Theology of Nature*, University of California Press, Berkeley, CA.

Trainer, T. 1985, *Abandon Affluence*, Zed, London.

Turkle, S. 1984, *The Second Self: Computers and the Human Spirit*, Simon & Schuster, New York.

—— 1985, 'The Psychology of Personal Computers', in T. Forester (ed.) *The Information Technology Revolution*, Blackwell, Oxford.

Turner, M. 1991, *Reading Minds: the Study of English in the Age of Cognitive Science*, Princeton University Press, Princeton, NJ.

Tyler, D. 1993, 'Making Children Better', in D. Meredyth & D. Tyler (ed.) *Child and Citizen: Genealogies of Schooling and Subjectivity*, ICPS, Brisbane.

Urmson, J. O. 1961, 'On Grading', in A. Flew (ed.) *Language and Logic* (Second Series), Blackwell, Oxford.

Urry, J. 1990, *The Tourist Gaze: Leisure and Travel in Contemporary Societies*, Sage, London.

Usher, R. & Edwards, R. 1994, *Postmodernism and Education*, Routledge, London.

Uspensky, B. 1973, *A Poetics of Composition: The Structure of the Artistic Text and the Typology of Compositional Form*, University of California Press, Berkeley, CA.

Veblen, T. 1970, *The Theory of the Leisure Class: An Economic Study of Institution*, George Allen & Unwin, London.

Véliz, C. 1994, *The New World of the Gothic Fox: Culture and Economy in English and Spanish America*, University of California Press, Berkeley, CA.

Waddington, C. H. 1977, *Tools for Thought*, Paladin, London.

Walkerdine, V. 1983, 'It's Only Natural: Rethinking Child-Centred Pedagogy', in A. M. Wolpe & J. Donald (eds) *Is There Anyone Here from Education?* Pluto Press, London.

—— 1984, 'Developmental Psychology and the Child-Centred Pedagogy: The Insertion of Piaget into Early Education', in J. Henriques, W. Hollway, C. Urwin, C. Venn, C. & V. Walkerdine (eds) *Changing the Subject: Psychology, Social Regulation and Subjectivity*, Methuen, London.

—— 1989, *Democracy in the Kitchen: Regulating Mothers and Socialising Daughter*, Virago, London.

—— 1990, *Schoolgirl Fictions*, Verso, London.

Walsh, K. 1992, *The Representation of the Past: Museums and Heritage in the Post-Modern World*, Routledge, London.

Walton, J. (ed.) 1963, *The Secondary School Timetable*, Ward Lock, London.

Walton, J. 1963, 'The Secondary Curriculum and Its Organization Prior to the 1944 Act', in J. Walton (ed.) *The Secondary School Timetable*, Ward Lock, London.

Walzer, M. 1983, *Spheres of Justice*, Blackwell, Oxford.

Warnock, M. 1975, 'The Concept of Equality in Education', *Oxford Review of Education*, vol. 1, no. 1, pp. 3–8.

Watkins, P. 1986, *Time, Organization and the Administration of Education*, Deakin University Press, Victoria.

—— 1987, *An Analysis of the History of Work*, Curriculum Development Centre, Canberra.

—— 1989, 'Economic Restructuring at the End of Organised Capitalism? Education and the Flexible Workplace', *Unicorn*, vol. 15, no. 3, August, pp. 139–45.

Watson, I. 1985, *Double Depression*, George Allen & Unwin, Sydney.

Watts, A. G., Jamieson, I. & Miller, A. 1987, 'School Work Tasks as Simulated Work Experience', *British Journal of Work and Education*, vol. 1, no. 1.

Weber, M. 1958, *The Protestant Ethic and the Spirit of Capitalism*, Charles Scribners, New York.

Weiler, K. 1988, *Women Teaching for Change: Gender, Class and Power*, Bergin & Garvey, South Hadley, Mass.

Weizenbaum, J. 1981, *Computer Power and Human Reason*, W. H. Freeman, San Francisco, CA.

Wells, D. & Singer, P. 1984, *The Reproduction Revolution: A New Way of Making Babies*, Oxford University Press, Melbourne.
Wernick, A. 1991, *Promotional Culture: Advertising, Ideology and Symbolic Expression*, Sage, London.
West, E. G. 1963, 'The Role of Education in Nineteenth-Century Doctrines of Political Economy', *British Journal of Educational Studies*, vol. 12, pp. 161–172.
Western, J. W. 1983, *Social Inequality and Australian Society*, Macmillan, Melbourne.
Wexler, P. 1982, 'Body and Soul: Sources of Social Change and Strategies of Education', *Journal of Curriculum Theorizing*, vol. 4, no. 2, Summer, pp. 160–80.
White, J. 1973, *Towards a Compulsory Curriculum*, Routledge & Kegan Paul, London.
White, L. 1975, 'Medieval Engineering and the Sociology of Knowledge', *Pacific Historical Review*, vol. 44, pp. 1–21.
White, R. 1987, 'Creating the Ideal Worker', *Education Links*, 31, Spring, pp. 7–10.
White, R. with Brockington, D. (ed.) 1983, *Tales Out of School: Consumers' Views of British Education*, Routledge & Kegan Paul, London.
Whitty, G. & Young, M. (eds) 1976, *Explorations in the Politics of School Knowledge*, Nafferton Books, Driffield, pp. 65–74.
Wilenski, P. 1986, *Public Power and Public Administration*, Hale & Iremonger, Sydney.
Wilkinson, R. 1964, *The Prefects: British Leadership and the Public School Tradition*, Oxford University Press, London.
Williams, N. P. 1988, 'Research on Poverty and Education: Report no. 1 of Poverty, Education and the DSP Project', Macquarie University, Sydney.
Williams, R. 1974, 'Social Darwinism', in Benthall, J. (ed.) *The Limits of Human Nature: Essays Based on a Course of Lectures Given at the Institute of Contemporary Arts*, E. P. Dutton, New York.
—— 1977, *Culture and Society, 1789–1950*, Penguin, Harmondsworth.
—— 1981, *Keywords: a Vocabulary of Culture and Society*, Fontana, London.
Willis, P. 1979, *Learning to Labour: How Working Class Kids Get Working Class Jobs*, Saxon House, Farnborough.
Wilson, J. & Cowell, B. 1989, *Taking Education Seriously*, Athlone Press, London.
Winner, L. 1977, *Autonomous Technology: Technics-Out-Of-Control as a Theme in Political Thought*, MIT Press, Cambridge, Mass.
Wirt, F. M. & Harman, G. 1986, *Education, Recession and the World Village*, Falmer Press, London.
Wirth, A. G. 1966, *John Dewey as an Educator*, John Wiley, New York.
—— 1972, *Education in the Technological Society*, Intext Educational Publishers, San Francisco, CA.
—— 1983, *Productive Work-in Industry and Schools: Becoming Persons Again*, University of America Press, Lanham, MD.

Woods, R. G. & Barrow, R. St. C. 1975, *An Introduction to Philosophy of Education*, Methuen, London.

Wren, B. 1981, *Education for Justice*, SCM Press, London.

Wright, N. 1989, *Assessing Radical Education: A Critical Review of the Radical Movement in English Schooling, 1960–1980*, Open University Press, Milton-Keynes, Bucks.

Wringe, C. 1984, *Democracy, Schooling and Political Education*, George Allen & Unwin, London.

—— 1981, 'Education, Schooling and the World of Work', *British Journal of Educational Studies*, vol. 24, no. 2, June.

Young, I. M., 1980, 'Throwing Like a Girl: A Phenomenology of Feminine Body Comportment, Motility and Spatiality', *Human Studies*, vol. 3, pp. 137–56.

—— 1987, 'The New Right and the Old Left: A Plague on Both Their Houses', *Discourse*, vol. 8, no. 1, October, pp. 48–60.

—— 1990, *Justice and the Politics of Distribution*, Princeton University Press, Princeton, NJ.

Young, M. 1958, *The Rise of the Meritocracy 1870–2000*, Thames & Hudson, London.

Young, M. 1988, *The Metronomic Society: Natural Rhythms and Human Timetables*, Thames & Hudson, London.

—— 1993, 'A Curriculum for the 21st Century? Towards a New Basis for Overcoming Academic/Vocational Divisions', *British Journal of Educational Studies*, vol. 41, no. 3 September, pp. 205–213

Young, R. E. 1989, *A Critical Theory of Education: Habermas and Our Children's Future*, Harvester Wheatsheaf, New York.

Zerubavel, E. 1981, *Hidden Rhythms: Schedules and Calendars in Social Life*, University of Chicago Press, Chicago.

Zukin, S. 1995, *The Cultures of Cities*, Blackwell, Cambridge, Mass.

Names index

Abercrombie, M. L. J. 9
Adam, B. 31, 100, 172, 174, 185
Adams, H. 37, 59
Adelstein, D. 53
Adler, M. 63, 65, 96
Adorno, T. W. 252
Althusser, L. xi
Anderson, D. & Vervoorn, A. 113
Anthony, P. D. 153
Apple, M. 69, 83, 117–18, 241, 256, 260, 261
Archambault, R. G. 79, 156
Arcilla, R. N. 40
Arendt, H. 149
Ariès, P. 59, 143, 171, 185, 201, 204, 208
Aristotle, 96, 120
Arnold, Matthew 96
Aronowitz, S. 13, 252
Aronowitz, S. & Giroux, H. 266–67, 284
Ashenden, D. & Milligan, S. 227
Aspin, D. 241
Auster, Paul 24, 35
Atweh, W., Hickling-Hudson, A. & Preston, N. 261, 281
Augustine, St. 105
Bagguley, P. 150

Bailey, C. H. 63, 68, 76, 105
Ball, S. 26, 152
Ball, S., Hull, R., Skelton, M. & Tudor, R. 190
Bantock, G. H. 64, 84
Barcan, A. 49
Barnard, Henry 206, 211
Barnes, D. & Seed, J. 231
Barrow, R. 95
Barrow, R. & White, P. 95
Barthes, Roland 28
Baudrillard, J. 25, 36, 199, 252
Bauman, Z. 25, 36, 253
Beck, C. 282

Beck, J. 83, 156
Beck, U. 25, 246, 248
Becker, G. S. 180
Becker, H. 3
Bell, Andrew 206
Bell, Daniel 13, 86, 90
Bell, D. 173
Ben-David, J. 11
Bennett, T. 198
Bentham, Jeremy 30, 50, 207
Berg, L. 152
Berger, P. & Luckman, T. 189
Bernstein, B., Elvin, H. L. & Peters, R. S. 213
Bernstein, B. 98
Biggins, D. 144
Bigum, C. et al. 281
Birch, C. 249
Birch, I. & Smart, D. 53
Bishop, S. 66
Blishen, E. 192
Bloom, A. 96, 252
Blyton, P. 179
Boden, M. 264
Bottomore, T. 20
Boulding, K. 269
Bourdieu, P. 16, 39, 173, 195, 199, 201
Bourdieu, P. & Passeron, J. C. 242
Bowen, J. & Hobson, P. R. 40, 70
Bowers, C. A. 9, 57–58, 65, 69
Bowles, S. & Gintis, H. 15, 7, 157–59, 222
Branson, J. & Miller, D. 113
Braverman, H. 108, 147, 162
Bremer, J. & Moschzisker, M. van. 218, 278
Brent, A. 104
Broadfoot, P. 243–44, 280
Brown, P. & Lauder, H. 151
Browne, K. 162, 164
Brubacher, J. S. 188
Bruner, J. S. 83

Buckley, J. H. 16
Bullough, R. Goldstein, S. & Holt, L. 69, 269
Burchell, L. 209
Burt, Sir Cyril, 12

Cadogan, M. & Craig, P. 16
Cagan, E. 278
Callinicos, A. 196
Calvin, J. 153–54, 249
Camilleri, J. et al. 289
Campbell, C. 145
Capra, F. 27, 247
Carlstein, T., Parkes, D. & Thrift, N. 169
Carmichael, L. 68, 98, 150
Carr, D. 229
Castles, F. & Mitchell, D. 257
Castles, S. & Wüstenberg, W. 146, 166, 270, 278
Cavell, S. 64
Cherryholmes, C. 53, 77, 83, 88, 226, 287
Christie, M. J. 175
Clarke, J. & Critcher, C. 145
Claus, J. F. 123
Cohen, B. 76, 120
Coleridge, Samuel Taylor, 48
Collis, B. 261
Colquhuon, D. 216
Connell, R. W. 85, 112–13, 116, 118, 132, 161, 282
Cook, Thomas 49
Cooley, M. 141, 147–48, 255
Cooper, B. 89
Corrigan, P. 47, 159, 212
Craig, P. 16
Crane, D. 11
Cross, G. 145, 184
Csikszentmihalyi, M. & Rochberg-Halton, E. 212

Dale, R. 183, 216
Daniels, N. 123
Davidson, K. 47, 127
Davies, B. 10
Davies, B. & Ellison, L. 213

Davison, G. 178–79
Dawkins, J. S. 53–54, 97, 116, 227
de Castell, S. & Luke, A. 96
de Certeau, M. 14
de Grazia, S. 176–77
de Saussure, F. 28
Denham, C. & Lieberman, A. 170
Derrida, J. 32
Dewey, J. 71, 79. 156
Dilnot, A. 133
Donzelot, J. 31
Doob, L. W. 173
Dore, R. 285
Dretske, F. I. 9
Dummett, M. 110
Dunlop, B. 196

Easlea, B. 250
Eco, U. 110
Edelman, M. 225
Eisner, E. 84, 224
Elias, N. 64. 169, 204
Elliot, R. 218, 251
Elliot, R. & Gare, A. 251
Ellsworth, E. 76
Ellul, J. 256
Erikson, E. 72
Euclid, 193
Evans, K. 202
Evans, R. 218
Evans-Pritchard, E. 173
Everhart, R.B. 159

Fairclough, N. 117
Featherstone, M. 25, 251, 254
Feifer, M. 49
Feinberg, W. 14, 115, 122, 156
Feinberg, W. & Soltis, J. F. 142
Fenstermacher, G. D. & Soltis, J. F. 71
Feyerabend, P. 12
Finch, L. 59
Finkelstein, J. 203
Finn, B. 68, 98, 151
Ford, G. W. 151
Forty, A. 154, 201
Foucault, M. xv–xvi, 7, 28–33, 51,

72, 77, 90, 144. 175, 186, 190, 196, 211, 218, 226, 233
Franklin, Benjamin, 177, 192
Fraser, J. J. 23
Fraser, N. 29, 77–78,169
Frayn, M. 168
Freire, P. 40–41, 52, 56–58, 288, 290
Freire, P. & Shor, I. 75, 277–78, 284
Frow, J. 13

Galton, Francis 235
Gee, J. 22
Gee, J. Hull, G. & Lankshear, C. 257
Geuss, R. 20
Gibson, R. 6, 21, 56, 68
Giddens, A. 25, 51, 196
Gilbert, P. & Taylor, S. 278
Ginsburg, M. 79, 286
Giroux, H. 52, 56, 73–74, 77–79, 284, 286, 288
Giroux, H. & Aronowitz, S. 73
Giroux, H. & McLaren, P. 283
Giroux, H. & Simon, R. 73
Gleick, J. 27, 110
Godfrey, J. A. & Castle, C. R. 200
Goffman, E. 51, 181, 201, 204, 239
Goldstrom, J. M. 50
Gollan, A. 289
Gooding, D. 10,
Goodman, N. 110
Goodson, I. F. 82, 101, 109
Goodson, I. F. & Ball, S. J. 102
Gordon, C. 7, 35, 210
Gordon, P. & Lawton, D. 229
Gore, J. 280
Gorz, A. 255, 257–58
Goss, J. 199, 214
Gottdiener, M. 28, 196
Gould, S. J. 232
Grace, G. 161
Gramsci, A. xi, 73, 284
Green, H. 139
Gregory, B. 133

Gross, D. 196
Grundy, S. 67, 76, 84
Gutek, G. L. 40

Habermas, J. xvi, 21, 23, 27, 33, 35, 77, 253
Hacking, I. 29, 83, 232
Hagerstrand, T. 196
Hall, E. J. 195
Halliwell, G. 76
Hamilton, D. 32, 84, 101, 107, 170, 206, 208–209
Hannan, B. 223
Hanson, N.R. 9
Hargreaves, A. 172, 179, 244
Hargreaves, D. H. 141, 145
Harley, J.B. 86
Harris, H. & Lipman, A. 214
Harris, K. 42–43, 53, 81, 114, 161, 163, 179, 182, 190, 193, 260–61, 273
Hartnett, A. & Naish, M. 34
Harvey, D. 20, 25, 35, 172, 190, 195
Hatton, E. 113
Hatton, E. & Elliot, R. 121, 124
Hay, A. 54
Hebdige, D. 24
Heilbroner, R. L. 269
Held, D. 20
Heller, A. 171, 195
Hempel, C. G. 7
Henry, M., Knight, J., Lingard, R. & Taylor, S. 43, 113–14
Hepburn, E. 248
Herbst, P. B. 148, 150
Hesse, H. 61
Hextall, I. 222, 236
Hextall, I. & Sarup, M. 108
Heyck, T. W. 96
Hill, C. 177
Hill, S. 256
Hirsch, E. D. 96, 111
Hirsch, F. 3, 115
Hirst, P. 16, 74, 95
Hobbes, Thomas, 29
Hobsbawm, E. & Ranger, T. 200

Hollis, M. 115
Holmes, M. 180
Holt, J. 190, 238
Holt, M. 68
Hooton, J. 16
Horvath, A. 211
Hoskin, K. W. 190
Hoskin, K. W. & Macve, 230
Howie, G. 105
Humphries, S. 51, 184, 237
Hunter, I. et al. 97
Hunter, I. 47, 208, 215, 274
Hurt, J. S. 82, 216
Hutton, P. 64, 152
Hyams, B. K. & Bessant, B. 62
Hyland, T. 228

Illich, I. 15, 59, 107, 139, 143, 269, 278
Inglis, F. 16, 82, 87, 92, 186, 237

James, William, 79
Jenks, C. 46
Johnson, L. 170
Joiner, D. 214
Jonathan, R. 129
Jones, B. 96, 113, 149, 178, 256
Jones, K. & Williamson, K. 48, 186, 206
Junor, A. 112

Karmel, P. 90
Keating, P. 151
Kemmis, S. 248
Kemmis, S. & Carr, W. 20
Kemmis, S., Cole, P. & Suggett, D. 74
Kemp, D. 76, 116
Kenway, J. with Bigum, C. & Fitzclarence, L. 26
Kirk, D. & Tinning, R. 106
Kirschenbaum, H. & Simon, S.B. 71
Kleinig, J. 53, 55
Kline, S. 46
Kociumbas, J. 59
Kohlberg, L. 72, 273

Kramer, L. 68
Kristeva, J. 174
Kritzman, L. D. 35
Kuhn, T. S. 8
Kukathes, C. & Pettit, P. 123

Lacan, J. 32
Landes, D. S. 172, 175–77
Lanham, R. A. 91, 266
Laqueur, T. 43, 48–49
Larick, K. T. & Fischer, J. 261
Lash, S. & Urry, J. 25, 152, 253
Latour, B. 232, 234
Lave, J. 236
Lawrence, D. H. 81
Lawton, D. 96
Leadbeatter, C. 257
Levin, H. 180
Lingard, B. 76, 119, 132
Liston, D. P. 79, 121
Livingstone, D. W. 157
Lloyd, G. 10, 103, 114
Locke, John 48
Lodge, D. 16
Lotman, J. 237
Luke, C. 45, 260–61
Lunn, E. 21
Lyon, D. 30
Lyotard, J. F. 24–27, 35, 89, 91, 253, 265–66
Lysenko, T. D. 12

MacIntyre, A. 20
MacLeod, R. 230
MacLure, S. 211
Mangan, J. A. 47
Marchello, J. 66, 267
Marginson, S. 6, 26, 62, 115, 228
Markus, R. 238
Marsh, P., Rosser, E. & Harré, R. 207
Marshall, J. 63, 65
Martin, J. R. 43, 65
Marx, K. 22, 28–29, 139, 142, 149, 195
Maslow, A. 71, 98
Matthews, M. 83, 158

Mauss, M. 108
Mayer, E. 68, 98, 151, 282
McCarthy, C. 47
McClintock, J. & R. 206, 211
McIntyre, S. 116
McLaren, P. 27, 77, 79, 276, 283, 288
McLuhan, M. 247
McPeck, J. F. 56
McWilliam, E. 13
Meadmore, D. 224, 234
Merchant, C. 250
Meredyth, D. & Tyler, D. 46
Metcalfe, A. W. 30, 233
Meyrowitz, J. 46
Middleton, M. 190, 192
Mill, John Stuart, 97, 229
Miller, P. 50, 184, 237
Modjeska, D. 199
Moline, J. N. 129–30
Moore, T. W. 40
Moretti, F. 16
Morris, William 149
Mumford, L. 177
Murdoch, Rupert 253
Murray, R. 159
Musgrave, P. W. 16

Neill, A. S. 70–71, 80, 98–99, 221
Neilsen, K. 121
Newcombe, B. & Humphries, D. 192
Newman, J. H. 97
Nicholson, C. 27
Nidditch, P. H. 88
Nietzsche, F. 24, 28
Noble, P. D. 253
Norris, C. 27, 121
Norris, N. 228
Nozick, R. 122
Nyberg, D. 29
Nyberg, D. & Egan, K. 42

O'Brien, M. 10
O'Connor, D. J. 14
Oakeshott, M. 64, 94, 156
Oakley, A. 16

Okin, S. M. 103
Olson, D. 11
Ong, W. J. 39, 91, 229, 231
Opie, I. & Opie, P. 16
Orme, J. 170–71
Orwell, G. 19
Owen, Robert 166
Ozolins, U. 238

Parkes, D. & Thrift, N. 185
Passmore, J. 13, 249
Peters, M. 19, 24–25, 28, 197
Peters, M. & Marshall, J. 25, 117
Peters, R. S. 52-3, 96–97
Peters, T. 22
Phenix, P. 95
Piaget, J. 72, 170, 233
Piore, M. J. & Sabel, C. F. 150
Plato, 26, 96, 102, 104, 109, 124–25, 142, 162
Polanyi, M. 15, 241
Pollock, L. 59
Popper, K. 8, 110
Poster, M. 248
Postman, N. 46
Poynton, K. 109
Pred, A. 196
Preston, N. 88, 248, 262, 282
Pudwell, C. F. 239
Purpel, D. 79
Purvis, J. 48
Pusey, M. 117

Quine, W. V. 110, 169, 194

Raban, J. 199
Raper, M. 113
Rawls, J. 123–25, 127–31
Reekie, G. 196
Reich, R. B. 90
Reich, W. 99
Reiger, K. M. 46
Reimer, E. 59
Reynolds, H. 269
Rich, P. J. 47
Richmond, W. K. 41

Robson, E. R. 194, 200, 206
Rodwell, G. 211
Rogers, C. 71, 98
Rojek, C. 144
Roobeck, A. J. M. , 140
Rorty, R. 35, 64, 79, 80
Rose, N. 24, 29, 223–24, 255
Roszak, T. 101, 248, 253, 261–62, 264
Roth, J. 181
Rousseau, Jean Jacques 48
Rowland, R. 248
Russell, B. 70
Russell, D. 70–71, 98
Rux, M. 28, 33, 35
Ryan, A. 123

Saint, A. 211
Sarup, M. 78
Schell, J. 269
Schmidt, A. 143
Schneidewind, N. 280
Schultz, T. W. 67
Schumacher, E. F. 149
Scruton, R. 198
Scull, A. 205
Seaborne, M. 208
Seaborne, M. & Lowe, R. 200, 211, 213
Sharp, R. 286
Sharp, R. & Green, A. 181
Sherwin, M. 46
Shields, R. 196
Shilling, C. 109
Shor, I. 52, 56
Singer, P. 115, 123, 248
Sivanandan, A. 152
Sklair, L. 93
Smark, P. 192
Smart, J. J. C. 169
Smiles, S. 192
Smith, Adam 107, 148–49
Snook, I. 76
Soja, E. W. 195
Sommer, R. 218
Spring, J. 160
Starrett, R. J. 278

Sterba, J. P. 121
Stoppard, T. 3
Stow, David, 208, 214
Stradling, R., Noctor, M. & Baines, B. 282
Strike, K. & Soltis, J. F. 282
Sultana, R. G. 197–98

Tate, F. 62
Taylor, P. W. 252
Taylor, S. 164, 280
Taylor, S., Rivzi, F., Lingard, B. & Henry, M. 5
Thagard, P. 7
Theile, B. 10
Theophanous, A. 123
Thompson, E. P. 175–77
Thrift, N. 175, 191
Tolstoy, L. 141
Toulmin, S. 20, 27, 31, 282
Trainer, T. 269
Turkle, S. 265
Turner, M. , 237
Twain, Mark 44, 59
Tyler, D. 210
Urmson, J. O. 240
Urry, J. 196
Usher, R. & Edwards, R. 9, 32, 47, 229, 275
Uspensky, B. 237

Veblen, T. 165
Véliz, C. 47

Waddington, C. H. 86
Walkerdine, V. 46, 72, 224
Walsh, K. 198
Walton, J. 186, 192
Walzer, M. 121
Warnock, M. 120
Waters, M. 257
Watkins, P. 143, 169, 191, 267
Watson, I. 163
Watts, A. G., Jamieson, I. & Miller, A. 161
Weber, M. 29, 152–53, 192
Weiler, K. 10, 79

Weizenbaum, J. 264
Wells, D. & Singer, P. 248
Wernick, A. 117
West, E. G. 50, 149
Western, J. W. 113
Wexler, P. 16
White, J. 95
White, L. 147
White, R. 157
White, R. with Brockington, D. 157, 192, 222
Whitty, G. & Young, M.
Whitman, G. 116-7
Wilenski, P. 127
Wilkinson, R. 47
Williams, N. P. 133
Williams, R. 85, 115
Willis, P. 52, 159, 174

Wilson, J. & Cowell, B. 12
Winner, L. 256
Wirt, F.M. & Harman, G. 54
Wirth, A. G. 63, 66, 83, 84, 148, 150
Woods, R. G. & Barrow, R. St. C. 85
Wren, B. 57, 66
Wright, N. 59
Wringe, C. A. 120, 123, 155

Young, I. M. 120, 125, 216
Young, M. 114
Young, M. 68, 86, 171, 184, 247
Young, R. E. 23

Zerubavel, E. 177, 182
Zukin, S. 196

Subject index

ABC, 288–89
ability, 114, 129, 183, 223, 225, 246
Aboriginal studies, 88, 89
Aborigines, 44, 59, 89, 114–15, 130, 269
academic paper, 11
advertising, 25; and education, 117, 200, 214
aesthetics and art, 21, 24–25, 198–99, 237, 242
affirmative action, 119, 130, 275
alienation, 43, 149, 180, 288
'anatomo-politics' and 'biopower', 30, 174, 186, 188–89, 197, 204, 215–16, 234
ancien régime, 290
anthropocentricism and technology, 78, 249–50
architecture and buildings, 196–99; semiotics of, 199
  see also school architecture and buildings
artificial intelligence, 248, 264
  see also computer technology
art education, 241
art gallery, 198
assessment, 31, 221–23, 228, 233, 235, 239, 280; and metatextuality, 239; and subjectivity, 241–42; as a genre, 236–38; criterion-based, 235, 241; language of, 225, 240; genre of, 206–207,
  see also credentialism, dividing practices, grading, marking
attendance, 51, 142, 178, 189
  see also moral economy, truancy
Australia Reconstructed, 151
asylums, 28, 29, 43, 181, 196, 205
Australian Council of Educational Research (ACER), 228
Australian Education Council, 90

'back regions', 179, 204–205, 214–15
  see also 'front regions'
'banking education', 57, 64, 231

behavioural pathologies, 232
biotechnology, 248
blackboards, 208
'blaming the victim', 154, 163
  see also individualism and individuality
boredom, 142, 160, 171, 180
body, 30, 64, 105, 186, 216; and education, 108–109
  see also physical capital
boys, 108, 215
Burdekin Report, 118
business education, 281

calendar and holidays, 153, 170, 172, 176
Calvinism, 49, 249
capitalism, xi, 20–21, 22, 63, 96, 266, 290; and work, 142–44, 152
Carmichael Report, 68, 98, 151
Cartesian thought, 31
chaos theory, 27, 110
child-centred pedagogy, 70, 71, 98
child development, 233
children and childhood, xiv, 4, 9, 45–46, 59, 87, 143, 277; and time, 169–70
Chrestomathia, 207
citizenry and citizenship, 5, 42, 55, 65, 170, 264, 287
'civilising process', 64
classes, 107, 208
classification and categorisation of populations, 142–43, 206, 208, 225, 273;
  see also assessment, difference, dividing practices, examinations
classrooms, xiv, 196–97, 208–10; open 197
'clever country', 53, 62, 67, 128
clocks, 170–72; 175–77,
  see also time
Coca-Cola, 25, 253
Colditz, 207
colleges, 4; of advanced education, 106

327

'communicative competence', 33
competency, 62, 69, 228–29, 241
competition, 107–108, 115, 117, 223
  see also co-operation
compulsory schooling, 4, 82, 182
computer literacy and education,
  100–101, 260–63, 265, 267, 278,
  280–81; and girls 237
computer technology, 26, 27, 90,
  248, 255, 260–64
connoisseurship and judgement, 224
'conscientisation' 52, 56, 290
consumer guides and education, 227
consumer society and consumerism,
  140, 145, 254–55, 279
convergency, 282
'conviviality', 278
co-operation, 237, 280
  see also competition
corporeal practices, 64–65, 108
  see also body
correspondence principle, 165
  see also reproduction theory
counter-hegemonic practice, 14, 52,
  70, 73, 75, 102, 277, 284, 286, 288
credentialism, 4, 11, 39 112, 116,
  233, 285,
  see also 'diploma inflation'
critical pedagogy, xv, 52, 56, 73, 78,
  79, 127, 277–80, 288; and
  'cultural nihilism', 58
  see also emancipatory perspective,
  socially-critical school
Critical Theory, xi, 20–24, 25, 27,
  77, 252, 287
  see also Frankfurt School
CSIRO, 10
'cultural capital' (Bourdieu), 39, 129
cultural etymology, xiii, xv, 38, 83,
  84, 169, 186, 273
cultural heritage and values, 3–4, 64
cultural studies, xiii
culture, 85, and nature 64; and
  schools, 3–4
curriculum, xv, 69, 82–102, 277,
  279; and dangerous knowledge
  and, 87–88; and instrumentalism,
  69; and its cultural etymology 84;
  and leisure pursuits, 144; and
Plato, 102–106; and ruling ideas,
  88; and marginal 'cultural voices',
  89; and national interest, 90; and
  the regulation of, 88; as an
  'intellectual civil war', 87, 89; as a
  selective tradition, 57, 88–89;
  social justice aspects, 132
  see also hidden curriculum,
  inclusive curriculum, knowledge,
  null curriculum
curriculum vitae, 110, 233
  see also dossiers

Dalton Plan, 188
Darwinism, 115
Deakin University, 77
deconstruction, xi, 38, 290
deference, 83, 142, 274, 287
  see also moral economy
deferred gratification, 174
deschooling, 15, 44, 58, 73
  see also radical tradition
deskilling, 148, 286
desks, 208, 215–16
devolution, 132
dialectic, 290
difference, 24, 120, 274; with
  deference, 142, 274, 287
  see also dividing practices
'diploma inflation', 103, 116, 285
  see also credentialism
Disadvantaged Schools Project, 132
disciplinary matrix, 8, 11
disciplinary perspective, xii, xv, 15,
  23–24, 40, 50, 57, 61, 69, 72,
  112, 191, 276
disciplinary society, xii, xiv–xv, 23,
  28–32, 82–83, 154, 170, 197, 273
disciplines, xvi, 6–7, 9, 12, 32, 64,
  81, 93–94,
  see also knowledge
discourses and subjectivity, 31, 33,
  290
distributive justice, 123–25
'dividing practices', 142, 217
docile bodies, 30, 222
  see also deference
domesticating education, 40, 57
  see also banking education

dossiers, 31, 183, 226, 233
dreamtime, 173
drill, 29, 178, 216
dualism, 10, 31, 77

Eastern Europe and totalitarianism, 17, 23, 34
ecological catastrophe, 249, 274
economic rationalism, 115, 117, 128–29, 155, 227, 253, 286
education, ix, 4, 6–7, 9, 11, 13, 21–22, 26, 31–32, 37–42, 43, 56, 61, 133, 168, 190, 264, 275, 287; and the economy, 53,62, 67; and expenditure, 118; and knowledge, 81; as 'cultural mobilisation', 16; as intrinsically worthwhile, 52–53, 66; as social control and socialisation, 41–43; language of, 84; normative aspects of, 38, 40, 53–55, 63, 66, 70
see also instrumentalism and education, schools and schooling
educational practice, 6, 14
educational research theory, xi, xiii-xiv, 6, 13, 14, 40
educationalists, 5
educationworld, ix, 3, 10, 15, 82, 211, 225
efficiency, 22, 26, 124, 134
egalitarianism and education, 121, 287
emancipatory perspective, xii, xv, 15, 23, 52, 55, 61, 72–78, 99, 112, 120, 127, 192, 218, 221, 258, 266, 268, 274, 276, 280, 286–87
see also critical pedagogy, socially-critical education
empiricism, 6
empowerment, 22, 120, 241, 276–77, 281
Encyclopaedia Britannica, 85–86
English, 231
Enlightenment, xiii, 9–10, 24, 26–27, 32, 34, 40, 77, 121, 195, 249, 253, 268, 287, 290 19, 67, 173, 218
environmentalism, xi, 24, 251, 265; and ethics, 251

epistemology, 92–93, 290
see also knowledge
'epochal break', 19–20
equality, xv, 15, 119–20; and discourse, 119; and power, 120; of opportunity, 112–13, 119, 120, 122–23, 276; of outcomes, 122
see also meritocracy natural lottery effects, social justice
equity, 116, 127; and human capital, 90
ethics, 21, 27, 248, 265, 282, 287
ethics and education, 40, 79, 133, 221, 264, 278, 282
ethnography, 52, 291; and schools, xiv, 15
examinations, 31, 183, 217, 221–22, 224, 229–32, 234, 236–37, 244; and time, 236, medical, 234
see also assessment
excellence, 65, 67, 128–29
'eye of power', 30, 207

fair-go, 122
fast capitalism, 22, 257
Feminist theory, xi-iii, 10, 23, 32, 77
feminist pedagogy, 73, 280
Finn Report, 68, 98, 151
'flexible specialisation', 150–51
Fordism, 148, 150, 178
see also Taylorism
frame theory, 237–38
Frankfurt School, 20–24, 73
free schools, 71
'front regions' 204
see also back regions
furniture, 197, 201, 214; and power in the school, 33, 204, 208, 212, 217

Gaia principle, 251
gay rights, 24
gender, 16, 49, 113; and curriculum, 108–109; and time 174; and work 143–44
see also boys, girls and education, women
general education, 146, 164
see also liberal education

giftedness, 129
  see also excellence
girls and education, 72, 107–108, 113, 216
globalisation, ix, 11, 20, 25, 54, 62, 151–52, 172, 247, 249, 291
grades and grading systems, 222, 225–26, 230, 240
  see also assessment, marking
'governing the soul', 224, 255
'governmentality', 20, 34, 46, 83, 89–90, 175, 212
grand theory, 23–24
Gulf War, 252

health, 26
hegemony, 291
hermeneutics, 291
hidden curriculum, 43, 75, 97, 107–108, 132, 181, 278
'hierarchical observation', 22, 207, 243
higher education and social class, 113, 116; the fictional representation of, 26–27
history, 7, 88
historiography, 291
home economics, 100, 106
homeschooling, 190
homework, 160–61, 190
hospitals, 29, 154, 181, 205, 284
houses, 201
'human capital', viii, 54, 67, 97, 155
  see also instrumentalism and education
human sciences, 31–32, 152
Humanism, xiii, 24, 31, 40, 64, 291
humanistic perspective, 71, 267
  see also progressive education
hygiene and school buildings, 210
hyperreal, 25, 252
Hypertext, 91

identity, 3; and work, 141
idleness, 145, 153–54, 186
  see also work
immanent forms, 104
  see also Plato
inclusive curriculum, 143

individualism and individualistic logic, 65, 99, 114, 120, 154, 160, 162–63, 213, 223, 278
industrial revolution, 29, 81–82, 140, 172, 175, 253
inequality, 112–14
information technology, 14, 27, 247–48, 251, 263–66
  see also computer technology,
Institute of Family Studies, 10
'instrumental rationality', 22, 83
instrumentalism and education, 52–55, 63, 66–71, 96–98, 105, 130, 146, 182, 191, 228, 267, 279, 286; critique of 58–59
  see also training, vocational education
intellectuals, 156, 284; and teachers, 285, 287,
intelligence tests, 232
'intergenerational continuity', 14, 44, 81, 102
Internet, 14, 17, 25, 252, 265 285
'invisible colleges', 11

jobs, 143, 256–57
journals, 12, 84
justice, theories of, 121–26, 276

Kabyle and time, 173–74
knowing, 57
knowledge, 7–9, 29, 276; and commodification, 13, 91; and its classification, 85; and perception, 8–9, 107; and power, 29, 32; as 'story telling', 92, 94; explosion, 86; forms of, 7, 9, 16; industry, 6, 13, 25, 90, 92; symbolic aspects, 37; the intellectual quality control of, 11
  see also epistemology

Labor governments and education, 53–54, 62, 67, 113, 116, 151
labour and work, 149
labour, the division of, 21, 106, 142–43
  see also Fordism, post-Fordism, Taylorism, unemployment, work
Larousse, 85

learning, 48, 236, 278
leisure, 49, 144–46, 177, 184
lessons, 101, 179, 184, 188, 190, 216
  see also timetables
Liberal Arts, 45, 88, 95
liberal education, 63, 68, 76, 96–97, 105, 146; critique of 65
  see also Paideia Proposal
liberal perspective, 33, 63–66, 83, 96, 104–105 146, 267–68, 279
Liberalism, 9, 65, 268
libertarian education, 70, 98–99
libertarians and society, 121
libraries and librarians, 4, 91, 198, 284
'limits to growth', 269

MACOS (Man a Course of Study), 88
'male-stream thought' (O'Brien), 10, 280
manual/mental division, 105–106, 147, 162–66
'market place of ideas', xii, 6
marketisation, 25–26, 291; and education, ix, 92, 117, 200, 203
marking, 235–41
Marxism, xi, xv, 15, 19–23, 77; and justice, 121
mass-media, 252
mathematics, 102, 104–105
Mayer Report, 68, 98 151, 282
Melrose Place, 253
'meritocracy', 114, 213, 222, 229, 233, 274
  see also ability, assessment, credentialism, examinations
memory, 231–32
metaphysics, 291
micro-institutional practices, xv, xvii, 29–31, 33
'minimal state', 122
modernism and modernisation, 4, 20, 24, 31, 82
monasteries and monastic life, 110, 176, 185, 200
monitorial schools, 206
moral economy, 48, 222
  see also attendance, deference, punctuality

'moral imagination', 40, 55, 82
moral technology, 33, 39, 48
Muirfield Technology High School, 262
'muscular Christianity', 47
museums, 4, 198

A nation at risk, 89
natural capital, 275
natural lottery effects, 15, 106, 122–23, 232
  see also equality
nature, 64, 85, 249–50
neo-Pragmatists, 64, 79
'new right' and Coalition government, 122
Newtonianism, 20, 27, 31
normal curve, 234–35
'normalising judgment', 31, 223, 234, 238, 243
normality, 224, 274
normative concepts, 39, 225, 275
null curriculum, 88

'opus', 149–50, 258
oral culture, 91, 229, 231
oral examination, 229
'organic intellectuals', 284
organisational culture, 3, 181

Paideia Proposal, 63–64, 96
panopticon, 30, 203, 207, 210, 214, 218, 227
  see also surveillance
paradigms, xiii, 8–10. 12, 19, 92
parents, 5, 37, 82
pedagogy, xiii-xiv, 14–15, 72, 75–76, 274, 277
  see also feminist pedagogy, critical pedagogy
performance indicators and outcomes, 69, 207, 228–29
performativity, 26–27, 91, 227
personal space, 195
phenomenology, 291
Philadelphia Parkway Program, 218
philosophy, 6, 32, 41, 64, 265; and women, 114
philosophy of education, 56, 95;

331

analytic, 52–53
'physical capital', 109
physical education, 98, 100, 109, 216, 218
playground, 212, 214–15
poetry and literature, 96
policy and education, 4–5, 41, 55, 62, 67–68, 89–90, 120, 126, 132, 151, 268
polity, 291
popular culture, 4, 252, 279
Port Arthur, 30
'positional good' (Hirsch), 115
positional advantage, 3–4, 103, 116
positivism, 6, 21, 291
post-colonialism and justice, 125
post-compulsory education, 44, 63, 68, 151, 182
'post-industrial society', 13, 65, 90, 257
post-Fordism, ix, 54, 69, 119, 140–42, 150–52, 160, 162, 165, 178, 188, 257, 292
'postmodern condition', 20, 25
postmodernist theory, ix, xi, 9, 20, 24–27, 40, 58, 64, 77, 287–88
post-structuralist theory, ix, xi, 9, 24, 28, 58, 196
poverty and the work ethic, 153
power, 29, 30, 43, 77, 99, 175, 185, 212, 278
praxis, 56–57, 75, 79, 127, 280, 286–87
prisons, 29–30, 43, 181, 196, 207
private schools, 65, 76, 199
progressive perspective, 22, 70–72, 98–99
progressive workers, 283–84
Protestant work ethic, 47, 49, 141, 152–53; and development of time consciousness, 176,
see also work ethic
psychoanalysis, xi, 20–21
psychologism, 224–25
psychometry, 232, 235
punctuality, 142, 173, 174, 178, 189–90
pupil, 32

quadrivium, 95
qualitarianism and education, 128

race, 15, 112
radical tradition, 277
rationality, 9, 104, 253
reference books, 85–86
'regimes of truth', xiii, 7, 93
reproduction theory, 15, 157–59
The Republic, 102–106, 142
research culture, 6–7, 10–13, 16, 34
resistance, 51–52, 159, 204
résumés, 233
    see also curriculum vitae, dossiers
retention rates, 113
'risk society', 274, 288
romantic naturalism, 70
rural and isolated students, 113

Saint Monday, 176
school administration, 43, 69, 180, 191, 213
school architecture and buildings, 33, 100, 190, 197–200, 208–209, 211, 273, 277, 285; in Australia, 208–209
school badges and mottoes, 47, 84, 159–60; calendar 100, 183–84; handbooks and prospectuses, xii, 33, 72, 189, 203, 215; iconography, 47, 212–213; novels, 16; time, 102, 157, 179–81; uniforms and dress, 47, 160, 185, 202–203, 209–210, 218; work, 160; the invention of, 47, 49; types of, 44
School renewal, 67
schools and schooling, 3, 13–15, 23, 29, 32–34, 37–41, 43–44, 52, 81–82, 112, 146, 190, 273, 275, 277, 285
sciences and scientists, 7–8, 21, 32, 88, 100, 282
'selective tradition', 66
semiotics and sign systems, 28, 292
sexuality, 21, 71, 99, 144, 204, 211
'shadow work', 139; in the school, 158

shopping malls, 30, 196
simulacra, 25, 252
social action, 286
social class and education, 113
Social Darwinism, 115
social justice, ix, 72, 125, 266, 283, 274
  see also equality
socialisation and education, 41–42
socially-critical education, 73–74, 78, 156, 266, 268
  see also critical pedagogy, emancipatory perspective
socio-technical theory, 150
space, 194; and metaphors, 195; and social theory, 195
'spacetable', 209, 278
'spatial apartheid' and schools, 202
staffroom, 212
streaming, 108, 183
students 3, 5, 32, 37, 158, 179, 181, 196, 204, 221–22, 247, 253, 256, 279
  see also pupil
student strikes, 51
Sunday schools, 47–48, 50, 206
surveillance xv-xvi, 30–31, 40, 72, 158, 186, 196, 202–204, 207, 217
  see also panopticon
'symbolic architecture', 47, 84

tacit component, 15, 148
Taylorism, 148–49, 151, 162, 178, 188, 261
teacher education, xii, 71, 191, 286–87
teachers and teaching, ix, 3, 5–6, 37–38, 62, 94, 101, 158, 160, 179, 181, 202, 204, 221, 233, 276, 279, 282–83
technocratic rationality, xvi, 21, 22, 100
technocratic consciousness and culture, 66, 69, 259, 265
technological determinism, 224
technology, xvi, 246–49, 255–56; and ethics, 248, 262; and nature, 249–50

technology of self and subjectivity, xvi, 31, 142, 223
teleological, 292
tertiary entrance, 113, 116
textuality, 11, 32, 91, 279
Thatcherism, 257
theory and practice, 102, 105–106
theory and theories, 6–10
Third World, 274
time, 168–91; and clocks, 170–72; and language 169, 194; and money, 175; and work, 169, 176–77; consciousness, 171–72, 175–76, 191; in non-Western societies, 169, 173
time geography, 196, 201
time thrift, 177–78, 189, 191
timetables, xiv, 33, 102, 176, 180, 183–88, 192, 201, 209, 278; innovative 180
  see also spacetable
toilets, 205, 214
Toshiba, 262
'total institutions', 202
tourism, 49, 196
trade unionism, 283, 286
training, 52, 78, 97, 155
  see also vocational education, instrumental education
transformative intellectuals, 55, 72, 283
trivium, 95
truancy, 184, 190
  see also attendance, resistance
tuck-shop ladies, 158
Tvind school, 270
typologies, 61–62, 95

unemployment, 68, 113, 116, 140–41, 145, 257
universities, 4, 10, 13, 16, 81, 84, 97
Utilitarianism, 50, 229
Utopia and utopian perspectives, xii, 78 292

ventilation, 210
vestibules, 213
vocational education, 53, 65, 67–68,

SCHOOLS AND CLASSROOMS

74, 97, 130, 155–56, 165, 267, 281
see also instrumental education, training

warrantable discrimination, 119, 130, 275
wealth, distribution of, 134
web sites, 281
wisdom and knowledge, 264

women, 10, 103, 114, 127
work, 139–42, 149, 256, 273; and capitalism, 142–44; and education, 152–61
see also post-Fordism, labour, unemployment
work ethic, 97, 143, 157, 159–60, 165–66, 175, 191, 208, 226
see also Protestant work ethic